THE TALE OF

T0048108

R. B. PARKINSON was trained at The Queen's College, Oxford, and was subsequently Lady Wallis Budge Junior Research Fellow at University College, Oxford, 1990-1. He was formerly Assistant Keeper in the Department of Egyptian Antiquities at the British Museum, and is now Professor of Egyptology at the University of Oxford. His research interests centre around the interpretation of Middle Kingdom literature. Previous books include an edition of *The Tale of the Eloquent Peasant* (1991), and *Voices from Ancient Egypt: An Anthology of Middle Kingdom Writings* (1991).

OXFORD WORLD'S CLASSICS

*For over 100 years Oxford World's Classics have brought
readers closer to the world's great literature. Now with over 700
titles—from the 4,000-year-old myths of Mesopotamia to the
twentieth century's greatest novels—the series makes available
lesser-known as well as celebrated writing.*

*The pocket-sized hardbacks of the early years contained
introductions by Virginia Woolf, T. S. Eliot, Graham Greene,
and other literary figures which enriched the experience of reading.
Today the series is recognized for its fine scholarship and
reliability in texts that span world literature, drama and poetry,
religion, philosophy and politics. Each edition includes perceptive
commentary and essential background information to meet the
changing needs of readers.*

OXFORD WORLD'S CLASSICS

The Tale of Sinuhe

and Other Ancient Egyptian Poems
1940–1640 BC

Translated with an Introduction and Notes by
R. B. PARKINSON

OXFORD
UNIVERSITY PRESS

OXFORD

UNIVERSITY PRESS

Great Clarendon Street, Oxford OX2 6DP

Oxford University Press is a department of the University of Oxford.
It furthers the University's objective of excellence in research, scholarship,
and education by publishing worldwide in

Oxford New York

Athens Auckland Bangkok Bogotá Buenos Aires Cape Town
Chennai Dar es Salaam Delhi Florence Hong Kong Istanbul Karachi
Kolkata Kuala Lumpur Madrid Melbourne Mexico City Mumbai Nairobi
Paris São Paulo Shanghai Singapore Taipei Tokyo Toronto Warsaw

with associated companies in Berlin Ibadan

Oxford is a registered trade mark of Oxford University Press
in the UK and in certain other countries

Published in the United States
by Oxford University Press Inc., New York

First published as a World's Classics paperback 1998
Reissued 2009

British Library Cataloguing in Publication Data

Data available

Library of Congress Cataloging in Publication Data

Data available

ISBN 978-0-19-955562-8

20

Printed in Great Britain by
Clays Ltd, Elcograf S.p.A.

Gli occhi mie vaghi delle cose belle
e l'alma insieme della suo salute
non hanno altra virtute
c'ascenda al ciel, che mirar tutte quelle.
Dalle più alte stelle
discende uno splendore
che' l desir tira a quelle,
e qui si chiama amore.
Né altro ha il gentil core
che l'innamori e ardu, e che' l consigli,
c'un volto che negli occhi lor somigli.

Michelangelo Buonarroti (AD c.1540)

CONTENTS

CONTENTS

PREFACE

This anthology contains those literary works from Middle Kingdom
Egypt that are not too obscured by problems of preservation, textual
corruption, or philological difficulties. Only relatively complete
works are translated, but a selection of other fragments is included
in a final section. Although these texts have been long acknowl-
edged as 'literary' in some sense of the word, they remain unknown
to many people familiar with other ancient classics. The English
anthologies of William Kelly Simpson and Miriam Lichtheim have
ended their confinement to a specialized discipline, and I hope to
continue this process of making them accessible for the general
reader. Thus, my translations are meant to be free enough for gen-
eral readers and literal enough to help those reading the original;
as with period performances of Western music, a balance between
strict authenticity and spontaneous passion is desirable. Like all
readers of Egyptian, I owe much to Lichtheim's renderings, which
touch the very heart of the originals, and are models of style and
clarity.

These translations do not aspire to the Egyptological impossible
state of being definitive, but I hope that they embody the present
state of our understanding of the texts. Many texts lack full critical
editions and commentaries, and there is still no fully comprehensive
dictionary of Egyptian, although we now have Rainer Hannig's
valuable *Großes Handwörterbuch Ägyptisch-Deutsch* (Mainz, 1995).
My translations and notes do not include any technical and philo-
logical comments, or indications of uncertainties: the notes would
otherwise have been overburdened with alternatives, doubts, qual-
ifications, and specific references. It should be clear enough to an
Egyptological reader what philological interpretations I have
adopted; I list in the Select Bibliography the studies on which
my readings are based (I do not indicate which renderings follow
earlier studies and which are my own innovations). I have drawn
freely on the work of many scholars; such imitation is an act of

grateful homage, since it was reading Adolf Erman's translation of *Sinuhe* at school that introduced me to Middle Kingdom literature. In the notes I concentrate on what I consider to be a present priority—the basic literary meaning; this approach belongs to what William Kelly Simpson has termed 'the new British school' of Egyptian literary studies.

The translations were begun while preparing a commentary on *The Tale of the Eloquent Peasant*. Much of the initial work was done while holding the Lady Wallis Budge Junior Research Fellowship at University College, Oxford, and I am indebted to that College for more than it suspects. The text has been completed in the Department of Egyptian Antiquities at the British Museum, amid its magnificent collection of literary papyri.

I am grateful particularly to John Baines, who has always been invaluable as teacher, mentor, colleague, and friend; I cannot hope to repay in full the debt I owe him. Generous and patient as ever, he has read the whole text and offered countless insights and comments.

My thanks are also due to Vivian Davies, William Kelly Simpson, and Antonio Loprieno for much kindness, encouragement, and advice; to the inhabitants of the Griffith Institute in Oxford, and of the Department of Egyptian Antiquities at the British Museum; and to the following valued colleagues and friends for general and specific help: Carol Andrews, E. Blumenthal, Mark Collier, Alec Dakin, C. J. Eyre, Hans-Werner Fischer-Elfert, Detlef Franke, Annie Gasse, Rainer Hannig, Yvonne Harpur, Anthony and Lisa M. Leahy, Andrea McDowell, Diana Magee, Jaromir Malek, Gerald Moers, Ingeborg Müller, Mary Newman, Stephen Quirke, Bruce Reid, Mark Robinson, Mark Smith, Deborah Sweeney, Pat Terry, Claire Thorne, Pascal Vernus, and Helen Whitehouse.

Hans-Werner Fischer-Elfert has very kindly read the translations, making many invaluable suggestions and pointing out numerous oversights. Tim Reid has read the whole manuscript, and his comments on form and content have saved the general reader from much suffering, and have improved every page. The remaining errors, mistranslations, and misunderstandings are entirely mine; I can only hope that the ancient poets whose works I have traduced will forgive me. Needless to say, I am indebted to Hilary O'Shea for commissioning these translations, to Liz Alsop for overseeing the text's preparation, and to Hilary Walford for her copy-editing.

It is a great pleasure to express once again my gratitude both to my much-loved, dear father, who taught the primacy of a work of art over all paraphrase and whose boyhood enthusiasm for Egypt sparked mine, and to my much-loved and noble-hearted mother, for their unfailing love and support. Such people can never be forgotten.

Scholarship alone is not enough to resurrect these ancient works; they have a personal voice that can be summoned up only with 'il nome dello straniero', and thus a most heart-felt debt is to Tim Reid, master-muse and only begetter of this book.

R.B.P.

Darlington and Barnard Castle
October 1995

NOTE ON THE TRANSLATIONS

Rather than trying to guess at the effect of the original and recreate this in modern poetry, I have made my translations deliberately literal. The spare style of many of the poems hinders comprehension, and I have therefore inserted 'and's and 'but's to help the reader follow the train of thought that would have been obvious to the ancient reader, while trying to keep this falsification of the style to a minimum. The poems make much use of wordplay between homonyms and homophones, and the more significant instances of this are remarked on in the notes. The diction is quite restricted, and a word will often be repeated through a passage with slightly different meanings; I have tried to preserve this repetition wherever possible, without making the rendering too stilted. I note where these repeats, echoes, and 'keywords' are significant for the meaning.

When only New Kingdom manuscripts are extant I have considered it necessary to draw on conflated texts, and I have not usually followed one manuscript exclusively; I have also silently replaced the New Kingdom version of the colophon with the Middle Kingdom version.

I have made no attempt to render the poems into modern verse, but have marked the end of each ancient line of verse with a new line, following the metrical principles proposed by Gerhard Fecht (see Select Bibliography, p. xvii), but with some modifications. I refer to these units as 'verses', to groups of verses as 'stanzas'. 'Line' refers to a (horizontal or vertical) line of the ancient manuscript; in some manuscripts the horizontal lines of the text are arranged into columns, which I refer to as 'pages'.

Ancient Egyptian verse is almost always written out continuously, and so the lines of text on a papyrus do not correspond to lines of verse; line-breaks can occur in the middle of a verse, a clause, or a word. In the outer margins of the translations I supply numbers referring to the line or section of the original text; these numbers are given only at appropriate intervals to avoid distracting the reader with indications of every new line or section of the text. The numbers in the margin follow the conventions of the standard modern edition of the poem. They give either the line numbers or page and line numbers (e.g. R 1.1) of the principal manuscript, or the section numbers adopted by the standard parallel text edition; in the latter case, subsections are indicated where necessary by a letter or another number following the practice of the edition (thus, the first subsection of section 5 is referred to as 5a or 5.1). When the numbering is that of a parallel text edition, I supply the line numbers of the principal manuscript in parentheses where appropriate. The numbers in the margin do not correspond to the lines of verse in the translations; in the notes I cross-refer to the lines or sections of the text, for the ease of those reading the original text, rather than to the verses of my translations.

As stated in the Preface, there are no indications of uncertainties in translation. Sigla have likewise been kept to the minimum, and are included when only one manuscript survives. I have paid particular attention to lacunae, to considering possible reconstructions, and to assessing the amount of text that is lost, basing my assessments on factors including the surviving traces, the physical size of the lacuna, and the metrical structure. The importance of assessing what and how much of a composition may have been lost has often been underestimated. Losses, omissions, and restorations are indicated as follows.

Square brackets [ ] indicate gaps due to damage to the manuscript. The text inside the brackets is a restoration by the modern editor, either on the basis of the remaining traces of text or on the basis of the context, often drawing on parallel passages in other texts. When restoration is impossible, dots give a visual indication of the amount of text that is missing; [. . .] indicates that a single syllable or complete word is lost in lacuna, and brackets with four or more dots indicate that a phrase of varying length is lost. The dots do not represent a specific number of signs or words. A row of dots in square brackets on a separate line indicates that a complete line of verse, of varying length, is lost. For a loss of three or more verses the following convention is followed: a lacuna of three verses is indicated thus:

[. . . . .]
[*total of 3 verses lost*]
[. . . . .]

If an uncertain number of verses is lost at the start of a text, the translation is headed with:

. . . .]

Angled brackets ⟨ ⟩ indicate an erroneous omission by the ancient copyist. The text inside the brackets is supplied by the modern editor. When restoration is impossible, dots give a visual indication of the amount of text that is missing, as with square brackets.

In the notes, particular words from the passage which are being discussed are set in italics; these lemmata are, however, not always in exactly the same form of the word in the original text. The note is placed at the end of the first verse of the passage that it discusses, and usually at the end of the first verse of a stanza or section of a stanza. Thus, the lemma in the note is usually in the subsequent verses, and only occasionally in the preceding ones.

The notes provide different levels of commentary for various texts. Some of the narratives and much of the didactic writing are clear to follow, as are the 'laments' which have a single theme consistently expounded. Other passages, especially those which are reflective or discursive, need extensive notes to explain the often allusive trains of thought. This requires a certain measure of paraphrase. I do not attempt to indicate the full diversity of possible reactions to the poems, but try to provide pointers towards a unified reading of a remarkably rich and coherent corpus. Since I hope to make the poems accessible to readers of the comparatively modern Western canon such as myself, I have not explored the culturally specific aspects of the ancient corpus in depth. This strategy may underplay the 'otherness' of the poems, but I consider it a necessary step to bring out the distinctive nature of their discourse that is closer to early modern concepts of 'literature' than the reader may at first assume.

SELECT BIBLIOGRAPHY

The Select Bibliography is arranged in two parts. The first provides discussions about general issues raised in the Introduction, divided into studies of the cultural and historical background, and of Egyptian literature (including some general literary studies of relevance to problems in Egyptian literary studies); a list of related anthologies in English follows. The second part lists editions and studies for each text translated here. Only items of major importance to the translations are given, as well as some stimulating studies from whose conclusions I differ.

Abbreviations for frequently cited periodicals, series, and volumes:

ÄA	Ägyptologische Abhandlungen (Wiesbaden)
ÄUAT	Ägypten und Altes Testament (Wiesbaden)
BEHE	Bibliothèque de l'École pratique des hautes études (Paris)
BiOr	Bibliotheca Orientalis
BSEG	Bulletin de la Société d'égyptologie de Genève
CdE	Chronique d'Égypte
DE	Discussions in Egyptology
GM	Göttinger Miszellen
JARCE	Journal of the American Research Center in Egypt
JEA	Journal of Egyptian Archaeology
JSSEA	Journal of the Society for the Study of Egyptian Antiquities
KÄT	Kleine Ägyptische Texte (Wiesbaden)
LÄ	W. Helck et al. (eds.), Lexikon der Ägyptologie (7 vols.; Wiesbaden, 1975–92)
MDAIK	Mitteilungen des Deutschen Archäologischen Instituts, Abteilung Kairo
Or.	Orientalia (NS)
RdE	Revue d'égyptologie
SAK	Studien zur Altägyptischen Kultur
TUAT	Texte aus der Umwelt des Alten Testaments (Gütersloh), ed. O. Kaiser
VA	Varia Aegyptiaca
WdO	Die Welt des Orients
ZÄS	Zeitschrift für ägyptische Sprache und Altertumskunde

Introduction

The Cultural and Historical Background

ARNOLD, DOROTHEA, 'Amenemhat I and the Early Twelfth Dynasty at Thebes', *Metropolitan Museum Journal*, 26 (1991), 5-48.

ASSMANN, J., *Ägypten: Theologie und Frömmigkeit einer frühen Hochkultur* (Stuttgart, 1984).

—— *Ma'at: Gerechtigkeit und Unsterblichkeit im Alten Ägypten* (Munich, 1990).

—— 'Maat und die gespaltene Welt oder: Ägyptertum und Pessimismus', *GM* 140 (1994), 93-100.

—— *Ägypten: Eine Sinngeschichte* (Munich, 1996).

BAINES, J., 'Society, Morality, and Religious Practice', in B. E. Schafer (ed.), *Religion in Ancient Egypt: Gods Myths and Personal Practice* (Ithaca, NY, 1991), 123-200.

BICKEL, S., *La Cosmogonie égyptienne avant le Nouvel Empire* (Orbus Biblicus et Orientalis, 134; Fribourg, 1994)

BOURRIAU, J., *Pharaohs and Mortals: Egyptian Art in the Middle Kingdom* (exhibition catalogue; Cambridge, 1988).

FRANKE, D., *Das Heiligtum des Heqaib auf Elephantine: Geschichte eines Provinzheiligtums im Mittleren Reich* (Studien zur Archäologie und Geschichte Altägyptens, 9; Heidelberg, 1994).

KEMP, B. J., *Ancient Egypt: Anatomy of a Civilization* (London, 1989).

QUIRKE, S. (ed.), *Middle Kingdom Studies* (New Malden, 1991).

RICHARDS, J. E., 'Mortuary Variability and Social Differentiation in Middle Kingdom Egypt', dissertation (Ann Arbor, 1992).

WILDUNG, D., *Sesostris und Amenemhat: Ägypten im Mittleren Reich* (Munich, 1984).

Egyptian Literature

ASSMANN, J., 'Der literarische Text im alten Ägypten: Versuch einer Begriffsbestimmung', *Orientalistiche Literaturzeitung*, 69 (1974), 117-26.

—— 'Königsdogma und Heilserwartung: Politische und kultische Chaosbeschreibungen', in J. Assmann, *Stein und Zeit: Mensch und Gesellschaft im alten Ägypten* (Munich, 1991), 259-87 [repr. from D. Hellholm (ed.), *Apocalypticism in the Mediterranean World and the Near East* (Tübingen, 1983), 345-77].

—— 'Schrift, Tod und Identität: Das Grab als Vorschule der Literatur', in ibid. 169-99 [repr. from A. Assmann *et al.* (eds.), *Schrift und Gedächtnis: Beiträge zur Archäologie der literarischen Kommunikation* (Munich, 1983), 64-93].

—— 'Gibt es eine "Klassik" in der ägyptischen Literaturgeschichte? Ein Beitrag zur Geistesgeschichte der Ramessidenzeit', *Zeitschrift der Deutschen Morgenländischen Gesellschaft*, suppl. 6 (1985), 35-52.

ASSMANN, J., 'Egyptian Literature' in D. N. Freedman (ed.), *The Anchor Bible Dictionary*, ii (New York, 1992), 378–90.

BAINES, J., 'Interpreting Sinuhe', *JEA* 68 (1982), 31–44.

—— 'Literacy and Ancient Egyptian Society', *Man* (n.s.) 18 (1983), 572–99.

—— and EYRE, C. J., 'Four Notes on Literacy', *GM* 61 (1983), 65–96.

BJÖRKMAN, G., 'Egyptology and Historical Method', *Orientalia Suecana*, 13 (1964), 9–23.

EYRE, C. J. and BAINES, J., 'Interactions between Orality and Literacy in Ancient Egypt', in K. Schousboe and M. T. Larsen (eds.), *Literacy and Society* (Copenhagen, 1989), 91–119.

FECHT, G., 'Die Wiedergewinnung der altägyptischen Verskunst', *MDAIK* 19 (1963), 54–96.

—— 'The Structural Principle of Ancient Egyptian Elevated Language', in J. C. de Moor and W. G. E. Watson (eds.), *Verse in Ancient Near Eastern Prose* (ÄUAT 42; Wiesbaden, 1993), 69–94.

FISCHER-ELFERT, H.-W., 'Synchrone und diachrone Interferenzen in literarischen Werken des Mittleren und Neuen Reiches', *Or.* 61 (1992), 354–72.

GREENBLATT, S., *Shakespearean Negotiations: The Circulation of Social Energy in Renaissance England* (Oxford, 1988).

HIRSCH, E. D., *Validity in Interpretation* (New Haven, 1967).

ISER, W., *Prospecting: From Reader Response to Literary Anthropology* (Baltimore, 1989).

JEFFERSON, A., and ROBEY, D. (eds.), *Modern Literary Theory: A Comparative Introduction* (London, 1986).

LICHTHEIM, M., 'Have the Principles of Ancient Egyptian Metrics been Discovered?', *JARCE* 9 (1971), 103–10.

LOPRIENO, A., *Topos und Mimesis: Zum Ausländer in der ägyptischen Literatur* (ÄA 48; Wiesbaden, 1988).

—— 'The Sign of Literature in the Shipwrecked Sailor', in U. Verhoeven and E. Graefe (eds.), *Religion und Philosophie im alten Ägypten: Festgabe für Philippe Derchain zu seinem 65. Geburtstag am 24. Juli 1991* (Orientalia Lovaniensia Analecta, 39; Louvain, 1991), 209–18.

—— 'Defining Egyptian Literature: Ancient Texts and Modern Literary Theory', in J. S. Cooper and G. Schwartz (eds.), *The Study of the Ancient Near East in the 21st Century* (Winona Lake Ind., forthcoming).

—— *Ancient Egyptian: A Linguistic Introduction* (Cambridge, 1995).

—— (ed.), *Ancient Egyptian Literature: History and Forms* (Leiden, 1996)

MOERS, G., and LOPRIENO, A. (eds.), *Definitely: Egyptian Literature. Proceedings of the Symposium 'Ancient Egyptian Literature. History and Forms' Los Angeles, March 24–26, 1995* (Lingua Aegyptia Series Monographica, 2; Göttingen, forthcoming).

NEWTON, K. M., *Interpreting the Text: A Critical Introduction to the Theory and Practice of Literary Interpretation* (London, 1990).

PARKINSON, R. B., 'Teachings, Discourses and Tales from the Middle Kingdom', in S. Quirke (ed.), *Middle Kingdom Studies* (New Malden, 1991), 91–122.

—— 'The Dream and the Knot: Contextualizing Middle Kingdom Literature', in G. Moers and A. Loprieno (eds.), *Definitely: Egyptian Literature. Proceedings of the Symposium 'Ancient Egyptian Literature. History and Forms' Los Angeles, March 24–26, 1995* (Lingua Aegyptia Series Monographica, 2; Göttingen, forthcoming).

POSENER, G., 'Les Richesses inconnues de la littérature égyptienne (Recherches littéraires I)', *RdE* 6 (1951), 27–48.

—— *Littérature et politique dans l'Égypte de la XIIᵉ dynastie* (BEHE 307; Paris, 1957).

Anthologies of Egyptian texts in English

LICHTHEIM, M., *Ancient Egyptian Literature: A Book of Readings*, i. *The Old and Middle Kingdoms* (Berkeley and Los Angeles, 1973).

—— *Ancient Egyptian Biographies Chiefly of the Middle Kingdom: A Study and an Anthology* (Orbus Biblicus et Orientalis, 84; Fribourg, 1988).

PARKINSON, R. B., *Voices from Ancient Egypt: An Anthology of Middle Kingdom Writings* (London, 1991).

SIMPSON, W. K. (ed.), *The Literature of Ancient Egypt: An Anthology of Stories, Instructions, and Poetry*² (New Haven, 1973).

The Texts

1 The Tale of Sinuhe

Text KOCH, R., *Die Erzählung des Sinuhe* (Bibliotheca Aegyptiaca, 17; Brussels, 1990).

ALLAM, S., 'Sinuhe's Foreign Wife (reconsidered)', *DE* 4 (1986), 15–16.

ASSMANN, J., 'Die Rubren in der Überlieferung der Sinuhe-Erzählung', in M. Görg (ed.), *Fontes atque Pontes: Eine Festgabe für Hellmut Brunner* (ÄUAT 5; Wiesbaden, 1983), 18–41.

BAINES, J., 'Interpreting Sinuhe', *JEA* 68 (1982), 31–44.

BARNS, J. W. B., *The Ashmolean Ostracon of Sinuhe* (London, 1952).

—— 'Sinuhe's Message to the King: A Reply to a Recent Article', *JEA* 53 (1967), 6–14.

—— 'Some Readings and Interpretations in Sundry Egyptian Texts', *JEA* 58 (1972), 159–66, esp. 160–1.

BARTA, W., 'Der "Vorwurf an Gott" in der Lebensgeschichte des Sinuhe', in B. Schmitz and A. Eggebrecht (eds.), *Festschrift Jürgen von Beckerath: zum*

70. Geburtstag am 19. Februar 1990 (Hildesheimer ägyptologische Beiträge, 30; Hildesheim, 1990), 21-7.

BEHRENS, P., 'Sinuhe B 134 ff oder die Psychologie eines Zweikampfes', *GM* 44 (1981), 7-11.

BERG, D., 'Note on Sinuhe B 5-7', *GM* 79 (1984), 11-13.

BLUMENTHAL, E., 'Zu Sinuhes Zweikampf mit dem Starken von Retjenu', in M. Görg (ed.), *Fontes atque Pontes: Eine Festgabe für Hellmut Brunner* (ÄUAT 5; Wiesbaden, 1983), 42-6.

—— 'Die Erzählung des Sinuhe', in E. Blumenthal *et al.*, *Mythen und Epen*, iii (TUAT III.5; Gütersloh, 1995), 884-911 [translation with notes and references].

BRUNNER, H., 'Das Besänftigungslied im Sinuhe (B 269-279)', *ZÄS* 80 (1955), 5-11.

CANNUYER, C., 'Note à propos de *Sinouhé B 133-4*', *GM* 88 (1985), 11-13.

DAVIES, W. V., 'Readings in the Story of Sinuhe and other Egyptian Texts', *JEA* 61 (1975), 45-53.

DEFOSSEZ, M. 'Note lexicographique sur le mot *ḥwtf*', in *RdE* 38 (1987), 187-90.

DERCHAIN, P., 'La réception de Sinouhé à la cour de Sésostris Ier', *RdE* 22 (1970), 79-83.

—— 'Sinouhé et Ammounech', *GM* 87 (1985), 7-13.

DONADONI, S. F., 'L'"ispirazione divina" di Sinuhe', in *Cultura del'antico Egitto: Scritti di Sergio F. Donadoni* (Rome, 1986), 289-91.

FECHT, G., 'Sinuhes Zweikampf als Handlungskern des dritten Kapitels des Sinuhe-"Romans" ', in F. Junge (ed.), *Studien zu Sprache und Religion Ägyptens zu Ehren von Wolfhart Westendorf* (Göttingen, 1984), i. 465-84.

FISCHER, H. G., *Egyptian Studies*, i *Varia* (New York, 1976), 97-9.

FOSTER, J. L., 'Cleaning up *Sinuhe*', *JSSEA* 12 (1982), 81-5.

GARDINER, A. H., *Notes on the Story of Sinuhe* (Paris, 1916).

GOEDICKE, H., 'Sinuhe's Duel', *JARCE* 21 (1984), 197-201.

—— 'The Riddle of Sinuhe's Flight', *RdE* 35 (1984), 95-103.

—— 'Sinuhe's Foreign Wife', *BSEG* 9-10 (1984-5), 103-7.

—— 'The Encomium of Sesostris I', *SAK* 12 (1985), 5-28.

—— 'Three Passages in the *Story of Sinuhe*', *JARCE* 23 (1986), 167-74.

—— 'Readings V: Sinuhe B 10', *VA* 4 (1988), 201-6.

—— 'Sinuhe's Self-Realization (Sinuhe B 113-27)', *ZÄS* 117 (1990), 129-39.

—— 'Where did Sinuhe stay in "Asia"? (Sinuhe B 29-31)', *CdE* 67/133 (1992), 28-40.

GRAPOW H., *Der stilistische Bau der Geschichte des Sinuhe* (Untersuchungen zur ägyptischen Stilistik, I; Berlin, 1952).

GREEN, M., 'The Word *ngȝw* in Sinuhe B 13', *GM* 70 (1984), 27-9.

—— 'The Syrian and Lebanese Topographical Data in the Story of Sinuhe', *CdE* 58/115-16 (1983), 38-59.

KITCHEN, K. A., 'Sinuhe B.219-223' in 'Sinuhe's Foreign Friends, and Papyri (Coptic) Greenhill 1-4', in C. J. Eyre *et al.* (eds.), *The Unbroken Reed: Studies in the Culture and Heritage of Ancient Egypt in Honour of A. F. Shore* (Egypt Exploration Society Occasional Publications, 11; London, 1994), 161-4.

LOPRIENO, A., *Topos und Mimesis: Zum Ausländer in der ägyptischen Literatur* (ÄA 48; Wiesbaden, 1988), 41-59.

PARANT, R., *L'Affaire Sinouhé: Tentative d'approche de la justice répresssive égyptienne au début du IIe millénaire av.J.C.* (Aurillac, 1982).

PATANÈ, M., 'Quelques remarques sur Sinouhé', *BSEG* 13 (1989), 131-3.

POSENER, G., *Littérature et politique dans l'Égypte de la XIIe dynastie* (BEHE 307; Paris, 1957), 87-115.

PURDY, S., 'Sinuhe and the Question of Literary Types', *ZÄS* 104 (1977), 112-27.

SCHENKEL, W., 'Sonst-Jetzt: Variationen eines literarischen Formelements', *WdO* 15 (1984), 51-61.

SHIRUN-GRUMACH, I., 'Sinuhe R 24—Wer Rief?', in F. Junge (ed.), *Studien zu Sprache und Religion Ägyptens zu Ehren von Wolfhart Westendorf* (Göttingen, 1984), i. 621-9.

SIMPSON, W. K., 'Sinuhe', in *LÄ* V (1984), 950-5.

THÉODORIDÈS, A., 'L'Amnistie et la raison d'état dans les "Aventures de Sinouhé" (début du IIe millénaire av. J.-C.)', *Revue internationale des droits de l'antiquité*, 3rd ser., 31 (1984), 75-144.

TOBIN, V. A., 'The Secret of Sinuhe', *JARCE* 32 (1995), 161-78.

YOYOTTE, J., 'A propos du panthéon de Sinouhé (B 205-212)', *Kêmi* 17 (1964), 69-73.

WESTENDORF, W., 'Einst—Jetzt—Einst oder: Die Rückkehr zum Ursprung', *WdO* 17 (1986), 5-8.

2 The Tale of the Eloquent Peasant

Text: PARKINSON, R. B., *The Tale of the Eloquent Peasant* (Oxford, 1991).

BERLEV, O. D., 'The Date of the "Eloquent Peasant" ', in J. Osing and G. Dreyer (eds.), *Form und Mass: Beiträge zur Literatur, Sprache und Kunst des Alten Ägypten. Festschrift für Gerhard Fecht* (ÄUAT 12; Wiesbaden, 1987), 78-83.

DÉVAUCHELLE, D., 'Le *Paysan* déraciné', *CdE* 70/139-40 (1995), 34-40.

FECHT, G., 'Bauerngeschichte', in *LÄ* i (1975), 638-51.

—— 'Der beredte Bauer: Die zweite Klage' in P. Der Manuelian (ed.), *Studies in Honor of William Kelly Simpson* (Boston, forthcoming).

GARDINER, A. H., 'The Eloquent Peasant', *JEA* 9 (1923), 5-25.

HERRMANN, S., 'Die Auseinandersetzung mit dem Schöpfergott', in J. Assmann *et al.* (eds.), *Fragen an die altägyptische Literatur: Studien zum Gedenken an Eberhard Otto* (Wiesbaden, 1977), 257-73.

LEPROHON, R. J., 'The Wages of the Eloquent Peasant', *JARCE* 12 (1975), 97–8.

PARKINSON, R. B., 'The Tale of The Eloquent Peasant: A Commentary', doctoral thesis (Oxford, 1988).

—— 'The Date of the "Tale of the Eloquent Peasant" ', *RdE* 42 (1992), 167–77.

—— 'Literary Form and the *Tale of the Eloquent Peasant*', *JEA* 78 (1992), 163–78.

SIMPSON, W. K., 'The Political Background of the Eloquent Peasant', *GM* 120 (1990), 95–9.

VERNUS, P., 'La Date du *Paysan Eloquent*', in S. I. Groll (ed.), *Studies in Egyptology Presented to Miriam Lichtheim* (Jerusalem, 1990), ii. 1033–47.

3 The Tale of the Shipwrecked Sailor

Text BLACKMAN, A. M., *Middle Egyptian Stories* (Bibliotheca Aegyptiaca, 2; Brussels, 1932), 41–8.

ALTENMÜLLER, H., 'Die "Geschichte des Schiffbrüchigen"—ein Aufruf zum Loyalismus?', in H. Altenmüller and R. Germer (eds.), *Miscellanea Aegyptologica: Wolfgang Helck zum 75. Geburtstag* (Hamburg, 1989), 7–21.

BAINES, J., 'Interpreting the Story of the Shipwrecked Sailor', *JEA* 76 (1990), 55–72.

BERG, D., 'Syntax, Semantics and Physics: The Shipwrecked Sailor's Fire', *JEA* 76 (1990), 168–70.

BOLSHAKOV, A. O., 'Some *De Visu* Observations on P. Hermitage 1115', *JEA* 79 (1993), 254–9.

BRADBURY, L., 'Reflections on Traveling to "God's Land" and Punt in the Middle Kingdom', *JARCE* 25 (1988), 127–56, esp. 139–40.

BRYAN, B., 'The Hero of the "Shipwrecked Sailor" ', *Serapis*, 5 (1980), 3–13.

BURKARD, G., *Überlegungen zur Form der ägyptischen Literatur: Die Geschichte des Schiffbrüchigen als literarisches Kunstwerk* (ÄUAT 22; Wiesbaden, 1993).

CANNUYER, C., 'Encore le naufrage du *Naufragé*', *BSEG* 14 (1990), 15–21.

DERCHAIN-URTEL, M.-T., 'Die Schlange des "Schiffbrüchigen" ', *SAK* 1 (1974), 83–104.

DÉVAUD, E., 'Le Conte du naufragé: Remarques grammatiques, lexicographiques, paléographiques, etc.', *Recueil de Travaux*, 38 (1916–17), 188–210.

FOSTER, J. L., 'The Shipwrecked Sailor: Prose or Verse?', *SAK* 15 (1988), 69–109.

GILULA, M., 'Shipwrecked Sailor, Lines 184–85', in J. Johnson and E. F. Wente (eds.), *Studies in Honor of George R. Hughes* (Studies in Ancient Oriental Civilization, 39; Chicago, 1977), 75–82.

HELCK, W., 'Die "Geschichte des Schiffbrüchigen"—eine Stimme der Opposition?' in J. Osing and E. R. Nielsen (eds.), *The Heritage of Ancient Egypt: Studies in Honour of Erik Iversen* (CNI Publications, 13; Copenhagen, 1992), 73–6.

IGNATOV, S., 'Some Notes on the *Story of the Shipwrecked Sailor*', *JEA* 80 (1994), 195–8.

LOPRIENO, A., 'The Sign of Literature in the Shipwrecked Sailor', in U. Verhoeven and E. Graefe (eds.), *Religion und Philosophie im alten Ägypten: Festgabe für Phillippe Derchain zu seinem 65. Geburtstag am 24. Juli 1991* (Orientalia Lovaniensia, 39; Louvain, 1991), 209–18.

MANUELIAN, P. DER, 'Interpreting "The Shipwrecked Sailor"', in I. Gamer-Wallert and W. Helck (eds.) *Gegengabe: Festschrift für Emma Brunner-Traut* (Tübingen, 1992), 223–33.

SIMPSON, W. K., 'Schiffbrüchiger', in *LÄ* v (1984), 619–22.

SPALINGER, A., 'An Alarming Parallel to the End of the Shipwrecked Sailor', *GM* 73 (1984), 91–5.

VANDERSLEYEN, C., 'En relisant le Naufragé', in S. Israelit-Groll (ed.), *Studies in Egyptology Presented to Miriam Lichtheim* (Jerusalem, 1990), ii. 1019–24.

WESTENDORF, W., 'Die Insel des Schiffbrüchigen—keine Halbinsel!', in S. Israelit-Groll (ed.), *Studies in Egyptology Presented to Miriam Lichtheim* (Jerusalem, 1990), ii. 1056–64.

4 The Tale of King Cheops' Court

Text BLACKMAN, A. M., *The Story of King Kheops and the Magicians: Transcribed from Papyrus Westcar, Berlin Papyrus 3033*, ed. W. V. Davies (Reading, 1988).

BAROCAS, C., 'Les Contes du Papyrus Westcar', *SAK Beiheft* 3 (1988), 121–9.

BORGHOUTS, J. F., 'Enigmatic Chests', *Jaarbericht van het Vooraziatisch-Egyptisch Genootschap (Gezelschap) 'Ex Oriente Lux'*, 23 (1975), 35–64 [of indirect relevance].

DERCHAIN, P., 'Snéferou et les rameuses', *RdE* 21 (1969), 19–25.

—— 'Deux notules à propos du Papyrus Westcar', *GM* 89 (1986), 15–21.

EDEL, E., 'Der Kanal der beiden Fische', *DE* 16 (1990), 31–3.

EYRE, C. J., 'Fate, Crocodiles and Judgement of the Dead: Some Mythological Allusions in Egyptian Literature', *SAK* 4 (1976), 103–14.

—— 'Yet Again the Wax Crocodile: P. Westcar 3, 12ff.', *JEA* 78 (1992), 280–1.

FISCHER, H. G., 'Some Iconographic and Literary Comparisons', in J. Assmann *et al.* (eds.), *Fragen an die altägyptische Literatur: Studien zum Gedenken an Eberhard Otto* (Weisbaden, 1977), 155–70.

GOEDICKE, H., 'Rudjedet's Delivery', *VA* 1 (1985), 19–26.

—— 'Gentlemen's Salutations', *VA* 2 (1986), 161-70.

—— 'Thoughts about the Papyrus Westcar', *ZÄS* 120 (1992), 23-36.

HORNUNG, E., 'Die "Kammern" des Thot-Heiligtumes', *ZÄS* 100 (1974), 33-5.

MELTZER, E. S., 'The Art of the Storyteller in Papyrus Westcar: An Egyptian Mark Twain?', in B. Bryan and D. Lorton (eds.), *Essays in Egyptology in Honor of Hans Goedicke* (San Antonio, Tex., 1994), 169-75.

SIMPSON W. K., 'Pap. Westcar', in *LÄ* iv (1982), 744-6.

STAEHELIN, E., 'Bindung und Entbindung: Erwägungen zu Papyrus Westcar 10,2', *ZÄS* 96 (1970), 125-39.

5 The Words of Neferti

Text HELCK, W., *Die Prophezeiung des Nfr.tj* (KÄT; Wiesbaden, 1970).

BLUMENTHAL, E., 'Neferti, Prophezeiung des', in *LÄ* iv (1982), 380-1.

—— 'Die Prophezeiung des Neferti', *ZÄS* 109 (1982), 1-27.

EYRE, C. J., 'Why was Egyptian Literature?', in *Sesto Congresso Internazionale di Egittologia: Atti*, ii (Turin, 1993), 115-27.

GOEDICKE, H., *The Protocol of Neferyt* (Baltimore, 1977).

GRAEFE, E., 'Die gute Reputation des Königs "Snofru" ', in S. Israelit-Groll (ed.), *Studies in Egyptology Presented to Miriam Lichtheim* (Jerusalem, 1990), i. 257-63.

KAMMERZELL, F., 'Die Prophezeiung des Neferti', in M. Dietrich *et al.*, *Deutungen der Zukunft in Briefen, Oraklen und Omina* (TUAT II.1; Gütersloh, 1986), 102-10 [translation with references].

POSENER, G., *Littérature et politique dans l'Égypte de la XIIᵉ dynastie* (BEHE 307; Paris, 1957), 21-60, 145-57.

QUACK, J. F., 'Beiträge zur Textkritik der Prophezeihung des Neferti', *GM* 135 (1993), 77-9.

6 The Words of Khakheperreseneb

Text GARDINER, A. H., *The Admonitions of an Ancient Egyptian Sage, from a Hieratic Papyrus in Leiden* (Leipzig, 1909), 95-112, pls. 17-18.

PARKINSON, R. B., 'The Text of *Khakheperreseneb*: New Readings of EA 5645 and an Unpublished Ostracon' (forthcoming).

CHAPPAZ, J.-L., 'Un manifeste littéraire du Moyen Empire—Les lamentations de Kha-khéper-ré-seneb', *BSEG* 2 (1979), 3-12.

HELCK, W., 'Lehre des Cha-cheper-Re-seneb', in *LÄ* iii (1980), 977.

KADISH, G. E., 'British Museum Writing Board 5645: The Complaints of Kha-kheper-Rēʿ-senebu', *JEA* 59 (1973), 77-90.

OCKINGA, B., 'The Burden of Khaʿkheperrēʿsonbu', *JEA* 69 (1983), 88-95.

Отто, E., 'Chacheperreseneb', in *LÄ* i (1975), 896-7.

PARKINSON, R. B., *'Khakheperreseneb* and Traditional Belles Lettres' in P. Der Manuelian (ed.), *Studies in Honor of William Kelly Simpson* (Boston, forthcoming).

VERNUS, P., 'L'Intuition de Khâkheperrêseneb', in Vernus, *Essai sur la conscience de l'Histoire dans l'Égypte pharaonique* (Paris, 1995), 1-33.

7 *The Dialogue of a Man and his Soul*

Text FAULKNER, R. O., 'The Man who was Tired of Life', *JEA* 42 (1956), 21-40.

BARTA, W., *Das Gespräch eines Mannes mit seinem BA* (*Papyrus Berlin 3024*) (Münchner Ägyptologische Studien, 18; Berlin, 1969).

BRUNNER-TRAUT, E., 'Der Lebensmüde und sein Ba', *ZÄS* 94 (1967), 6-15.

FECHT, G., 'Die Belehrung des Ba und der "Lebensmüde" ', *MDAIK* 47 (1991), 113-26.

FOX, M. V., 'A Study of Antef', *Or.* 46 (1977), 393-423 [of indirect relevance].

GOEDICKE, H., *The Report about the Dispute of a Man with his Ba:* (*P Berlin 3024*) (Baltimore, 1970).

HANNIG, R., 'Die erste Parabel des "Lebensmüden" (LM 68-80)', *Journal of Ancient Civilizations* (IHAC), 6 (1991), 23-31.

LEAHY, A., 'Death by Fire in Ancient Egypt', *Journal of the Economic and Social History of the Orient*, 27 (1984), 199-206 [of indirect relevance].

LETELLIER, B., 'De la vanité des biens de ce monde: L'Évocation d'un personnage de fable dans le "Désespéré" (P. Berlin 3024, col. 30-39)', *Cahier de recherches de l'Institut de papyrologie et égyptologie de Lille*, 13 (1991), 99-105.

MATHIEU, B., 'Se souvenir de l'Occident (*sḫ3 Jmnt.t*): Une expression de la piété religieuse au Moyen Empire', *RdE* 42 (1991), 262-3 [of indirect relevance].

OSING, J., ' "Gespräch des Lebensmüden" ', in *LÄ* ii (1977), 571-3.

RENAUD, O., *Le Dialogue du Désespéré avec son Âme: Une interprétation littéraire* (Cahiers de la Société d'égyptologie, 1; Geneva, 1991).

TOBIN, V. A., 'A Re-assessment of the *Lebensmüde*', *BiOr* 48 (1991), 341-63.

WILLIAMS, R. J., 'Reflections on the *Lebensmüde*', *JEA* 48 (1962), 49-56.

8 *The Dialogue of Ipuur and the Lord of All*

Text GARDINER, A. H., *The Admonitions of an Ancient Egyptian Sage, from a Hieratic Papyrus in Leiden* (Leipzig, 1909).

HELCK, W., *Die "Admonitions" Pap. Leiden I 344 recto* (KÄT 11; Wiesbaden, 1995). This edition incorporates speculative emendations and restorations, and is unreliable; I retain many of Gardiner's readings, and those suggested by Fecht, cited below. The fragmentary state of the manuscript makes the reading of many passages uncertain.

BARTA, W., 'Das Gespräch des Ipuwer mit dem Schöpfergott', *SAK* 1 (1974), 19-33.

FECHT, G., *Der Vorwurf an Gott in den 'Mahnworten des Ipu-wer'* (Abhandlungen der Heidelberger Akademie der Wissenschaften, Phil.-hist. Kl. 1972, 1; Heidelberg, 1972).

—— 'Ägyptische Zweifel am Sinn des Opfers: Admonitions 5,7-9', *ZÄS* 100 (1974), 6-16.

FAULKNER, R. O., 'Notes on "The Admonitions of an Egyptian Sage" ', *JEA* 50 (1964), 24-36.

GILULA, M., 'Does God Exist?', in D. W. Young (ed.), *Studies Presented to Hans Jakob Polotsky* (Beacon Hill, Mass., 1981), 390-400.

OTTO, E., *Der Vorwurf an Gott: zur Entstehung der ägyptischen Auseinandersetzungsliteratur* (Vorträge der orientalistischen Tagung in Marburg: Ägyptologie; Hildesheim, 1951).

POSENER, G., 'Admonitions 3¹⁴', *RdE* 5 (1946), 254-5.

ROCCATI, A., '[šmw šḥnw]', in C. Berger *et al.* (eds.), *Hommages à Jean Leclant* (Cairo, 1994), i. 493-7.

SCHORR, E., 'Admonitions 9,3', *GM* 13 (1974), 29-30.

SPIEGEL, J., 'Admonitions', in *LÄ* I (1975), 65-6.

9 The Teaching of King Amenemhat

Text HELCK, W., *Der Text der 'Lehre Amenemhets I. für seinen Sohn'* (KÄT; Wiesbaden, 1969). (Additional manuscripts included in publications listed below.)

BLUMENTHAL, E., 'Lehre Amenemhets I.', in *LÄ* iii (1980), 968-71.

—— 'Die Lehre des Königs Amenemhet', *ZÄS* 111 (1984), 85-107; 112 (1985), 104-15.

BURKARD, G., *Textkritische Untersuchungen zu altägyptischen Weisheitslehren des Alten und Mittleren Reiches* (ÄA 34; Wiesbaden, 1977), 31-44, 99-102, 124-6, 164-70, 187-9, 212-16, 264-6, 307-10.

FISCHER-ELFERT, H.-W., 'Textkritische Kleinigkeiten zur "Lehre des Amenemhet" ', *GM* 70 (1984), 89-90.

FOSTER, J. L., 'The Conclusion to *The Testament of Ammenemes, King of Egypt*', *JEA* 67 (1981), 35-47.

GOEDICKE, H., *Studies in 'The Instruction of King Amenemhet I for his Son'* (Varia Aegyptiaca, suppl. 2; San Antonio, Tex., 1988).

GRIMAL, N., 'Le Sage, l'eau et le roi', in B. Menu (ed.), *Les Problèmes institutionnels de l'eau en Égypte ancienne et dans l'Antiquité méditerranéenne*

(Colloque AIDEA Vogüé 1992, Bibliothèque d'étude 110; Cairo, [1995]), 195–203.

—— 'Corégence et association au trône: l'*Enseignement d'Amenemhat Ier*', *BIFAO* 95 (1995), 273–80.

OBSOMER, C., *Sésostris Ier*: *Étude chronologique et historique du règne* (Brussels, 1995), esp. 112–33.

POSENER, G., *Littérature et politique dans l'Égypte de la XIIe dynastie* (BEHE 307; Paris, 1957), 61–86.

SCHAEFER, A., 'Zur Entstehung der Mitregentschaft als Legitimationsprinzip von Herrschaft', *ZÄS* 113 (1986), 44–55.

THÉRIAULT, C. A., 'The Instruction of Amenemhat as Propaganda', *JARCE* 30 (1993), 151–60.

WESTENDORF, W., 'Die Menschen als Ebenbilder Pharaos: Bemerkungen zur "Lehre des Amenemhet" (Abschnitt V)', *GM* 46 (1981), 33–42.

10 The Teaching for King Merikare

Text HELCK, W., *Die Lehre für König Merikare* (KÄT; Wiesbaden, 1977).
   QUACK, J. F., *Studien zur Lehre für Merikare* (Göttinger Orientforschungen iv. 23; Wiesbaden, 1992).

BLUMENTHAL, E., 'Die Lehre für König Merikare', *ZÄS* 107 (1980), 5–41.

BURKARD, G., *Textkritische Untersuchungen zu altägyptischen Weisheitslehren des Alten und Mittleren Reiches* (ÄA 34; Wiesbaden, 1977), 18–31, 94–8, 120–4, 154–64, 209–12, 256–64, 303–7.

DEMEDCHIK, A., 'A Note to §141 of Sir A. H. Gardiner's "Egyptian Grammar"', *GM* 134 (1993), 29–30.

DERCHAIN, P., 'Éloquence et politique: L'Opinion d'Akhtoy', *RdE* 40 (1989), 37–47.

DONADONI, S. F., 'À propos de l'histoire du texte de "Merikarê"', in *Cultura dell'antico Egitto: Scritti di Sergio F. Donadoni* (Rome, 1986), 129–36.

LÒPEZ, J., 'L'Auteur de l'Enseignement pour Mérikarê', *RdE* 25 (1973), 178–91.

POSENER, G., 'Trois passages de l'Enseignement à Mérikarê', *RdE* 7 (1950), 176–80.

—— 'Lehre für Merikare', in *LÄ* iii (1980), 986–9.

—— 'L'Enseignement pour le roi Mérikarê' [summary of course], *Annuaire du Collège de France* 62 (1962), 290–95; 63 (1963), 303–5; 64 (1964), 305–7; 65 (1965), 343–6; 66 (1966), 342–5.

QUACK, J. F., 'Zwei Ostraka-Identifizierungen', *GM* 115 (1990), 83–4.

ROWINSKA, E., and WINNICKI, J. K., 'Staatausdehnung (P 67–68) und Massnahmen zur Verstärkung der Nordostgrenze (P 106–109) in der "Lehre für den König Merikare"', *ZÄS* 119 (1992), 130–43.

11 *The 'Loyalist' Teaching*

Text POSENER, G., *L'Enseignement loyaliste*: *Sagesse égyptienne du Moyen Empire* (Centre de recherches d'histoire et de philologie II—Hautes études orientales, 5; Geneva, 1976).

BERLEV, O. D., [review of W. K. Simpson, *The Terrace of the Great God at Abydos*], *BiOr* 33 (1976), 324-6, esp. 325.

FISCHER-ELFERT, H.-W., 'Vermischtes III: Loyalistische Lehre und Totenbrief (*Cairo Bowl*) im Vergleich', *GM* 143 (1994), 41-4.

POSENER, G., 'Lehre, loyalistische', in *LÄ* iii (1980), 982-4.

SIMPSON, W. K., 'Mentuhotep, Vizier of Sesostris I, Patron of Art and Architecture', *MDAIK* 47 (1991), 331-40, esp. 337.

12 *The Teaching of the Vizier Ptahhotep*

Text ŽÁBA, Z., *Les Maximes de Ptahhotep* (Académie tchécoslovaque des sciences, section de la linguistique et de la littérature; Prague, 1956).
CAMINOS, R., *Literary Fragments in the Hieratic Script* (Oxford, 1956), 52-3, pls. 28 30.

BLUMENTHAL, E., 'Ptahhotep und der "Stab des Alters"', in J. Osing and G. Dreyer (eds.), *Form und Mass: Beiträge zur Literatur, Sprache und Kunst des Alten Ägypten*; *Festschrift für Gerhard Fecht* (ÄUAT 12; Wiesbaden, 1987), 84-97.

BRUNNER, H., 'Lehre des Ptahhotep', in *LÄ* iii (1980), 989-91.

BURKARD, G., 'Ptahhotep und das Alter', *ZÄS* 115 (1988), 19-30.

—— *Textkritische Untersuchungen zu altägyptischen Weisheitslehren des Alten und Mittleren Reiches* (ÄA 34; Wiesbaden, 1977), 10-18, 73-93, 117-20, 146-54, 192-209, 230-42, 247-56, 287-302.

CANNUYER, C., 'L'Obèse de Ptahhotep et de Samuel', *ZÄS* 113 (1986), 92-103.

FECHT, G., *Der Habgierige und die Maat in der Lehre des Ptahhotep (5. und 19. Maxime)* (Abhandlungen des Deutschen Archäologischen Instituts Kairo, 1; Glückstadt, 1958).

—— 'Ptahhotep und die Disputierer (Lehre des Ptahhotep nach Pap. Prisse, Max. 2-4, Dév. 60-83)', *MDAIK* 37 (1981), 143-150 [with errata sheet in *MDAIK* 38 (1982)].

—— 'Cruces Interpretum in der Lehre des Ptahhotep (Maximen 7, 9, 13, 14) und das Alter der Lehre', in A. Guillaumont (ed.), *Hommages à François Daumas* (Montpellier, 1986), i. 227-51.

FISCHER-ELFERT, H.-W., 'Vermischtes III: Zwei neue Ptahhotep-Spuren', *GM* 143 (1994), 45-7.

PARKINSON, R. B., '"Homosexual" Desire and Middle Kingdom Literature', *JEA* 81 (1995), 57-76, esp. 68-70.

TROY, L., 'Good and Bad Women: Maxim 18/284–288 of the Instructions of Ptahhotep', *GM* 80 (1984), 77–81.

VERNUS, P., 'L'Intertextualité dans la culture pharaonique: l'Enseignement de Ptahhotep et le graffito d'jmny (Ouâdi Hammâmât n° 3042)', *GM* 147 (1995), 103–9.

13 *The Teaching of Khety*

Text HELCK, W., *Die Lehre des Dw3-Ḥtjj* (2 vols.; KÄT; Wiesbaden, 1970).

BRUNNER, H., 'Lehre des Cheti' in *LÄ* iii (1980), 977–8.

BURKARD, G., *Textkritische Untersuchungen zu altägyptischen Weisheitslehren des Alten und Mittleren Reiches* (ÄA 34; Wiesbaden, 1977), 44–65, 102–8, 126–39, 170–85, 189–90, 216–29, 266–82, 310–15.

HOCH, J. E., 'The Teaching of Dua-Kheti: A New Look at the Satire of the Trades', *JSSEA* 21/22 (1991/1992), 88–100.

POSENER, G., 'L'Auteur de la Satire des Métiers', in J. Vercoutter (ed.), *Livre du Centenaire: 1880–1980* (Mémoires publiés par les membres de l'Institut français d'archéologie orientale du Cairo, 104; Cairo, 1980), 55–9.

QUACK, J. F., 'Zwei Ostraka-Identifizierungen', *GM* 115 (1990), 83–4.

ROCCATI, A., *Sapienza egizia: La letteratura educativa in Egitto durante il II millennio a. C.* (Brescia, 1994), 79–87 [translation incorporating an unpublished papyrus in Museo Egizio, Turin].

SEIBERT, P., *Die Charakteristik: Untersuchungen zu einer altägyptischen Sprechsitte und ihren Ausprägungen in Folklore und Literatur. Teil I: Philologische Bearbeitung der Bezeugungen* (ÄA 17; Wiesbaden, 1967).

THÉODORIDÈS, A., 'La "Satire des Métiers" et les marchands', *Annuaire de l'Institut de Philologie et d'Histoire Orientales et Slaves* 15 (1958–60), 39–69.

WESTENDORF, W., 'Eine Formel des Totenbuches als Schreibfehler in der "Lehre des (Dua-)Cheti" ', *GM* 5 (1973), 43–5.

14 *Phrases and Fragments*

The Tale of the Herdsman

GARDINER, A. H., *Die Erzählung des Sinuhe und die Hirtengeschichte* (Literarische Texte des Mittleren Reiches, 2; Leipzig, 1909), 6, 15, pls. 16–17. This publication does not include the erased lines; my reading of these is based on an examination of the original. The erased lines are unnumbered.

GILULA, M., '*Hirtengeschichte* 17–22 = CT VII 36m–r', *GM* 29 (1978), 21–2.

GOEDICKE, H., 'The Story of the Herdsman', *CdE* 45/90 (1970), 244–66.

OGDON, J. R., 'CT VII, 36i–r = Spell 836', *GM* 58 (1982), 59–64.

OGDON, J. R., 'A Hitherto Unrecognised Metaphor of Death in Papyrus Berlin 3024', *GM* 100 (1987), 73–80.

The Tale of King Neferkare and Sasenet (P. Chassinat I X+3.x+2–10)

KAMMERZELL, F., 'Von der Affäre um König Nafirku'ri'a und seinen General', in E. Blumenthal *et al.*, *Mythen und Epen*, iii (TUAT III.5; Gütersloh, 1995), 965–9.

PARKINSON, R. B., ' "Homosexual" Desire and Middle Kingdom Literature', *JEA* 81 (1995), 57–76, esp. 71–4.

POSENER, G., 'Le Conte de Néferkarè et du general Siséné (Recherches littéraires IV)', *RdE* 11 (1957), 119–37.

VAN DIJK, J, 'The Nocturnal Wanderings of King Neferkarē'' in C. Berger *et al.* (eds.), *Hommages à Jean Leclant* (Cairo, 1994), iv. 387–93.

The Tale of P. Lythgoe (recto ll. 2–5)

SIMPSON, W. K., 'Papyrus Lythgoe: A Fragment of a Literary Text of the Middle Kingdom from el-Lisht', *JEA* 46 (1960), 65–70.

The Tale of a King and a Ghost (P. Chassinat II Frag. A+B.x+7–x+8)

POSENER, G., 'Une nouvelle histoire de revenant (Recherches littéraries, VII)', *RdE* 12 (1960), 75–82.

The Discourse of Sasobek (P. Ramesseum I A.17–19)

BARNS, J. W. B., *Five Ramesseum Papyri* (Oxford, 1956), 1–10, pls. 1–6.

The Discourse of the Fowler (P. British Museum EA 10274 verso, ll. 16–21)

GRIFFITH, F. Ll., 'Fragments of Old Egyptian Stories from the BM and Amherst Collections', *Proceedings of the Society for Biblical Archaeology*, 14 (1892), 451–72, esp. 458, pls. 3–[5]. The translation is based on an examination of the original.
This may be the same composition as the one whose title is preserved on a papyrus in Moscow: see G. Posener, 'Fragment littéraire de Moscou', *MDAIK* 25 (1969), 101–6.

The Teaching for Kagemni (P. Prisse 1.1–2.9)

GARDINER, A. H., 'The Instruction addressed to Kagemni and his Brethren', *JEA* 32 (1946), 71–4.
—— 'Kagemni Once Again', *JEA* 37 (1951), 109–10.
MORSCHAUSER, S., 'The Opening Lines of K3-gm.n.i (P. Prisse I, 1–3a)', in B. Bryan and D. Lorton (eds.), *Essays in Egyptology in Honor of Hans Goedicke* (San Antonio, Tex., 1994), 177–85.

The Teaching of Hordedef (2.1–4 [ed. Helck])

HELCK, W., *Die Lehre des Djedefhor und die Lehre eines Vaters an seinen Sohn* (KÄT; Wiesbaden, 1984), 1–24.

POSENER, G., 'Lehre des Djedefhor', in *LÄ* iii (Wiesbaden, 1980), 978–80.

The Teaching of a Man for his Son (1.1–2.1, 18.5–7 [ed. Helck] = 0.1–1.5, 24.7–10 [ed. Fischer-Elfert])

HELCK, W., *Die Lehre des Djedefhor und die Lehre eines Vaters an seinen Sohn* (KÄT; Wiesbaden, 1984), 25–72.

A new edition containing much more of the text is being prepared by H.-W. Fischer-Elfert; see Fischer-Elfert, '*Die Lehre eines Mannes für seinen Sohn*': *Eine Etappe auf dem 'Gottesweg' des loyalen Beamten der frühen 12. Dynastie*, Habilitationschrift (Würzburg, 1993).

The Maxims of P. Ramesseum II (recto i.1, iii.5, iv.3)

BARNS, J. W. B., *Five Ramesseum Papyri* (Oxford, 1956), 11–14, pls. 7–9.

The Account of the Sporting King (P. Moscow [unnumbered] B 2.4–9), and *The Account of the Pleasures of Fishing and Fowling* (P. Moscow [unnumbered] A 2.1–3, B 2.9–11, B 4.2–5)

CAMINOS, R., *Literary Fragments in the Hieratic Script* (Oxford, 1956), 1–39, pls. 1–16.

See also W. Decker, *Quellentexte zu Sport und Körperkultur im Alten Ägypten* (Sankt Augustin, 1975), 31–44.

Further Reading in Oxford World's Classics

The Bhagavad Gita, trans. and ed. W. J. Johnson.
HESIOD, *Theogony and Works and Days*, trans. and ed. M. L. West.
HOMER, *The Iliad*, trans. Robert Fitzgerald, ed. G. S. Kirk.
—— *The Odyssey*, trans. Walter Shewring, ed. G. S. Kirk.
Myths from Mesopotamia, trans. and ed. Stephanie Dalley.

CHRONOLOGY

All dates are approximate

The Tenth Dynasty, ruling in the north	2080–1987
Various kings called Khety, including:	
Nebkaure Khety	
Merikare Khety	

The Eleventh Dynasty, initially ruling in the south	
Intef I	2081–2065
Intef II	2065–2016
Intef III	2016–2008

Rulers of all Egypt	
Nebhetepre Montuhotep (II)	2008–1957
Sankhkare Montuhotep (III)	1957–1945
Nebtawire Montuhotep (IV)	1945–1939

The Twelfth Dynasty	
(Overlapping dates indicate co-regencies)	
Amenemhat I	1938–1908
Senwosret I	1918–1875
Amenemhat II	1876–1842
Senwosret II	1844–1837
Senwosret III	1836–1818
Amenemhat III	1818–1770
Amenemhat IV	1770–1760
Queen Neferusobek	1760–1756

The Thirteenth Dynasty   1756–1640
A series of ephemeral kings; only the most important are listed,
with their approximate position in the Dynasty, according to the
Turin Royal Canon
  4 Sekhemkare Amenemhat (V)
12 Khaankhre Sobekhotep (I)

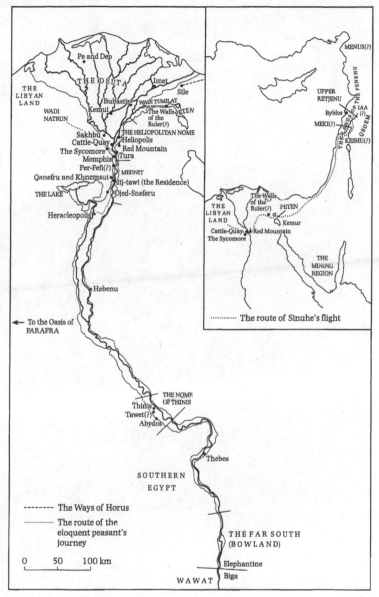

MAP. Egypt and the surrounding areas showing places named in the poems.

INTRODUCTION

Or duopo è d'un gran core e d'un bel canto.

A. Striggio, *L'Orfeo* (1607), III

An Ancient Egyptian Reader

Around 1800 BC in the reign of the great king Amenemhat III, a man lived at Thebes whose position in the state bureaucracy was high enough for him to build a tomb on the west bank of the Nile—probably the sort of man who could also dedicate a small but tasteful statue of himself in the local temple. Like others of his position and education, he was proud of his knowledge of literature, and he copied out on a reused roll of papyrus in his own professional hand, the highly regarded *Tale of Sinuhe*, which had been composed at the royal court in the north in his grandfather's time. He also made his own copy, with some enthusiasm and haste, of another fine work, *The Tale of the Eloquent Peasant*; this copy lacked the end of the poem, but he later managed to acquire part of a roll that included the final stanzas. He also possessed a roll with the poetic *Dialogue of a Man and his Soul*, perhaps copied by a friend who had been trained by the same master-scribe as himself; this manuscript had to be patched with a sheet from a discarded roll that contained another old, but less well-liked, Tale. When he died, his collection of four manuscripts seems to have been buried with him, and it survived to be discovered in unrecorded circumstances and subsequently auctioned in London in 1843.

We know almost nothing about this man, not even his name, his rank, or the exact location of his tomb. The preceding speculative account of his existence is based entirely on the surviving papyri.[1] The most certain thing that we know about him, apart from his

---

[1] Now P. Berlin 3022-5. My imaginative reconstruction draws on various features of the group of papyri; see R. B. Parkinson, *The Tale of the Eloquent Peasant* (Oxford, 1991), p. ix–xxx. For the Tale on the reused roll see pp. 287-8.

handwriting, is that he was a person of high literary taste, for his manuscripts contain three masterpieces that are among the supreme achievements of his culture. These manuscripts remained unread, however, for over three-and-a-half millennia, and during this period all knowledge of their poetry vanished as completely as his name.

Approaching Ancient Egyptian Literature

From antiquity, Ancient Egypt exerted a fascination as a land of strange gods, impenetrable symbols, magicians, and tyrants, and it was only in the 1820s that decipherment revealed that hieroglyphs were not allegorical mysteries, but a practical script used for a wide range of writings, including literature. Ancient Egyptian poems, with their frivolity and pessimism, challenged the scholars' preconceptions about that civilization, and still have an allure for us as the voices of the dead speaking their thoughts and feelings with enduring artistry.

The rediscovery of Ancient Egyptian literature can be dated precisely to the 22 July 1828, when Jean-François Champollion, the decipherer of the hieroglyphic script, viewed the collection of François Sallier on his way to Egypt, and saw Papyrus Sallier II (now in the British Museum), which contains a copy of *The Teaching of King Amenemhat*, composed c.1900 BC. However, he did not recognize its literary character, since at that date preclassical literature—with the exception of the Bible—was little regarded. Until quite recently, Egyptian poems were read largely for their adventitious historical interest and their supposed documentary information, and they are a strange mixture of the familiar and of elements that now seem very unliterary. Literature is not only older than is often assumed, but more varied.[2]

Egyptian writing is very rich, and the poems translated here are a small section belonging to a larger tradition much of which has literary or poetic qualities. No criticism survives from Ancient Egypt, nor any explicit indications of how the Egyptians assessed 'literature', for which there was no specific Egyptian term. In an attempt to define literature, one is left with deductions from the contexts of the manuscripts and from the works themselves. The extant literary

---

[2] For example, *The Teaching of King Amenemhat* was still being copied in Egypt when Sappho was composing her more familiar-sounding lyrics.

corpus existed side by side with a much larger and rather better pre-
served body of religious texts, which it often resembles in style and
in density of meaning. From various features, one can suggest that
literature is an institution which is defined and created by its cul-
ture; whether a text is part of the institution or not is determined
by formal criteria—that is, by genres. A linguistic approach is also
valuable in identifying features that are characteristic of literature,
if not unique to it.

Egyptian literary texts exhibit various distinctive features: they
mingle the general and the particular; they are self-conscious and
concerned with self-definition and expression; they are not bound
to any context or situation; aesthetic considerations are of central
value; the speaker–hearer relationship is dramatized with framing
devices. Perhaps most importantly, they are fictional. This last fea-
ture distinguishes them from commemorative texts, which were
intended to be accurate—if idealized—accounts, and from religious
texts, which were intended to be authentic reflections of the uni-
verse. Fiction, however, allows its audience a vision of a different
reality and an experience of alternative possibilities. Egyptian liter-
ature was also a predominantly secular mode of discourse, being
concerned with the 'here and now', but it was one which spanned
various spheres, and crossed the secular–sacred and royal–private
divides; it was not limited to a particular single function. This
feature is reflected in its physical mobility: it was copied on privately
owned rolls of papyrus, not stelae, or tomb or temple walls.
Literature was not like the funerary texts, whose numerous copies
drew—with local variants—from a fairly restricted set of religious
utterances; the literary papyri are the results of individuals choos-
ing to copy individual works. Most ancient settlements are now
under cultivation and waterlogged, so that usually only those
papyri that were placed in dry tombs or stored in some other desert
location have survived. These papyri are often little more than
scraps, and very few copies are free from major gaps.

After three millennia, the survival of any manuscripts is remark-
able. Thirteen poems are translated here, of the thirty-five or so
works that are preserved to any extent and can be dated to the 300-
year period of the Middle Kingdom, c.1940–1640 BC. This is equiv-
alent in length to the period in English history between the birth of
Chaucer and the composition of *Paradise Lost*, or from the birth of
Shakespeare to the death of Charlotte Brontë, although Egyptian

society was much smaller, less literate, and less productive of literature than the English society of these periods. It is unknown how many works are lost; whole genres may not have survived, but the relative coherence of what remains makes this unlikely, even though there is not a single complete copy of some types of text. The relative chronology of the compositions also remains uncertain. As excavations continue, and museum collections are studied in greater detail, new texts will appear that are bound to modify current analyses.

Contemporaneous papyri are not the only sources. Some Middle Kingdom works became established classics in the following New Kingdom (c.1550–1070 BC), and some survive only in later papyri. In addition, short excerpts were copied onto flakes of limestone, often by apprentice scribes for whom the classic works were set texts. This practice increases the textual problems for the modern scholar, not only because young scribes made errors in copying a poetic language that was by then far distant from everyday language, but also because they sometimes had no access to a coherent or comprehensible textual tradition.[3] *The Teaching of Khety*, for example, was the most copied work on the syllabus as it extolled the profession of the scribe, but all the copies are so corrupt that it must have been virtually unintelligible. It is tempting to think that the texts of which numerous copies are known, such as *The Tale of Sinuhe*, were held in some particular esteem. It would be some consolation to the modern researcher to suppose that the surviving copies represent the major ancient classics, but a New Kingdom Miscellany text listing sages of wisdom literature makes it clear that some of the most famous works have not survived,[4] while the chances of preservation are so random that a poem's survival in a single manuscript does not mean that it was not highly regarded.[5]

Philology still has a central role in providing the critic with the means to shape expectations and assess the probability of competing interpretations, and is crucial in attempting any evaluation. Problems attend the most basic questions of translating and interpreting what survives. Many details of grammar and vocabulary remain obscure and controversial. After surviving so much, the poems remain confined by these academic difficulties, and have not

---

[3] For textual reasons, the fragmentary *Teaching of a Man for his Son*, which is being reassembled by H.-W. Fischer-Elfert, is excluded; see pp. 292–3.

[4] See n. 24.   [5] Such as *The Dialogue of a Man and his Soul*.

yet become, as early Egyptologists once hoped, 'a part of the stock-in-trade of literary criticism'.[6] Despite these difficulties, the artistry of the poems retains the power to fascinate; we can read them together with people who have been dead for more than 3,000 years.

The Historical and Social Context

Literature creates its own world, but it is still an artefact of a particular culture. Egyptian culture was so different from our own that some historical background is essential for understanding, although it is easy to overestimate the direct relationship between the poems and historical events. The dating of many works is still uncertain, but it is now generally agreed that those translated here belong to the Middle Kingdom.

The Middle Kingdom was preceded by a period of less centralized power, when the country was divided, and its literature remained very aware of the dangers of civil unrest and the chaos of the interregnum. A period of military conflict between the royal dynasty at Heracleopolis (the Tenth Dynasty) and the rulers at Thebes (the Eleventh Dynasty) in the south ended in victory for the Theban Dynasty c.1987 BC. The new rulers remained at Thebes for some fifty years, until a new family, the Twelfth Dynasty, took control of the kingdom with the accession of Amenemhat I in c.1938 BC. His reign saw the eventual movement of the royal line to a new residence in the north named with the royal epithet 'Seizer of the Two Lands' (Itj-tawi), and the Twelfth Dynasty was later known as the 'kings of the Residence of Itj-tawi'. After a turbulent beginning, a policy of cultural centralization was gradually imposed on the whole country.

The Middle Kingdom is often seen in terms of a struggle between central power and local rulers, a highly developed bureaucracy, and convulsive administrative reforms. Political developments, however, remain obscure; many of the period's most characteristic features appear after more than a century, in the reign of Amenemhat III. After a rule of 180 years, the family trailed off in dynastic worries, and was succeeded by what Egyptian historiographers termed the 'kings who followed the House of Sehotepibre (Amenemhat I)'. This,

[6] S. R. K. Glanville, quoted by G. Posener in J. R. Harris (ed.), *The Legacy of Egypt*[2] (Oxford, 1971), 220.

the Thirteenth Dynasty, was essentially a continuation, but it witnessed a gradual failing of authority and influence under a long sequence of ephemeral kings. While there was no political disintegration, there was a levelling in general prosperity, and state works of art show a decline in quality. Eventually foreigners in the eastern Delta formed a culturally distinct power base, until the country became divided between the 'rulers of foreign countries' in the north (the so-called 'Hyksos' dynasties) and the Theban state in the south, around 1640 BC. Another turbulent period ensued before the unity of Egyptian culture was reasserted from the south, around 1540 BC.

Invasion by foreigners was regarded by the Egyptians as an overwhelming of the established order by representatives of chaos. For most of the Middle Kingdom, it is unknown how extensive foreign influence on Egypt actually was, but the general impression is of a unified state quite self-contained, despite campaigns and trading links abroad, and the conquest of Nubia to the south. Egyptian art and religion were one with the central state in articulating the order of the élite; the life of most of society is now unknown, except where archaeology can provide a corrective to the partial evidence of ideological artefacts. Despite the images of gracious living found in élite tombs, life was brutal for most people, and adults who survived childhood could expect to live only until about 35. Administrative texts, which are less concerned with direct expression of the state ideology and more with practical matters, give an impression of workhouses, corvée labour, and a highly ordered bureaucracy, although the range of different types of burials in the cemeteries suggests that society was more varied and differentiated than the documents imply.

Egyptian fictional literature appears at the start of the troubled but effective Twelfth Dynasty. It was not a direct result of the disturbances of the First Intermediate Period, but its origins can perhaps be sought in social changes, such as the rise of a class of free commoners, with wealth and respect for intellectual 'excellence'. Burials of the period show an increased access to religious writings, which is both a change in cultural decorum and a sign of growing literacy. By the start of the Middle Kingdom, written tomb Autobiographies were no longer the prerogative of the highest élite, and this will have offered one model for the expansion of written forms in general.

The written literature, which was clearly composed for dissemination in written form, must have existed against a background of oral poetry, but we cannot know what the relationship between the two was. The extent of literacy has been tentatively estimated at less than 1 per cent of the population, and all the evidence implies that the surviving compositions were to some extent court poetry, although they were also circulated far away from the royal residence. Some manuscripts owned by individuals were placed in tombs, but we should not imagine a private person reading alone; rather—and perhaps primarily—the compositions were probably recited at a formal gathering, like a soirée. The poems had an audience rather than a reader, to judge by the way they describe their own settings: in *The Words of Neferti*, a sage is commissioned to improvise a composition before the court of King Sneferu, and it is written down as he speaks. The names of the actual poets were not recorded, although the wisdom texts, which rely on personal authority, were usually attributed to historical or pseudo-historical characters from the past. In a semi-oral context, and without any personal prominence for the actual 'author', there was little concern with 'authorized' texts, and different contemporaneous copies of a poem can show some variants.

Literary Genres

Many of the literary motifs will seem familiar to the modern reader, but the significance of these motifs is very different from what modern expectations would suggest. *The Tale of the Shipwrecked Sailor* is, for example, remarkably similar in many ways to Coleridge's *The Ryme of the Ancient Mariner*; in both a sailor tells of strange adventures in which he met representatives of another world, but their aesthetic and intellectual concerns are different, as are the genres.

The literary canon comprises a group of fictional texts, belonging to three main genres: the narrative, which shows great formal variety, and two types of wisdom text. The Tales are the easiest to appreciate, and display a taste for narrative skill and fantastic events that is relatively timeless. Wisdom texts are, however, an unfamiliar form to the modern reader. Of the two types of wisdom literature, the Teaching (*sebayet*) is the most formally unified; in it a wise father speaks to his son, presenting the fruits of his experience in didactic and reflective utterances. There are two sub-genres: the private teaching, where the teacher is a high official, and the royal teaching, where the teacher is a king at the end of his reign, so that the teaching becomes a *speculum regnis* in which the king's experience embraces a universal range. The other type of wisdom text is more reflective and takes various forms, including the Discourse (*medet*) and the Dialogue; they are all, however, to some extent pessimistic and form 'complaints' or 'elegies' lamenting the vicissitudes of life.

The canon displays great interweaving and combination of different genres drawn from the whole of Egyptian writing, and a flexibility which allows the creation of hybrid genres. The titles used to refer to many poems are modern inventions. Only the Teachings were invariably given titles, starting 'Beginning of the Teaching . . .'; some Discourses have titles, but they often open with narrative prologues. Tales characteristically start without a title.

Egyptian literature lacks dramatic and epic genres, although performative ritual texts and commemorative texts occupy these roles to some extent outside the narrowly literary corpus. Comedy is muted, although satire runs rather fitfully throughout the poetry. In the Middle Kingdom, lyric songs seem not to have been part of the written canon in their own right, but they could be included in other written poems; they were performative oral poetry, and bound to particular contexts. They are preserved only as captions on tomb walls, or, if sacred, in copies derived from temple libraries, such as a papyrus from the settlement of el-Lahun, which contains ritual hymns to King Senwosret III:

> How your [descendants] rejoice!
> You have fixed their borders.
> How your ancestors of old rejoice!
> You have made great their portion.
> How the Egyptians rejoice at your strength!
> You have protected the ancient heritage.[7]

Texts that match many modern readers' expectations of lyric poetry entered the written literary canon only in the New Kingdom. Their immediate charm, can be exemplified in a snatch of a love-song that was scribbled on the back of an apprentice's papyrus (*c.*1220 BC):

[7] Text: K. Sethe, *Ägyptische Lesestücke*[2] (Leipzig, 1928), 66, ll. 14–17.

If the wind comes, he's for the sycomore;
if you come ⟨you're for me⟩.[8]

The prominence given here to landscape and to the description of emotions, especially love, is lacking in the Middle Kingdom; its literature is, in modern terms, not pastoral or lyrical, but rather didactic. The poems are generally unromantic in all senses of the word, but they are not impersonal or abstract; they have an intimate mode of address and deal with personal themes, being concerned with the human heart. Man's ethical life is their central concern, and not the cultivation of subjectivity, or personal emotions such as romantic love.

The Style and Range of Literature

Although the narratives are now the most familiar-seeming type of literature, even they reveal very alien conventions of style. They are direct and uncluttered by any description of superfluous detail. They are objectively narrated, even when related in the first person, and, while extreme changes in emotion are noted, the shifting moods of a conversation are left to speak for themselves. The audience's response is guided by literary form rather than by explicit authorial comment. The discursive wisdom poetry in particular moves by syntax rather than by metaphor, despite elaborate sequences of occasionally extreme images and the presence of continuous strands of imagery. There is a tendency towards simile rather than metaphor. The style is repetitive and formulaic, and calls to mind biblical rather than classical parallels. The use of formulae may look dull on the page, but is very helpful and stimulating when a work is performed.

The language of literature was archaic, and fairly remote from everyday speech, with a very formal diction and grammar which only occasionally displays colloquial features. This does not mean that poetry was necessarily inaccessible to common people, only that it was distinct from normal speech. The diction is recherché, sometimes convoluted, but it is not sensuous, exotic, or 'purple'. It has a spare elegance, with an occasional density of wordplay that recalls the Shakespearian. Wordplay is often with different forms of

[8] P. Anastasi II, verso 5; the second verse is only half-written, as if the apprentice were distracted or interrupted. Text: M. V. Fox, *The Song of Songs and the Ancient Egyptian Love Songs* (Madison, Wis., 1985), 404.

the same word, but allusions to homonymous and homophonous words can add another layer of meaning. Although pronunciation cannot be reconstructed with any assurance, it is clear that assonance will have given the poems an incantatory quality, as a verse from *The Teaching of King Amenemhat* shows:

> *jw-ms-msyt-ꜥšꜣwt m-mrrwt*
> (i.e. *iu-mes-mesyt-ashaut em-mererut*)
> Yet now the children of the masses are in the street.

A tendency towards epigrammatic or proverbial utterance is particularly strong in the didactic and reflective poems, which present generalizing formulations of wisdom that are sparing and witty. These wisdom texts are prescriptive, explicitly moralistic, and rhetorical. Ambiguity and amphiboly also produce resonance within individual verses and in the structure of works as a whole: stanzas draw compressed parallels and contrasts, but differing attitudes are balanced, sometimes ironically, throughout whole compositions, producing a sense of semantic multifariousness.

Many aspects of the works' original appeal, including rhetorical virtuosity, metrical skill, and the sheer *cantabile* quality of their music, can no longer be appreciated by a modern audience. The nature of Egyptian verse in particular has been much debated; the prevalent analysis of Gerhard Fecht proposes that it was based on the counting of stress units, rather than on the alternation of long and short syllables; the difference between it and 'prose' is one of degree rather than of kind. The principles of scansion have been reconstructed by him,[9] but the parallel of Coptic (the descendant of Egyptian) suggests that there were many exceptions to these grammatically derived prosodic rules, due to the influence of the spoken language. This may explain the occasional divergence between the verses of poetry as reconstructed and the red dots ('verse-points') that mark off short sections of text in many New Kingdom copies. These points occur first in the late Twelfth Dynasty, in ritual texts whose recitation had to be exact,[10] and were introduced into copies of literary texts in the early New Kingdom when stress counting in recitation had probably become an acquired rather than an instinctive skill, as the spoken form of words became progressively

---

[9] See Select Bibliography.
[10] An unpublished papyrus from el-Lahun in University College London (to be published by M. Collier and S. Quirke).

reduced. As they mark pauses, they may sometimes indicate a sort of caesura rather than the end of a verse.

One important stylistic feature of metrical form is the use of balanced phrases—the 'parallelism of members' familiar from biblical verse. This seems to be a stylistic feature which heightens the poetry, and it does not occur consistently throughout a composition. Verse often favours strongly antithetical statements, rising to paradoxes. Such statements are characteristic of a form of pessimistic wisdom poetry known as laments, which was derived from descriptions of reversal, as in death or in changes of season; their role is analogous to the elegy of Western literature.

The poems' complexity involves a display, a variety, and a hierarchy of style, ranging from simple narratives to complex lyrical passages. Refrains, which were characteristic of ritual lyrics, probably indicate a formal and elevated tone. Many poems are supremely unified compositions, although their unity is different from what a modern reader might expect; the more diffuse examples of high style, such as the lengthy laments of *The Dialogue of Ipuur and the Lord of All*, have consequently proved less accessible to modern audiences. Verbal profusion, to an extent that we would consider superfluous, was a virtue in Egypt, as in many other semi-oral societies. Nevertheless, a mastery of form can still be appreciated in the internal symmetry of tightly structured poems such as *The Tale of Sinuhe*. That structure and (on a more minor scale) the use of repetition give the work a great resonance and profundity; passages and incidents echo one another, illuminating the narrative and its significance. The repetition of phrases can give an effect of integrity and authority, presenting the same subject in a variety of complementary ways, but it can also produce a polyphonic interweaving of imagery and motifs that embody the richness and complexity of the poem's subject matter. In wisdom Discourses, this interweaving creates the impression of a rapid train of thought, exploring and developing understanding with proliferating images and formulations.

The poems often present themselves as monologues, and many compositions would have gained tension from being recited in performance. They show elements of 'dramatic' presentation and characterization,[11] although this is on a different level from modern

---

[11] For example, the end of *The Teaching of Amenemhat*, or *The Tale of the Eloquent Peasant*. The performative potential of the latter is effectively realized in *Der*

expectations: characterization is more concerned with public per-
sonae than with shifting individual emotions. *The Tale of Sinuhe*, for
example, is unusually detailed in its descriptions of emotions, but
these are presented in moral rather then purely personal terms. The
poems are, nevertheless, more concerned with individuality and
subjectivity than other types of Egyptian writing.

The form, the moral tone, and the classical language of most of
the surviving examples of Middle Kingdom literature suggest that
they embody a culturally central, or high, tradition. As the process
of preservation was restricted by the élite's dominance over literacy,
this is not surprising. Despite the unity of the whole literary corpus,
a few fragmentary texts, such as a collection of maxims,[12] show
that literature was not rigidly restricted to these courtly genres.
Some works, particulary tales, reveal looser structures, more collo-
quial language, and are less serious; these suggest the existence of
more culturally peripheral or low traditions, where decorum was
looser. *The Tale of King Cheops' Court* is the best evidence for this. It
is a typical member of the genre, but is more diffuse and picaresque,
less rigid and concentrically structured, and in a much less formal
language; its themes are similarly less elevated, although often a
parody of more serious treatments. Its anecdotes of wonders are
more frivolous and 'sexy' than anything from the high tradition;
merry King Sneferu, for example, is presented in them in a less
admirable light (in terms of serious cultural values) than he is in *The
Words of Neferti*. *Neferti* is a much earlier work, but it seems likely
that these differences are not just a matter of date and that this vari-
ety was always part of literature. This less elevated tradition may
have been a little closer to oral poetry, but it seems likely that the
written and oral forms were remote and separate from each other:
the 'little' tradition of the peasants, as opposed to the 'great' tradi-
tion of the literate élite, is completely lost.

Less elevated features were more widely adopted in the written
compositions of the late New Kingdom, when the more colloquial
Late Egyptian was used as a written language for documents. The
characteristic composition of that period was no longer the wisdom
text, but the more episodic narrative, as well as the Miscellany—a
collection of varied types of composition forming a didactic anthol-

redekundige Bauer, a melodrama for speaker and small orchestra by H.-P. Müller-
Kieling (first performed 2 Sept. 1993, Freiburg im Breisgau).

[12] See p. 293.

ogy. Literature's boundaries seem to have moved to embrace a wider decorum, and the Middle Kingdom texts were hallowed, by their age and their language, into classics that formed a canon for apprentice scribes and continued to be transmitted alongside the new and more varied genres.

The Role of Literature

The poems of the high tradition of the Middle Kingdom were conceived as 'monuments to unageing intellect',[13] and many show the direct influence of funerary inscriptions and official texts. They teach, meditate on, and relate the 'nature of mankind' and the 'nature of eternity'.[14] Literature was already *aere perennius*, and aimed at eternal renown beyond the endurance of physical monuments.[15] The wisdom texts, in particular, demonstrated what the Egyptians termed *Maat*, 'Truth'. This was the order of society and, by extension, of the cosmos, ethical and moral righteousness, and Truth as an abstract ideal. According to one late Middle Kingdom inscription:

> The reward of the man who does what is done to him:
> in the heart of God, this is *Maat*.[16]

Maat is a loyalistic virtue, and an expression of society's solidarity that reflects the solidarity of the cosmos in time and space, a principle that operates through laws of reciprocity and retribution. In the Teachings there are frequent injunctions to 'do' and 'say' Truth in public and private contexts. This enacting of Truth is also described in a general manner, on a cosmic level, and with examples from specific situations.

Like representational art and cultural artefacts, literature was dominated by inherent rules of decorum. Egyptian ideology, as formulated in official documents and inscriptions, presents an ordered coherent view of life, a paradigmatic construction of reality that ignored the untoward events of life and concealed contradictions. The poetry that was produced by and for office-holders naturally

[13] W. B. Yeats, 'Sailing to Byzantium', l. 8.
[14] *The Teaching for Kagemni*, 2.3–4 (see pp. 291–2); *The 'Loyalist' Teaching*, 1. 6.
[15] This is most explicit in a passage of the Late New Kingdom P. Chester Beatty IV, quoted below, see n. 24.
[16] Stela of King Neferhotep, l. 40; text: W. Helck, *Historisch-Biographische Texte der 2. Zwischenzeit und neue Texte der 18. Dynastie*[2] (Wiesbaden, 1983), 29, ll. 14–15.

voiced a similar self-definition of the culture. Its themes are, for the most part, state themes, just as the diction is usually formal and courtly. The Teachings, for example, are almost always addressed by a member of the élite, to the élite, and concern their ethical behaviour. One exception is the comparatively peripheral *Teaching of Khety*, where satirical vignettes of low life make the didactic point that scribedom is best; eternal virtue is reduced to the enduring quality of writing. The modern lack of any comparable 'state' literature makes a response to this element of cultural self-presentation rather difficult: at least for his own time, the modern poet has become a rebel rather than a laureate. This aspect led some scholars, most notably Georges Posener, to consider the poems 'propaganda', but recent studies have recognized that this is too reductive a term for these complex works. While they have a strong tendency to affirm loyalistic values, and many of them are didactic 'cultural texts', they do not affirm cultural values in a simple or propagandistic manner. They formulate and examine basic principles of the Egyptian world-view, and central political concerns, such as the relationship between power and culture, rather than particular political events. In addition, literature was concerned with, and was composed by, individuals; it was about individual wisdom and experience, not that of undifferentiated 'aristocratic' representatives of the state. It belonged to the relative privacy of official life, not to the unremittingly universal world of religious and monumental achievements. The founding of the Twelfth Dynasty, amid considerable opposition and an increase in cultural individualism, seems to have provided the impetus to compose and circulate written literature, as a vehicle for transmitting and examining intellectual culture, and for exploring man's interpretation of an ever-problematic reality.

Literature's fictionality and its use of historical settings gave it a freedom to discuss aspects of life, such as unashamed frivolity, that were excluded from more ideologically constrained modes of discourse. Since literature was a culturally central artefact in the Middle Kingdom, it is not surprising that it has a generally serious tendency, diverging from the official normative order usually towards the darker, rather than the lighter, side. Even the generally positive Teachings warn of the dangers and difficulties facing the wise in a complex world. The most extreme example of this high pessimism is in the wisdom discourses. In *The Words of Neferti*, for example, when the king demands literary entertainment, he is presented with a grim vision of chaos that eventually resolves in a prophecy. The discourses are not prescriptive but reflective, and they are addressed to specific members of the élite or to an indefinite audience, often by lowly people. They express a complaint about the imperfection of individuals, society, and the very cosmos; against *Maat* they set falsehood, wrong, disorder, and chaos. They raise questions about the existence of imperfection and of suffering—themes seen most fully in a later religious text that expounds the Egyptians' belief in a negative cosmology, by which the universe has a tendency towards chaos and decay.[17] These poems explore that problem and question the justice of the gods. They express this theodic question more forcefully than any religious texts, which voice the problem only by presenting the answer of the creator-god, that imperfection was allowed into the created world by mankind's own heart, against his will, and that mankind's flawed nature cannot be held against its creator.[18] The reflective poems are characteristic of the Middle Kingdom and have no direct successors in the subsequent period. Their descriptions of agony were intended to be a source of aesthetic pleasure, presumably in a manner similar to the sufferings enacted in western tragedy.

The Tales of the great tradition reflect these questioning concerns in both form and motif. The concerns underlie, for example, *The Tale of Sinuhe* and *The Tale of the Eloquent Peasant*, and are explicit even in the apparently simple *Tale of the Shipwrecked Sailor*. Narratives are more specific in their treatment of these issues, and they allow grand themes to be mingled with more everyday aspects of life, such as humour: mankind's imperfection can be a source of laughter, as well as despair.

This untoward tone permeates literature, and is one of its most distinctive features. Royal inscriptions never mention the fallibility of a king, but the fictional Teachings present it in a most intimate manner; tomb Autobiographies present unqualified, absolute self-declarations of the culture's virtues and the tomb-owners conformity to them, whereas the 'Autobiography' of *Sinuhe* is in part a

---

[17] E. Hornung, *Der ägyptische Mythos von der Himmelskuh*: *Eine Ätiologie des Unvollkommenen* (Orbus Biblicus et Orientalis, 46; Fribourg, 1982).

[18] Coffin Text spell 1130; text: A. de Buck, *The Ancient Egyptian Coffin Texts*, vii (Chicago, 1961), 461–71; recent translation: R. B. Parkinson, *Voices from Ancient Egypt* (London, 1991), 32–4.

catalogue of fallibility. Homosexual desire had no place in the Egyptian ideal society, and all signs of it are lacking in the mortuary, religious, and commemorative texts, but it features prominently in several literary works. The contradictions between the ideal extolled by the ideology and the imperfect actuality of the present life are not articulated in official texts, whereas literature addresses these contradictions, mediating between the ideal and the actual.[19]

The questioning poems, however, always reach a reconciliation—at least wherever the ending is extant—and they do not end by undermining cultural values. Nowhere is there any trace of intellectual rebellion or dissent; any socially peripheral characters are judged by élite standards and values, and there is a lack of any alternative voice speaking independently, despite the undercurrents of potential dissent.[20] Potential dissent seems to be articulated almost in order to be accommodated, contained, and constrained by the poetry. A combination of factors at the start of the Middle Kingdom may have allowed the creation of the distinctive questioning voice of literature; factors such as expanding literacy may have created a potential for dissent to be formulated, and literature may be seen as a response, which allowed this to be articulated and contained within the status quo of the court and its officials. Such a presentation of the untoward could programmatically validate the harsh measures imposed by the state to enforce its ideal, but literature's presentation is not made in a programmatic fashion, or in order to entrap the untoward. Instead, the poetry revels in and creates sympathy for the untoward, the individual, and the unideal. Although there is always a positive resolution to the most pessimistic texts, questions such as the justice of the gods are posed forcefully, and never answered glibly. The poems' eventual resolutions are achieved in a complex and subtle manner. In *The Tale of the Eloquent Peasant*, the audience's attitude is suspended between sympathy and ironic detachment for over 600 lines; the energies of the discourse of ideas are not exhausted by the resolution, and the issues remain problematic. In their ambiguity, these compositions embody a profound awareness of the 'dark side to perfection'.[21]

[19] Cf. the remarks of B. Smith, *Homosexual Desire in Shakespeare's England: A Cultural Poetics* (Chicago, 1991), 22.

[20] A more familiar parallel is Vergil's *Aeneid*, where the alternative values of Dido and Turnus are accommodated within the affirmation of state values presented by the whole.

[21] M. Piper, libretto for Benjamin Britten's *Death in Venice* (1973), I. v.

Through its acknowledgement of life's anomalies, randomness, and complexities, Middle Kingdom literature allowed its privileged audience to explore or enact various possible complementary realities, as the poets taught, meditated on, or narrated their interpretations of the nature both of humanity and of the divine. As the audience listened to the poetry of imagined princes and peasants, they playfully expanded their own experiences and lived out the experiences of different individuals from different worlds. The 'travesties' of these fictional individuals—both peasants and princes were very different from the actual audience's rank—will have distanced the audience from the experiences that were narrated to it. The audience will thus have both experienced and stepped away from difficulties of life, and have gained 'relief', a sense of transcending them in something that was 'perfect to their hearts', as several poems phrase it. Monumental commemorative inscriptions address a discourse of permanent perfection to eternity; literature seeks eternity through humanity, and creates a space for entertainment as well as wisdom. In the hands of the poets, the knotty difficulties and choices of life become a sort of enchantment, and the nightmares of troubled experience become for the audience an entertaining reverie or revelation of grace, without losing their untoward, disturbing qualities. Poetry transforms an imperfect world into 'perfect speech'.

Reading Egyptian Literature

Literature's playful and untoward nature provides a unique record from Ancient Egypt of man's (self)-consciousness and his exploration of the problematic reality that faced him. This is not its only aspect, but it is the one to which the modern reader can most easily relate. Cultures change, but many of life's problems remain universal experiences that defy comprehension. In their treatment of these themes, the poems reveal a complex sensibility which we recognize as a sign of artistic value.

The first duty of the critic is to publish and analyse these texts. They are sources for a cultural poetics of Ancient Egypt, rather than for the more empirical history of the 'old historicist' scholars. Such interpretation requires great objectivity, involving a suspension of modern attitudes; attempts at absolute objectivity, however, run the danger of leaving the poetry lifeless. Literature was a powerful medium of cultural self-definition, which was designed to be an eternal memorial: 'every poem an epitaph'.[22] Literature was, in the words of *The Teaching of the Vizier Ptahhotep*, composed in order to 'speak to the future', and it was also a very personal medium. The poems were written for individual enjoyment and self-exploration, and not to be scholarly exercises—although they had partially become this by the New Kingdom—or historical curiosities.

In view of this, we should remember to read the poems for plea-sure, while appreciating the conventions of their different world. We should aim not only at a critical reading—a distancing process—but also at a creative act of reconstructing, and appreciating the 'perfect speech' of these poems. This beauty demands not only scholarship but also responsive love. The reader needs the same quality that Marguerite Yourcenar required for her fictional recre-ation of the emperor Hadrian, whose love transfigured Antinous into an Egyptian god, and who is thus a particularly appropriate fig-ure to invoke here. For Yourcenar, such work needs 'un pied dans l'érudition, l'autre dans la magie, ou plus exactement, et sans métaphore, dans cette *magie sympathique* qui consiste à se trans-porter en pensée à l'intérieur de quelqu'un'.[23] Her concern with summoning up the voices of the beloved dead captures the spirit of the Egyptians' own attitude to their authors, as expressed in a eulogy to dead writers from *c.*1190 BC. In this, the Middle Kingdom writers are described as dispensing with funeral preparations in favour of the more potent magic of their art:

> These sage scribes . . .
> their names endure for eternity,
> although they are gone, although they have completed their
>   lifetimes, and all their people are forgotten.
> They did not make for themselves pyramids of bronze
> with stelae of iron . . .
> they made heirs for themselves
> as the writings and Teachings that they begat . . .
> Departing life has made their names forgotten;
> writings alone make them remembered.[24]

---

[22] T. S. Eliot, *Little Gidding*, l. 225.

[23] *Carnets de notes de "Mémoires d'Hadrien"* in *Oeuvres romanesques* (Paris, 1982), 526.

[24] P. Chester Beatty IV, verso 3.7-11; text: A. H. Gardiner, *Hieratic Papyri in the British Museum*: 3rd ser., *Chester Beatty Gift*, ii, pls. 18-19; recent translation: Parkinson, *Voices from Ancient Egypt*, 148-50.

TALES

[1]

The Tale of Sinuhe

Introduction

The Tale of Sinuhe is a tale of adventure in foreign lands, but one which encourages reflection on the nature of Egyptian life, particularly on an individual's relationship to the king. The king was quasi-divine, the political and ideological centre of Egyptian culture, and the representative of all its values. The king was the direct heir of the creator-god, who, according to one (possibly contemporaneous) religious text, had appointed him to rule

> for judging men, for appeasing the Gods,
> for creating Truth, for destroying Evil.[1]

Sinuhe was composed in the first half of the Twelfth Dynasty, probably shortly after the end of the reign of Senwosret I (*c.*1875 BC). The earliest surviving manuscripts date from the reign of Amenemhat III, and later copies show that it was read for at least 750 years.

The Tale is presented as a funerary Autobiography from the start of the Twelfth Dynasty. In these commemorative tomb inscriptions the dead man addressed the passer-by with an idealized description of his virtues, as manifested in his life and career, in order to preserve his reputation and his funerary cult. Sinuhe is, as his inscription immediately makes clear, a royal courtier, but for him the usual pattern of an official's ideal life was destroyed by a moment of panic in which he fled from Egypt, and most of the Tale describes experiences away from the court that are often extremely untoward. From the moment of his panic, the style moves away from that of an Autobiography, and encompasses a wide range of genres and

---

[1] Text: J. Assmann, *Der König als Sonnenpriester: Ein kosmographischer Begleittext zur kultischen Sonnenhymnik in thebanischen Tempeln und Gräbern* (Abhandlungen der Deutschen Archäologischen Instituts Kairo, 7; Glückstadt, 1970); also M. C. Betrò, *I testi solari del portale de Pascherientaisu (BN2)* (Saqqara, 3; Pisa 1990), 27–50. Recent translation: R. B. Parkinson, *Voices from Ancient Egypt* (London, 1991), 38–40.

techniques: narratives of conquest and combat, eulogies of the king, a royal decree, meditative prayers, and ceremonial lyrics, culminating in the description of the tomb in which Sinuhe's Autobiography is supposedly inscribed. The narrative of Sinuhe's flight from Egypt and his return matches the form of the Tale, in which the Autobiographical style is shattered by his flight, and is only firmly re-established as his life returns to order in the final stanzas. Instead of commemorating an ideal life 'in truth', the literary Tale deals with 'dreams', 'half-truths', and things that are 'unrepeatable'. The Tale displays a perfection of form, as well as spare and concise composition; the manuscripts divide the text into forty stanzas, and these form five concentric groups. The Tale's virtuosity is manifest in allusions and self-echoes rather than in florid diction, although this is elegant and rather recherché in idiom. Throughout, there is a constant tension between the ideal and the actual, and a questioning of Sinuhe's motivation that is unparalleled in actual Autobiographies.

In the opening lines of the Tale Sinuhe speaks from his tomb in Egypt: the ending of his life is thus implicit in the beginning of his tale. The calm elevated style appropriate to an Autobiographical narrative is gradually broken down in the first part of the Tale (R 1–B 34) as Sinuhe leaves Egypt. He overhears that the old king has unexpectedly died, is struck by a blind panic, and flees his homeland with what is, in effect, an unwitting renunciation of all its values. The horror of this moment is described in detail, and images of night-time suggest its broader significance: the Egyptian world-view was fundamentally pessimistic; chaos was thought to be ever present and waiting to overwhelm the ordered cosmos, and Sinuhe's terror is an experience of this.[2]

Sinuhe abandons the fixed security of Egypt for the impermanence of life amidst the nomadic 'sandfarers'. This fatal transition is symbolized by his near death from thirst, from which he is rescued by a passing sheikh, and he ends up being carried off by a Palestinian prince, Amunenshi.

In the second part of the Tale (B 34–92), narrative gives way to discourse as Sinuhe converses with his foreign rescuer, and

---

[2] This episode has been the subject of much fruitless discussion among Egyptologists, who have often tried to interpret the Tale as if it were a historical document (referring to a palace conspiracy) or a novel with modern characterization (providing a single unspoken rational motivation for Sinuhe's flight): see Select Bibliography.

Amunenshi asks why he has come to Retjenu. The dialogue is dominated by Sinuhe's lengthy answer, which is a eulogy of the new king Senwosret; this establishes Sinuhe's continued loyalty to the Egyptian king, despite his flight. He extols the king's fearsomeness against foreign lands, dramatically enacting his terror of the king's ferocity towards deserters such as himself. In this exchange, Amunenshi is presented as pseudo-Egyptian, and he rewards Sinuhe's praise song with generosity, as if he were the Egyptian king. His land is described as a place where Sinuhe tries to find a substitute Egypt, and to replace the life he has lost. The settings of the Tale form a symmetrical pattern of Egypt–Retjenu–Egypt, and this is reinforced with many ironic verbal echoes and contrasts, which combine to heighten the difference between the real with the substitute life, his true and substitute identity. As R. A. Brooks has remarked of the *Aeneid*, the Tale is a 'web of antithetic symbols, of tensions and oppositions never finally resolved'.[3]

Abroad, Sinuhe attempts to rationalize and overcome the consequences of his fatal panic, and the third part (B 92–177) relates his struggles to establish a social identity in the midst of an alien herd. This includes a duel with a local challenger, which is structurally the central incident of the Tale, and the turning-point of the plot. It embodies the conflict between the real and the substitute, between Egypt and the desert. His victory in this armed combat brings him greater wealth but also, ironically, an awareness of his alienation, and it leads to an inner conflict. He recounts his triumph in a lyrical manner, and in doing so he attempts finally to distance himself from the consequences of his flight, to deny that he is a fugitive in exile. His speech initially echoes the Autobiographical style with measured parallel cadences and motifs, but, at the very moment of apparent self-justification, he collapses into a desperate prayer. It is a dramatic interior monologue, leading to a realization of his true state: life outside Egypt is meaningless. The third part of the Tale ends with the almost miraculous statement that the king has heard of Sinuhe's state and has sent an answer to his private prayer.

Just as the second part was the conversation between Sinuhe and Prince Amunenshi about the king, the fourth part contains his correspondence with the true king (B 178–243). It opens directly with

[3] '*Discolor Aura*: Reflections on the Golden Bough' in Steele Commager (ed.), *Virgil: A Collection of Critical Essays* (Englewood Cliffs, NJ, 1966), 158.

a copy of the royal decree summoning him home. In the letter the king restates the problem of Sinuhe's motivation more forcefully, and asks directly for the reason for his flight. Sinuhe has already proved himself unable to explain his actions, and his unaccountable, unintentioned fault raises broader questions about whether the gods can be just: for how could the powers above allow an innocent man to transgress and still be just? The king is a representative of the gods and in some sense a god himself, and in his letter he distances himself from any responsibility for Sinuhe's suffering and assigns all responsibility to the man's own fallible heart.

The climax of the reassuring letter comes as the king enjoins Sinuhe to return for burial in Egypt. This is a joyous description of a transition to eternal verity—an ultimate homecoming. The juxtaposition of death and joy would have been to the original audience a happy paradox. A contemporaneous harpist's song describes the tomb as a home

> built for festival,
> planned for happiness.[4]

A later harpist's song extols the 'land of eternity' as 'righteous and just', elevated from all 'strife'.[5] The otherworld is a refuge from the struggles of life, and the home of the absolute and ideal.

The inclusion of a royal letter is a motif of Autobiographical inscriptions and marks the start of a gradual reassertion of order on a formal level. Sinuhe's receipt of the letter is briefly narrated, and then a copy of his reply follows. In this he denies conscious responsibility for his flight, and abandons himself to the king's grace. The letter's profusion of stately wishes for the king's well-being recalls his earlier eulogy spoken to Amunenshi.

The fourth part of the Tale ends as Sinuhe travels to the border of Egypt, and the fifth part (B 244–311) returns him to the court and the enduring security of the state, in a vivid and climactic scene. Sinuhe at last finds himself face to face with the king who has been the centre of all his preceding narration. The meeting is marked by a panic 'like that which created the fated flight', and his re-entry into Egyptian life is marked by a death-like collapse,

---

[4] Stela Leiden V.68; text: K. Sethe, *Ägyptische Lesestücke*[2] (Leipzig, 1928), 87, ll. 1–2.

[5] Text: R. Hari, *La Tombe thébaine du père divin Neferhotep (TT 50)* (Geneva, 1985), pl. 4, ll. 4–5.

similar to that which marked his leaving Egypt. This time, however, his unconsciousness is banished not by nomads, but by the royal children, who are reintroduced to their long-lost attendant. Despite moments of humour, as they fail to recognize him, there is a break with the tone of the preceding stanzas as Sinuhe enters the realms of royalty and divinity. The princesses enact a ritual of renewal with a song to the king that is intensely religious, lyrical, and erotic. In the song the princesses beg grace for Sinuhe, whom they describe as 'a barbarian born in the Homeland'; they articulate the Tale's central paradox of how an Egyptian can be a foreigner, and how a virtuous man can find himself a traitor and deserter. This is a final summation of the Tale's theme of the problematic justice of the gods. Sinuhe's irrational panic was the incursion of chaos which underlies the whole plot, and the antithesis of the order of the court, but here it is accommodated within that order. His panic is rearticulated as a 'fear', which is a natural, orderly response to the king's 'fearsomeness'. The king dismisses the chaos and the preceding events with the words 'he shall not fear', and Sinuhe is recreated as a courtier.

He is then cleansed and rejuvenated, and the final stanzas lead the audience swiftly from this moment of revelation through a series of courtly dwellings, into a description of the tomb which the king bestows as a sign of his favour. The Tale ends as it began, with Sinuhe in his tomb, addressing the tomb-visitor.

The profusion of genres in the Tale gives an encyclopaedic feel, suggesting a full range of human experience, but all run parallel to the basic plot in terms of form. In tone, however, the whole is more complex, because of the richness with which Sinuhe's experiences abroad are described. The modulations of the patterns of the Egyptian official text *par excellence*, the Autobiography, articulate a questioning of Egyptian culture. In one sense, nothing has happened—the trip to Retjenu is a 'dream', and Sinuhe is purged of his experiences abroad—and yet everything in the Tale has happened in this dream. The horror of the nightmare that is Sinuhe's life is vividly expressed with a poetry that makes it for the audience an entertaining reverie as well as a disturbing narrative. The Tale reassuringly presents the value of the Egyptian way of life, but the possibility of a world elsewhere lingers in the audience's mind, as does the question of his motivation: how can the gods allow the heart of

man to be so unstable that it can lead him astray so unintention-
ally? This ambivalence is reflected in the setting of the Tale in a
tomb, which is a link between the imperfect world of men and the
perfection of the otherworld.

Four papyrus copies are known from Middle Kingdom, and, along
with *The Tale of the Eloquent Peasant*, *Sinuhe* is one of the best-
attested works in manuscripts from that period. There are some
twenty-eight later copies. It is now widely regarded as the master-
piece of Egyptian literature. The numbers in the text give line
numbers of the principle manuscript available at that point: R (P.
Ramesseum A = P. Berlin 10499), then B (P. Berlin 3022).

The Tale of Sinuhe

The Patrician and Count,[1]   R 1
Governor of the Sovereign's Domains in the Syrian lands,
the True Acquaintance of the King, whom he loves,
the Follower, Sinuhe says,
'I was a Follower who followed his lord,
a servant of the Royal Chambers
and of the Patrician Lady, the greatly praised,
the Queen of Senwosret in Khnemsut,
the Princess of Amenemhat in Qanefru,   R 5
Nefru, the blessed lady.

REGNAL YEAR 30, MONTH 3 OF THE INUNDATION SEASON, DAY 7:[2]
The God ascended to his horizon;
the Dual King Sehotepibre
mounted to heaven,
and was united with the sun,
the divine flesh mingling with its creator.
The Residence was in silence,[3]
hearts were in mourning,
the Great Portal was shut,
the entourage was bowed down,   R 10
and the patricians were in grief.

Now his Majesty had sent out an expedition to the Libyan
   land,[4]
with his eldest son at its head,
the Perfected God Senwosret;
but now he was returning, having carried off Libyan
   captives   R 15
and all sorts of cattle without number.
The Friends of the Court[5]
sent to the western border
to inform the prince
of the affair which had happened in the Audience Hall.

On the road the messengers found him.[6]
They reached him at nightfall.   R 20
Not a moment did he wait;
the falcon flew off with his followers,

without informing his expedition.
Now, when the royal children
accompanying him on this expedition were sent to,
B 1   one of them was summoned.
Now, when I was standing on duty,[7]
I heard his voice as he spoke,
as I was a little way off.
My heart staggered, my arms spread out;
trembling fell on every limb.
I removed myself, leaping,
to look for a hiding place.
B 5   I put myself between two bushes,
until the traveller had parted from the road.

I travelled southwards.[8]
I did not plan to reach this Residence,
expecting strife would happen;
I did not think to live after him.
I went across Lake Maaty in the region of the Sycomore.[9]
I came to the Isle of Sneferu.
B 10   I passed a day on the edge of a field.
When it was daylight again, I made an early start.
I met a man standing in my way.
He saluted me, though I was afraid of him.
When it was supper-time,
I had arrived at Cattle-Quay.

I crossed in a rudderless barge[10]
blown by the west wind.
B 15   I passed east of Iaku,
above Lady of the Red Mountain.
I gave my feet a northwards path,[11]
and I reached The Walls of the Ruler,
made to beat back the Syrians.
I crouched down in a bush
for fear of being seen by the watcher
on duty upon the wall.

B 20   I travelled in the night-time.[12]
When it was dawn I had reached Peten.
I alighted on an island of Kemur.

Thirst's attack overtook me,
and I was scorched, my throat parched.
I said, "This is the taste of death."
But I lifted up my heart, and gathered my limbs together,[13]
as I heard the noise of cattle lowing, caught sight of Syrians,   B 25
and a leader of theirs, who had once been
in Egypt, recognized me.

Then he gave me water,[14]
while he boiled milk for me.
I went with him to his tribe,
and what they did was good.
Country gave me to country.[15]
I set out for Byblos; I got to Qedem.
I had spent half a year there,
when Amunenshi carried me off.   B 30
He was the ruler of upper Retjenu,
and he told me, "You'll be happy with me,
for you'll hear the speech of Egypt."
He said this, knowing my character
and having heard of my understanding,
and the Egyptians who were with him there
had vouched for me.

*

Then he said to me, "Why did you come here?[16]   B 35
Has anything happened in the Residence?"
Then I said to him, "It's that the Dual King Sehotepibre[17]
has gone to the horizon,
and how this all happened is unknown."
But I spoke in half-truths.
"I have come from the expedition to the Libyan land:
it was reported to me, and my heart failed
and carried me off on the ways of flight.   B 40
I had not been talked of, and my face had not been spat
     upon;
I had heard no reproaches; my name had not been heard
     in the herald's mouth.
I do not know what brought me to this country—it is like a
     plan of God."

Then he said unto me, "So how is that land[18]
without him—that worthy God,
B 45 fear of whom is throughout the countries
like Sekhmet's in a plague year?"
I spoke thus to him, answering him,
"Indeed, his son has already entered the palace,[19]
and has taken up his father's inheritance.
Now, he is a God who is peerless,
before whom no other exists.
He is a lord of understanding, excellent of plans, effective of
  orders;
B 50 coming and going are by his command.
He subjugates the countries.
His father stayed within his palace,
and he reported to him that what he had ordained was done.

Now, he is a hero, active with his strong arm,[20]
a champion without compare,
seen descending on barbarians, approaching the combat.
He curbs horns, weakens hands;
B 55 his foes cannot marshall troops.
He is vengeful, a smasher of foreheads;
close to him no one can stand.
He is far-striding, destroying the fugitive;
there is no end for the man who shows him his back.
He is firm-hearted at the moment of forcing retreat.
He turns back again and again; he shows not his own back.
B 60 He is stout-hearted, seeing the masses;
he allows no rest around his heart.

He is bold, descending on Easterners;[21]
his joy is to plunder barbarians.
As soon as he takes up his shield, he tramples;
he needs no second blow to slay.
None can escape his arrow, none draw his bow.
As before the power of the Great One,
barbarians flee before him.
B 65 Having foreseen the end, he fights heedless of all else.

He is a lord of kindness, great of sweetness.[22]
Through love he has conquered.

His city loves him more than its own members;
it rejoices at him more than at its God.
Men and women pass by, exulting at him.
He is a king, who conquered in the egg,
his eyes on it from birth.
He makes those born with him plentiful.
He is unique, God-given.   B 70
How joyful this land, since he has ruled!
He extends its borders.

He will conquer southern lands, without yet considering
        northern countries.[23]
He was begotten to strike Syrians, to trample Sand-farers.
Send to him, let him know your name,
as a man far from his Majesty who enquires!
He will not fail to do good   B 75
for a country that will be loyal to him."

And he said unto me, "Well, Egypt is certainly happy,[24]
knowing of his success.
But look, you are here,
and you will stay with me; I shall do you good."
He placed me at the head of his children.
He joined me to his eldest daughter.
He had me make my choice of his country,
from the choicest of what was his,   B 80
on his border with another country.
It was a good land,[25]
called Iaa.
Figs were in it, and grapes;
its wine was more copious than its water;
great its honey, plentiful its moringa-oil,
with all kinds of fruit on its trees.
Barley was there, and emmer, and numberless were its
        cattle of all kinds.   B 85
Now, what came to me as a favourite was great.
He appointed me the ruler of a tribe
of the choicest of his country.

Provisions and strong drinks were made for me,[26]
with wine as a daily supply, and cooked flesh,

and roast fowl, as well as wild game.
B 90 They would snare and lay it all out for me,
as well as the catch of my own hounds.
Many sweets were made for me,
with milk in every cooked dish.

*

I spent many years there,[27]
and my children became heroes,
each man subjugating his tribe.
The messenger who went north and south to the Residence
B 95 would tarry for me. I would make all men tarry.
I would give water to the thirsty,
and I returned the wanderer to his path and rescued the
    robbed.
The Syrians who became so bold
as to resist the countries' rulers—I countered their
    movements.
B 100 This ruler of Retjenu[28]
would have me do many missions
as the commander of his army.
Every country for which I set out,
I made my attack on it,
and it was driven from its grasslands and wells;
I plundered its cattle and carried off its inhabitants,
and their food was taken away.
B 105 I killed the people in it with my strong arm, my bow,
my movements, and my excellent plans.

In his heart I attained high regard;[29]
he loved me, knowing my valour.
He placed me at the head of his children, having seen the
    strength of my arms.
A hero of Retjenu came
B 110 to provoke me in my tent;
he was a peerless champion, who had subjugated all the
    land.
He said he would fight with me, he planned to rob me,
and thought to plunder my cattle, on the advice of his tribe.
That ruler conferred with me;[30]

I spoke thus, "I do not know him.
So am I some ally of his, to walk around in his camp? B 115
Or does this mean that I've opened his private quarters,
    overturned his stockade?
It is resentment at seeing me do your missions.

How like am I to a bull of the roaming cattle in the midst
    of another herd,[31]
whom the bull of that little herd attacks,
whom that long-horned bull is charging! B 120
Can an inferior ever be loved as a superior?[32]
No barbarian can ever ally with a Delta man;
what can establish the papyrus on the mountain?
Does that bull want to fight,[33]
or does that champion bull want to sound a retreat
in terror of being equalled?

If he has the will to fight, let him speak his wish![34] B 125
Does God not know what He has fated,
or does He know how it stands?"
When it was night I strung my bow and tried my arrows,[35]
sharpened my sword and polished my weapons.
When it was dawn, all Retjenu had come,
having incited its tribes and gathered its neighbouring
    countries, B 130
for it had planned this fight; and yet every breast burned
    for me,
the wives jabbered, and every heart was sore for me,
saying, "Is there another man mighty enough to fight him?"

Then his shield, his axe,[36]
his armful of javelins fell to me: B 135
after I had escaped his weapons and made them pass by me,
with his arrows spent in vain,
one after the other,
he approached me, and I shot him;
my arrow stuck in his neck,
he cried out, and fell on his face.
I felled him with his own axe, B 140
and gave my war cry on his back,
while every Asiatic was bellowing.

To Montu I gave praises,
while his supporters mourned for him.
This ruler Amunenshi
took me into his arms.
Then I carried off his property and plundered his cattle.[37]
B 145   What he planned to do to me, I did to him;
I seized what was in his tent, and stripped his camp.
With this I became great, and grew copious of wealth,
and grew plentiful of cattle.

For now God has acted so as to be gracious to one with
    whom He was offended,[38]
whom He led astray to another country.
Today, He is satisfied.
B 150   A fugitive takes flight because of his surroundings;[39]
    but my reputation is in the Residence.
A creeping man creeps off because of hunger;
    but I give bread to my neighbour.
A man leaves his land because of nakedness;
    but I have bright linen, white linen.
A man runs off because of the lack of someone to send;
B 155   but I am plentiful of serfs.
Good is my house, spacious my dwelling place,
    and memory of me is in the palace.
Whatever God fated this flight[40]
—be gracious, and bring me home!
Surely You will let me see the place where my heart still stays!
What matters more than my being buried
B 160   in the land where I was born?
This is my prayer for help, that the good event befall,
    that God give me grace!
May He act in this way, to make well the end of someone
    whom He made helpless,
His heart sore for someone He compelled
to live in a foreign country!
Does this mean that He is so gracious today as to hear the
    prayer of someone far off
who shall then turn from where he has roamed the earth
to the place from which he was carried away?

May the king of Egypt be gracious to me,[41]   B 165
that I may live on his grace!
May I greet the Mistress of the Land who is in his palace,
and hear her children's messages!
So shall my limbs grow young again, for now old age has
    fallen:[42]
weakness has overtaken me,
my eyes are heavy, and my arms weak;
my legs have ceased to follow, and my heart is weary;   B 170
I am near to dying.
May they lead me to the cities of eternity![43]
May I follow the Lady of All,
and then she shall tell me that all is well with her children!
May she pass eternity above me!

Now the Majesty of the Dual King Kheperkare was told[44]
about the state of affairs in which I was.
And his Majesty sent to me,   B 175
with bounty of royal giving,
to gladden the heart of this humble servant
like any ruler of a country,
and the royal children who were in his palace let me hear
    their messages.

❋

Copy of the Decree Brought to this Humble Servant[45]
about his Being Brought Back to Egypt:
"Horus Living-of-Incarnations;
Two Ladies Living-of-Incarnations;
Golden Horus Living-of-Incarnations;
Dual King Kheperkare;
Son of Re Senwosret   B 180
—may he live for all time and eternity!
Royal Decree to the Follower Sinuhe:[46]
Look, this decree of the king is brought to you
to inform you that your roving through countries,
going from Qedem to Retjenu,
country giving you to country,
was at the counsel of your own heart.

What had you done, that you should be acted against?
You had not cursed, that your speech should be punished.
You had not spoken in the officials' council, that your
    utterances should be opposed.

B 185 This idea carried off your heart—
it was not in my heart against you.
This your Heaven, who is in my palace, endures[47]
and flourishes in the kingship of the land
today as she did before,
and her children are in the Audience Hall.

You will store up the wealth given by them,[48]
and live on their bounty.
Return to Egypt!
And you will see the Residence where you grew up,
kiss the earth at the Great Portal,
and join the Friends.
For today you have already begun to be old, have lost your
B 190   virility,
and have in mind the day of burial,
the passing to blessedness.

A night vigil will be assigned to you, with holy oils[49]
and wrappings from the hands of Tayet.
A funeral procession will be made for you on the day of
    joining the earth,
with a mummy case of gold,
a mask of lapis lazuli,
a heaven over you, and you placed in a hearse,
with oxen dragging you,
and singers going before you.
The dance of the Oblivious ones will be done at the mouth
B 195   of your tomb-chamber,[50]
and the offering-invocation recited for you;
sacrifices will be made at the mouth of your offering-chapel,
and your pillars will be built of white stone
in the midst of the royal children's.
Your death will not happen in a foreign country;[51]
Asiatics will not lay you to rest;
you will not be put in a ram's skin when your coffin is
    made.

This is too long to be roaming the earth!
Think of your corpse—and return!"

As I stood in the middle of my tribe, this decree reached
    me.[52]

It was read to me and I prostrated myself,
I touched the earth
and scattered it on my chest;
I roved round my camp, shouting and saying,
"How can this be done for a servant
whose heart led him astray to strange countries?
So good is the kindness which saves me from death!
Your spirit will let me make my end
with my limbs at home!"

Copy of the Reply to this Decree:[53]
"The servant of the palace, Sinuhe says,
'Most happy welcome!

Concerning this flight which your humble servant made in
    his ignorance:
It is your spirit, Perfected God, Lord of the Two Lands,[54]
which is loved by the Sungod, and favoured by Montu Lord
    of Thebes;
Amun Lord of the Throne of the Two Lands,[55]
Sobek-Re, Horus, Hathor,
Atum and his company of Gods,
Sopdu-Neferbau-Semseru the eastern Horus,
the Lady of Imet—may she enfold your head!—
the divine Council upon the Flood,
Min-Horus in the midst of the countries,
Wereret Lady of Punt,
Nut, Haroeris-Re,

and all the Gods of the Homeland and the islands of the Sea—
may they give life and dominion to your nostrils,
endow you with their bounty,
and give you eternity without limit,
all time without end!
May fear of you resound in lands and countries,
with the circuit of the sun curbed by you!
This is the prayer of a humble servant for his lord,[56]
who saves from the West.

The lord of perception, perceiver of the people,[57]

B 215 perceives as the Majesty of the Court

what your humble servant was afraid to say—

it is like an unrepeatably great matter.

O great God, equal of the Sungod in understanding

someone who willingly serves him!

Your humble servant is in the hand of him who enquires

after him:[58]

these things are placed at your disposal.

Your Majesty is Horus the conqueror;

your arms are mighty against all lands.

Now, may your Majesty command that he be made to bring

the Meki man from Qedem,[59]

B 220 the settler from out of Keshu,

and the Menus man from the lands of the Fenkhu.

They are rulers who are well known,

who live by love of you.

Without calling Retjenu to mind—it is yours, even like your

hounds!

This flight which your humble servant made—[60]

I had not planned it. It was not in my heart.

I had not thought of it. I know not what parted me from

my place.

B 225 It was like the nature of a dream,

like a Delta man seeing himself in Elephantine,

a man of the marshy lagoons in Southern Egypt.

I had no cause to be afraid; no one had run after me.

I had heard no reproaches; my name had not been heard in

the herald's mouth.

Only—that shuddering of my limbs,[61]

my feet hastening,

my heart overmastering me,

B 230 the God who fated this flight dragging me away!

I was not presumptuous before,[62]

for a man respects him who is acknowledged by his land,

and the Sungod has put respect for you throughout the

land,

and terror of you in every country.

Whether I am at home,

whether I am in this place—
it is you who veils this horizon of mine.
The sun shines for love of you;
the water of the river
is drunk when you wish;
the air of heaven
is breathed when you say.

Your humble servant will hand over to the chicks[63]
which your humble servant has begotten in this place.
A journey has been made for your humble servant!
May your Majesty do as you desire!
Men live on the breath of your giving:[64]
may the Sungod, Horus, and Hathor love
these your noble nostrils,
which Montu Lord of Thebes desires
to live for all time!' "
I was allowed to spend a day in Iaa,[65]
handing over my property to my children;
my eldest son was in charge of my tribe,
and all my property was his—
my servants, all my cattle,
my fruit, and all my orchard trees.
This humble servant then came southwards,[66]
and I halted at the Ways of Horus.
The commander there who was in charge of the garrison
sent a message to the Residence to inform them.

B 235

B 240

*

And his Majesty caused a worthy Overseer of the Peasants
    of the Royal Household to come,[67]
accompanied by laden boats,
and bearing bounty of royal giving
for the Syrians who had come with me,
leading me to the Ways of Horus;
and I announced each one by his name.
Every serving man was at his duty.[68]
I set sail,
with kneading and brewing beside me,
until I reached the harbour of Itj-tawi.

B 245

When it was dawn, very early,
they came and summoned me;
ten men coming,
ten men going,
ushering me to the palace.

I touched the ground between the sphinxes,[69]
B 250 as the royal children stood in the portal, receiving me;
and the Friends who usher to the Pillared Hall
were showing me the way to the Audience Hall.
I found his Majesty on the great throne
in the portal of electrum.
Then I was stretched out prostrate,
unconscious of myself in front of him,
while this God was addressing me amicably.
I was like a man seized in the dusk,
B 255 my soul had perished, my limbs failed,
my heart was not in my body.
I did not know life from death.

And his Majesty said to one of these Friends,[70]
"Raise him up, let him speak to me!"
And his Majesty said, "Look, you have returned after
            roaming foreign countries,
after flight has made its attack on you;
you are now elderly, and have reached old age.
Your burial is no small matter;
you will not be laid to rest by barbarians.
Act against yourself, act against yourself no more!
B 260 You did not speak when your name was announced—
are you afraid of punishment?"
I answered this with the answer of a frightened man:[71]
"What does my lord say to me, that I can answer?
For this is no disrespect towards God, but is a terror
which is in my body like that which created the fated flight.
Look, I am in front of you, and life is yours;
may your Majesty do as he desires!"

And the royal children were ushered in,[72]
and his Majesty said to the Queen,
B 265 "Look, Sinuhe has returned as an Asiatic,

an offspring of the Syrians!"
She gave a very great cry,
and the royal children shrieked as one.
And they said unto his Majesty,
"Is it really he,
sovereign, my lord?"
And his Majesty said, "It is really he."
Now they had brought with them their necklaces,[73]
their rattles and their sistra.
And they presented them to his Majesty:
"Your hands upon this beauty, enduring king,[74]   B 270
these insignia of the Lady of Heaven!
May the Golden One give life to your nostrils,
the Lady of Stars enfold you!
South-crown fares north, North-crown south,[75]
joined and made one
in the words of your Majesty,
on whose brow the uraeus is placed!

You have delivered the poor from evil.[76]
So may the Sungod, Lord of the Two Lands, be gracious
    to you!
Hail to you, as to the Lady of All!
Slacken your bow, withdraw your shaft!
Give breath to him who suffocates!   B 275
Give back the good we give on this good day—[77]
present us with North Wind's Son,
the barbarian born in the Homeland!
Through fear of you he took flight,[78]
through terror of you he left the land.
A face that has seen your face shall not pale!
An eye that has gazed at you shall not fear!"

And his Majesty said, "He shall not fear,[79]
he shall not gibber in terror!   B 280
He will be a Friend among the officials,
and he will be appointed amongst the entourage.
Proceed to the Robing Chamber to attend on him!"
I went forth from the Audience Hall,
with the royal children giving me their hands.
And afterwards, we went through the Great Portal.   B 285

I was appointed to the house of a prince,[80]
with costly things in it, with a bathroom in it
and divine images of the horizon,
with treasures from the Treasury in it,
clothes of royal linen,
myrrh and kingly fine oil,
B 290 with officials whom the king loved in every room,
and every serving man at his duty.

The years were made to pass from my limbs;[81]
I became clean-shaven, and my hair was combed.
A load was given back to the foreign country,
and clothes back to the Sand-farers.
I was clad in fine linen;
I was anointed with fine oil.
I slept in a bed.
I returned the sand to those who are upon it
B 295 and the tree oil to those smeared with it.

I was given the house of a Governor,[82]
such as belongs to a Friend.
Many craftsmen were building it,
all its trees were freshly planted.
Meals were brought to me from the palace,
three and four times a day,
as well as what the royal children gave,
without making a moment's ceasing.
B 300 A pyramid of stone was built for me,[83]
in the midst of the pyramids.
The masons who construct the pyramid measured out its
        foundations;
the draughtsman drew in it;
the overseer of sculptors carved in it;
the overseer of the works which are in the burial grounds
        busied himself with it.
B 305 All the equipment to be put in a tomb shaft—
its share of these things was made.
I was given funerary priests;
a funerary demesne was made for me,
with fields in it and a garden in its proper place,
as is done for a Chief Friend.

My image was overlaid with gold,
and its kilt with electrum.
It is his Majesty who has caused this to be done.[84]
There is no other lowly man for whom the like was done.
I was in the favours of the king's giving,   B 310
until the day of landing came.'

So it ends, from start to finish,[85]
as found in writing.

Notes

1. The Tale begins as a funerary Autobiography with the titles held by Sinuhe at the end of his life. The first two mark him as a person of high rank, though not of hereditary nobility; that of *Governor* . . . anticipates his activities abroad. *True Acquaintance* refers to Sinuhe as a member of the court, and articulates the importance of a person's relationship with their king in the Tale. The title of *Follower* (i.e. retainer) is repeated in Sinuhe's opening statement as he starts to recount his life; it indicates his original (lower) status, and, like that of *Governor*, is ironic when viewed with hindsight. The name *Sinuhe* means 'Son of the Sycomore', referring to the most characteristic tree of Egypt, and one associated with Hathor, the goddess of fertility and rebirth, who features throughout the Tale. He describes himself as a palace servant of the late Queen *Nefru*, who was a daughter of Amenemhat I (*c.*1938–1908 BC) and the wife of Senwosret I (*c.*1918–1875 BC). *Khnemsut* and *Qanefru* are the cultic enclosures attached to the pyramids of Senwosret and Amenemhat respectively, near modern el-Lisht, some 30 km south of Memphis. The whole stanza has a formal, elevated, and funerary tone, as befits an Autobiography.

2. *Regnal year 30* is the date of Sehotepibre Amenemhat I's sudden death, which the following stately verses record as a withdrawal of the divine king from humanity into the world of the gods. *His horizon* is the royal pyramid, already alluded to in the preceding stanza (see n. 1).

3. The second half of the stanza moves to the human sphere, while maintaining a calm and monumental style; grief is described in terms of the élite. The *Residence* is the dwelling place of the king, the capital of the Twelfth Dynasty, called Itj-tawi, near modern el-Lisht (see n. 1). Here the *Great Portal* of the palace is shut to the audience, and is reopened only towards the end of the Tale.

4. The *Libyan land* is the desert country west of Egypt. The narrative now begins its move to more specific events. The title *Perfected God* is a royal epithet referring to the king's being made divine at his accession; the succession of the new king is presented smoothly, as if already achieved. The account of his victorious *return* is in the language of commemorative inscriptions: all as it should be, despite the king's death.

5. The *Friends* are the inner members of the royal court: the title is derived from close-ness to the king. The narrative alludes circumspectly to the shock of the king's death, and moves very gently from the ideal state of affairs to a harsher reality.

6. The mention of *night-fall* evokes the potentially chaotic nature of the events sur-rounding a king's death. The *falcon* is the new king, an embodiment of the falcon-god Horus. He secretly leaves for the Residence to ensure his succession; a message is then *sent* by him to his siblings (on whom Sinuhe is waiting) to

inform them of their father's death, and one of them is *summoned*, to assist him in his accession.

7. In the second part of the stanza, Sinuhe describes for the first time his own actions: chaos and panic irrupt on a personal level, as he unofficially overhears the news of the king's death while in attendance on the royal children. The original audience would have known what the Tale leaves unspoken: that this news told how the king had been assassinated (see *The Teaching of King Amenemhat*, pp. 203-11). Sinuhe hides himself like a common thief until the coast is clear (the *traveller* is the royal child on his way to the Residence).

8. A stanza of rapid flight, providing a detailed description of constant movement over two days (see Map, p. xxxiii). Sinuhe explains that he fled away from the court, in terror of the interregnum (*him* is the old king).

9. The *Sycomore* is probably a tree sanctuary to Hathor at Giza, and *Maaty* a lake or canal nearby. As the name Sinuhe means 'Son of the Sycomore', and Maaty is 'Right-place', these place names evoke the home and the values which Sinuhe is leaving behind. The *Isle of Sneferu* is a funerary estate that was established by a famous and benevolent Fourth Dynasty king. The confused meeting with a man gives the flight an aspect of social chaos and reversal (recalling the themes of contemporaneous literary Discourses). *Cattle-Quay* was probably a small village opposite modern Gebel Ahmar—a sharp contrast to the royal Residence.

10. The wind-blown *rudderless barge*, an intervention of chance, forces Sinuhe to flee eastward instead of continuing his planned flight to the south; a rudderless ship is a common image of the state in chaos. *Iaku* is a settlement to the west of the quarries of the *Red Mountain* (modern Gebel Ahmar), where there was a shrine, referred to here, of the goddess Hathor (the *Lady*), the patroness of foreign places and quarrying (see n. 1).

11. Sinuhe now moves north-east towards what was the edge of the civilized world. *The Walls of the Ruler* was a fortress built by Amenemhat I to guard the eastern border, in the region of the Wadi Tumilat. He behaves like a barbarian, terrified of being spotted; the echo of his earlier hiding in a *bush* (B 4-5) gives the impression of continuing flight. The mention of *Syrians*, Egypt's barbarous enemies, anticipates later developments.

12. The *travelling in the night-time* of this third stanza of flight reverses his previous pattern of travel, and evokes the chaos which caused Senwosret to return to Egypt by night (R 20-2). *Peten* is an otherwise unknown location, on the way to *Kemur*, the bitter lakes (including Lake Timsah); it was presumably the area at the end of the Wadi Tumilat. As Sinuhe crosses the boundary out of Egypt, this symbolically charged moment is marked by his near *death* (described in the central verse of the stanza).

13. Another sudden change in fortune occurs, reversing the effects of his earlier panic (B 2-3). The stanza's concluding allusion to *Egypt* and Sinuhe's being once again *recognized* suggests how inescapable his identity and responsibility are. The fact that this is by a *Syrian* who had been in Egypt anticipates the mixture of cultures that is to come.

14. *Water* is given as an immediate help, while more substantial *milk* is being prepared (this latter is a touch of local colour). In Autobiographies 'giving water to the thirsty' is a virtuous act done by the narrator; here the conventions and roles of an ideal Egyptian life are reversed.

15. The rapid uncontrolled movement away from Egypt continues, through foreign *countries* (as if too numerous to be named). *Byblos* was a Syrian port with traditional Egyptian connections, while *Qedem* is probably the wooded area east of the Lebanon mountain range. Sinuhe is then captured by a local ruler; *upper*

Retjenu is probably the land along the upper reaches of the river Litani, and is mentioned in contemporaneous inscriptions as an enemy state. Although Amunenshi, whose name may also be read Amunesh, has not been to Egypt (unlike the sheikh of B 25-6), he can speak Egyptian and has *Egyptians* with him, who may be other exiles, or messengers passing through. His land is presented as an Egyptianized foreign chiefdom. At this point, the first part of the Tale ends with verses whose frequent mentions of Egypt suggest that Sinuhe's own cultural and personal identity cannot be renounced by voluntary exile.

16. The second part of the Tale opens with a return to the events with which the Tale began (Amenemhat's death). Amunenshi naturally questions Sinuhe's motivation, which is a major concern of the plot. As an Egyptianizing chief, he is also curious, out of self-interest, to know if Egypt is still stable.

17. Sinuhe's account repeats the stately description of R 6-8 (see n. 2), but adds the significant detail that the circumstances are unknown: the audience knows that Sinuhe overheard more about these circumstances than he admits to Amunenshi (this is his *half-truth*). The following verses also are duplicitous, as the death was not *reported* to Sinuhe, but overheard (B 1-2). He defensively stresses that his exile was not imposed on him, but was the result of his own *heart* or of an unknown power, and he proclaims his lack of guilt, perhaps implying a lack of involvement in the king's death. (In most manuscripts, the simile at the end of the stanza continues as it does in B 225 6.)

18. Amunenshi now develops his question, taking up Sinuhe's mention of *God* and turning it to the divine king Amenemhat. His Egyptian-style phraseology shows that he is a loyal ally: the baleful goddess *Sekhmet*, the Lady of *plague*, is a protectress of Egypt; in a eulogy of the period, the king is a 'Sekhmet against those who touch his borders'.

19. Sinuhe echoes the words of Amunenshi's question exactly, to stress that the new king is at least the equal of the old. His reply is an extensive praise song to the new king. Eulogy was an important poetic genre, characterized by sequences of descriptive epithets. The eulogy is an integral part of the Tale, since the king represents the culture that Sinuhe has abandoned, and is also very relevant to the addressee, who is ruler of a foreign country such as the new king *subjugates*. The stanza ends, as it began, with a description of the close relationship between the old and the new order.

20. Two stanzas now acclaim the king's military prowess against foreigners. The dichotomy between victorious Egypt and the craven *barbarians* is strongly drawn, as in official discourse. The king's power against defectors is grimly appropriate to the fugitive Sinuhe: his description dramatically expresses his own fear of royal punishment.

21. The opening verse of the third stanza of the eulogy is implicitly pertinent to Amunenshi, who is an *Easterner*. The choice of the king's weapon is appropriate as *barbarians* are literally 'Bowmen'. The *Great One* is the uraeus serpent on the Sungod's forehead; as an avenging goddess, she recalls the earlier mention of Sekhmet, an archer-goddess (B 45 and n. 18).

22. The eulogy now shifts to the king's grace; the two contrasting aspects of the king's power are paradoxically united in the second verse of this stanza. The stanza is full of mentions of *birth* and increase, as opposed to the death of the preceding stanzas (*in the egg* is an idiom for extreme youth). The king's grace is presented in terms of Egypt's social prosperity: the people who benefit live in *cities*, not in tribes. Sinuhe, however, seems completely transported by his own eulogy, and speaks as if he were still in Egypt, referring to it as *this land*. The stanza concludes with the expansion of Egypt (a phrase used in many royal inscriptions), which is ironical here, since Sinuhe has gone beyond its *borders*.

23. The concluding stanza of the eulogy resumes the military and hostile ethos of the opening stanzas. Sinuhe makes its relevance to Amunenshi explicit, treating him as a vassal of the Egyptian king, whose grace will be extended to foreign lands in return for loyalty.

24. Amunenshi ignores the recommendation in a laconic reply, which reassures Sinuhe, but also brings him back to earth, pointing out the dichotomy between his position and Egypt. There is ironic use of the word for *happy/good*: while Egypt's *good* relies on the king, Sinuhe's *good* must come from Amunenshi. This promise is fulfilled in the rest of the stanza, as Amunenshi adopts him.

25. At the centre of the stanza is *Iaa*, whose description as a *good/happy* land ironically echoes the happiness of Egypt. It is a paradise (cf. the island in *The Tale of the Shipwrecked Sailor*, p. 93) whose name may mean 'Rushy place'; it is possibly fictional, although the name occurs in much later lists of foreign lands.

26. The second part of the Tale ends with a stanza of plentiful sustenance, continuing the description of Sinuhe's well-being. The prominence of *wild game* in the list keeps his foreign (desert) position in mind, as does the culinary reference to *milk*—a touch of authentic local colour (recalling his rescue by nomads in B 26–7; see also n. 14).

27. The stanza that opens the new part of the Tale—the repetition of *many* provides a link with the preceding one—recounts Sinuhe's rise to power over a long time period, during which he retains indirect contact with the Egyptian court. His encouraging all to *tarry* is an indication of his desperate isolation, as well as of his virtue in providing hospitality. In the following verses he returns to the formulaic declarations of virtuous acts as found in Autobiographies: he asserts that he is established in his own pseudo-Egyptian world.

28. His achievements abroad are recounted as in Autobiographies. This expresses Sinuhe's ambivalent position, since the phrases are normally used of Egyptians attacking foreigners; the description of his military deeds also shows how he is loyally conforming to the model provided by the Egyptian king: his triumph recalls that of Senwosret over Libya (R 15–16), and his *excellent plans* recall Senwosret's (B 48–9). Since his eulogy of Senwosret, the style of his narrative has resumed much of its stateliness.

29. This stanza opens with more Autobiographical-sounding phrases, but Sinuhe's influence is soon shown to be unstable. This episode is the central one of the Tale—a face-to-face combat between Egyptian and foreign values. It is introduced as in a commemorative inscription, and the *hero* is presented as a scheming enemy.

30. The fact that the challenge to Sinuhe makes Amunenshi feel the need to *confer* with him is a sign of Sinuhe's importance. Sinuhe denies any knowledge of the disruptive mighty man, either as an ally or as someone who has given offence (the *private quarters* imply interference with the man's women).

31. Sinuhe's speech becomes more reflective in a stanza that begins and ends with imagery of bullfights. Cattle are not only plunder (as in B 112), but are often an image for humanity, and this metaphor expands the individual incident beyond one man's experience. The *roaming* cattle are relevant to the wandering Sinuhe, who is living among nomads.

32. To Retjenu Sinuhe is an *inferior* outsider, but he has become a resented *superior*. As Sinuhe meditates, the imagery moves from the specific to the general and the geographical, to express the fundamental incompatibility of Egypt (the *papyrus*) with barbarians (the desert *mountain*). This proverbial-sounding verse is structured by wordplay: *papyrus* and *mountain* are homophones.

33. Sinuhe's questions turn on the enemy to imply that the enemy's motives are as chaotic and unsure as they are veiled; the man's indirect challenge suggests that he may wish to back out.

34. Sinuhe states unequivocally that he is willing to fight and places his faith in the certainty of divine justice. A final pair of rhetorical questions affirms that god must know the preordained result of the combat, contrasting with the previous pair's expression of uncertainty.

35. His preparations in the *night* contrast with his earlier irresolute night-time activities (the flight: see nn. 6, 12), suggesting the extent to which he has regained strength of character. In the second half of the stanza he narrates the anticipation of the duel. Even the natives pity Sinuhe, and the *wives* come to watch (presumably only the tribe's married women would be allowed to do this). Their sympathy encourages the audience's, and the sequence of questions heightens the suspense as the turning-point of the Tale approaches. (In the final question *him* is the foreign champion).

36. The stanza narrating the duel begins suddenly and continues swiftly. The champion's moves are described in complicated and extended syntax, but then Sinuhe's easy victory is narrated in laconic simple statements. The word *stuck* is (ironically) the same root as 'establish' in Sinuhe's earlier question 'what can establish the papyrus on the mountain?' (B 122–3, see n. 32). The irony of felling the enemy with his own *axe* is developed later, and prepares for a wider and unexpected change in Sinuhe's fortunes. The mention of *every Asiatic* brings out the foreignness of the surroundings, but Sinuhe the Egyptian reappears in the incident: his accuracy recalls the king's (B 62–3), and he thanks *Montu*, a falcon and bull-god of battle associated with Thebes (pertinent to the cattle imagery here, as is the word *bellowing*).

37. The stanza progresses from the rapidly described fight to Autobiography-like statements of Sinuhe's triumph, as order returns to his life; after the interruption of the duel the description of his achievements resumes.

38. The narrative moves from a past narrative into the present (*today*), as Sinuhe reflects in a dramatic monologue on his god-given good fortune. He places responsibility for both his flight and his present success on god, giving a (short-lived) sense of reconciliation.

39. Sinuhe hymns his triumph with a formal lyric. He contrasts his present state with the actions of various types of *fugitive*, and thus distances himself from his flight. His claim to have given *bread* echoes the ethical ideals claimed in funerary Autobiographies; *white linen* is the characteristic dress of successful Egyptians. The lyric ends as it began with a reference to the royal *Residence*, and the couplets are patterned by contrasts which point the contrast between two locations—Sinuhe's foreign *dwelling place* and Egypt. He can only formulate his foreign prosperity in terms of Egypt, and this suggests the self-contradictory nature of his happiness, which he gradually realizes even as he proclaims it.

40. The dichotomy produces a breakdown, as Sinuhe realizes how desperate his position is. The second half of the stanza is full of convoluted syntax, desperate cries and rhetorical questions, and the language has grown more passionate. Like the first half, it starts with mention of *God*'s responsibility and his *grace*, but here grace is not yet attained. The *good event* is his return to Egypt for burial (the phrase can be a euphemism for 'death'). Earlier, he was pitied even by foreigners (B 131–3; see n. 35): surely god must pity him now. Before, he distanced himself from his flight, but here he moves to a deeper level, acknowledging his exile's reality but distancing himself from the motivation.

41. This stanza continues his concern with *grace*, moving from god to his deputy, the *king* and his family. After the moment of self-realization, Sinuhe expresses his wishes to be in Egypt more directly and more calmly.

42. At the centre of the stanza is a description of his decrepitude, which echoes his near-death as he left Egypt (B 21–3); here a more lasting rescue is wished for.

His _legs ceasing to follow_ is very ironically appropriate, given his flight. _Weariness of heart_ is a euphemism for the lethargy of death: his life is a living death.

43. The _cities of eternity_ are the Egyptian necropoleis, which are an otherworldly court in layout (_they_ are either his legs and heart, or the royal children). Burial is often an image of the permanence of Egyptian values. The queen, Sinuhe's patroness, is here not just the Mistress of the Land, but the _Lady of All_—which is an epithet of Hathor and Sekhmet as a universal goddess in religious texts. The imagery of the final verse merges her with the sky-goddess, by alluding to the symbolism of the coffin lid—_above_ the dead man—as representing this goddess who provides rebirth. Her _children_ are a sign of Egypt's continuance: Sinuhe hopes to follow his queen after death, when she will tell him how they prosper on earth. (The wishes are linked together by repetition of the word _follow_, and by the fact that _lead_ and _pass_ are homonyms.)

44. As soon as this prayer is uttered, heard only by the Tale's audience, the king answers it: the _children_ send the desired _messages_, and Sinuhe's _heart_, weary before (B 170), is revived. _The humble servant_ is an epistolary formula for 'I', which prepares for the actual royal letter in the next part of the Tale.

45. Royal letters (_decrees_) are occasionally included in actual Autobiographies; here a title presents the decree as an exact transcript. The title makes the main purpose immediately apparent; the letter is _brought_ to reverse Sinuhe's being 'brought'/'carried away' into foreign lands (B 164) and bring him home. The letter itself opens with the full titulary of king, comprising five titles (see Glossary).

46. The use of the title _Follower_ in the address is ironic (cf. n. 1). The king immediately assigns responsibility for Sinuhe's exile to his own heart; whereas Sinuhe had earlier placed his responsibility with god (B 147–9), the king, himself a god, denies this, and draws a contrast between Sinuhe's fallible heart and his own. The king reaffirms Sinuhe's earlier denial of being consciously blameworthy. For _Qedem_, see n. 15.

47. The king assures Sinuhe that his patroness is still in favour; since the plot leading to the old king's death seems to have originated in the Women's Chambers in the palace, this would probably have seemed a necessary reassurance to the original audience. The image of the queen as Sinuhe's _Heaven_ continues the imagery of B 172–3 (see n. 43)—the tale is moving to a cosmic level.

48. Another stanza of assurances, developing the topic. The king repeats Sinuhe's description of old age, as if he had heard Sinuhe's own thoughts (note the echo of _today_ from the previous stanza). This description is a tacit promise, which is developed in the following stanza. To _have in mind the day of burial_ is not just a sign of old age, but also of piety (_memento mori_).

49. The king assures Sinuhe a full courtly burial, the privilege of the élite. The preparations, including the funeral procession, occupy much of the first half of the stanza. The _night_ is here a period of funerary ceremonies, and as such is a transformation of the usually negative associations of night-time in the narrative. The funeral is a union with the gods: the mummy-wrappings come directly from _Tayet_, the goddess of weaving. The _lapis lazuli_ is inlaid in the mummy _mask_ to represent hair. The _singers_ are a band who perform mourning songs. The _heaven_ is the lid of the mummy case, imagined as the sky-goddess (a symbol of rebirth, evoking the queen's role as Sinuhe's patroness (see n. 47)); this fulfils Sinuhe's earlier wish (see B 172–3 and n. 43).

50. The assurance now moves on to the rites performed at the entrance of the tomb, and the subsequent funerary cult performed in the _pillared_ chapel next to the pyramid. The _dance of the Oblivious ones_ is a ritual performance portraying spirits welcoming the dead man into the other world. The _offering-invocation_ is a

recitation summoning up offerings for the dead to live on, which accompanied the *sacrifice* of animals. Sinuhe will be buried in the same enclosure as the royal family, a privilege of the highest courtiers. This central position in eternity contrasts with his peripheral and transient state among Asiatics, as is described in the following verses.

51. *Ram's skin* is impermanent and unclean, in contrast to the security and magnificence of an Egyptian burial, amid *white stone* (limestone), which will ensure his resurrection and save him from death. After assuring Sinuhe of an eternal homecoming, the letter ends with a summarizing couplet which reiterates the climactic command to *return*.

52. In contrast with the promised bliss, the letter is received *in the midst of* a foreign *tribe* (not royal children). Sinuhe abases himself before the royal might. In his cry of joy, he now admits the responsibility of his own *heart* for his flight, in accordance with the king's view.

53. In Autobiographies royal letters need no reply, but here one is necessary. Sinuhe presents himself using a title that expresses his continuing loyalty, as does the epistolary formula *your humble servant* (cf. n. 44). In the opening heading, Sinuhe characterizes his flight as not a conscious decision; this explanation of his motivation is developed in the letter, and his *ignorance* is contrasted with the king's all-knowing wisdom.

54. The letter begins with standard epistolary wishes on the grandest scale, with a great list of deities forming a rhetorical declaration of loyalty. The mention of the king's *spirit* recalls the previous stanza (B 203). *Montu* is a god of war (see n. 36) and a state god of *Thebes*, the original religious centre of the Twelfth Dynasty.

55. *Amun Lord of the Throne of the Two Lands* is the king of the gods and the god of kings, and a state god of Thebes, the lord of the temple of Karnak. He heads a wide-ranging list of gods: *Sobek-Re* is a fusion of the potent crocodile-god and the Sungod, and a patron of the Twelfth Dynasty; *Horus* is the kingly god, appropriate to the addressee; *Hathor* is a cosmic goddess, but also the goddess of foreign lands (see n. 10); *Atum* is the creator-god who, together with his children, the *company* of nine gods, forms the divine dynasty. All these deities are a group that is sometimes associated with Thebes, and which occurs in the formulae of actual Middle Kingdom letters. The following gods are associated with foreign lands and with the routes towards them: *Sopdu–Neferbau–Semseru the eastern Horus* is a compound god associated with the eastern desert (into which Sinuhe fled); the *Lady of Imet* is the goddess Buto, who appears on the king's *head* as the royal uraeus (*Imet* is modern Tell Farun, north-east of Cairo, and on the route to the eastern countries); the *divine Council upon the Flood* is a cosmic group with powers over the Nile and other bodies of water (part of Sinuhe's flight was by water); *Min-Horus* is another compound deity, again a patron of foreign countries; *Wereret* is the uraeus-goddess of the Crown, and *Punt* is a land of exotic marvels in Africa. The list concludes with two cosmic gods: *Nut* the sky-goddess and *Haroeris-Re* the elder Sungod. The group of deities shows the king's universal significance—including foreign lands, relevant to Sinuhe; this is summarized by the final generalized and all-inclusive verse; the *Sea* is that to the north of Egypt (a final foreign reference). The gods are invoked in wishes which affirm Sinuhe's loyalty to the king, and which acclaim his power as unbounded in both space and time.

56. Sinuhe's prayers for the god's gifts are a reciprocal response to the king's gift of mercy (the theme of reciprocity is fundamental to Egyptian concepts of truth and justice (cf. n. 76)). The couplet echoes Sinuhe's earlier acclamation of the king's mercy (B 202–3). The *West* is the death from which the promised funeral and

tomb will save him, by ensuring his eternal rebirth. (It is also paradoxically a rescue from his living death in the east.)

57. After the introduction, Sinuhe acclaims the king's *perception*—an intellectual power used in the creation of the cosmos—of his exile and of his desire to return. The king displays the perception that Sinuhe lacked when he fled (cf. B 205), and the unspeakable flight is introduced with circumlocution. Sinuhe draws attention to the inexpressible (*unrepeatable*) nature of his predicament, which underlies the whole Tale.

58. He affirms his dependence on the king (*enquires* echoes B 74), and pertinently acclaims him as a divine *conqueror* of foreign lands. Now that the true king has entered the Tale, Amunenshi disappears from view, as more important matters occupy the audience's attention.

59. Before turning to his personal concerns, Sinuhe diplomatically lists peoples who show that he has served the king by spreading his influence. The foreign dignitaries who can be *brought* by him to pay their respects are referred to by their places of origin or rule, rather than their names. *Meki* is perhaps the southern Beqa, and is part of *Qedem* (for which see n. 15); *Keshu* is perhaps the biblical Geshur, a north-western part of the region of Bashan. Meki and Keshu are included in contemporaneous lists of potential enemy states. *Menus* is perhaps the Amanus mountain range, now in south-eastern Turkey, although the Cretan Minos has also been suggested. The *Fenkhu* are the people of the Lebanese coastal plain, later known as the Phoenicians. The diction of the final verse mentioning the more general region of *Retjenu* is rather florid.

60. Sinuhe admits his responsibility for the flight (and significantly starts to use the first person), but asserts that it was neither intentional nor caused by past blame. The stanza recapitulates the various earlier attempts to explain his flight: it was an inexplicable, unconscious, confused event, like a *dream* of geographical confusion; the *Delta* marshes and the southern *Elephantine* are at the opposite ends of Egypt.

61. The syntax moves from simple sentences to a longer and more complex sequence of clauses as Sinuhe truthfully relates his experience. In speaking to the king, he can formulate the truth of what happened more than hitherto, and he now reconciles the two distinct motives which he has mentioned earlier at various points—the external force of *God* and the internal one of his *heart*—by placing them in parallel juxtaposition. The heart was sometimes described as the 'God within a man', and here the two motives complement each other to convey a sense that the flight was by him and yet not by him.

62. Sinuhe claims he could not have been *presumptuous*, so as to deserve reproaches, because the king is too awe-inspiring. This description of the king presents a vision of *the land* of Egypt, where respect is paid where it is due, very different from the confused jostling for power in Retjenu (B 120-1), or from Sinuhe's ambiguous position during his flight (B 10-11). The *Sungod* is the king's divine father, who authorizes the power of his son. Sinuhe implicitly acknowledges that Egypt is his *home*, and states the king's sole power over his world (the reference to his *horizon* extends the reference to the other world (see n. 2)). The lyrical stanza concludes by extolling the king's control of all the basic necessities of life: light, water, and air; his power implicitly has a caring aspect.

63. At the very end of his reply, Sinuhe assures the king that he will not hesitate to relinquish his possessions; his intention to return is unstated but is implicit in his obedience. Although his foreign home is dismissed simply as *this place*, the description of his mature children as *chicks* is tender; such language keeps the audience vividly aware of the importance of the preceding events.

64. The concluding epistolary wishes include the most important gods from the

opening of the letter (B 205–12 and n. 54): the cosmic *Sungod*, the royal *Horus*, *Hathor* the goddess of foreign places, and the warrior *Montu*. Sinuhe returns to the themes of breath and reciprocity, praying that the king will be given life by the gods in return for his gift of life to Sinuhe.

65. *Iaa* is dismissed from the Tale with a description of what is being relinquished, and a cycle is completed: the land has not been mentioned since Sinuhe's arrival in it (B 81). Sinuhe's swift departure reveals that only Egypt is of importance now. The motif of a father handing over to his son when he retired or died was the Egyptian ideal: all is as it should be.

66. At the end of the fourth part of the Tale, Sinuhe arrives at the *Ways of Horus*, the royal road leading from Egypt's border at Sile (modern Tell Abu Sefa) to the north-east; the toponym implies that he is back on 'the way of true living', and not 'the ways of flight' (B 39–40; *Horus* also recalls the eulogy of the king in B 217–18). His journey reverses his earlier one, which was, in contrast, solitary, uncontrolled, and towards death. The narrative moves forward rapidly through the gradual stages of his reassimilation. The *commander* is the first of a series of intermediaries who accompany Sinuhe back to the king; the mention of a military *garrison* may ironically recall the fortresses past which he fled earlier (B 16–19).

67. The final part of the Tale is occupied with Sinuhe's reintegration. The title of the official who meets him is appropriate, as *peasants* were marginal members of society, as he is now. The *Syrians* are presumably the men mentioned in Sinuhe's letter (B 219–22), but their *names* are not given to the audience here: as he re-enters Egypt, they recede into the background.

68. The voyage to the royal capital (*Itj-tawi* (see n. 3)) is a picture of idyllic social order. The mention of a *harbour* recalls Sinuhe's previous voyage (B 12–14). The stanza ends with his gradual progress into the palace itself, the repetitive description heightening the sense of expectation as the confrontation between Sinuhe and the king approaches. (Sinuhe's *ushering* reverses his having been 'dragged away' by god, B 230: the same word is used for both movements.)

69. At the great *portal* flanked by statues of *sphinxes*, Sinuhe is introduced to the palace, amid the full panoply of the court as a foreign ambassador: the *royal children* greet him without recognizing him (as is later apparent). The repetition of *portal* gives a sense of his progress; the second *portal* may refer to the canopy of the king's throne or to the portal between the Pillared Hall and the Audience Hall, where the king is enthroned. His terrified bow before the king re-enacts his original panic-stricken collapse when he was literally *seized in the dusk* by panic (B 2–4), and is also a second near-death, echoing his experience of death as he left Egypt (B 23).

70. Courtiers lift him up now, unlike his first near-death, when nomads helped him. The king's address summarizes his letter, and blames Sinuhe for his own suffering (echoing Sinuhe's prayer at B 159, and his own decree at B 197).

71. Sinuhe's respectful reply describes both his irrational flight and his hesitation in replying now as the result of blind—but not disrespectful—panic. Once again he abandons himself to the king's grace.

72. The formal atmosphere is lightened by a moment of charm and humour. The queen's failure to recognize Sinuhe dramatically shows how much he has changed; the court itself, however, seems unchanging—the princesses still seem young, whereas Sinuhe has aged. Their cry poses the plot's central question of Sinuhe's true identity—is he really (literally 'in truth') barbarian or Egyptian?—which the king immediately resolves.

73. The *rattles and sistra* are musical instruments shaken by women in cultic rituals. Like the *necklaces* (also shakeable) they are particularly associated with

Hathor (see n. 74). By presenting them, the princesses enact a lyrical ceremony of renewal before the king (similar to those shown on tomb walls (see R. B. Parkinson, *Voices from Ancient Egypt* (London, 1991), 78–81)).

74. The *Lady of Heaven* recalls the epithets used of Sinuhe's patroness (B 172, 185–6, and nn.43, 47), but refers to Hathor, the goddess of love and rebirth, and the lady of the sycomore (see n. 1) and of foreign lands (see n. 10). *Golden One* and *Lady of Stars* are epithets of the radiant and celestial Hathor. The song is one of rebirth, and has an erotic charge, evoking the king's union with Hathor, who is merged with the queen, to ensure his own rebirth and continued vitality; the worlds of the court and of the gods are fused. Here the song ensures Sinuhe's rebirth.

75. The king unites the two parts of Egypt—the *North* and *South*—and upholds the unity of the state, expressed with images of royal insignia (appropriate to the ritual context). The phrasing echoes the opening of the tale where the old king's death united him with the gods (R 6–8); here the union is achieved within the court of his successor.

76. The princesses urge the king to be gracious, so that the *Sungod*, his divine father, shall be gracious to him, evoking the principle of reciprocity. The *Lord of the Two Lands* is a title held by both king and god. They then hail him in a deliberately ambiguous verse: the *Lady of All* is either the queen or the goddess (see nn. 74, 43), so it is both: 'Hail to you, as to Hathor', and 'Hail to you and also to your queen'. The goddess's role as protectress of Egypt is taken up in the following verses, as the princesses make their request. The imagery of archery echoes Sinuhe's duel (B 137–9), as well as his eulogy of the king (B 62–3).

77. The princesses use the principle of reciprocity (expressed in the repetition of *give*, and of *good*) to request a reward in return for the special offering of their performance: this reward is their beloved Sinuhe. These verses echo the king's last speech (B 260) and are a summation of the paradox of Sinuhe's plight. They rename him at this rebirth *North Wind's Son*—an allusion to his exile in the north—instead of his old name 'Son of the Sycomore' (see n. 1). An additional paradox is that Hathor is the Lady of both the Sycomore and the North Wind.

78. The princesses now provide a final explanation of Sinuhe's flight, in which his irrational panic becomes a sign of the king's power and fearsomeness, and the abnormality of his actions is made into an expression of the natural order of the state. A final couplet expresses their faith in the king's protective care.

79. The king's response is both a natural remark in the situation, and a grand dismissal of the chaos and terror of the preceding plot. The rest of the Tale is a rapid progression from this climactic moment to the practical preparations for his ultimate homecoming, his death.

80. Sinuhe's reintegration takes place in a royal dwelling. The following verses allude to Sinuhe's possessions abroad: the wealth of this dwelling replaces that of the land of Iaa, and the building itself contrasts with the nomads' stockades and tents (B 115–16, 145–6). The *bathroom* is a mark of prestige, and appropriate when Sinuhe is about to be cleansed of his experience. *Images of the horizon* are probably images of gods, either statues or wall-paintings; the idiom moves the audience towards Sinuhe's own *horizon* (tomb) and eternity.

81. This stanza describes what Sinuhe had attempted in his central monologue (B 149–56)—the negation of his flight. He now literally casts off the *load* of his debilitating foreign experiences; beards were worn by foreigners, not Egyptians. The stanza is structured by a stately series of direct antitheses: foreign *clothes* and Egyptian *fine linen*; crude *tree oil* and *fine oil*.

82. After his transitional dwelling, Sinuhe is given a permanent residence. The rank of *Governor* is now bestowed on him, echoing the very start of the tale (R 1 and

n. 1). These stanzas present a panoramic series of dwellings, moving towards an eternal residence. The *meals* ironically recall Sinuhe's plenty when abroad (B 87–92), which is now surpassed and nullified through royal bounty.

83. The *pyramid* is Sinuhe's eternal home; it is in the royal enclosure around the pyramid of Senwosret I at el-Lisht, which contained subsidiary pyramids for family members and the highest members of the élite. The repetitive description gives a sense that all is as it should be, forming a progression through the building and equipping of the tomb to the establishment of the funerary cult, with priests and a *demesne* as its endowment. Sinuhe has now attained the rank of a *Chief Friend*, at the very centre of the court (see n. 5). The *image* of Sinuhe is his statue in the tomb, the object of the funerary cult and the subject of the Autobiography; it is an image of permanent personality, transcending the mutability of his earlier life.

84. As Sinuhe regains his true identity, the narrative resumes the form of an Autobiography, a development that is completed in the final verses. The description of tomb-building and the statement that these favours come from the king are standard elements in Autobiographies. The movement of the final stanzas ends here, and the audience is back where it started at the beginning of the Tale, listening to Sinuhe speak from his tomb. The Tale ends, as an Autobiography, by relating Sinuhe's death—his *landing*. This widespread metaphor is particularly appropriate for his journeying life.

85. The colophon states that the literary text was copied accurately in its entirety.

2

The Tale of the Eloquent Peasant

Introduction

The Tale of the Eloquent Peasant is found with *The Tale of Sinuhe* in two Middle Kingdom manuscripts, displays a comparable complexity of form and style, and was probably composed at approximately the same time. Like *Sinuhe*, it concerns problems of motivation, and of suffering and its justification, but it is mostly concerned with exploring the significance of a single event, rather than with narrating a sequence of events.

The plot of the Tale is deceptively simple, like a folk tale: once upon a time a clever peasant was robbed, spoke eloquent protests, and got his goods back because of his eloquent appealing for justice. The narrative is a clear and precise relation of the event, which is developed with swift dialogue, and is then left hanging at the point of crisis as the peasant's appeals remain unanswered. The style has a studied simplicity, but the exchanges between the peasant and the official who robs him are highly literary, and this prepares the audience for the rhetoric of the peasant's subsequent appeals. The narrative avoids anything fantastic, and its general naturalism helps accommodate the inherent improbability of the plot—the studied eloquence of the provincial peasant, who is presented as a sort of noble savage.

The peasant's appeals occupy most of the poem, and are a complaint against the falseness of the world. They are partly reflective, but, since they are inspired by a specific crime and are directed against a specific individual, they have considerable didactic force: the *Eloquent Peasant* is a wisdom text as well as a Tale. The peasant's appeals comprise nine separate petitions, which create an episodic and cyclical presentation in which a single theme is variously and repeatedly expounded; this complexity contrasts with the unitary progression and simplicity of the narrative. Much of the Tale's meaning is presented through viewing the same theme in different ways, revealing new implications and associations of the fundamental subject matter—Truth and justice. The range of genres and styles expresses the universality of the Tale's contention, that Truth is a prerogative of all mankind.

The style of the petitions is highly wrought, exuberant, and profuse; the continuous ingenuity of the speeches is one sign of the speaker's eloquence, and attention is repeatedly drawn to the virtuosity of the style. The petitions display a rapid play of ideas and a high level of imagery, with frequent repetition of keywords, syntactic patterns (such as series of negative constructions), motifs of imagery, and heightened recollections of earlier phrases. These features increase the forcefulness of the petitions. Shifts in emotional tone—from eulogy to denunciation, from subtle criticisms to direct abuse—mark the peasant's desperate recourse to different approaches, and are patterned to express his mounting anxiety. This rhetorical exuberance is in part the point of the Tale; it is a dazzling display of poetry as entertainment and impassioned expression.

The Tale is, however, very ambiguous as a whole: it is a treatise on the value of Truth, and yet also in part a satire on the difficulties of dealing with the Egyptian bureaucracy that was meant to uphold this value. It is a moral anecdote, but one fissured with a deep irony. The eloquence which ensures the peasant's success is also the cause of his prolonged suffering: he is so eloquent that, after the first introductory petition, the king commands that no response be given, simply to force him to continue talking. The peasant assumes that his words are unheard and so speaks on, while his audience withholds any acknowledgement, prolonging his misery. As he speaks, his complaint about a theft becomes a larger questioning of why society ignores justice.

There is a continuous dichotomy between the actual audience's awareness of the situation (shared with the fictional audience of the High Steward) and the peasant's awareness. This is articulated in the stylistic dichotomy between the rhetoric of his appeals and the simplicity of the narrative: one is highly subjective, the other objective. The irony of the plot is intense, as the peasant's discourse concerns Truth, and the value of his eloquence is in its revelation of Truth, but his speeches are founded on a misconception. Most of his underlying accusations against officialdom are false, although one early episode, in which a group of officials sides with the villain, justifies his complaint to some extent.

The peasant appeals to an absolute standard of justice, and evokes images of the gods, and of the otherworld as the place where Truth itself dwells. There is, however, no divine intervention in the Tale, and this conspicuous absence implies the question: if the gods will not intervene to save a man who suffers innocently, can they be just? The Tale raises this problem both through metaphors from the world of the gods and by establishing a hierarchy of authority which should also form a hierarchy of perfection; this runs from the lowly peasant, through various attendant officials, to the High Steward to whom the peasant appeals, from him to the aloof king and, beyond him, to the gods. The mortal official is poised halfway between the gods and the lowest forms of life. His non-intervention calls into question the aims of his superiors in allowing evil to flourish and the just to suffer, and his ultimate superior is the creator-god. Thus, in the third petition, the peasant likens the High Steward both to the all-powerful creator-gods and to the most wretched members of society: an individual's ethical choices involve the whole of this hierarchy. The involvement of this range of hierarchy parallels the involvement of specific events and absolute generalized principles, and informs the style of the whole, which intermingles abstract and concrete. The peasant's poetry draws on metaphors in which Truth is both a pair of scales and a cosmic creation of order, is both the very breath of life and a pile of grain. The imagery of grain also alludes to the dramatic situation, in which the peasant has been deprived of his means of subsistence, grain, ostensibly because one of his asses had eaten a mouthful of grain; in this it is dramatically ironic, as he is being secretly sustained by the High Steward with grain.

If the peasant is driven to question the justice of the gods, he exonerates them of responsibility for his suffering, and justifies it by distinguishing between the absolute justice of the otherworld and the partial embodiments of this ideal that are found in the officials of the mortal world. The belief that this world is imperfect, and that man is both potentially perfect and inherently inclined towards chaos, is implicit throughout his speeches. The later petitions reiterate previous ones, but they move towards a treatment of justice that is at once more personal and more generalized and abstract. They also become more desperate, and culminate in the ninth petition, which is a final statement of the peasant's faith in the absolute Truth that cannot be found in this world. This petition provides a paradoxical definition of the relationship of Truth and Falsehood, in which Falsehood is the withdrawal of Truth, and evil exists only as a negation of the transcendant Truth. In this way the justice of the gods is upheld. These themes are couched in more abstract terms than earlier, reflecting the peasant's abandonment of this world, and his desperate recourse to the beyond. He is driven to suicide in his pursuit of the ideal, but at this moment the High Steward intervenes and reveals that the ideal and the actual coincide more closely than the peasant realizes.

He tells the peasant that his speeches have been heard and have been recorded on a 'new roll'. The subject matter of the text is very much its own production: the 'roll' which he shows the peasant is the model for the roll from which the Tale would have been read to the actual audience. Literary production is also an image of the embodiment of Truth, which is here finally actualized. The High Steward's neglectful silence is now revealed to have been the very listening that the peasant has been beseeching. He does not provide an explicit answer to the peasant's complaints, and no justification of authority is didactically stated; instead the formal change to narrative itself provides a response. After this interchange there is no need for further dialogue, and the peasant is finally quiet. A concluding section of descriptive narrative provides a resolution to the Tale. Just as the villain's evil is contained within the ultimately just established order, so the narrative encloses the discourse's nightmare vision of the world in chaos, without negating its force.

Whereas, in *Sinuhe*, the structural significance of the various genres runs parallel to the action of the plot, in this Tale tension is maintained between the passionate suffering of the petitions and the irony of the narrative plot. Because of this irony, the Tale is no simple allegory in which the peasant represents a suffering mankind in search of justice from an official who represents god. The legitimation of suffering advanced by the peasant is made equivocal by its problematic presentation, and the Tale's examination of justice implies that there is no simple answer. The subtlety of its form articulates the complexity of living and the difficulty of the problem of suffering, while its literary virtuosity makes it a source of entertainment.

The only known copies of the Tale are four Middle Kingdom papyri, but it was still being quoted in the Ramesside Period, c.1160 BC. Numbers give the line numbers of principal manuscripts: first R (P. Ramesseum A = P. Berlin 10499), then B1, then its companion manuscript B2 (P. Berlin 3023 and 3025).

The Tale of the Eloquent Peasant

R 1.1 There was once a man[1]
called Khunanup;
he was a peasant of the Wadi Natrun,
whose wife was called Meret.
And this peasant said to this wife of his,
'Look, I am going to Egypt
to buy provisions there for my children.
Go and measure for me
the grain which is left in the storehouse from [yesterday].'
And he measured out for her six gallons of grain.

R 1.5 And this peasant said to this wife of his,
'Look, twenty gallons of grain [are given] to you
and your children for provisions.
But you shall make these six gallons of grain
into bread and beer
for every day, for me to live on.'

This peasant then went down to Egypt,[2]

B1 1 having loaded his asses with reeds and fan palms,
natron and salt,

B1 5 sticks from [. . .]tiu
and staffs from Farafra,
leopard skins
and wolf hides,

B1 10 [pebbles] and [serpentine],
wild mint-plants and *inbi*-fruits,
tebu- and *uben*-plants,

B1 15 —with all the fair produce of Wadi Natrun.

This peasant then went[3]
south to Heracleopolis.
He then arrived
in the area of Per-Fefi, north of Mednit.
There he met a man, called Nemtinakht,[4]
standing on the riverbank.

B1 20 He was the son of a gentleman called Isry;
they were liegemen of the High Steward
Meru's son Rensi.

And this Nemtinakht, when he saw this peasant's asses[5]
which tempted his heart, said,
'If only I had some effective charm,
with which to steal this peasant's belongings!'
Now the house of this Nemtinakht was on the water edge,
    which was a path.   B1 25
It was narrow; it was not broad,
but only as wide as a kilt.
One of its sides was under water,
and the other under grain.
And this Nemtinakht said to his follower,
'Go bring me a sheet from my house!'
It was brought immediately.
Then he spread the sheet on the water-edge pathway.
And its fringe rested on the water,   B1 30
with its hem on the barley.
And this peasant came on the public path.
And this Nemtinakht said, 'Take care, peasant![6]
Will you tread on my clothes?'
And this peasant said, 'I'll do as you wish; my way is good.'
He then went upwards.   B1 35
And this Nemtinakht said, 'Will my barley be your path?'
And this peasant said, 'My way is good,
for the bank is high and the way under barley,
and you block our path with clothes.
Won't you even let us go past the path?'

Then one of the asses took a mouthful[7]   B1 40
from a clump of barley.
And this Nemtinakht said, 'Look, peasant, I will take your
    ass,
for eating my barley,
and it will tread grain for its offence.'
And this peasant said, 'My way is good;[8]
one clump is destroyed—
one destroying ten!   B1 45
For ten units I bought my ass
and you seize it for a mouthful
of a clump of grain!
Now, I know the lord of this estate;

it belongs to the High Steward Meru's son Rensi.
Now, he punishes every robber in this entire land.
Am I robbed in his estate?'

B1 50 And this Nemtinakht said, 'Isn't this[9]
the proverb that people say—
"A wretch's name is uttered only because of his master"?
Even though it's the High Steward you recall,
I'm the one who speaks to you.'

Then he took a stick of fresh tamarisk to him.[10]
Then he beat all his limbs with it,

B1 55 and his asses were taken, and entered into his estate.
And this peasant now wept very much,
for the pain of what was being done to him.
And this Nemtinakht said, 'Don't raise your voice, peasant,[11]
or, look, you're for the harbour of the Lord of Silence!'
And this peasant said, 'You beat me and steal my belongings?

B1 60 And then you'll rob my mouth of complaint?
O Lord of Silence, may You give me back my belongings,
so I shan't cry out to Your fearsomeness!'
And this peasant spent a full week[12]
petitioning this Nemtinakht, but he paid no attention.

This peasant then went[13]
to Heracleopolis to petition

B1 65 the High Steward Meru's son Rensi.
He met him coming out
of the door of his house,
about to board his official barge.
And this peasant said, 'Might I acquaint you with this
complaint!
There is a reason to send one of your choice followers
to me, about which I shall send him back to you.'

B1 70 And the High Steward Meru's son Rensi sent
a choice follower to him,
and this peasant sent him back
about this matter in every detail.
And the High Steward Meru's son Rensi
accused this Nemtinakht to the officials who were with him.

B1 75 And they said to him, 'Surely it's only a peasant of his[14]
who's run off to someone else.

Look, this is what people do to their peasants
who run off to others.
Is there cause to punish this Nemtinakht
for a little natron,
and a little salt?
Order him to repay it, and he'll repay it.'   B1 80
The High Steward Meru's son Rensi
was then quiet.
He answered neither the officials,
nor the peasant.

*

And this peasant came to petition[15]
the High Steward Meru's son Rensi,
and said, 'High Steward, my lord!
Great of the great,
leader of all that is not and all that is!   B1 85

If you go down to the Sea of Truth,[16]
you will sail on it with true fair wind;
the bunt will not strip off your sails, nor your boat delay;
nor will misfortune come upon your mast, nor your yards
      break;
you will not go headlong, and be grounded;
nor will the flood carry you off;   B1 90
nor will you taste the river's evil, nor stare in the face of fear.
But to you the fish will come caught;
you will catch fatted fowl.

For you are a father to the orphan[17]
and a husband to the widow,
a brother to the divorced,
an apron to the motherless.   B1 95
Let me make your name in this land, with every good law:
Leader free from selfishness!
Great one free from baseness!
Destroyer of Falsehood! Creator of Truth!
Who comes at the voice of the caller!

I speak so that you will hear.[18]
Do Truth, praised one whom the praised praise!   B1 100

Drive off my need—look, I am weighed down!
Examine me—look, I am at a loss!'

*

Now this peasant made this speech[19]
in the reign of the Majesty of the Dual King Nebkaure, the
justified.
The High Steward Meru's son Rensi
B1 105 then went before his Majesty
and said, 'My lord, I have found one of the peasants,
whose speech is truly perfect, and whose goods have been
stolen.
And, look, he has come to me to appeal about it.'

And his Majesty said, 'As you wish to see me in health[20]
B1 110 you shall delay him here,
without answering anything he says!
For the sake of his speaking, be quiet!
Then we shall be brought it in writing, and we shall hear it.
But provide sustenance for his wife and children!
Look, one of these peasants only comes
to Egypt when his house is all but empty.
Also, provide sustenance for this peasant himself!
You shall have the provisions given to him
B1 115 without letting him know that you are giving him them!'

And he was given ten loaves of bread,[21]
and two jars of beer daily.
The High Steward Meru's son
Rensi gave them—
gave them to his friend, and his friend gave them to him.
Then the High Steward Meru's son Rensi sent
to the mayor of the Wadi Natrun
about making provisions for this peasant's wife,
three gallons daily.

*

And this peasant came to appeal to him a second time,[22]
and said, 'High Steward, my lord!
Greatest of the great![23]

Richest of the rich!   BI 120
Whose great ones have one greater!
whose rich, one richer!
Helm of heaven![24]
Beam of earth!
Plumbline bearing the weight!
Helm, drift not!
Beam, tilt not!
Plumbline, go not wrong!
For a lord great through taking what is ownerless[25]
is now robbing someone, while your share is in your
     house.
A jar of beer and three loaves of bread—   BI 125
what else need you give out to satisfy your dependents?
A mortal must die with his underlings.

Will you then be a man of eternity?[26]
Yet is it not wrong?—the scales tilting,
the weight wandering
the truly upright man turned aside?
Look, Truth flees from under you,[27]
exiled from its place;
the officials are doing evil;
the standard of speech[28]
is now partial,
and the judges snatch when it carries things off—   BI 130
this means that he who twists speech from its rightness
makes himself go wrong thereby;
the breath-giver is now at a loss on the ground;[29]
he who breathes calmly makes people pant;
the apportioner is greedy,
the dispeller of need is the commander of its making,
and the harbour is its own flood;
the punisher of wrong does evil.'

And the High Steward Meru's son Rensi said,[30]
'Are your belongings more important to you   BI 135
than my follower's seizing you?'
And this peasant said, 'And the measurer of heaps now
     defrauds for himself;
the measurer for others now despoils his surroundings;

the lawful leader now commands theft—
who then will beat off wretchedness
when the dispeller of infirmity is going wrong?
One man is exact about being crooked;[31]
another acclaims the evildoer. Do you not profit yourself
    thus?

BI 140 The redress is short, the evil long;[32]
yet good character returns to its place of yesterday.
This is an ordinance: Act for the man who acts, to cause him
    to act.
This is thanking him for what he does;
this is parrying a thing before shooting;
this is commissioning something from a master craftsman.
O for a moment that destroys,[33]
downfall in your bird-nets,
loss in your fowl,
waste in your marshbirds!
For the watcher has turned out blind,
the hearer deaf,
BI 145 the leader a misleader!

You depositary! Have you not gone too far?[34]
Why do you act against yourself so?
Look, you are mighty, powerful,[35]
your arm active, your heart selfish, and mercy has passed
    you by!
How miserable is the poor man you destroy!
BI 150 For you are like the messenger of Khenty.
Look, you surpass the Lady of Plague;
what is not for you is not for her;
what not against her, not against you;
you shall not act, she shall not!
A lord of bread should be merciful, whereas might belongs
    to the deprived;[36]
theft suits one without belongings,
when the belongings are snatched by the deprived;
BI 155 but the bad act without want—should it not be blamed? It
    is self-seeking.

You, however, are sated with your bread,[37]
drunk with your beer;

you are rich with all [things].
The steersman faces forward,
yet the boat drifts as it wills.
The king is within the palace,
and the steering-oar is in your hand,
yet evil is placed all around you.
Long is the appealer's task, profound the divide;[38]   B1 160
"What's up with him?" will be said.
Give shelter so that your shore will be sound, for look,
     your harbour is swarming with crocodiles!
Be your tongue righteous, so that you will not stray;[39]
that limb of a man is his bane.

Do not speak falsehood! Beware the officials![40]
Those hearers and winnowers are a basket,
but their fodder is speaking falsehood,   B1 165
so that it seems a light concern for their hearts.
Sage of all men,[41]
do you ignore only my affairs?
You who take care of all at sea—
look, I am under way, but boatless!
Bringer to land of all who drown—rescue the wrecked,
for I am anguished at your very side!'   B1 170

*

And this peasant came to appeal to him a third time[42]
and said, 'High Steward, my lord!
You are a Sungod, lord of heaven, with your entourage.[43]
Everyone's portion is with you, like a flood.
You are a Nileflood who revives the water-meadows, and
     restores the ravaged mounds.
Punisher of the robber, protector of the poor—   B1 175
become not a torrent against the appealer!

Take heed of eternity's approach! Wish to endure,[44]
as is said, "Doing Truth is the breath of life."
Deal punishment to the punishable!
May your standard never be equalled!
Do the scales wander?[45]
Is the balance partial?   B1 180
And is Thoth lenient? If so, then you should do evil!

You should bestow yourself as the twin of these three![46]
If the three are lenient, then you can be lenient.
Do not answer good with bad!
Do not put one thing in another's place!
Or speech will grow, even than weeds,[47]

BI 185 to reach the smeller with its answer.
The man who waters evil to make deception grow—
this is three times to make him act.

Steer according to the sail![48]
Remove the torrent to do Truth!
Beware turning back while at the tiller!

BI 190 Maintaining earth's rightness is doing Truth.
Speak not falsehood, for you are great![49]
Be not light, for you are weighty!
Speak not falsehood, you are the scales!
Stray not, you are the standard!
Look, you yourself are the very scales:[50]
if they tilt, then you can tilt.
Drift not, but steer!

BI 195 Rescue with the tiller rope!
Seize not, but act against the seizer!
A selfish great one is not truly great.
But your tongue is the plummet;[51]
your heart is the weight;
your lips are its arms.
So if you disregard the fierce, who will beat off wretchedness?

BI 200 Look, you are a wretched washerman,[52]
a selfish one who destroys friendship,
and forsakes his faithful companion for his client—
anyone who comes and supplies him is his brother.
Look, you are a ferryman who ferries only fareholders,
a doer of right whose righteousness is flawed.

BI 205 Look, you are a storehouse keeper,
who does not let someone in penury escape a debt.

Look, you are a hawk to the folk,[53]
who lives on the wretched birds.
Look, you are a butcher
whose joy is slaughter, without feeling any of the carnage.

Look, you are a shepherd—
is it not a wrong for me that you cannot reckon?
If not, then you can create loss—a predatory crocodile,   BI 210
a shelter which has abandoned the harbour of the whole
    land!

Hearer, you do not hear![54]
So why do you not hear?
Is it because the predator has today already been beaten off
    for me?
The crocodile retreats?
What use for you is this?
The mystery of Truth will be found, and Falsehood cast
    down on the ground!
Do not plan tomorrow before it comes; the evil in it cannot
    be known!'   BI 215

*

Now the peasant spoke this speech[55]
⟨to⟩ the High Steward Meru's son Rensi
at the entrance of the office.
Then he set two attendants on him with whips.
Then they beat all his limbs with them.

And this peasant said, 'So shall Meru's son still err,[56]
his face blind to what he sees,
and deaf to what he hears,
his heart straying from what is recalled to him.   BI 220
Look, you are a town without a mayor,[57]
like a generation without a great man,
like a boat with no controller,
a gang without a leader.
Look, you are a stealing officer,
a bribed mayor,
a district-overseer who should beat off the plunderer
who has become an archetype for the evildoer.'

*

And this peasant came to appeal to him a fourth time;[58]   BI 225
⟨he⟩ met him coming out of the gate[59]

of the temple of Herishef,
and said, 'O praised one, may Herishef
from whose temple you have come, praise you!

Destroyed is goodness, it has no unity,[60]
and nothing can hurl Falsehood to the ground.

B1 230 Has this ferry not gone down? So who can be taken across,
when crossing is made hateful?
Crossing the river on foot—
is that a good crossing? No!
So who now can sleep till dawn?[61]
For destroyed is going by night
and travelling by day,
and making a man attend his good true right.

B1 235 Look, it is no use to tell you this,
for mercy has passed you by: how miserable is the poor man
you destroy!

Look, you are a hunter who slakes his desire,[62]
who reaches out and does what he wants,
who harpoons hippopotami and shoots wild bulls,
catches fish and snares fowl.

B1 240 Yet none hasty-mouthed is free from recklessness;[63]
none light of heart is cautious of intent.
Your heart should be patient, so that you will know Truth!
Suppress your choice for the good of him who would depart
quietly![64]
No rapid man cleaves to excellence; no hasty-hearted man
will exist.

Stretch out to act, now your eyes are opened![65]
Inform the heart!

B1 245 Be not harsh because you are powerful, so that evil may
not reach you!
Pass over a misdeed, and it will be two.
Only the eater tastes;[66]
so the accused replies.
Only the sleeper sees the dream;
so the punishable judge
is an archetype for the evildoer.

Fool, look now you are caught![67]   BI 250
Ignoramus, look now you are accused!
Bilge-baler, look now you are noticed!
Helmsman, do not mis-steer your ship![68]
Life-giver, let not die!
Destroyer, let not perish!
Shade, be not sun-blaze!
Shelter, let not the crocodile seize!   BI 255
A fourth time appealing to you! Shall I continue at it all
    day?'

*

And this peasant came to appeal to him a fifth time[69]
and said, 'High Steward, my lord!
The netter is [. . .]ing the [*mehyt*]-fish,[70]
the [. . .]er killing the Comer-fish,
the fish-spearer harpooning the *ubbu*-fish,   BI 260
and the trawler is after the *paqru*-fish.
The catcher ravages the river.

Look, you are like them![71]
Do not rob a wretch of his belongings!
Helplessness—you know what it is:
a pauper's belongings are his breath—
taking them is suffocating him.   BI 265

You were appointed to hear cases,[72]
to judge contenders, to punish the thief.
Look, your way is to weigh for the robber.
You are trusted—and are become a misleader.
You were appointed as a dyke for the pauper—
beware lest he drown!
Look, you are his lake, you who drag under!'   BI 270

*

And this peasant came to appeal to him a sixth time,[73]
and said, 'High Steward, my lord!
A lord diminishes falsehood: a creator of Truth,[74]
who creates all goodness, and destroys evil!

Like the coming of satiety, ending hunger,
Bɪ 275 of clothes, ending nakedness;
like the sky's calm after high wind, which warms all the
        cold;
like fire which cooks the raw;
like water which quenches thirst!
See for yourself:[75]
Bɪ 280 the apportioner is robbing,
the appeaser making suffer,
the perfecter making anguish!

Making defects lessens Truth:[76]
so measure well!
For Truth has not been damaged, nor has overflown.
If you acquire, then give to your brother,
Bɪ 285 for jawing is devoid of right.
My sorrow leads only to separation;[77]
my accusation brings departure:
what is in the heart is unknowable.
Be not remiss: you should act with a view to report!
You divide—who will then reconcile?[78]
For the helmstaff is in your hand, like a pole to open a way
when mischance befalls at sea.
Bɪ 290 But if the boat goes down it is robbed;
its load perishes on the ground on every shore.

You are educated; you are skilled;[79]
you are perfected—but not for robbing!
You act the same as everyone;
your surroundings are awry, you who should be right!
Defect-maker of the whole land!
For a gardener of wretchedness[80]
Bɪ 295 is now watering his plot with bad,
to make his plot grow with falsehood,
to water the evil of the entire estate.'

                              *

And this peasant came to appeal to him a seventh time,[81]
and said, 'High Steward, my lord!
You are the helm of the whole land.[82]

The land sails as you command.
You are the twin of Thoth,
the judge without partiality.   BI 300

Lord, may you endure,[83]
that a man may be summoned for his true right!
Be not quarrelsome: it is not for you!
The confident man becomes miserable—
do not scheme for what has not yet come,
do not rejoice in what has not yet happened!
Patience extends friendship,
destroying an evil deed which has occurred.
What is in the heart is unknowable.
The law-hacker, the standard-destroyer—[84]   BI 305
there is no wretch whom he has plundered still living.
Has Truth not addressed him?
Now, my body is full, my heart laden,[85]
and what comes from my body due to its state
is the breach of a dyke, whose waters have flown out,
as my mouth opens to speak.
So, I have now plied my pole, baled out my water,[86]   BI 310
unloaded what was in my body, washed my soiled
      clothes!
My plaint is done, my wretchedness ended before you—
what more do you want?

Your neglect will mislead you,[87]
your selfishness befool you,
your greed create you foes,
but will you find another peasant like me?
Or will the negligent man, now a pleader, stand   BI 315
waiting at the door of his house?

There is none quiet whom you made speak,[88]
none sleeping whom you roused,
none obtuse whom you enlightened,
none with shut mouth whom you opened,
none ignorant whom you made wise,
none foolish whom you educated.
Officials are men who beat back evil, they are lords of
      goodness,[89]

Bı 320 they are craftsmen of creating what is, joiners of the
              severed head!'

                                    *

              And this peasant came to appeal to him an eighth time,[90]
              and said, 'High Steward, my lord!
              One falls far for greed.[91]
              The selfish man is free from success;
              his success belongs to failure.
              You are selfish—it is not for you;
              you steal—it is not good for you,
              you who should make a man attend his good true right!
Bı 325 In fact, your portion is in your house, and your belly
              full,[92]
              while the grain measure brims over and overflows
              so that its excess perishes on the ground.

              Seizer of the robbed, taker![93]
              The officials who were appointed
              to outlaw evil
              are a shelter against the predator—
              those officials who were appointed
              to outlaw Falsehood!
              Yet your fearsomeness does not make me appeal to you; you
                  do not perceive my heart.[94]
Bı 330 The quiet man who turns to complain to you—
              he does not fear the man he supplicates,
              though no brother of his can be summoned against you out
                  of the street.
              Your plots of land are in the country,[95]
              your wealth in the estate,
              your provisions in the storehouse!
              Officials are giving to you,
              and you are still taking. So are you a thief?
              —when people are ushered in before you,
              and troops are with you, for the division of land plots!

Bı 335 Do Truth for the Lord of Truth,[96]
              whose truth has Truth!
              Pen, roll, palette of Thoth,

may you avoid doing evil! Only the goodness of the good
   man is good beyond him.
But Truth itself is for eternity.[97]
To the necropolis in its doer's hand it descends;
he is entombed, earth joins with him;   B1 340
but his name is not effaced on earth.
He is remembered for his goodness.
It is the standard of God's word.
If it is scales, it tilts not;[98]
if a balance, it is not partial.
Look, I will come, or look, another will come,[99]   B1 345
so that you will make accusation; but do not respond
by accusing a quiet man, nor attack one who cannot!
You do not pity, nor suffer, nor yet destroy!
You do not repay me for this perfect speech,   B1 350
which comes forth from the mouth of the Sungod himself!
So speak Truth! Do Truth![100]
For it is mighty, great, enduring.
Its revelation will be found good, it will conduct to
   blessedness!

Can the scales tilt, when theirs are the pans which weigh
   things?[101]   B1 355
There cannot be excess for the standard.
A vile deed cannot reach harbour,
nor the cargo-bearer landfall.'

*

And this peasant came to appeal to him a ninth time,[102]   B2 91
and said, 'High Steward, my lord!
The tongue of men is their balance;[103]
and scales are what detect deficiency,
dealing punishment to the punishable: let the standard be
   like you!

Even when its portion exists, Falsehood [sallies forth],[104]   B2 95
but Truth turns back to confront it;
Truth is the property of Falsehood,
which lets it flourish, but Falsehood has never been
   gathered in.

If Falsehood sets out, it strays;[105]
it cannot cross in a ferry, and has not altered its course.

B2 100 He who is rich with it has no children,[106]
and no heirs on earth.
And he who sails with it cannot touch land,
his boat cannot moor in its harbour.

Be heavy no more, you have not yet been light![107]
Delay no more, you have not yet been swift!

B2 105 Be not partial! Do not listen to the heart!
Do not disregard one you know!
Do not blind yourself against one who looks to you! Do not
fend off a supplicator!

You should abandon this negligence, so that your sentence
will be renowned![108]
Act for him who acts for you
and listen to none against him,
so that a man will be summoned according to his true right!
There is no yesterday for the negligent,[109]

B2 110 no friend for him who is deaf to Truth,
no holiday for the selfish.
The accuser becomes wretched,[110]
more wretched than when a pleader,
and the opponent becomes a murderer.
Look, I am pleading to you, and you do not hear—

B2 115 I will go and plead about you to Anubis.'

*

And the High Steward Meru's son Rensi[111]
sent two attendants to turn him back.
And this peasant was afraid, thinking this was done
to punish him for the speech he had made.
And this peasant said, 'The thirsty man
approaching water,

B2 120 the nurseling reaching his mouth
for milk—they die,
while for him who longs to see it come,
death comes slowly.'

And the High Steward Meru's son Rensi said,[112]
'Don't be afraid peasant!
Look, you will be dealing with me.'
And this peasant swore an oath,
'So, shall I live on your bread,   B2 125
and drink your beer for ever?'
And the High Steward Meru's son Rensi said,
'Now wait here and hear your petitions!'[113]
And he caused every petition to be read out
from a fresh roll according to [its] content.
And the High Steward Meru's son Rensi had them
        presented[114]   B2 130
before the Majesty of the Dual King Nebkaure, the justified.
And they seemed more perfect to his heart
than anything in this entire land.
And his Majesty said, 'Judge yourself, Meru's son!'

And the High Steward Meru's son Rensi[115]
sent two attendants to [bring this Nemtinakht].
Then he was brought, and an inventory made [of his
        household].   B2 135
Then he found six persons, as well as [his . . .],
his barley, his emmer,
his donkeys, his swine, and his flocks.
And this Nemtinakht [was given] to this peasant,
[with all his property, all his] ser[vants],   B2 140
[and all the belongings] of this Nemtinakht.

So it ends, [from start to finish,
as found in writing].

Notes

1. The Tale begins as a simple narrative. The *Wadi Natrun* is an oasis *c.*100 km
   north-west of modern Cairo: the *peasant* is a rustic, on the edge of society. (For
   his name, see B2 115 and n. 110). He tells his wife to fetch all the food that they
   have left, and he then assigns rather low rations for himself and his family.
2. The list of goods shows that he is a trader, not a farmer. *Natron* and *salt* are the
   characteristic products of the Wadi Natrun; many of the other goods are slightly
   exotic imports from the various oases. *Farafra* is an oasis, *c.*300 km west of the
   Nile Valley. *Inbi* is a garden fruit or hedge plant. *Tebu* and *uben* are unidentified
   plants.

3. *Heracleopolis* was the capital of Egypt in the Ninth and Tenth Dynasties; this location implies the setting which is given in full in B1 102–4. *Mednit* is the 22nd Upper Egyptian nome, *c.* 50 km north of Heracleopolis. *Per-Fefi* ('the Estate of Fefi') is an otherwise unknown place, perhaps near Dahshur, *c.* 80 km north of the capital (see Map, p. xxxiii).

4. *Nemtinakht's* name means 'Nemti is mighty', alluding to a minor god who was possibly a patron of travellers—an ironic touch, as this man is about to harass a traveller. The *High Steward* was one of the highest officials under the king in the Twelfth Dynasty (the title is an anachronism in the Heracleopolitan setting). His name suggests his virtue: his patronym, *Meru's son*, is homophonous with the epithet 'Beloved Son'—a type of virtuous man, and *Rensi* word-plays with 'renown'. The villain of the Tale is thus introduced as a servant of a benevolent figure of authority, suggesting that good and evil are inextricably linked.

5. Nemtinakht's speech immediately reveals his conscious villainy. The following scenic description is important for the plot, as Nemtinakht is blocking, and thus laying claim to, a public right of way (a *kilt* is *c.* 50 cm wide). His order to his retainer is very autocratic in tone. His actions against the public in general prepare for the wider implications of the whole affair.

6. When challenged, the peasant replies with the standard answer of obedient servants. As the dialogue becomes more heated the peasant's responses become more pointed and highly wrought. The dialogue ends with an unanswered question, prefiguring the peasant's fate—to petition without any response.

7. The new development which precipitates the crisis is not chance but an inevitable consequence of Nemtinakht's plot.

8. The peasant protests at the inequality of the exchange, and appeals to a higher authority (cf. n. 4), moving to wider issues.

9. Nemtinakht cites a proverbial utterance, but only to dismiss the wider issues raised by the peasant: a *poor man* exists only in so far as he has a lord, and he is now the peasant's lord, not the distant protector invoked by the peasant.

10. The wood's *freshness* makes it more stinging. *Tamarisk* is homophonous with Nemtinakht's patronym (Isry's son); wordplay makes an aggressive act his defining characteristic.

11. *The Lord of Silence* is the god of the dead, Osiris; this speech is a threat to *silence* the peasant by death. The peasant's reply reverses Nemtinakht's image, appeals to a higher *lord*, and invokes *silence* as a sign of contentment; he sees the world of the gods as his last refuge.

12. This length of time (Egypt had a ten-day 'week') shows that the peasant behaves decorously, and that it is only Nemtinakht's lack of *attention* (often a metaphor for ethical evil and deafness to wisdom) that makes him petition a higher authority in a series of petitions that occupy another week.

13. Rensi's location in the capital, and the presence of an intermediary, are indications of his high rank. His judgement is immediate, and just. This breaks the pattern of the unproductive dialogue between Nemtinakht and the peasant.

14. The *officials*, however, respond cynically and materialistically, ignoring (like Nemtinakht) the wider issues, and assuming that the peasant is simply fleeing his rightful master, Nemtinakht. Their defence of the villain prevents the case being settled immediately by Rensi. *Repayment* is an ironic allusion to the

principle of reciprocity, which is parodied here. Rensi's *quietness* associates him with the divine Lord of Silence (see n. 11); quietness is a sign of virtue in wisdom literature, but here his silence is also the problematic motor of the plot.

15. The peasant starts to *petition* Rensi in person to hear his case. His first speech is an introduction to the whole sequence, and is the most simply argued petition. After addressing Rensi by his usual title, the peasant coins epithets evoking his power in universal terms. Despite the eulogistic tone, the negative (*all that is not*) is given precedence over the positive (*all that is*).

16. Enacting *Truth* (*Maat*) is imagined as a hunting voyage (the metaphor adds a touch of local colour, as there was a sacred lake called Maaty at Heracleopolis). This image has great resonance, as the hunt is a symbol of overcoming chaos on tomb and temple walls. The metaphor is formulated in negative terms: the water is an image of Truth, yet full of dangers; the *face* belongs to a crocodile. The last couplet presents a (contrasting) positive climax to the voyage, as the hunted animals come to Rensi voluntarily.

17. A formal eulogy follows, with four standard epithets describing selfless social virtue, which are known from funeral Autobiographies (an allusion to justice *sub specie aeternitatis*). The peasant then proclaims a set of epithets forming a quasi-royal titulary, as a regal acclamation of Rensi. *Selfishness* alludes to Nemtinakht's crime, and the second pair of epithets puts the issue in absolute terms of *Falsehood* and *Truth*.

18. A coda develops the last verse of the eulogy, and urges Rensi to act in the peasant's specific case.

19. The Tale's setting is now given in more detail: *Nebkaure* was a king of the Heracleopolitan Dynasty (*c.*2080–1987 BC). He is presented in general terms here. He implicitly accepts the peasant's innocence. *Perfect speech* is a standard description of literature's aesthetic and ethical qualities.

20. The king's oath presents the central paradox behind the plot: the state's apparent neglect of the peasant's case is in fact an act in support of just speech and justice. (For the metaphorical significance of putting literature into writing, see B1 336, and nn. 96, 113). The king's terse command of silence towards the peasant associates him with the gods (cf. B1 58–60 and n. 11); he, unlike the officials and Nemtinakht, has a caring attitude towards the peasantry.

21. This is a basic wage, such as is appropriate for a lowly peasant (whose suspicions must not be aroused by overgenerous treatment). Distributing grain is later a metaphor for true conduct; here, the High Steward's action is both literal and a metaphor for the state's (covert) support of justice.

22. The second petition is by far the longest, and marks a shift in the poem from narrative to discourse. Its length allows complex presentation of arguments that cautiously approach the central issue of Rensi's responsibility. The petition avoids any initial direct denunciation of him as a thief—the implied accusation is made gradually and with inescapable conviction. Patterns of allusive repetition and parody (especially in the increasingly ambivalent eulogies) articulate this indirect denunciation, which is supported by the explicit affirmation of responsibility: the only resolution of the dilemmas and paradoxes presented is for Rensi to intervene and help the peasant. The modes of address are more varied and tightly interwoven than in the first petition, presenting a complex pattern of invocation, injunction, description, imagery, and argument,

developed in later petitions. The petition is dramatically effective, as the peasant's vehemence rises from specific to universal concerns.

23. The petition opens with an hyperbolistic invocation acclaiming Rensi as above all compromise and qualifications. The juxtaposition of *greatness* and *richness* implies his privilege and its attendant responsibility. Wide issues are involved in the peasant's plight.

24. Rensi is acclaimed with metaphors expressing his authority as absolute and universal. The first evokes the orderly sailing of the heavenly bodies; the *beam* is an architectural support, but also one for scales and *plumbline* (an image of justice). Rensi's authority upholds both *heaven* and *earth*. The imagery of sailing (echoing the first petition B1 85–93) and weighing is returned to again and again. The injunctions to shun evil set the tone of the petition; for the first time the peasant raises the possibility of Rensi's doing wrong.

25. This description of the peasant's (*someone's*) state implies that Rensi's prosperity should make him sympathetic; the allusion to Nemtinakht as a great *lord* echoes the eulogy of Rensi, and associates the two. The peasant then moves to more specific matters: a little recompense, equivalent to a helping of *beer* and *bread*, will satisfy the peasant, and justice will cost Rensi nothing. In the dramatic context, this is ironic, as the peasant remains unaware that Rensi is actually provisioning him. A concluding verse states that the fate of a man and his *underlings* are bound together, implying that Rensi must help his inferior.

26. The question contrasts Rensi's desire for *eternity* with the mortality of the preceding stanza. A further contrast is developed between Rensi's aspirations and the actual state of affairs which threatens to undermine him. The peasant turns to consider the imperfection with which Rensi is surrounded.

27. This verse introduces a long descriptive lament about how good is perverted to evil, with antitheses between the world as it is now and as it should be.

28. The peasant argues that a single crime can undermine the whole *standard* of justice. A couplet (*this means* . . .) gives a gloss on these verses: a judge's prevarication in speech affects justice and is thus as bad as the robber's crime.

29. The petition continues with antithetical descriptions of reversal, and concludes by describing wrong as cataclysmic (*flood*), and with a phrase that is directed against Rensi (the *punisher of wrong*).

30. Rensi intervenes to maintain the credibility of his position and to provoke further speech. He accuses the peasant of the materialism and selfishness that he has detected in others. The peasant simply continues his descriptive denunciations of *theft*, alluding more strongly to Rensi's involvement. *Measurer* introduces the metaphor of grain, in which the distribution of food represents that of justice, to imply that Truth is the stuff of life.

31. Evil and hypocrisy in society are such that men's apparent correct behaviour is for the sake of wrong and they give praise accordingly. In the final question of this stanza the peasant answers Rensi's challenge by accusing him of self-interest and complicity in the theft.

32. The peasant turns his attention to retribution, and the second half of the petition begins by asserting the cogency of good action, described in a more abstract and figurative fashion than hitherto. The opening line associates the lack of *redress* with the dominance of *evil* (described earlier), but asserts that the principle of reciprocity remains valid in spite of this, for *good character* is ultimately

immutable. This infallibility is expressed as a god-given *ordinance* concerning reciprocity and retribution, a central aspect of Truth. The principle of reciprocity is then exemplified in three metaphors, which present it as ensuring continuity by rewarding (*thanking*) a man's deeds, as a way of thus avoiding evil (*parrying*), and of gaining good (*commissioning* a work of art).

33. The negative side of the principle of reciprocity is now applied to Rensi with an extended violent exclamation. A short *moment* of retribution is invoked to destroy his ill-gotten wealth; the imagery ironically recalls the hunt of B1 85–93, where *fowl* were the reward of the just (see n. 16). Antithetical denunciations then justify this savage wish.

34. Rensi is now addressed as a *depositary* (literally 'basket'), being a source of wealth. This stanza develops the association of wealth with responsibility. Questions allude to his actions as self-destructive, as well as criminal.

35. The peasant affirms Rensi's power with eulogistic but increasingly ambivalent declarations, in which his power is also a source of his abuse of privilege and aggression; the verses suggestively echo the earlier descriptions of retribution. The *poor man* alludes to the peasant. Rensi is now likened to a demon of *Khenty*, a crocodile-god of death, and the following verses develop this more extravagantly—he has *surpassed* the baleful *plague* goddess *Sekhmet*. His injustice evokes savage gods as if calling the benevolence of the divine into question.

36. The problem of culpability is now argued more specifically and socially, in less passionate terms: the *deprived* can justifiably take, but the rich man *without want* (i.e. Rensi) is at fault to behave likewise, and should be *merciful*: the concluding verse justifies the peasant's denunciations.

37. This stanza opens by describing Rensi's great wealth in order to drive home the extent of his fault. The peasant then continues with calmer antithetical descriptions of the lack of order surrounding Rensi. The *boat* represents the state (echoing the cosmic 'helm' of B1 121, see also n. 24). The central problem is that, although power that should not be abused has been entrusted to Rensi by the aloof *king*, he is apparently surrounded by *evil*.

38. The peasant's (the *appealer's*) petition is presented as a force against this wrong, which will endure as *long* as the evil (the *divide*) that it confronts. Through attracting attention the plaint threatens to be a public rebuke for Rensi. As the petition nears its end, Rensi is enjoined to return to justice. The imagery of *shore* and *harbour* develops the nautical themes of the previous stanza.

39. The peasant warns that retribution is the inherent consequence of evil action: a man's own *tongue* can bring about his downfall.

40. A final stanza develops the social aspects of the preceding one and its concern with speech; the opening injunction warns against the *officials'* neglect of true speech. The image presents *officials* who *hear* cases as *winnowing* baskets, yet, because they deal with and live off falsehood, injustice is of little concern to them. The peasant denounces their neglect of evil, and again correlates sustenance with justice.

41. The peasant enjoins Rensi to distinguish himself as a just judge. The previous descriptions and denunciations are subsumed in a return to eulogy. The imagery of shipwreck was earlier applied to Rensi, but here the peasant uses it of his own suffering (emphasizing the close ties between the protagonists). The concluding

impassioned cries forcefully present the shock of Rensi's apparent indifference to the peasant's plaint.

42. The third petition presents a less complex interweaving of types of discourse, and the imagery is grouped into more unified patterns of gods, balance, navigation, professions, and animals. It is less argumentative and descriptive, but more animated; it concentrates on Rensi's person more exclusively to present in extreme terms the paradox of his responsibility; metaphoric exaltation and debasement are violently juxtaposed. As a member of the hierarchy, Rensi acts as a representative of the king and can take it upon himself to represent the creator without losing his human individuality; by the same principle he is responsible for the crime of his subordinate, and thus can be addressed as the robber.

43. The opening eulogy is on a grand, cosmic, scale; it assimilates Rensi with the greatest god, the creator *Sungod*. His universal bounty, providing people with their daily rations (*portion*), is likened to a *flood*, which moves to the next assimilation—the god of the annual *Nileflood*; the two gods are the sources of two necessities of life. The imagery also gives a sense of Rensi's ambivalent position: he is both an inundation of benefit, and a flood that destroyed the *mounds* on which settlements were built, before restoring them. The ambivalence of the image comes to the fore in a concluding injunction.

44. The peasant now warns of *eternity's approach*, by proclaiming a generally held proposition that only virtue can create enduring life and elevate Rensi to the level of the eternal.

45. Three rhetorical questions imply that eternal justice is unswerving, and that Rensi must be so too. *Thoth* is the god of wisdom, writing, and judgement, and is an agent of the Sungod. The eulogistic assimilation with the divine is reformulated as an ironic injunction to behave like the gods. These sarcastic questions suggest that the divine has a potentially ambivalent role too: if Rensi can be unjust, perhaps the gods can too.

46. The third stanza directly enjoins Rensi to behave like Thoth, the scales, and the balances, with significant play on the number *three* (appropriate in this third petition).

47. If Rensi ignores the peasant, he will find a response more prolific than *weeds*, which grow even as they are smelled. This image of growth associates speech with the regenerating power of the Nileflood, but in the next verses it also represents Rensi's designs, which cultivate *deception*. This double use of imagery presents the interrelationship of unjust provocation and justified complaint. The final verse juxtaposes the peasant's just intentions with Rensi's apparently ignoble inaction; the repetition of *three* associates the 'occasions' of petitioning with the three representatives of true judgement mentioned in B1 181-2 (see n. 46).

48. The peasant now expresses his injunction still more forcefully, resuming the navigational imagery of the first petition (where it concerned justice), and the water imagery (*torrent*) of the opening invocation (B1 173 and n. 43).

49. A sequence of negative commands intensifies the sense of urgency. The balancing eulogistic clauses provide the rationales; Rensi is urged to behave as the absolute ideal (*standard*) of justice.

50. Rensi is identified with the *scales*, rearticulating and condensing the extended and more indirect identification of previous verses. Two strands of imagery— nautical and scales—are then interwoven in commands forbidding divergence.

Through the idea of *seizing*, which recalls a rapacious flood, the petition returns from imperatives to a more descriptive treatment of robbery and the selfless nature of true *greatness*.

51. This is the most daringly expressed identification of Rensi with the scales (comprising *plummet* and *weight*, suspended from the scales' *arms*)—an image of the ideal greatness. Ideal and actual are contrasted in an expansively phrased and climactic question about Rensi's failure to act according to the ideal.

52. The mood now changes to direct denunciations, with a bitingly sarcastic parody of the opening eulogy (the repetition of *wretched* from B1 199 establishes continuity). The laments of the previous petition (B1 128-39 and nn. 27-31) are reformulated as direct accusations which evoke the corruption of the world. The images refer back to previous motifs: e.g. the *washerman* is concerned with the river of B1 172-4 (n. 43), with the mock heroic diction of *faithful companion* adding to the scorn; the *ferryman* echoes the nautical imagery (B1 85-93) and parodies Autobiographies in which a virtuous man claims to have ferried over people without fares; the *storehouse keeper* recalls the imagery of Truth as grain (see n. 30). All these menial workers are, like Rensi, reprehensible, despite apparent professional propriety.

53. The imagery includes animals as well as human society. In official iconography the *hawk* is a royal bird, but here it preys on humanity. The stanza culminates in a despairing and sarcastic question with the metaphor of a *shepherd*, who cannot *reckon* (i.e. count his flock, or, metaphorically, judge); the shepherd should represent caring authority. The image of a *crocodile* (echoing B1 149-50 and n. 35) presents Rensi as a predator instead of a protector. The final address states that Rensi's betrayal of responsibility affects the *whole land*, as seen in the previous verses' evocation of general woe.

54. Rensi is now accused with greater assurance, and his motives, more than just his behaviour, are questioned. The only justification for his inaction would be if all aggression (the *crocodile*, i.e. Rensi himself) against the peasant had already ceased (which it has not). In the final verses, which are formal in tone, the peasant returns to the theme of nemesis: Rensi's behaviour cannot benefit him, for the *Falsehood* on which he relies will be overthrown, and earthly life is uncertain (*comes* and *evil* are homonyms).

55. After this direct abuse, Rensi intervenes again; see n. 30. The beating recalls Nemtinakht's actions (B1 53-4) and it effectively provokes the peasant further. This narrative interlude is the last significant portion of narrative in the Tale before the resolution.

56. After the hope with which the preceding petition ended (B1 213-15), the peasant again despairs, and describes Rensi's indifference as a complete lack of perception.

57. The peasant continues the denunciations of the third petition, but now they are shorter, swifter, and more direct, articulating social chaos and corruption. The first sequence likens Rensi to ineffective groups of men in order to suggest the self-destructive nature of his negligence; the increasingly demeaning comparisons move from a *town* to a *gang*. In the second half the antitheses refer more directly to his abuse of authority.

58. The fourth petition begins the second group of petitions. It returns to a more complex interweaving of stylistic modes and forms of address, to lament-motifs

and to direct denunciations. The images are varied and complex, drawing on previous formulations, but they share a common theme of movement, through which Rensi's aggression is described in psychological terms. The petition reaffirms the concerns of the preceding ones and relates these more personally to the question of Rensi's motivation, culminating in impassioned and despairing pleas.

59. The *temple gate* was a place of judgement and legal appeal. Local references remind the audience of the dramatic setting: *Herishef* is the god of Heracleopolis, and is—appropriately for the peasant—associated with the vindication of the suffering god Osiris. The peasant returns to unqualified eulogy in a fresh start after the third petition; the greeting is a return to a more formal, decorous style. These verses associate Rensi's ideal moral purity with that of a vindicator god, enjoining him to act like god. Rensi comes purified from the temple; he is the link between the peasant and the gods.

60. In contrast to the harmony implicit in the temple, this stanza is a despairing lament about the disintegration of right in society. Nautical imagery, which is intensified by repetition, rhetorical questions, and exclamatory answers, implicitly continues the previous denunciation of Rensi as a ferryman and the helm of the state (B1 121, 157–9, 202–3). The motif of *crossing the river on foot* articulates the impossibility of achieving success in such circumstances, and ironically recalls the image of life as a voyage. The situation has been caused by the sunken *ferry*, i.e. Rensi.

61. *Sleeping till dawn* is a proverbial sign of well-being and security. The description of the land in chaos continues with the impossibility of travel by land (note the repetition of *destroyed*); the land is smitten with moral paralysis. A third verse returns to legal concerns. The repetition in the final despairing couplet of phrases from the second petition (B1 148–9) emphasizes the lack of progress or movement.

62. The second half of the petition opens with a bitter address to Rensi. After the immobility of the first half, Rensi is presented in a swift burst of action, and is addressed forcefully as a *hunter*. His actions are usually prestigious activities, but have aggressive overtones here: the godlike sportsman of B1 85–93 is now a predator; implicitly the peasant is the prey. Although the hunt is potentially symbolic of the triumph of Right (see n. 16), it is here motivated by selfish aims.

63. Swiftness is now an ethical issue, and a danger; the rapid hunt becomes *recklessness*, which is contrasted with what is *cautious* and *patient*, as the peasant concentrates on Rensi's psychological motivation.

64. Only selfless action is urged, and for the benefit of someone (the peasant) whose *quietness* (cf. n. 14) makes him an antithesis of the 'hasty-mouthed' (B1 239) and the *hasty-hearted*. The peasant alludes to retribution: unvirtuous recklessness is impermanent, unlike Truth.

65. Positive action, including perception, is now urged, as is its correlate, the avoidance of abusive action. The peasant now presents retribution less as divine intervention, more as an inevitable and inherent consequence of bad action.

66. Five verses articulate the underlying subject of the cogency of action, actor, and consequence in terms of basic life situations. The image of Rensi as an *eater* alludes to the image of Truth as sustenance (cf. n. 30); that of Rensi as a *sleeper* suffering bad dreams recalls the lack of calm sleep in the land (B1 232 and

n. 61); his nightmare is an image of the way in which proliferating evil, caused by Rensi's moral sleep (i.e. negligence), will disturb him.

67. The full force of invective is suddenly and personally turned against Rensi: the judge is now judged. *Bilge-baler* echoes the preceding nautical imagery in a demeaning manner. These verses gain resonance from their double meaning and interwoven imagery: *bilge-baler* can also mean 'one who can only dish out water (instead of words or provisions)' or 'one who bails out his own urine'; to *be noticed* is homonymous with 'to be sunk'.

68. Epithets with images of protection and sustenance form a violent parody of the eulogistic titulary of the first petition (B1 95–9); the number of five alludes to the fivefold form of king's titulary. The strong antitheses articulate the contradiction of Rensi's position. The petition ends with a cry of despair and exasperation, a realization by the peasant that his perception of Rensi's character is not enough to end his suffering.

69. The fifth petition moves from description, through argumentative presentation, to denunciation. The imagery is unified, simple, and intense, presenting Rensi's wrong in both social and figurative terms. His social wrong is defined plainly, tersely, and explicitly, with renewed emphasis on his deputized responsibility. The brevity and simplicity of this petition reflect its structural role as the central petition, with a largely descriptive summary of the underlying problem.

70. The petition opens with a description of lowly and savage riverine activity (far from the earlier aristocratic hunts of B1 85–93, 236–9; see also nn. 16, 62), which continues the derogatory images of lowly professions. Aggression now engulfs the whole *river*. The five statements about catching various (unidentified) fishes ironically echo the earlier fivefold titulary (B1 252–5 and n. 68); this is also the fifth petition.

71. This stanza makes clear the relevance of the preceding one: it defines the nature of the peasant's wretchedness, and confronts Rensi with the seriousness of his plight. *Breath* is elsewhere a metaphor for justice (B1 177) as well as life.

72. A stanza on Rensi's legal responsibilities develops the preceding allusion to justice, symmetrically arranged around the rebuke of *You are trusted*. *Dykes* were vital protection against the flooding Nile, and this image climaxes in the final line, which reverses the images of earth and water; the metaphor of the *lake* returns to the imagery of the opening verses of the petition (B1 257–62).

73. The sixth petition is structured by progression from the ideal to its contrary within each section. It moves from description, through highly allusive argument, to more direct address of Rensi. Thematically, it rearticulates motifs already presented, but with greater emphasis on their ramifications. This happens on both an abstract generalizing level, and with more specific reference to the peasant himself. This shift marks a growing emphasis on the interrelationship of the two protagonists as well as on Truth and its contraries.

74. The petition opens with a nine-line, rhetorical quasi-invocation which juxtaposes (but does not assimilate) Rensi and an ideal *lord*. These verses identify the (re)creation of virtue with the ending of evil, and are followed by four similes from basic life situations. The images include phrases reminiscent of the ethical ideals of Autobiographies, and metaphors of sustenance. The broad images of resolution give a sense of relief after the preceding descriptions of social wrong.

75. The peasant now commands Rensi to perceive the evils which remain undispelled: the brief descriptions recall the earlier laments.

76. The petition continues with broad statements; *measuring* evokes the imagery of *Truth* as grain. Wrong's attack on Truth is described in a paradox: although Truth is lessened in the world, it is itself never *damaged*: it is an ideal despite its flawed embodiments, and the ideal remains an exact and enduring equilibrium. *Overflow* is a term used of grain; the next verses continue this imagery more specifically, and urge the just distribution of food rather than selfish *jawing* (which includes eating and talking). These verses enjoin Rensi to refrain from greed, implying both the brotherhood of man and the ideal that Truth is common property.

77. The peasant laments how his just actions bring only unjustified suffering, and further alienation from the principle of reciprocity, in contrast to Rensi's *acquiring* two verses earlier. The *unknowableness* of the heart relates to the contrast between the ideal situation and the actual: wrong springs from the human heart, but one cannot know why a man (Rensi) chooses it.

78. Five verses employ images of navigation to articulate Rensi's unique responsibility to fight evil (and thus echo earlier imagery). Rensi's *helmstaff* is a force to redress disaster. The image of *robbing* a wreck implies that, if the case under Rensi's charge is wrecked, he too will suffer because of the loss.

79. Rensi's ability is now acclaimed in terms of personal capacities. His distinction is incompatible with theft, and is contrasted with his culpably undistinguished behaviour. This stanza summarizes the paradox of Rensi, which involves his individual qualities and his surroundings: his wrong act makes him an evil influence on *the whole land*.

80. An elaborate concluding image justifies the expansiveness of the preceding verse, showing how one deed cultivates universal evil. The imagery of growth increases from a single *gardener* and his small *plot*, to his affect on the whole *estate* (*estate* has funerary associations, evoking eternal concerns). The *gardener* is implicitly Rensi, but the image of a corrupt and *wretched* profession also evokes a corrupt society. It is a parody of the petition's opening description of the 'lord' and his creative potential (B1 272–3).

81. The seventh petition begins a third group of petitions. It is a return to a more decorous address, and it moves from eulogy through argumentative statements to an oblique denunciation which reformulates the opening eulogy in an ironic manner. The personal interaction of the protagonists is now more extensively related to Truth on a cosmic and a social level: the peasant increasingly emphasizes how abstract principles of right and wrong are embodied in himself and in Rensi. He justifies his complaint more explicitly, and he predicts with greater certainty that retribution is an inherent consequence of wrong. The images, the ambivalence of the final eulogy, and the allusively significant descriptions present the contrast between right and wrong, together with their ramifications.

82. As in the third petition, the opening is an unqualified eulogy, but this one is significantly less elevated (now Rensi is a god's *twin*, not a god himself). It returns to the imagery of the navigation of the *land* (from B1 289–91), weighing, and *Thoth* (see n. 45).

83. The second stanza is a fresh address to the peasant's *lord*. He urges him to be patient, and two triplets on this virtue flank a central triplet on the consequence

of its contrary, impatient confidence. Implicit in this warning against unforeseen nemesis is the choice Rensi must make between these alternatives. The third triplet on patience concludes with a reflection on the *unknowable* nature of the *heart* that determines the choice (cf. B1 287).

84. The peasant now denounces the man (Rensi) who, regardless of the preceding warnings, destroys the *wretched* man (the peasant) whose protection and well-being are integral to Truth. *Truth* is now an active accusing force, and is associated with the peasant, not Rensi.

85. The peasant justifies his accusation and shows that, as it is enforced by suffering, it is compatible with the patience he enjoins. The imagery is ironic—his belly is *full* but with suffering, not sustenance. Images of satiety and oppression culminate in that of a breached *dyke* (ironically alluding to that of Rensi as a protective dyke at the end of the fifth petition (B1 268-9)).

86. The peasant's attempts to repel his wretchedness are expressed as resistance to shipwreck and as physical hardship. These verses are layered and complex, a rapid fusion of images of a sinking ship and the excretion of woe (incontinence and *soiled clothes*). He then states that the articulation of his agony is complete. His question, which stresses that Rensi is forcing him to continue, is ironic beyond his knowledge.

87. The second half of the petition considers Rensi's future, forcefully affirming that his *neglect* of Truth will be his nemesis. A triplet predicts his fall, and then another predicts his regret as he realizes what he has lost in the *peasant*: the *negligent* Rensi will then stand begging to meet *another* such petitioner.

88. This stanza continues the forceful symmetry of the preceding one with a eulogy that is ambivalent and bitter: there is *none* that he has aided who is still helpless, but there is no helpless person whom he has aided. There are other layers of irony in the opening line: *quietness* is desirable (see n. 14), but Rensi is forcing the peasant to speak; the faults Rensi can dispel are those that he embodies himself.

89. In contrast with the preceding six verses, the petition ends with an unqualified eulogy of ideal *officials*, who—unlike Rensi—act as *creators*. The final phrase has darker implications: it links the ideal official with a miraculous—that is, impossible—event, highlighting the dichotomy between the ideal and the actual.

90. The eighth petition continues to develop the interrelationship of the protagonists in abstract terms. The first major section has a predominantly social aspect, which contrasts with the otherworldly nature of the next part. The inevitable downfall of evil is reaffirmed, but much of the central portion presents Truth as a positive force, now associated with the peasant, and not Rensi (this change builds upon previous tension). This is the longest explicit discussion of Truth: appropriately, the petition is long, comparatively restrained in imagery, and it describes the protagonists' behaviour in relation to general principles. The series of descriptive statements juxtaposes and interweaves the specific situation with the universal aspect of Truth, throwing this latter into relief.

91. The petition opens with a statement about the downfall of greed, which is developed in the following verses. These describe the failure of vice, and then relate this directly to Rensi, climaxing in a vocative, which implicitly denounces vice as incompatible with his duty.

92. Rensi's wealth is now described as culpably excessive and misused, highlighting the wrongness of his greed.

93. A second stanza opens with a passionate address repeating the accusations of greed, and alluding to Rensi's abuse of his position in relation to the *robbed*. Contrasted with this is a description of *officials'* ideal duty in terms of social redress.

94. The peasant describes the interaction of the two protagonists and his own motivation more explicitly. His (the *quiet man's*) virtue in opposing Rensi is independent of concern and respect for social status, and is maintained despite his lack of any help (*brother*).

95. A forceful series of verses describes Rensi's social status and wealth. The series reaches a climax as the peasant turns on Rensi with an ironic question, justifying his lack of respect. Rensi has no excuse to act as a thief, when he has such authority: he is attended by *troops* as he administers the *division* of landed property despite his corruption.

96. The second half of the petition turns to abstract injunctions to *do Truth* in terms implying a complex scale of virtue from the absolute ideal to actual embodiments of relative virtue: there is true justice and greatness which belong to the creator-god (the *Lord of Truth*), but there are also imperfect embodiments of these ideals—apparent justice. Rensi is acclaimed as the writing equipment of *Thoth* (see n. 45): writing is a way of embodying an ideal. This image implies that Rensi is the agent of a higher, and absolute, authority—a hierarchy from *the Lord of Truth*, through his scribe *Thoth*, to Rensi. The allusive quatrain concludes with an injunction to *avoid doing evil*, which is juxtaposed with a definition of *goodness* (which is associated with Truth). This definition uses dense wordplay to express how the absolute ideal of goodness surpasses the limited actual capacities of a *good man*, and is what ensures his virtue.

97. *Truth* itself contrasts with the limited value of relative good, and the stanza continues by describing the power of absolute Truth to help its doer, transcending this world and its social order. The result of justice is now presented in otherworldly terms.

98. A central couplet relates the *scales* of justice to the ideal of Truth, whose immutability they reflect. The scales allude to Rensi as judge (cf. B1 196–8 and n. 51), to the judgement of the peasant's case, and also to the weighing of all men after death in the scales of god.

99. The relationship of the protagonists is rephrased, as the peasant urges that Rensi must eventually respond to him, and *accuse* the villain, not the *quiet* peasant. Rensi is not immutable like Truth, nor fearless like the peasant, but merely unresponsive in any way: he is self-alienated from Truth. The peasant here adopts a prophetic role: his *perfect speech* (cf. B1 105–7 and n. 19) is an embodiment of the Truth spoken by the creator *Sungod*, and peasant and god are aligned against the impious Rensi, who is no longer a representative of the divine. To *repay* is fundamental to the principle of Truth, involving the doctrines of reciprocity and retribution.

100. A complementary injunction to *speak Truth* now follows. Truth's true greatness and endurance contrast with Rensi's transitory wealth, and the ultimate predominance of Truth is asserted as absolute, otherworldly *blessedness*.

101. A coda summarizes the immutability of the ideal (the *standard*) in generalized imagery of the *scales* and of voyaging. If Rensi fails to match the ideal, he will perish: the final image of *landfall*, which defines success as journey's end and

simultaneously as death, concludes the petition on an otherworldly, ideal level.

102. Nine is a number symbolic of multiplicity and of totality, and the ninth petition concludes and summarizes the peasant's case in the most abstract formulation of his appeal. In the first half he proclaims the supremacy of Truth, and Falsehood's downfall, and then commands Rensi to renounce evil. The relationship of Truth and Falsehood dominates the second half and is reflected in the stylistic structure, which juxtaposes generalizing verses and ones with personal references to the protagonists. The culmination is a grim triumph: while the ideal of justice ultimately holds sway, in this imperfect world Rensi is unjust, and the peasant turns to the beyond, the home of the perfect, the ideal, and the divine.

103. The opening reaffirms the inherency of judgement (continuing the preceding petition's imagery): men are judged by their own *tongues* (cf. B1 162–3), and this judgement is manifested in their downfall. The peasant wishes once more that Rensi would be just.

104. Personifications of *Truth* and *Falsehood* are contrasted in an image of Falsehood making an avaricious expedition. The next couplet elaborates their relationship: Falsehood cannot exist without Truth, and, while it may own and prey on Truth, it cannot ultimately prevail. Although the vocabulary recalls the specific context (*property*), this is the peasant's most abstract statement and his profoundest articulation of Truth's supremacy: Falsehood is merely the negation of Truth and is dependent on it for its prosperity.

105. The *straying* of Falsehood presents its downfall as inherent in its actions. The image of *crossing* draws together previous navigational imagery to present an image of the fate of invariable Falsehood in the journey of life.

106. The fates of Falsehood's minions (this is an allusion to Rensi) are embodiments of Falsehood's nature. Their ineffectiveness is presented first in terms of earthly *riches* and their failure to endure (through *heirs* who would maintain a man's funerary cult), and then with the image of the voyage of life (the *harbour* is often an image of the otherworld).

107. A desperate series of forceful and antithetical negative imperatives summarizes the preceding petitions, and relate directly to Rensi's situation. The first couplet concerns inertia and delay (inverting previous references to Rensi as *heavy*, i.e. sluggish, and *swift*), and the second concerns spurning a client (i.e. the peasant). *Partiality* is the concern of the central line, which represents Rensi's *heart* as the perverter of his action; the injunction against *listening* strikingly reformulates the peasant's usual injunctions to hear, and foregrounds the ambivalent role of the human *heart*.

108. This stanza opens with a summary of the injunctions and an appeal to repute. The ideal relationship of the protagonists is defined as reciprocity: the peasant, who has aided Rensi by articulating Truth, should be repaid with his *true right*.

109. The peasant now describes the lack of success of one who does not reform in accordance with the preceding verses, and lists the three fatal errors Rensi has displayed. These move from the past through to the future (*yesterday* is past reputation; a *holiday* can include funerary celebrations).

110. The ramification of such action for the *accuser* peasant and Rensi is now presented as a degeneration of the judicial process leading to *murder* in order to

silence the persistent *pleader*. The final couplet tersely reformulates these pre-
ceding verses with direct reference to the protagonists. *Anubis* is a god of death
and otherworldly judgement: the peasant threatens suicide. It is a dramatic
ending and a final despairing affirmation of faith in ideal Truth. The mention
of the god completes a huge circle, as the peasant's name (mentioned in the
first verses of the Tale) means 'One protected by Anubis'.

111. The poem returns to narrative for the resolution. The *two attendants* have
appeared earlier in the third petition (B1 217). The peasant's speech laments
the fact that Rensi has prevented him from suicide, and expands on his
thwarted longing for death. It briefly resumes the lyrical style of the petitions;
earlier similar images of sustenance referred to Truth (B1 272–8 and n. 74),
but here they express the desirability of life for most of mankind, and also iron-
ically reflect his desire for the absoluteness that he can attain only in death.

112. Rensi's speech reminds the audience that he is a benevolent figure of author-
ity, and he replaces Anubis (B2 115 and n. 110) as the person with whom the
peasant will deal. As the exchanges shorten, there is a reversal of roles: Rensi
becomes the addresser who enjoins action, while the peasant vehemently
spurns cooperation. His oath (referring to *bread* and *beer*) points to the irony of
the preceding petitions' food imagery—which he apparently still does not real-
ize—and his last word is a reference to eternity. (The oath is ambiguous; it
might also be translated: 'I will not live . . .').

113. The dialogue ends with a simple command, an implicit and dramatic denial of
all the peasant's accusations of deafness. The speaker is now the *hearer*, whose
growing awareness of the irony of the preceding situation remains implicit.
The writing down of the petitions (B1 109-11 and n. 20) is concluded here,
and the petitions are enclosed within the narrative. This writing down is a
standard successful conclusion of a literary text but here is dramatically, struc-
turally, and thematically necessary: writing is a symbol of how the ideal is
actualized (B1 336 and n. 96).

114. The following verses move swiftly to make the final judgement explicit on the
highest level of authority. The justness of the king's *heart*, which perceives the
perfection of the peasant's 'perfect speech', contrasts it with Nemtinakht's:
the heart is not invariably, inherently evil.

115. The ease of the ending throws into relief both the efficacy of authority to
uphold Truth and the central irony of the plot—that Rensi's ignoring of the
peasant has been a trick to keep him speaking. The exact restoration of the
final verses is uncertain. The list of goods echoes and replaces those stolen in
the opening narrative: the unjustly robbed is now the just taker. This sudden
change in fortune provides a tacit answer to the accusations against Rensi
which were made in paradoxical, peripatetic ('then-now') form. The peasant
remains quiet (an evocative state; see n. 14): he has at last no further need to
speak.

3

The Tale of the Shipwrecked Sailor

Introduction

The Tale begins in dramatic fashion, *in medias res,* as a clever retainer tries to comfort his master who is sailing back from an expedition in a state of despair, apparently at the failure of his mission. The retainer tells a tale about a previous voyage of his to show how catastrophe can be endured, in order to encourage his master in making his report to the king.

The Tale is an entertaining account of fantastic and exciting adventures. It gives the impression of a simple folk tale, but has a very sophisticated structure with an elaborate pattern of a tale within a tale within a tale, and alludes to esoteric knowledge to articulate its central message. Its mock simplicity is a virtue in itself, producing a sense of bare elegance, but it also drives home the Tale's universal moral and adds verisimilitude to the mariner's narrative.

Such verisimilitude is much needed, for the traveller, who was perhaps then (as now) a type considered to be a teller of tall tales, tells one including a tale told to him; as the audience moves from tale into tale, the experience becomes increasingly unreal. The fact that all the narrators remain nameless gives the Tale the feel of a timeless narration, of universal relevance. The repetition of incidents and phraseology, and the structuring of the whole by accounts of 'similar' happenings, give a sense of the universal similarity of experience, and suggest a world of metaphor and allegory. Voyaging is a common image for a person's journey through life, and the sailor's concern about landfall evokes the attainment of material and spiritual success in life. In the Tale, however, voyages are continually interrupted by disaster. Man's ability to speak (and to produce poetry) is his only safeguard against this, as is demonstrated by the sailor's tale, in which he attempts to allay his captain's fears about reporting to his sovereign by telling how he has had to face meetings with a numinous being as well as with the king.

Although the sailor's narrative of a shipwreck appears objectively straight forward, it is subtly suggestive: when he tells how he was cast onto a southern paradisal island ostensibly sited in the Red Sea, his description hints that the island is not as uninhabited as it seems. He then encounters the inhabitant, a giant human-headed serpent, whose shape declares him to be divine, but whose exact identity remains mysterious.

The sailor implied that his tale would advise bravery in the face of disaster, and he now reveals that his moral was learnt from this serpent, who told him how he had to endure the death of his kinsmen. The lost community of serpents totalled seventy-five, a number that alludes to a religious text, and suggests that the serpent is a metaphorical representative of the creator-god (see n. 17). His tale of catastrophe expands and deepens the lesson to be learnt from the sailor's experience, by suggesting that disaster is an inevitable part of existence that afflicts even the divine. The island was initially described by the serpent as a spirit isle, and now the serpent reveals that it will sink after the sailor is rescued; this alludes to the myth that the universe will end in a cosmic catastrophe, and that only the creator-god will survive, taking the form of a serpent (see n. 23). The serpent's narrative contains a further allusion: he mentions a daughter who was saved from catastrophe, which recalls the daughter of the creator-god, who is Truth, the personification of the ideal order of the universe.

These literary (and unliteral) allusions present an analogue of the nature of suffering. The thrust of the poem is that, since the whole cosmos—even the divine—is prey to disaster, all that one can do is to bear it bravely, attain a degree of self-realization and self-control, and 'view' one's experience without despair (there is much play with 'seeing'). The serpent's survival offers the audience some hope, which is embodied in the sailor's survival and the serpent's prophecy that he will return home safely with another shipload of sailors. In this survival, art has a role: the telling and retelling of misfortune enable people to overcome or to endure it. In the Tale as a whole, literature acts as a redress for suffering: the man saves himself by his quick and skilful speech. The Tale is thus about the value of telling tales, and the formal repetition of the Tale itself provides a reassuring regularity in the tales of disaster. The stanzas likewise fall into regular groups: the first five deal with the introduction and the journey to the island, the second five with the man's dialogue with the serpent he meets there, the next five with the serpent's tale and prophecy, while the remainder take the sailor back home, where he is rewarded with the title with which he was introduced at the start of the whole.

The repetition of incidents, however, also presents many sudden reversals of fortune, and differences between what should be and what actually happens; occasionally these are almost humorous, but they create an unsettling atmosphere. The reassuring narration is clouded by multiple ambiguities: the audience cannot tell the identity of the characters, or precisely why they are travelling; the serpent's identity is left ambiguous, as is his daughter's and (through wordplay) the exact nature of the island; and there are numerous incidental verbal ambiguities (see nn. 10, 14, 15, 18, 22). The various and cross-purposed allusions increase the sense of uncertainty and unreality for the audience.

Disorder reasserts itself with a final unexpected event, and the Tale ends with a reply by the sailor's master. The sailor's monologue has ended and there is no need for any response from his silent interlocutor, but his intricately structured lesson is swept aside with a brutal, cynically laconic response: the Count asks in a terse proverbial-sounding question how it can profit a doomed man to hope for help. Although shockingly sudden, this rejection has been subtly prepared for: the serpent has already brushed aside one of the sailor's declarations as laughable. The dismissal casts doubt on the validity of his moral, on the capacity of speech to change things, and thus perhaps on the reliability of the sailor as a narrator. For all its stoic assurances, the Tale ends on a question with a final unexpected twist, and all is left hanging. The only certainty is the art of the poem, and the Count's final question is left for the audience to answer.

The Tale is preserved in a single manuscript (P. St-Petersburg 1115), written in an archaizing hand in the middle of the Twelfth Dynasty, and was probably composed early in the Dynasty; the name of the copyist is preserved. Although the start of the manuscript has been tampered with to add a strengthening strip (now lost), there is little doubt that the text is complete. Numbers give line numbers of the manuscript.

The Tale of the Shipwrecked Sailor

1 A clever Follower speaks:[1]
  'May your heart be well, my Count!
  Look, we have reached home,
  and the mallet is taken, the mooring post driven in,
  and the prow-rope has been thrown on the ground;
  praises are given and God is thanked,
  every man is embracing his fellow,
  and our crew has come back safe,
  with no loss to our expedition.

10 We've reached the very end of Wawat, and passed Biga!
  Look, we have arrived in peace!
  Our own land, we've reached it!

  Listen to me, my Count![2]
  I am free ⟨from⟩ exaggeration.
  Wash yourself! Pour water on your hands!
  So you may reply when you are addressed,
  and speak to the king with self-possession,
  and answer without stammering.
  A man's utterance saves him.
  His speech turns anger away from him.

20 But you do as you wish![3]
  It is tiresome to speak to you!

  I shall tell you something similar,[4]
  which happened to me myself:
  I had gone to the Mining Region of the sovereign.
  I had gone down to the Sea,
  in a boat 120 cubits long,
  40 cubits broad,
  in which there were 120 sailors from the choicest of Egypt.
  They looked at the sky, they looked at the land,
30 and their hearts were stouter than lions'.

  Before it came, they could foretell a gale,[5]
  a storm before it existed;
  but a gale came up while we were at sea, before we had reached
    land.
  The wind rose, and made an endless howling,

and with it a swell of eight cubits.
Only the mast broke it for me.[6]
Then the boat died.
Those in it—not one of them survived.
Then I was given up onto an island   40
by a wave of the sea.
With my heart as my only companion,[7]
I spent three days alone.
I spent the nights inside
a shelter of wood, and embraced the shadows.
Then I stretched out my legs to learn what I could put in my
    mouth.

I found figs and grapes there, and every fine vegetable;[8]
and there were sycomore figs there, and also ripened ones,
and melons as if cultivated;   50
fish were there, and also fowl:
there was nothing which was not in it.
Then I ate my fill, and put aside
what was too much for my arms.
I took a fire drill, made fire,[9]
and made a burnt offering to the Gods.

Then I heard a noise of thunder; I thought it was a wave
    of the sea,[10]
for the trees were splintering,
the earth shaking;   60
I uncovered my face and found it was a serpent coming.
There were 30 cubits of him.
His beard was bigger than two cubits,
his flesh overlaid with gold,
and his eyebrows of true lapis lazuli.
He was rearing upwards.

He opened his mouth to me, while I was prostrate in front of
    him.[11]
He said to me, "Who brought you?
Who brought you, young man?   70
Who brought you?
If you delay in telling me
who brought you to this island,

I will make you know yourself to be ashes,
turned into invisibility!"

"You speak to me, without me hearing.[12]
I am in front of you, and do not know myself."
Then he put me in his mouth,
took me away to his dwelling place,
and laid me down without harming me.
80 I was safe, with no damage done to me.

He opened his mouth to me, while I was prostrate in front of
    him.
Then he said to me: "Who brought you?
Who brought you, young man?
Who brought you to this island of the sea,
with water on all sides?"
Then I answered this to him, my arms bent in front of him.[13]
I said to him, "It's because I was going down
90 to the Mining Region on a mission of the sovereign,
in a boat 120 cubits long,
40 cubits broad,
in which there were 120 sailors from the choicest of Egypt.
They looked at the sky, they looked at the land,
and their hearts were stouter than lions'.

Before it came, they could foretell a gale,
a storm before it existed;
each one of them—his heart was stouter,
100 his arm stronger, than his fellow's.
There was no fool among them.
And a gale came up while we were at sea, before we had
    reached land.
The wind rose, and made an endless howling,
and with it a swell of eight cubits.
Only the mast broke it for me.
Then the boat died.
Those in it—not one of them survived, except me.
And look, I am beside you.

Then I was brought to this island
110 by a wave of the sea."
And he said to me, "Fear not,[14]

fear not, young man!
Do not be pale, for you have reached me!
Look, God has let you live,
and has brought you to this island of the spirit;
there is nothing which is not within it,
and it is full of every good thing.
Look, you will spend month upon month,[15]
until you have completed four months in the interior of this
    island.
A ship will come from home,   120
with sailors in it whom you know,
and you will return home with them,
and die in your city.

How happy is he who can tell of his experience, so that the
    calamity passes![16]
I shall tell you something similar,
that happened on this island,
where I was with my kinsmen,
and with children amongst them.
With my offspring and my kinsmen, we were 75 serpents in all—[17]
I shall not evoke the little daughter,[18]
whom I had wisely brought away.

Then a star fell,[19]   130
and because of it they went up in flames.
Now this happened when I wasn't with them;
they were burnt when I wasn't among them.
Then I died for them, when I found them as a single heap of
    corpses.
If you are brave, master your heart,[20]
and you will fill your embrace with your children,
kiss your wife, and see your house!
This is better than anything.
You will reach home, and remain there,
amongst your kinsmen."
Stretched out prostrate was I,
and I touched the ground in front of him.

I said to him, "I shall tell your power to the sovereign.[21]
I shall cause him to comprehend your greatness.   140

I shall have them bring you laudanum and malabathrum,
terebinth and balsam,
and the incense of the temple estates with which every God is
     content.
I shall tell what has happened to me, as what I have seen of
     your power.
They will thank God for you in the city
before the council of the entire land.

I shall slaughter bulls for you as a burnt offering.[22]
I shall strangle fowls for you.
I shall have boats brought for you
laden with all the wealth of Egypt,
as is done for a God who loves mankind,
in a far land, unknown to mankind."

Then he laughed at me, at the things I had said,[23]
which were folly to his heart.
150 He said to me, "Do you have much myrrh,
or all existing types of incense?
For I am the ruler of Punt;
myrrh is mine;
that malabathrum you speak of bringing
is this island's plenty.
And once it happens that you have left this place,
you will never see this island again, which will have become
     water."

Then that boat came,[24]
as he had foretold previously.
Then I went and put myself up a tall tree,
and I recognized those inside it.
Then I went to report this,
and I found that he knew it.
Then he said to me, "Fare well,[25]
fare well, young man,
to your house, and see your children!
160 Spread my renown in your city! Look, this is my due
     from you."

Then I prostrated myself,[26]
my arms bent in front of him.

Then he gave me a cargo
of myrrh and malabathrum,
terebinth and balsam,
camphor, *shaasekh*-spice, and eye-paint,
tails of giraffes,
a great mound of incense,
elephant tusks,
hounds and monkeys,
apes and all good riches.

Then I loaded this onto the ship,[27]
and it was then that I prostrated myself to thank God for him.
Then he said to me, "Look, you will arrive
within two months!
You will fill your embrace with your children.
You will grow young again at home, and be buried."
Then I went down to the shore nearby this ship.   170
Then I called to the expedition which was in this ship,
and I on the shore gave praises
to the lord of this island,
and those who were aboard did the same.

We then sailed northwards,[28]
to the Residence of the sovereign,
and we reached home
in two months, exactly as he had said.
Then I entered before the sovereign,
and I presented him with this tribute
from the interior of this island.
Then he thanked God for me before the council of the entire land.
Then I was appointed as a Follower;
I was endowed with 200 persons.
Look at me, after I have reached land, and have viewed my
        past experience![29]   180
Listen to my [speech]!
Look, it is good to listen to men.'
Then he said to me, 'Don't act clever, my friend![30]
Who pours water [for] a goose,
when the day dawns for its slaughter on the morrow?'

So it ends, from start to finish,[31]
as found in writing,
[as] a writing of the scribe with clever fingers,
Ameny son of Amenyaa (l.p.h.!).

Notes

1. The Tale opens suddenly. For the ranks of Follower and Count, see The Tale of
   Sinuhe, n. 1. No more specific names or titles are provided, but the dramatic
   monologue specifies the location and indirectly provides all the necessary infor-
   mation about the setting. Wawat was Lower Nubia, and was the goal of many
   expeditions at the start of the Twelfth Dynasty. The island of Biga is in the First
   Cataract, just south of Elephantine (modern Aswan), the southern border of
   Egypt. The opening verses are reminiscent of commemorative inscriptions
   recording expeditions, which were a familiar motif in official Egyptian writings.
   The dramatic setting matches the subsequent narrative's theme of a successful
   homecoming.
2. As the Tale opens, the sailor reassures the audience of the reality of the fiction
   that follows; the claim is, however, ironic and perhaps humorous (see also n.
   3). He also attempts to reassure his Count: the washing marks his return home,
   and is perhaps also a preparation for his reception at court. These encourage-
   ments imply that all is not well with the Count, and that he will have to justify
   himself before the king, presumably for an ineffective expedition. The moral
   about speech is demonstrated by the whole Tale, which is about tale-telling, and
   ordering one's experience by speaking.
3. This testy couplet further indicates the state of the Count, and explains his
   silence, which allows the sailor's monologue to develop into a full narration. It
   is also an ironic touch, since the sailor now continues to speak at great length.
4. The sailor now begins to narrate an earlier journey. The Mining Region is the
   Sinai peninsula, to which he would have travelled by road from Egypt and then
   sailed from the Red Sea coast. The dimensions of the boat (21 × 63 m) are real-
   istic, but the number of sailors may be schematic. There is wordplay between
   the homonyms looking and lions (which were proverbially watchful animals).
5. This stanza is dominated by disaster, and the sailors' foreknowledge proves to
   be an inadequate protection (it also anticipates the sailor's later meeting with
   greater prophetic powers). The wave is 4 m tall.
6. An obscure phrase: it is probably the wave, so that the sense is that the mast
   sheltered the sailor from the storm. The pathetic fallacy of the next verse
   increases the sense of death—a subject which is taken up by a later narrator.
7. For three days the sailor is in shock and exhausted, without bothering to eat.
   To embrace the shadows probably means to be unconscious.
8. A stanza now describes what the sailor discovers. The island is a bountiful para-
   dise (similar to Iaa in The Tale of Sinuhe), and its lack of nothing makes it seem
   an image of all the created world (see n. 14). There are hints, however, that it
   is not uninhabited, since sycomore figs have to be notched by hand to ripen; the
   following verse contains another hint.
9. This pious offering to the gods is answered in the next stanza by the arrival of
   the numinous.
10. The sailor fears that he is about to be engulfed by another calamitous wave,
    despite being on land; the cause of the noise is yet more remarkable. The ser-
    pent seems to be human-headed, similar to the fire-spitting demi-gods seen on

contemporaneous magic wands. He is 15 m long, and has a metre-long beard (beards are distinguishing marks of kings and gods); he is described as are gilded images of gods. The phrase *rearing upwards* (i.e. raised up to attack) is ambiguous: it is homophonous with 'wise beforehand/exceedingly'.

11. A stanza of dialogue. The serpent's *young man* (literally 'little man') alludes to their difference in size and in social rank: he speaks like a noble talking to a commoner, and he subsequently always repeats his address (a common means of marking emphasis and exclamations).

12. The change in speaker is unmarked, to indicate that the man's response is immediate: his quick words save his life. He echoes the serpent's threat in a humble reply, declaring that he is overpowered by his grandeur.

13. A gesture of respect. The scene is similar to the expected meeting of the Count and his sovereign (n. 2). The sailor now retells his tale of shipwreck (see earlier notes), and his tale concludes with a couplet which finally answers the serpent's initial question. Although the repetition of his earlier account may help him seem a reliable narrator to the audience, there are slight elaborations on the first version.

14. Although the serpent is portrayed like a god (see nn. 10, 17), he here refers to God as a still higher authority. The serpent provides, for the first time, an identification of the island. The *spirit* (*ka*) was the link between life and death, so his description implies that the island exists halfway between this world and the next. There is also wordplay: an *island of the spirit* is homonymous with an 'island of abundance'. Its abundance (see n. 8) makes it a metaphor for the created world.

15. The serpent now reassures the sailor. There is ironically ambiguous wordplay between *the interior* and *home* (and later with 'within' and the 'Residence'); they are homonyms, but are used of radically different locations. The death promised to him is very different from all the previous ones described; this will be a homecoming and a resurrection, not a shipwreck.

16. This exclamation asserts a central moral of the Tale: that telling a misfortune can be cathartic. The serpent begins his narrative with the same words as the sailor used (21–3). This tale within a tale within a tale is the most central and densely allusive part of the poem; it tells of ultimate disaster, but is flanked by reassuring prophecies that the sailor will be spared such an experience.

17. The number of serpents is the same as the number of the forms of the Sungod in a later religious text, *The Litany of the Sungod*. This esoteric allusion suggests that the serpent is an image of the creator, although he has referred to 'God' as distinct from himself (113–14 and n. 14). The identity of the serpent is presented as an obscure metaphor.

18. The serpent's wise intuition recalls that of the sailors; although greater, following events show that his wisdom is insufficient to ward off calamity: he is unable to save his *kinsmen*, only his *daughter*, whom he had taken with him. In mythology the daughter of the creator Sungod is the goddess Truth, the central value of Egyptian culture. (The verse is allusive and ambiguous; it might also be translated: 'who was brought to me by prayer').

19. The stanza begins with a cosmic cataclysm. The serpents' vulnerability to suffering suggests that the divine, including even the creator-god, is not exempt from suffering and chaos (see Introduction, p. 90). Even the serpent 'dies' metaphorically.

20. The serpent shifts abruptly from a narrative of despair to positive injunction: his tale advocates and exemplifies stoic endurance and self-control (implying that the man's calamity is easier than his). The reference to *kinsmen* points the parallel between the serpent's loss and the sailor's. This reassurance is personal and

intimate, following on from the serpent's tale of personal suffering. Here the sailor's happy return implicitly depends on his accepting the serpent's lesson; wordplay links the two together: *brave* and *embrace* are homophones (*embrace* also recalls the sailor's earlier 'embracing the shadows' (44-5 and n. 7)). The sailor's own monologue began with a similar injunction not to despair (1-2).

21. The sailor enthusiastically promises to extol the serpent's divinity. (The royal audience that he envisages recalls the Count's coming audience, which provides the frame of the whole Tale.) He also promises offerings of spices and perfumes suitable for a god; not all of these are securely identifiable.

22. His continuing promises of sacrifices are natural in the circumstances, but are slightly extravagant to judge by the serpent's response. The last two verses of the stanza can also be rendered 'a god who loves mankind (i.e. Egyptians), in a distant land, whom mankind does not know': this ambiguity increases the sense of how impossible it is for the sailor to send anything to the isle and maintains the mysterious atmosphere of the whole Tale.

23. The serpent now gives two reasons why the sailor's offer is ridiculous: compared to the serpent he lacks the means to fulfil his promises; and he will be unable to return to the island. The serpent finally reveals something of his mystical identity: *Punt* was a semi-mythical land of riches, and the source of exotic goods; it was perhaps in the region of modern Eritrea and part of the semi-legendary regions known as 'God's Land'. The island's disappearance evokes its mystical and metaphorical nature: these verses are similar to the end of the created world as related in a later funerary text (*Book of the Dead*, spell 175). The serpent does not specify his own fate, but in that myth the creator-god survives the apocalypse as a primordial serpent in the waters of chaos.

24. At the start of the description of the homeward journey, the sailor meets sailors who compensate in part for the ones who had died (38-9). He recognizes them from past knowledge, whereas the more perceptive serpent perceived them by foreknowledge.

25. The serpent's speech promises a return to certainty and the familiar real world, adding the assurance of reunion with family. What he asks in return, merely the repetition of his fame, is the Tale itself, although there is a touch of irony: *renown* is literally 'name', and the serpent remains anonymous. As *renown* ensured the survival of the dead, the word also alludes to the fact that the serpent is not of this world.

26. The serpent now surpasses the sailor's earlier offer with a list of exotic products from his African kingdom of Punt.

27. In a stanza of leave-taking, the serpent repeats his reassuring prophecy; the mention of *two*, not four, months (118-19) gives a sense of time passing and the speed of his return. For the sailor death now has a positive aspect; the paradox of simultaneously growing young again and being buried is also found in Sinuhe's homecoming. *Children* are a sign of survival and continuity, as well as of family life.

28. In narrating his reception and reward, the sailor makes no mention of spreading the serpent's renown (cf. 159-60). His fulfilling his duty may be tacitly understood, but the lack of any explicit description may foreshadow the unsatisfactory response to the narration that is to come. Once again, the sailor's eloquence benefits him, and he is rewarded with an improbably large number of servants: his promotion to the rank of a *Follower* returns the audience to the start of the whole tale, as does the subsequent mention of *reaching land*.

29. This moralizing triplet is an appropriate ending to the sailor's tale, which was told to urge the value of speaking and experience. *Reaching land* is an evocative

phrase, suggestive of success (it is homonymous with 'endowed') and of a good death.

30. The Tale abruptly returns to the setting. The Count's laconic and unexpected answer makes a brutal ending, and shows that he has not listened to the sailor's moral. He asks who will support a doomed person like himself, and implies that no endurance will help him survive his catastrophe. His warning against *acting clever* alludes scornfully to the sailor's title of 'clever Follower' (1). His answer also echoes the offerings of fowl mentioned by the sailor (145-6) and the *pouring of water* advocated earlier (13-14 and n. 2). The mention of *slaughter* recalls curses against rebels in graffiti left by contemporaneous expeditions to Nubia, suggesting that the Count may expect to be accused of disloyalty.

31. In this colophon the use of (*l.p.h.!*) (see Glossary) after the copyist's name is a little grandiloquent (an occasional tendency in colophons). The mention of *clever fingers*—a standard epithet for scribes—is a witty touch, as 'clever'ness was mentioned in the final lines of the Tale.

[4]

The Tale of King Cheops' Court

Introduction

This entertaining Tale tells of wonders from the fabulous past, some seven centuries before its composition in the late Middle Kingdom. It consists of a cycle of tales within a single framing tale concerning the Fourth Dynasty builder of the Great Pyramid, King Cheops, and the birth of the kings who are to succeed his line. Its description of the origin of the Fifth Dynasty is very different from historical fact, even though the solar cult's increased prominence in that period may lie behind the role of the Sungod in the Tale. The portrayal of Cheops reflects the attitudes of the Middle Kingdom, rather than any historical reality. The high seriousness of other Tales is here avoided in favour of lighter qualities. The audience is told of the boredom of everyday life (felt by Sneferu and Cheops) and various senseless losses (of jewellery and of a wife's fidelity); through the act of storytelling these become sources of carefreeness, and sequences of events which create an enjoyable anticipation and suspense. Everyday life becomes full of 'wonders'.

About seventy verses may be lost from the start of the Tale, but it probably began with a statement that

> There was once a time when the Dual King, Cheops, the justified
> was the worthy king in this entire land

and then related how one day the king went around every chamber of his palace to find some 'relief' from his boredom, and, having failed, summoned his princes to entertain him.[1] The episodes in the palace at Memphis are almost a parody of the court scenes that feature in commemorative inscriptions, in which the king is eulogized as he sits among his courtiers. Here, a prince tells Cheops a

---

[1] This reconstruction is based on the start of the second tale told to Cheops (see n. 16), and on the opening of *The Words of Neferti*.

tale about a 'wonder' that happened under his ancestor King Djoser—but only the king's appreciative response is preserved. One tale was obviously not enough to satisfy him, and a second prince tells another tale of similar antiquity, about adultery. Then another prince tells one about Cheops' own good-natured father King Sneferu. This time the wonder is a more cheerful one, but no less bizarre. Each tale ends with a formal pious response from Cheops, who orders funerary offerings for the kings and their wonder-workers, and these set up an expectation of continuity.

These fantastic reports are, however, dismissed by the next son, who is Hordedef, famous in the Middle Kingdom and later as a wise man. He offers a wonder which Cheops can witness himself, and which will be performed by a contemporary commoner called Djedi, as opposed to dead priests. When the commoner and the king meet, it becomes clear that the commoner is more humane and aware of the king's responsibilities than is Cheops himself. Three wonders are performed, but Cheops' impatient presumption is still not satisfied, and he desires a wonder involving restricted knowledge that lies beyond his access. Djedi foretells the birth of the person who can bring him what he desires, but also tells him that he is someone who will oust Cheops' descendants from the throne.

A second strand of the narrative starts as the scene shifts and the audience hears the most marvellous wonder—the birth of three children of the Sungod to a mortal woman. This supernatural birth was part of Egyptian doctrine, in which each king was the son of the Sungod, but his direct paternity of these children implies that Cheops' line is not the true royal line. This wonder surpasses even the golden time of Sneferu, with a reality that excels the slightly frivolous masquerade of his reign; in the earlier wonders there were parodic allusions to myth and ritual, but these are now replaced with the real thing. There is also a change of setting: the Tale moves from the court to a wider world that includes both the court of the Sungod and the house of a private priest, and moves from the fantastic past into a present that is more wonderful and yet also more familiar, as the divine children are born into an increasingly troubled everyday world. At this point the manuscript breaks off.

The Tale offers its audience a sequence of wonderful episodes. The tales within the Tale are episodic and very different from those of the more elegantly and symmetrically patterned *Tale of the Ship-wrecked Sailor*. The style is consistently simple, always describing actions and deeds, and interspersed with rapid dialogue. It is descended from the folk-tale-like style employed in the narrative sections of *The Tale of the Eloquent Peasant*, but here the simplicity seems less studied; the construction of the Tale is as loose in details as the manuscript itself is careless. The language is more colloquial and 'prosaic' in style than in other tales, and the verse is less tightly structured, and less regular. The style is repetitive, and this has the virtue of creating and maintaining expectation—for example, in the second tale's narrative leading up to the transformation of the crocodile—and a sense of events developing. Recurring details draw attention to parallels between various incidents.

The Tale is more 'sexy' than other serious moralizing tales; it is amusing, with subjects including adultery, voyeurism, and the straightforward exotica of the priests' conjuring tricks. There are, however, underlying serious topics: the most frivolous incident, which sounds like the invention of fishnet tights, alludes to rituals for the goddess Hathor. Such esoteric allusions, however, are incidental (unlike the theological allusions of *The Tale of the Shipwrecked Sailor*, which are central to its meaning and structure), and they are presented for enjoyment, with parody and without much emphasis on edification. Nevertheless, they reinforce the impression that the Tale is not just an adventure about changing dynasties; the princely contest of who can demonstrate the nature of a true 'wonder' is part of a narrative about true and false things—the reputed as opposed to the witnessed wonders—and these include the central institution of kingship. A major contrast is drawn between the imperfect king Cheops and the good king Sneferu, both through the figure of Djedi, who spans both reigns, and through the various parallel episodes, such as the two rowing expeditions. The Tale also contains contrasts between a true and a false wife, between two crocodiles, and between groups of court beauties and goddesses in disguise. The series of comparable incidents helps to characterize the various protagonists, whose actions are described objectively and without explicit commentary, although the characterization is not unambivalent (see n. 66).

Many of these minor incidents serve to reinforce the main contrast between Cheops and the divine kings of the Fifth Dynasty, who were venerated as royal ancestors by the Middle Kingdom rulers. Later texts show a belief that the gods would cut short the reigns of impious kings, and this is the general implication here, but it is uncertain how the Tale would have ended. In the last episode set in the court, Cheops plans to visit the children's birthplace, perhaps with hostile intentions, and the manuscript breaks off as a malicious plot to inform him about the children fails. The arrival of a crocodile suggests that any further attempts to cause trouble for the children would not have passed unhindered by their divine father. This final extant episode may have helped lead the main narrative back to describing Cheops' actions, and the Tale may have continued to tell how he made his planned visit. The audience will have known, from history, that any attempt by Cheops to delay the succession of the three children would fail, and the Tale may have ended with his being reconciled to the fate of his dynasty, possibly through the intervention of the Sungod or Djedi.

The Tale is preserved on a single papyrus, now in Berlin, from *c.*1600 BC (P. Westcar — P. Berlin 3033). The beginning is badly damaged, and at least one page is lost. On the recto there are nine pages, and on the verso three further ones; after the third of these the copy ends abruptly, and the final episodes of the Tale are lost (see n. 67). Numbers give page and line numbers of the manuscript.

The Tale of King Cheops' Court

. . . .]'¹

1.12 And the Majesty of the Dual King [Che]ops, the justi[fied],
         said,
      ['Let an offering be made of a thousand loaves,]
      a hundred jars of be[er],
      [one ox and two balls of incense]
      [to] ⟨the Majesty of⟩ the Dual King Djoser, the justified!
1.15 [And let there be given a cake] and a [jug of beer],
      a big portion of meat,
      [and a ball of incense]
      [to the high lector priest Imhotep].
      [I have] seen his deed of wisdom.'
      [And it was] done [exactly as his Majesty] had commanded.

      Prince Chephren then stood up to speak,²
      [and said, 'I shall let] your Majesty [hear] a wonder
      which happened in the time of [your] forefather Nebka, the
         justified,
1.20 as he proceeded to the temple of Ptah, Lord of Life-of-the-
         Two-Lands.
      Now, his Majesty himself had gone to [make an offering at
         Memphis].
      His Majesty himself did the performance of the [rite],
      [and] the high lector priest Ubainer [was with him].³
      [Now,] the wife of Ubainer [loved] a c[ommoner]⁴
      [. . . . .]
      [total of 4 verses lost]
      [. . . . .]
2.1   [Then she had] a box [carri]ed to him,
      full of clothes [. . . . .]⁵
      He came back with the house[maid].
      [Now, some] days [after this]—
      there was a pav[ilion] in Ubainer's [garden]—
2.5   the commoner [said to Uba]iner's [wife],
      "But there's a pavilion [in Ubainer's garden], isn't there?
      Look, let's spend a little time in it!"
      [Then] Ubainer's [wife sent] to the steward [who looked after
         the garden],

[to say], "Let the pavilion [which is in the garden] be made
     ready [like a . . .]!"
and she passed the day there drinking
[with the commoner, until they were] content.   2.10
Now, when [it was evening],
he [came away].
And he went down to the pool.[6]
[And] the housemaid [waited on him at] the [pool],
[while the steward was nearby, and he said, "I]'ll go [to]
     Ubainer!"

[Now when the next day dawned],   2.15
[the steward] went
[to inform him about] this matter,
[and said, "Your wife's done a deed in] your pa[vilion],
[she and] the [commoner],
and he [then went down] ⟨to⟩ the pool.
[Then] he returned to his [home],
[having washed in] the shallows of the water."   2.20
Then that [. . . . .].[7]
Then [Ubainer said], "Go, bring me [my doc]uments
[in my chest] of ebony and electrum,
[and I'll] fash[ion and s]end [a] mess[enger!]"
[Then] he [modell]ed a [wax] crocodile, seven [fingers long].[8]
[And he] read out [a spell]
reading [it thus], "[As for the man] who will come to wash
     in my pool,
[you shall seize] that commoner [in your mouth]!"   3.1
Then he gave it to the [stew]ard,
and said to him, "Now, [wh]en the commoner has gone
     down to my pool,
as is his daily custom,
you shall throw [this] crocodile [into the water] after him!"
The [steward] then went,
and took the wax crocodile with him.   3.5
Then Ubainer's wife sent to the steward who looked after
     the [garden],
to say, "Have the pavilion in the garden made ready!
Look, I'm coming to relax in it."
Then the pavilion was made ready with every good thing.

[They] then went,[9]

3.10 and they made holiday with the commoner.
Now when it was evening,
the commoner then came away,
as was his daily custom.
Then the [steward] threw the wax crocodile
after him into the water.
Then it [became] a crocodile of seven cubits.[10]
Then it seized the commoner [in its mouth].

3.15 Now, Ubainer had to remain
with the Majesty of the Dual King Nebka, [the justified], for
    seven days,
while the commoner was in the dep[ths of the pool]
[without anything to] breathe [there].
Now, when it was the seventh day,
the Dual King Nebka, the justified, then proceeded [south-
    wards].
Then the high lector priest
Ubainer placed himself in the royal presence.
Then Ubainer said, "[Look, a deed] has been told to me!

3.20 May your Majesty proceed and see the wonder
which has happened [in] your Majesty's time—
a commoner [under water]!"
[Then his Majesty went with] Ubainer.
Then Ubainer [summoned the] crocodile,
saying, "Bring [the] commoner [immediately]!"
[The] crocodile [came] out,
[with the commoner in its mouth].
Then the high lector priest Ubainer said,
"[That commoner—release] him!" Then it [spat] him [out].
Then it put [him down without having harmed] him.

4.1 And the Majesty of the Dual King Nebka, the justified, said,
"This is surely a fierce crocodile!"
Ubainer then bent down.
Then he took hold of it.
And in his hand
it was a wax crocodile.
And the high lector priest Ubainer recounted the thing

4.5 that the commoner had been doing in his house with his
    wife,

to the Majesty of the Dual King Nebka, the justified.
Then his Majesty said to the crocodile,
"Take what is yours!"[11]
The crocodile then went down
to the [depths] of the lake;
no one ever knew where it had gone with him.
Then the [Majesty of] the Dual King Nebka, the justified, had
Ubainer's wife taken away to a plot
north of the Residence.
Then he had her burnt, [and she became] refuse for the
     river.[12]   4.10
Look, this is a wonder which happened
[in] the time of ⟨your⟩ forefather, the Dual King Nebka,
     ⟨the justified⟩,
something the high lector priest Ubainer did!'
And the Majesty of the Dual King Cheops, the justified, said,
'Let an offering be made of a thousand loaves,[13]
a hundred jars of beer,
one ox and two balls of incense
to the ⟨Majesty of⟩ the Dual King Nebka, the justified!
And let there be given a cake, a jug of beer,   4.15
a big portion of meat,
and a ball of incense,
to the high lector priest Ubainer.
I have seen his deed of wisdom.'
And it was done exactly as his Majesty had commanded.

⟨Prince⟩ Bauefre then stood up to speak,[14]
and said, 'I shall let [your] Majesty hear a wonder,
which happened in the time of your father Sneferu, [the
     justified],
[something] the high lector priest Djadjaemankh [did].   4.20
Yesterday illu[mines . . . . . .] success,[15]
[. . . . .]
[. . . up to to]day, these things which have not happened
     before.
[One day, the Dual King Sneferu, the justified,
was going round] every [chamber] of the Royal House (l.p.h.!)
to seek [some relief] for himself, [and he could not find any].
[And he said], "Go, bring me the high [lector priest]

and scribe [of the book Djadjaemankh!]"[16]
And he was brought to him immediately.
And [his Majesty] said to him,
"[I've gone round every chamber of the Royal] House
     [(l.p.h.!)],

5.1   to seek some relief for myself, and I cannot find any."
And Djadjaemankh said to him,
"O may your Majesty proceed to the lake of the Great House
     (l.p.h.!)!
Equip a barque for yourself
with all the beauties from inside your palace,
and the heart of your Majesty will gain relief
at seeing them row a rowing trip,

5.5   upstream and downstream.
And you'll see the beautiful pools of your lake-land.
And you'll see its countryside and its beautiful banks.
Your heart will gain relief by this."
"I'll certainly have a rowing trip![17]
Let me be brought twenty oars of ebony,
worked in gold,
with handles of sandal wood,
worked in electrum!
Let me be brought twenty women,

5.10 with beautiful limbs,
deep-breasted and braided,
who are not yet stretched with childbirth!
And let me be brought twenty nets;
and give these nets to the women, when their clothes have
     been laid aside!"
Then it was done exactly as his Majesty had commanded.

And they rowed upstream and downstream.

5.15 And his Majesty's heart was happy at seeing them row.
Then the woman who was at the stroke oar
got her braid entangled.
Then a fish-pendant of new turquoise[18]
fell in the water.
Then she was still, and did not row.

5.20 And her side was still, and did not row.
And his Majesty said, "Shouldn't you row?"

Then they said, "Our stroke's still, and isn't rowing!"
Then his Majesty said to her,
"[Why] aren't you rowing?"
Then she said, "[It's because a] fish-pendant of new
    [turquoise]
[has fallen] in the water."
Then he had [. . . . . . , and said to her],[19]
"[If you] want [it], it's replaced!"
Then she said, "I want my own thing, not one like it!"
And [his Majesty] said, "[Go bring me]
the [high] lector priest [Djadjaemankh!]"
[And he was brought to him immediately].
And his Majesty said, "Djadjaemankh, my brother!   6.1
I've done the things you said.
And the heart of my Majesty gained relief at seeing them row.
Then a fish-pendant of new turquoise,
belonging to one of the strokes,
fell in the water.
Then she was still, and did not row. And so it happened
    that she disrupted her side.
Then I said to her, 'Why aren't you rowing?'   6.5
Then she said to me, 'It's because a fish-pendant of new
    turquoise
has fallen into the water.'
Then I said to her, 'Row! Look, I'll replace it myself!'
Then she said to me, 'I want my own thing, not one like it!' "
Then the high lector priest Djadjaemankh said
his words of magic.
Then he put one side of the lake's water on top of the other,
and he found the fish-pendant lying on a sherd.   6.10
Then he brought it back, and it was given to its owner.
Now the water was twelve cubits in the middle,[20]
and it ended up as twenty-four cubits, once it was folded.
Then he said his words of magic.
Then he brought these waters of the lake back to their usual
    position,[21]
and his Majesty spent all the day making holiday,
with the entire Royal Household (l.p.h.!).
And so he rewarded the high lector priest Djadjaemankh
    with every good thing.   6.15

Look, this is a wonder which happened
in the time of your father the Dual King Sneferu, the justified,
something the high lector priest
and scribe of the book Djadjaemankh did!'
And the Majesty of the Dual King Cheops, the justified, said,[22]
'Let an offering be made of a thousand loaves,
a hundred jars of beer,
one ox and two balls of incense
to the Majesty of the Dual King Sneferu, the justified!

6.20 And let there be given a cake, a jug of beer,
a ball of incense,
to the high lector priest and scribe of the book Djadjaemankh.
I have seen his deed of wisdom.'
And it was done exactly as his Majesty had commanded.

Prince Hordedef then stood up to speak,[23]
and said, '[How to tell a past] deed
is something that only those who have passed away know.
Truth cannot be known from Falsehood.
[There is someone living under] your Majesty, in your own
       time,

6.25 who is ignorant [only of what does not exist and who knows
       all that does].'
And his Majesty said, 'What is this,[24]
Hor[dedef, my son]?'
[And Prince Hor]dedef [said],

7.1 'There is a commoner called Djedi,[25]
who resides in Djed-Sneferu.
He is a commoner, a hundred and ten years old.
He eats five hundred loaves of bread,
a shoulder of ox for meat,
and also drinks a hundred jars of beer,
up to this day.
He knows how to rejoin a severed head.[26]

7.5 He knows how to make a lion walk behind him with its
       leash on the ground.
He knows the number of the Chambers of the Sanctuary of
       Thoth.'[27]
Now, the Majesty of the Dual King Cheops, the justified, would
       spend all the day[28]

seeking for himself these Chambers
of the Sanctuary of Thoth,
in order to make himself ones like them for his Horizon.
And his Majesty said, 'You yourself,
Hordedef, my son, shall bring him to me!'
Then boats were made ready for Prince Hordedef.
He then went   7.10
southward to Djed-Sneferu.
When these boats had moored at the riverbank,
he then went overland,
reclining in a palanquin of ebony,[29]
with carrying poles of tamarisk wood
mounted in gold.
When he had reached Djedi, the palanquin was set down.
He then stood up to address him,
and found him lying on a mat,   7.15
on the threshold of his [porch],
with a servant holding his head, rubbing it for him,[30]
and another massaging his feet.
Then Prince Hordedef said,
'Your condition is like living before old age—[31]
though age is the time of death,
the time of burial, the time of joining the earth—
sleeping until dawn,
free from illness,
without the hacking of a cough.
Here are greetings for a blessed one!   7.20
I have come here to summon you
on a commission of my father Cheops, the justified.
You will eat fine things of the king's giving,
and the provisions of his retinue!
He will make you pass a good lifetime,
and reach your forefathers who are in the necropolis.'
And this Djedi said, 'Welcome! Welcome![32]
Hordedef, prince whom his father loves!
May your father Cheops, the justified, favour you!
May he advance your position among the elders!   7.25
May your spirit vent its anger against your enemy!
May your soul know the roads
which lead to the Portal of Him who Shrouds the Tired One!

8.1 Here are greetings for a prince!'
Then Prince Hordedef[33]
held out his arms to him. Then he raised him up.
He then proceeded with him to the riverbank,
giving him his arm.
Then Djedi said, 'Let me be given a barge,[34]
to bring me ⟨my⟩ children and also my writings!'
Then two boats and their crews were made to wait on him.

8.5 Djedi then came northwards
in the barque in which Prince Hordedef was.

Now, when he had reached the Residence,
Prince Hordedef then entered
to report to the Majesty of the Dual King Cheops, the justified.
And Prince Hordedef said,
'Sovereign, my lord! I have brought Djedi.'
And his Majesty said, 'Go bring him to me!'

8.10 His Majesty then proceeded to the Hall of the Great House
(l.p.h.!).
And Djedi was ushered in to him.
And his Majesty said, 'How is it,[35]
Djedi, that I have not seen you before?'
And Djedi said, 'He comes who is summoned,[36]
Sovereign, ⟨my lord⟩!
Summon me, and look, I've come!'
And his Majesty said, 'Is what they say true—
that you know how to rejoin a severed head?'
And Djedi said, 'Yes, I know how to,
Sovereign, my lord!'

8.15 And his Majesty said, 'Let me be brought[37]
the prisoner who is in the Stronghold, and inflict the injury on
him!'
And Djedi said, 'Not to mankind,
Sovereign, my lord!
Look, doing such a thing to the noble flock is not ordained!'
Then a goose was brought to him and its head was cut off.
Then the goose was placed at the west side of the Hall,

8.20 and its head at the east side of the Hall.
Then Djedi said his words of magic.
And the goose stood up, and waddled,

and its head likewise.
Now, when one reached the other,
the goose stood up and cackled.
Then he had a *khetaa*-goose brought to him,[38]
and he did the same to it.
Then his Majesty had a bull brought to him,
and its head was made to fall on the ground.   8.25
Then Djedi said his words of magic.
Then the bull stood up behind him,
with its leash still fallen on the ground.[39]   9.1
Then the King Cheops, the justified, said, 'And how about
        what they say,
that you know the number of the Chambers of the Sanctuary
        of Thoth?'
And Djedi said, 'May it please you, I don't know their number,[40]
Sovereign, my lord! But I do know where it is kept.'
And his Majesty said, 'Where?'
And this Djedi said, 'There is this casket,[41]   9.5
of flint, in a room,
called Sipti, in Heliopolis.
⟨Look, it is⟩ in the casket.'[42]
⟨And his Majesty said, 'Go bring me it!'⟩
And Djedi said, 'Sovereign, my lord!
Look, I'm not the one who'll bring you it.'
And his Majesty said, 'Who'll bring me it?'
And Djedi said, 'The eldest of the three children
in the womb of Ruddjedet will bring you it.'
And his Majesty said, 'But I want it!
These things you say—who is this Ruddjedet?'
And Djedi said, 'She is the wife of a priest of Re Lord of
        Sakhbu,[43]
who is pregnant with three children of Re Lord of Sakhbu.   9.10
He has said of them, "They will perform the worthy office
in this entire land.
The eldest of them
will be the Great Seer in Heliopolis." '
And his Majesty fell into a bad mood at this.
And Djedi said, 'What's this mood,[44]
Sovereign, my lord?
Is it because of the three children I mentioned?

Consider—first your son, then his son, then one of them.'
And his Majesty said,

9.15 'When will Ruddjedet give birth?'
'She will give birth on the fifteenth day of the first month of
the Season of Emergence.'[45]
And his Majesty said, 'That's when the sandbanks of Two-Fish
Canal are exposed.
My servant, if only I'd already crossed it myself,
to see the temple of Re Lord of Sakhbu!'
And Djedi said, 'Then I'll make there be four cubits of water[46]
on the sandbanks of Two-Fish Canal.'
His Majesty then proceeded to his palace.
And his Majesty said, 'Have Djedi assigned[47]

9.20 to the house of Prince Hordedef, and he will reside with him,
provided with provisions of a thousand loaves,
a hundred jars of beer,
one ox, and a hundred bundles of vegetables.'
And it was done exactly as his Majesty had commanded.

One of those days,[48]
Ruddjedet was suffering; her giving birth was painful.
And the Majesty of Re Lord of Sakhbu said
to Isis, Nephthys,
Meskhenet, Heqet, and Khnum,
'O may you go forth and make Ruddjedet give birth
to the three children who are in her womb,

9.25 who will perform the worthy office
in this entire land,
for they will build your temples, provision your altars,
make your libation-vessels flourish, and increase your divine
offerings!'
These Gods then proceeded,[49]

10.1 having taken the forms of musicians,
and Khnum was with Them carrying the baggage.
They then arrived at the house of Reusre,[50]
and They found him standing with his kilt upside down.
And They presented him with Their necklaces and sistra.
Then he said to Them, 'O my ladies!
Look, this is because a woman is suffering; her giving birth is
painful!'

Then They said, 'Let us see her! Look, we know about
    giving birth.' 10.5
Then he said to Them, 'Come in!'
They then entered before Ruddjedet.
Then They sealed the room with her and Them in it.[51]
Then Isis placed Herself before her, Nephthys behind her,
and Heqet was hastening the birth.
Then Isis said, 'May you not be powerful in her womb,[52]
in this your name of Userref!'
And this child slipped out onto Her arms,[53] 10.10
as a child of one cubit, with strong bones,
the appearance of whose limbs was gold,
whose head-cloth was true lapis lazuli.
And They washed him, when his navel cord had been cut,
and he was placed on a sheet as a pillow.
Then Meskhenet presented Herself to him.
Then She said, 'A king who will perform the kingship
in this entire land!'
⟨And⟩ Khnum made his limbs healthy.
And Isis placed Herself before her, Nephthys behind her, 10.15
and Heqet was hastening the birth.
And Isis said, 'May you not kick in her womb,[54]
in this your name of Sahure!'
And this child slipped out onto Her arms,
as a child of one cubit, with strong bones,
the appearance of whose limbs ⟨was gold⟩,
whose head-cloth was true lapis lazuli.
And They washed him, when his navel cord had been cut,
and he was placed on a sheet as a pillow. 10.20
Then Meskhenet presented Herself to him.
Then She said, 'A king who will perform the kingship
in this entire land!'
And Khnum made his limbs healthy.
And Isis placed Herself before her, Nephthys behind her,
and Heqet was hastening the birth.
And Isis said, 'May you not stay dark in her womb,[55]
in this your name of Keku!'
And this child slipped out onto Her arms, 10.25
as a child of one cubit, with strong bones,
the appearance of whose limbs was gold,

whose head-cloth was true lapis lazuli.
Then Meskhenet presented Herself to him.

11.1   Then She said, 'A king who will perform the kingship
in this entire land!'
And Khnum made his limbs healthy.
And They washed him, when his navel cord had been cut,[56]
and he was placed on a sheet as a pillow.
The Gods then went out,
having delivered Ruddjedet of the three children.

11.5   Then They said, 'Be glad, Reusre!
Look, three children are born to you!'
Then he said to Them 'My ladies!
What can I do for you?
Please give this ten gallons of grain to your porter[57]
and take it as a tip!'
And Khnum loaded Himself with the ten gallons of grain.

11.10   They then proceeded to where They had come from.
Then Isis said to the Gods,
'What did we come here for,
if we don't do a wonder for these children,
which we can report to their father who sent us here?'
Then They fashioned three lordly crowns (l.p.h.!).[58]
And They put them in the ten gallons of grain.
Then They made the sky change into wind and rain.

11.15   Then They turned back towards the house.
Then They said, 'Please put this ten gallons of grain
in a sealed room here,
until we return from making music ⟨in the⟩ north.'
Then They put the ten gallons of [grain] in a sealed room.
Then Ruddjedet became pure[59]
with the purification of fourteen days.

11.20   Then she said to her housemaid, 'Is the house made ready?'
Then she said, 'It's ready with every good thing,
except for the jars—they haven't been brought.'
Then Ruddjedet said, 'But why haven't the jars been
      brought?'
Then the housemaid said, 'There's absolutely nothing here to
      enhance them with,
except the musicians' ten gallons of grain,
and it's in a room under their seal.'

Then Ruddjedet said, 'Go down and bring it from there!   11.25
Then when Reusre returns he can give them[60]
repayment for it.'
The housemaid then went, and opened the room.   12.1
Then she heard in the room the noise of singing,
    music-making,
dancing, rejoicing,
and all that is done for a king.
She then went back.
And she repeated all she had heard to Ruddjedet.
And she went around the room, and she couldn't find where
    it was being made.[61]
Then she put her ear to the sack,
and she found that it was being made inside it.
Then she put ⟨it⟩ in a box,   12.5
which was placed inside another sealed container,
bound with leather;
she put it in the room
which contained her belongings, and she sealed it up.
Reusre then returned,[62]
coming from the water-meadow.
And Ruddjedet repeated this matter to him.
And he was exceedingly happy.
They then sat down and made holiday.

Now, some days after this,[63]
Ruddjedet quarrelled with the housemaid about something,   12.10
and she had her punished with a beating.
Then the housemaid said to the people in the household,
'Is this done—this, against me? She's born three kings—[64]
I'll go tell this
to the Majesty of the Dual King Cheops, the justified!'
She then went,
and she found her older close brother,
binding flax and yarn on the threshing floor.
Then he said to her, 'Where are you off to, little girl?'   12.15
And she repeated this matter to him.
Then her brother said to her,
'So doing what should be done means coming to me, and
    me joining in denunciations?'

Then he took a bundle of flax to her.
Then he gave her a nasty blow.
The housemaid then went
to get herself a handful of water.
Then a crocodile seized her.[65]
Her brother then went to tell this
12.20 to Ruddjedet,
and he found Ruddjedet sitting
bowed down in grief,
her mood exceedingly bad.[66]
Then he said to her, 'My lady,
why are you in this mood?'
Then she said, 'It's the little girl
who grew up in this house.
Look, but she's gone,
saying, "I'll go and denounce them!"'
Then he bent his head down.
Then he said, 'My lady,
she actually came to tell me [all that had happened],
12.25 so that she might go off together with me.
Then I gave her a nasty blow.
Then she went to draw
a little water for herself.
Then a crocodile seized her.'[67]
[. . . . .]

Notes

1. Eleven manuscript lines are lost from the first page—at least twenty verses. There
was probably also one other page before this (another fifty verses or so); see
Introduction (p. 102) for restoration. A first tale was told perhaps by Prince
Redjedef, who became the immediate successor of Cheops (c.2528–2520 BC).
Cheops himself (c.2551–2528 BC) was the second king of the Fourth Dynasty and
the builder of the Great Pyramid at Giza. He was later regarded as a tyrant
because of its overweening size, and the Tale presents him as an imperfect king.
Here he orders funerary offerings to be made in honour of the heroes of the tale
that he has just heard; the king gets far more than the magician, according to
court decorum. *Djoser* (c.2630–2611 BC) was the most famous king of the Third
Dynasty, about a century before Cheops and over eight centuries before the copy-
ing of P. Westcar. The *lector priest* or 'ritualist' was in charge of the sacred writ-
ings, and often appears in literature as a wise man or magician; *Imhotep*, the most
probable restoration, was a famous sage, and a historical high lector priest under
King Djoser.

2. *Chephren* was subsequently the fourth king of the Fourth Dynasty (*c.*2520–2494 BC), and builder of the second pyramid at Giza. He tells of a wonder under *Nebka* (*c.*2649–2630 BC) who was probably the predecessor of King Djoser, although the Tale implies that he was Djoser's successor; he is, like Djoser, a figure from the very start of the Old Kingdom. *Ptah* is the creator-god of Memphis, the capital of the Old Kingdom kings, near modern Cairo. *Life-of-the-Two-Lands* is a designation of the north-western area of Memphis; it alludes to the city's position at the meeting-point of Upper and Lower Egypt.

3. *Ubainer* is a fictional character, as are the subsequent wonder-workers.

4. While the wealthy Ubainer is away with the king performing a ritual, his wife commits adultery with a *commoner*, whom she seduces with a gift of *clothes*. Although Chephren's tale is very fragmentary, the main plot is clear.

5. Perhaps restore 'by her housemaid'?

6. i.e. for a post-coital bath.

7. Perhaps restore 'Ubainer became angry'?

8. Documents and chests are associated with magic throughout the Tale (see n. 41). The wax figure measures 13 cm; such figures were a common element in Egyptian magic. The *crocodile* is often an animal of death, especially as an agent of divine retribution. *Seven* is a magical number, and occurs throughout this tale (3.13, 3.15, 3.17).

9. *They* are the wife and her housemaid. *Making holiday* here includes having sex.

10. The crocodile is 3.65 m long. There is wordplay between *cubit* and *seize* (they are homophonous). The actions of the crocodile are realistic, as the reptile does kill its prey by drowning.

11. The king gives the death sentence, expressing it as giving the creature its due; a sense of decorum is maintained even in the face of fabulous events.

12. Fire is an attested means of execution, but in actual life adultery tended to be dealt with in a less extreme manner. Both of the adulterers end up in the water, a place often associated with the unburied dead.

13. For Cheops' response, see n. 1.

14. This prince is otherwise unknown, apart from a Middle Kingdom graffito with a list of royal names. Nevertheless he is perhaps a historical figure, possibly the prince of Cheops and vizier who is attested in Fourth Dynasty monuments as Horbaef. He provides a much more recent tale of wonder than his brothers. *Sneferu* was the father and predecessor of Cheops, and the first king of the Fourth Dynasty (*c.*2575–2551 BC). He also features in *The Words of Neferti* (*q.v.*) as a jovial 'good old king'.

15. Bauefre's opening remarks apparently concern the benefits conferred by the past, or perhaps the virtues of a tale from the more recent past. The *Royal House* and the *Great House* are terms for the king's palace.

16. It is likely that the tale here echoes the lost start of the whole Tale, and a contrast may have been intended between how the good king Sneferu dispelled his boredom and how Cheops attempts to.

17. Contrary to the usual practice, the change in speakers is not indicated, to suggest how quickly Sneferu replies. He elaborates on Djadjaemankh's suggestion with great glee and sumptuousness. The description of the court beauties evokes epithets of Hathor, the goddess of sexuality, implying that the expedition has a ritual aspect. Religious festivals, including Hathor's, involved rowing

expeditions. These parodic allusions to religious rites may make the incident more glorious or simply frivolous. *Nets* of beads were sometimes worn over dresses as jewellery, but Sneferu enthusiastically dispenses with the dresses, making the women near-nude.

18. *Catfish* amulets were common pieces of Middle Kingdom jewellery, and were worn from a braided plait of hair. They were perhaps amulets against drowning, suitable for rowers. *New turquoise* was especially valued, as turquoise was believed to discolour with age.

19. Perhaps restore: 'had [her put back at the oar and said to her]'. The frank informality of this exchange continues as the benevolent king addresses his sage in a merry, casual manner.

20. i.e. 6.3 m.

21. The tale ends with order restored and the court *making holiday*. The same activity was indulged in by the adulterous couple in the second tale (3.9–10 and n. 9), but to very different purpose; here it is a festival, not forbidden intercourse. Both tales involve water (cf. 4.6–7) and a figure of an animal (2.22–3).

22. For Cheops' response, see n. 1.

23. *Hordedef* was a historical prince, well known to the Middle Kingdom audience as the supposed author of a Teaching, and a famous sage (see p. 292); he did not succeed to the throne. His opening breaks the pattern of the previous tales, by implying that what is past is unreliable, and that one cannot be certain of the truthfulness of the other tales (cf. n. 15). His telling of a present wonder would be wittily ironic in such a historical setting for the actual Middle Kingdom audience. The way in which the wonder is introduced gives it a greater sense of the unknown than the other tales have.

24. Cheops' response further disrupts the pattern of an introduction followed by a narrative established in the other princes' speeches.

25. Hordedef's sage is no court ritualist; like many literary heroes he is a *commoner*. The contrast between the commoner and Cheops' court here prepares for the subsequent movement of the narrative away from the court. His rank also contrasts him with the adulterous *commoner* of the second tale (2.4–4.10). The name *Djedi* means the 'enduring one'—a positive quality. *Djed-Sneferu* ('Enduring is Sneferu') is a historical settlement linked to that king's pyramid at Maidum; the location associates Djedi with the good king Sneferu, under whose rule he will have spent much of his life, which amounts to the ideal age of 110. In this context, his being a *commoner* (literally 'little man') is a witty touch, as this word can also mean 'youth'. Djedi's diet, which is envisaged as his daily consumption, testifies to his keen appetite and his extraordinary health (a result of his virtue), and in itself makes him a wonderful figure.

26. The three wonders match in number the three previous tales of wonder. The first miraculous activity is quasi-divine, and is an act elsewhere associated with the creator-god. The next deed—dominance over wild animals—is symbolic of the containment of chaos, and recalls the animal magic of the second tale (2.22–4.7; also the fish-pendant of the third tale: 5.16–6.10). Although these wonders are potentially serious, they are presented primarily for the audience's entertainment.

27. The list of wonders concludes with an obscure reference to mysterious knowledge: *Thoth* is the god of wisdom and of judgement; his *Sanctuary* may be an

otherworldly, mythical place. The word for *Chambers* implies a private apartment. Hordedef may be claiming that Djedi knows how many chambers there are in the sanctuary, or *number* could mean 'measurements' or some other specifications. The word *Chambers*, however, could be used figuratively to mean small shrines. A royal search for the details of a particular divine image is a motif that is found in monumental inscriptions, which are parodied here. Whatever the meaning of this phrase (and the exact meaning may be irrelevant), the information is deliberately esoteric.

28. Cheops wishes to copy the chambers in his *Horizon*, i.e. his pyramid at Giza. Whereas Sneferu earlier roamed his palace for 'relief' (4.22–5.1), Cheops is seeking hidden knowledge.

29. This incidental echo of Sneferu's sumptuous oars (5.8–9) associates Djedi and Hordedef yet again with the good king; the materials also echo those of Ubainer's chest (2.21–2).

30. These serene and elegant activities (involving unguents) are shown being done to Vizier Ptahhotep II in his Sixth Dynasty tomb; they are the height of luxury, and an indication of Djedi's success.

31. Stately greetings compliment Djedi on both his youthful vigour and his extreme old age (the two are contrasted in a pair of threefold descriptions). *Sleeping until dawn* is a common description of the happy life of the virtuous. *Blessed one* is a term of respect often applied to the dead. The prince then makes two promises to Djedi, one for continuance of life, and one for its completion; the emphasis on food is pertinent for Djedi (see 7.2–4 and n. 25).

32. Literally 'In peace!' Djedi's greeting is elevated as befits a sage, and even more formal than the prince's. His four wishes repay Hordedef's promises twice over, and cover a wide spectrum. Two wishes refer to this life, the third is legalistic (but may have otherworldly reference), and the last refers to the otherworld: *He who Shrouds the Tired One* is the embalmer of the dead, and the *Portal* is one of the gateways in the underworld through which the dead must pass. Djedi, appropriately for an aged sage concerned with lasting wisdom, has one eye on eternity, and goes further than Hordedef in referring to the otherworld.

33. A striking gesture of respect from a prince to a commoner.

34. Djedi's *children* probably mean his pupils, who will assist him. Just as Djedi returned Hordedef's greetings by doubling them (see n. 32), so the prince gives him twice what he asked for. The two gentlemen are perfectly in accord.

35. Cheops earlier said he had metaphorically 'seen'—i.e. heard accounts of—the wonders told to him (1.16, 4.16–17, 6.21), but now he actually *sees* a wonderworker. His speech is, characteristically, an impatiently abrupt question.

36. Djedi's answer is respectful, but almost impertinently polite. The meeting contrasts sharply with the elegant and leisurely dialogue between him and the virtuous Hordedef (7.16–8.1), and the earlier ones between Sneferu, the maiden, and Djadjaemankh (5.20–6.7 and n. 19). It is already clear that the king will not get what he wants, but that this commoner will get the better of him.

37. Cheops peremptorily proceeds with the first of the promised wonders, which should be an act of restitution, not *injury*, as Cheops demands. The *Stronghold* is a place where people were confined, a sort of work camp, but although the victim of Cheops' entertainment is despicable, the king is clearly in the wrong, and Djedi directly contradicts his order with an evocative statement. The *noble*

flock is mankind, the 'flock of God' (*The Teaching for King Merikare*, 46a), and god *ordained* that mankind should be cared for. Djedi alludes to the idea of a king as the shepherd of mankind, and implies that Cheops should know better. He proceeds to satisfy Cheops' curiosity with a much smaller and less noble animal.

38. The *khetaa* is a larger type of goose, but is unidentified. Cheops proceeds to bring on bigger and better animals, but the slaughter is limited to animals, and not the 'noble flock'.

39. A problematic passage. It seems that, as the bull was decapitated, the *leash* fell on the ground, and remains there when the head is restored. On this reading, the promised miracle of making 'a lion walk with its leash behind it' (7.4–5) is not performed, and Cheops rushes impatiently to his chief concern. However, it is also possible that the copyist accidentally omitted the miracle of the lion, except for this concluding phrase (cf. the omission a few verses later: 9.5 and n. 42).

40. Djedi makes another negative reply to the king. His lack of knowledge about the *Chambers* (see n. 27)—which contradicts the prince's claim about his knowledge (7.5–6)—suggests that they must be extremely esoteric information.

41. As Cheops' impatience grows, the *Chambers* become more and more distant: now their number is hidden in a strange *flint* chest (as are books of magic in other tales). In funerary texts, chests are connected with the Sungod, who dominates the following episodes, as is flint (a fiery stone). *Sipti* means 'investigation', and the name may denote a room of inventories, although it may also allude to the 'investigation' of the soul after death. *Heliopolis* is the city sacred to the Sungod, and one with which *Thoth* too was associated. The whole description is deliberately obscure and evocative.

42. The copyist seems to have omitted a half verse and a whole verse here. As king, Cheops is nominally high priest of every temple, and so should have access to the room in Heliopolis. Either the author did not take this into account, or Cheops' inability (like his partial knowledge) is a sign of his failure to be an ideal king; Sneferu only needed a sage to tell him how to enjoy himself (4.22–5.13), but Cheops' failing is more serious in every respect.

43. Djedi's answer puts a conclusive stop to Cheops' questioning. *Sakhbu* was a cult centre of the Sungod *Re*, in the 2nd Lower Egyptian nome in the west Delta, near modern Zat el-Kom, *c.*40 km north-west of Memphis. *Ruddjedet*'s name recalls Djedi's, with its positive associations (see n. 25). The Sungod will have appeared to her in the form of her husband: subsequent events suggest she is unaware of her children's divine paternity. *The worthy office* is the kingship. *Great Seer* is the title of the High Priest of the Sungod in his city of *Heliopolis*; this office, which the eldest will hold before becoming king, gives him access to Sipti. In the Middle Kingdom the king's role as intermediary between men and gods was expressed both through his status as a sun-priest and through the title 'Son of Re'. Thus, the offices and parentage of the children imply that they are worthier to be king than Cheops is, and at this snub he falls into a sulk. The actual succession of the Fifth Dynasty is completely rewritten here in a folklore-like manner.

44. Djedi attempts to placate the king with a limited promise of the ideal pattern of filial succession. *Your son* is presumably Chephren (see n. 2), and *his son* is Mycerinus (*c.*2490–2472 BC), the builders of the second and third pyramids at Giza; the Tale passes over Cheops' immediate but short-lived actual successor

(Redjedef, see n. 1) and Mycerinus' (Shepseskaf). Cheops' response conspicuously ignores Djedi's reassurance (see n. 45).

45. There is no marker of a change in speaker, perhaps indicating Djedi's quick certainty. The *Season of Emergence* was when the fields were due to emerge from the Inundation—a season of creation, the Egyptian spring. There may have been some symbolism in the date, but it was probably chosen simply to cause Cheops difficulties reaching Sakhbu, and so advance the plot, since water is needed to cross *Two-Fish Canal*, which presumably lay south of Sakhbu, between it and the capital. Cheops addresses Djedi as *servant*, whereas the jovial Sneferu called his wonder-worker 'brother' (6.1). Cheops' response is probably disingenuous; after his peremptory behaviour with the earlier wonders, it seems likely that he has a specific and unworthy motive. This could be to take the chest for himself, but his attention seems to have shifted to the children: the narrative arouses in the audience suspicions that his journey is to ensure his own children's succession, or even perhaps to do away with the rival claimants to the throne. Whether such suspicions are justified would only have been answered in the missing final episodes of the Tale.

46. This promised wonder recalls Djadjaemankh's water-miracle during Sneferu's boating trip (6.7 13). Compared with the earlier wonder, Djedi will move a small amount of water—some two metres depth; this may suggest that Djedi's compliance is grudging. The earlier wonders are about to be surpassed by the divine birth.

47. The allowance is similar to the offerings bestowed on the dead kings (with *vegetables* instead of the ritual incense since Djedi is still alive (see 1.15 and n. 1)); it is in excess—roughly double—of even Djedi's lively appetite (7.2-4 (see n. 25)). Cheops acts in a proper manner here, and the endowment marks the end of this episode, but not necessarily the end of Djedi's role in the original complete Tale.

48. A narrative formula introduces a new stage in the Tale. The narrative moves from the imperfect court of Cheops to the divine court, ruled by the Sungod, the archetype of kingship (for *Sakhbu*, see n. 43). Re's announcement confirms Djedi's prophecies. *Isis* and *Nephthys* are the mother and aunt of the royal god Horus; *Meskhenet* is a goddess of birth and destiny; *Heqet* is a goddess of the primordial creation and birth; and *Khnum* is the creator-god who models human bodies in the womb. The gods are encouraged through reciprocity, a fundamental principle of virtue and piety: they should help the children as they will be pious kings. Their piety may contrast them with Cheops, whom much later Classical accounts describe as impious.

49. The goddesses' disguise as singing- and dancing-girls recalls the court beauties *en travesti* of the third tale (5.9-13).

50. *Reusre* ('Re-is-powerful') is a fitting name for a priest of Re. His disordered *kilt* is probably an indication that he is distraught, but it may allude to an act of sympathetic magic, in which undoing knots was supposed to ease giving birth. The *necklaces* and *sistra* are pieces of jewellery and musical instruments that are appropriate for goddesses in disguise: they would be carried by temple dancers in rituals, but were also worn by the goddesses in whose honour such rituals were performed. Thus presenting Reusre with these regalia is a greeting with a ritual aspect (cf. *The Tale of Sinuhe*, B 268-70 and n. 73).

51. Although childbirth was an exclusively female concern, the secrecy surrounding it here is probably due to the importance of the children. The description of the births is highly repetitive (still more so than elsewhere), which may be appropriate for these stately, ritual actions. The episode alludes to representations of the birth of the king at the hands of the gods, which are attested on temple walls only from later periods, but which probably already existed in the Middle Kingdom.

52. Egyptian birth names are often a wish, or have a meaning connected with the mother's experience of birth. Here folk etymologies are accordingly invented for the names of the actual kings, in the form of wishes for them to come peaceably out of Ruddjedet's womb. The first son's name recalls that of his earthly father, *Reusre* (see n. 50). To *be powerful* in Egyptian is *user*; the first king of the Fifth Dynasty was actually named Userkaf, meaning 'His spirit is powerful' (c.2465–2458 BC). The Tale treats the historical kings' names rather freely.

53. The children are 52 cm tall, rather large by natural standards. They are described, as befits their god-like status, as divine images, gilded and inlaid; the word *appearance* is synonymous with the word for the king's titulary; the *headcloth* was a royal headdress.

54. To *kick* in Egyptian is *sah*. Sahure was the second king of the Fifth Dynasty (c.2458–2446 BC)—a name that may mean 'One close to Re'.

55. To *stay dark* (i.e. to stay hidden in the womb) is in Egyptian *kek*. The third king of the Fifth Dynasty was Neferirkare Kakai (c.2446–2426 BC).

56. This difference in the order of events of the third birth is presumably a slip of the copyist.

57. *Tip* is literally 'the price of beer' (i.e. 'pour-boire'); Egyptian beer was made from partly baked bread (see n. 59). The tip is very generous; drunkenness often accompanied religious ceremonies as well as dances, so the tip is more appropriate than Reusre realizes.

58. The regal *crowns* are the specific wonder of this episode, whose general atmosphere is more marvellous than that of the preceding ones; the crowns are also necessary for the plot to continue, as they reveal the children's destiny to their mother, and thus indirectly provoke the next episode. The *rain* is created to prevent the transporting of the grain, and thus to give the gods an excuse to return.

59. A period of *purification* after giving birth. The making *ready* of the house and the mention of a *housemaid* recall the adulterous celebrations of the second tale (3.6–9). The grain will *enhance* the jars by being made into beer to fill them.

60. Ruddjedet is characterized as a dutiful wife who acts responsibly with the grain while her husband is away, but she breaks the goddesses' seal, and her plan to replace the grain later is less than ideal (to judge from the dissatisfaction at a similar repayment in 5.23–4): the divine children are born into an imperfect world, where there are family shortages and squabbling.

61. Her going *around* recalls Sneferu's search for pleasure (4.22, 25). The *box* recalls the mysterious chest in Heliopolis (9.4–5 and n. 41), and another mentioned earlier (2.21–2).

62. The mention of a pastoral landscape prepares for the couple's *holiday* mood. The episode recalls the couple of the second tale, whose holiday was, in contrast, adulterous (3.9–10 and n. 9), as well as the end of the third tale (6.13–14 and n. 21).

63. A new incident begins here (cf. n. 48). There is nothing unsympathetic in Ruddjedet's action: beatings were part of a servant's lot. Any doubts about this are dispelled by the girl's subsequent actions, for which she is beaten by her own brother (12.16–17). Nevertheless, the world of the Tale is becoming increasingly fraught and 'everyday'.

64. The maid sees a chance to cause trouble and revenge herself. The incident reminds the audience of Cheops' ambivalent intentions. The existence of more than one claimant to the throne was always a potential source of conflict, and the audience would assume that Ruddjedet wanted to keep her children secret from Cheops.

65. The housemaid is now punished by more potent forces than her brother. The *crocodile* recalls that of the second tale (2.22–4.7 and n. 8); here it is not of wax and the work of a man, but a real reptile, presumably an agent of vengeance from Re.

66. The phrase was earlier used of Cheops (9.12); this echo may contrast the wicked Cheops and the dutiful Ruddjedet, or may instead suggest that she is, like him, not perfect.

67. This is the end of the final surviving written page on the back of the roll; following it there is no lacuna, only a blank surface. The present incident ends conclusively here, but this is unlikely to be the end of the whole Tale, as Cheops has announced his wish to visit Sakhebu, with unstated intent. Either the papyrus was an incomplete copy or the rest of the Tale was erased from the papyrus; it is probable that there was at least one other page to the original Tale.

DISCOURSES

DISCOURSES

5

The Words of Neferti

Introduction

The Words of Neferti is a prophecy spoken by an Old Kingdom sage named Neferti. The poem opens with a simple narrative, similar to that of *The Tale of King Cheops' Court*. King Sneferu (c.2575–2551 BC) asks for entertainment in a jolly manner, his boredom leading to a spontaneous disruption of etiquette. His courtiers offer a provincial but learned priest, an individual who has earned his position by his merit. The poem was probably composed when written literature was a recent phenomenon and, perhaps significantly, deals with textualizing an oral performance: Sneferu himself writes down Neferti's speech. Although this setting is obviously fictional, it is the closest we can come to a description of the actual social context of literature in the Middle Kingdom, and the rank of the sage may well reflect, in some way, that of the actual authors.

When Neferti is introduced to the court, he asks the king what he wants, and then provides not the royal eulogy that is characteristic of such courtly settings, but a doom-laden prophecy addressed to his own heart. There is a sharp contrast between the tone and style of the two sections of the poem. The first half is relatively light-hearted, composed in simple language, in long, episodic, and repetitive stanzas with a high proportion of dialogue. The prophecy itself is in a more elaborate style, and in short stanzas. It is a tightly organized complaint about the vicissitudes of life, that interweaves various signs of chaos, such as invasion, geographical confusion, and social unrest. These are all features that occur in official descriptions of the interregnum, and they would have been topical concerns at the probable time of composition, which seems to have been soon after the troubled start of the Twelfth Dynasty (as is revealed later in the poem). The Discourse is, however, essentially a reflective text which mourns for the loss of culture, wisdom, and virtue. Such pessimistic meditations are an important genre of

Middle Kingdom literature, and their form suggests that they developed from funeral elegies.

The prologue makes it clear that Neferti is speaking a prophecy, but he presents his complaint as an immediate reality. The lament is expressed with dualities, as is much in Egyptian thought: chaos versus order, anarchy versus authority, foreigners versus Egypt, social upheaval versus the established hierarchy (in which the rise of the poor is a sign of social anarchy and a usurpation of positions of authority). The 'inventories' of woe embrace both the general and the particular. Neferti portrays himself as an isolated wise man who is alone in perceiving the state of the land in which all order and wisdom (including proper speech) has perished.

Cosmic, social, and personal chaos are interwoven, and various phrases recur, like refrains, scattered across the stanzas. A sense of continuity is also provided by the repetition of words from the end of one stanza at the beginning of the next. Despite this pattern of thematic complexity, the style is consistently and elegantly antithetical, and generalizing. In its use of repeated motifs, images, and individual words, the style is similar to that of the petitions of *The Tale of the Eloquent Peasant*, but without the dramatic aspect of that poem.

The sage's questioning lament ends with a description of Egypt as a godless land, prey to murder. His despair then vanishes, as he suddenly turns to prophesy the quasi-miraculous appearance of an ideal king, who will redeem the chaos, banish enemies, and set all to right. In this final part, there are strong eulogistic elements which suit the courtly setting of the whole; the style is here more regular and formal, and less flowing than in the lament. In official texts, court eulogies acclaim and commemorate their royal audience by name; this one, however, acclaims not Sneferu, but a future king called Ameny, 'the Hidden one'. The specific detail of 'The Walls of the Ruler' suggests that he represents the founder of the Twelfth Dynasty, Amenemhat, who is elsewhere described as the builder of this fortress. It is as if the history of the period between the Fourth Dynasty and the Twelfth is rewritten as a giant interregnum between two ideal kings, Sneferu and Amenemhat. The composition of the whole poem has thus been attributed to the reign of Amenemhat I, and it does have evident propagandistic elements; the new king may have needed validation, since he was of non-royal descent and may have come to power in a palace *coup*. The prominent concern with the north-east may reflect actual political problems of the period, since the capital moved to the north at that date. The general significance of the poem is, however, not limited by its historical inspiration.

The prophecy ends by foretelling how the contemporaneous audience will pay homage to the sage: the poem is guaranteed, both in textual terms and in its obviously fictional claim to be an ancient prophecy, by the royal authority of the person who transcribes it. The lament is given supreme state authority and accommodated within the orderly decorum of Sneferu's court: the chaos is confined by the agent of its recording and the setting in a golden age, as well as by the explicit resolution of the prophecy. This containment is enacted in the narrative prologue, where Sneferu's act of transcribing the poetry brings disorder under the king's hand. Nevertheless, the chaos is described much more extensively than the resolution, in nine stanzas—a number symbolic of multiplicity. It escapes confinement by being indefinite in its historical placement somewhere between Sneferu and 'Ameny', and by Neferti's being unspecific in his foretelling.

The state of the land and its regeneration is described without drawing any directly didactic moral. The poem provides a reflection on the nature of order and chaos which extols the virtue of authority, but in which the portrayal of the dark side of life predominates. It is notable that a king could consider such a searing and dark lament as 'entertainment', and the poet's art has a central role in this; it makes the 'undone' chaos into something 'perfect', and the imperfection of life and history becomes a source of aesthetic pleasure.

There are many Ramesside partial copies of the work, but the most complete manuscript is P. St Petersburg 1116B from the Eighteenth Dynasty. Numbers give section numbers of Wolgang Helck's edition (letters indicate the lines of these sections); the line numbers of P. St Petersburg 1116B are given in parentheses.

The Words of Neferti

1 (P 1) Now, there was once a time when the Majesty of the Dual
          King Sneferu, the justified,[1]
was the worthy king of this entire land.
On one of those days
the Council of the Residence entered
into the Great House (l.p.h.!) to pay their respects.
They then went out, having paid their respects,[2]
as was their daily custom.
And his Majesty (l.p.h.!) said to the functionary who was
          beside him,
'Go bring me the Council of the Residence,
who have just left here from today's respects!'
And they were ushered in to him immediately.
And they were once again prostrate
in front of his Majesty (l.p.h.!).
And his Majesty (l.p.h.!) said to them, 'Lads![3]
Look, I've had you called to make you seek me out
a son of yours who is a man of understanding,
a brother of yours who is a clever man,
a friend of yours who can achieve a perfect deed,
who will tell me a few perfect words,
choice verses,
which my Majesty will be entertained to hear.'
And they once again prostrated themselves,
in front of his Majesty (l.p.h.!).

2 (P 9) And they said unto his Majesty (l.p.h.!),
'Bastet has a chief lector priest,[4]
sovereign, our lord,
called Neferti.
He is a strong armed commoner,[5]
a scribe with clever fingers.
He is a wealthy man, who has greater riches than any of his
          equals.
O let him be brought for your Majesty to see!'
And his Majesty (l.p.h.!) said, 'Go bring him to me!'
And he was ushered in to him immediately.
And he was prostrate in front of his Majesty (l.p.h.!).

And his Majesty (l.p.h.!) said, 'Come now,[6]
Neferti, my friend,
and tell me a few perfect words,
choice verses,
which my Majesty will be entertained to hear!'
And the lector priest Neferti said,
'Of what has happened, or of what will happen,
sovereign, my lord?'
And his Majesty (l.p.h.!) said, 'But of what will happen,[7]
for today happens and then it is passed by!'
Then he stretched his hand out to a box of writing
    equipment.
Then he took for himself a roll and a palette.
And he was writing down
what the lector priest Neferti said.
He was a sage of the East;[8]
he belonged to Bastet in her Orient.
He was a child of the Heliopolitan nome.

He ponders the happenings in the land.[9]   3 (P 17)
He recalls the sad state of the East,
the Asiatics journeying in their strength,
terrorizing the hearts of the harvesters,
and seizing the cattle from ploughing.
He says, 'Stir, my heart,[10]
and beweep this land, in which you began,
for silence is what overwhelms!
Look, what should be denounced will be respected,
and look, the official will be laid low in the land!

Do not tire! Look, this is in front of you![11]   4 (P 21)
May you attend to what is before you!
Look, there will be no officials in the affairs of the land,
and what is done will be what is undone.
May the Sungod begin to recreate!
For the land has been ruined entirely, no remnant exists.
Not even the total of one fingernail will survive its fate.

Destroyed is this land, and no one cares about it,[12]   5 (P 24)
no one speaks out, no one sheds tears.
What is this land like?
For the sun is covered, and will not shine for folk to see.

They will not stay alive, when clouds cover.
And everyone will be numb for lack of it.
I will say what is in front of me; I prophesy nothing that
    will not come.

6 (P 26) And the river of Egypt is dry,[13]
so that water is crossed on foot;
water will be sought for ships to sail on,
for its course has become a sandbank.
The bank will be a flood,
and the water's place will be what was once the bank's.
The south wind will oppose the north wind;[14]
there is no sky with a single wind.
An alien bird will breed
in the lagoons of the Delta,
having made its nest upon its neighbours,
and the people will have to approach it through want.

7 (P 30) Destroyed indeed are those things of happiness—the
        fishpools,[15]
which were full of people gutting fish,
which overflowed full of fish and fowl;
all happiness has fled, and the land is laid low with pain,
by those feeding Syrians who go throughout the land.
Enemies have arisen in the East!
Asiatics have come down to Egypt;
a secure stronghold is lacking: someone else is close by
        without the guards hearing;[16]
a ladder will be waited for in the night,
the stronghold will be entered,
and slumber in the eyes will be swept away
just as the sleeper says, "I am awake!"

8 (P 35) And the flock of the foreign countries will drink[17]
at the river of Egypt.
They will cool themselves on their banks,
lacking anything to make them fearful.
This land will go to and fro;
the consequence is unknown, and what will happen is
        hidden,
like the saying, "See how the hearer is deaf!

The mute takes the lead!"
I shall show you the land in catastrophe,[18]
what should not happen, happening:
arms of war will be taken up,
and the land will live by uproar.

Arms will be made out of copper;[19]   9 (P 40)
bread will be asked for with blood;
a sick man will be laughed at out loud;
death will not be wept at;
the night will not be spent fasting for death,
for a man's heart is concerned only with himself.
Mourning will not be done today,
for the heart has turned away from it entirely.
A man will sit and bow his back
while one person is killing another.
I shall show you a son as a foe,
a brother as an enemy,
a man killing his own father.

Every mouth is full of "I want!",[20]   10 (P 45)
all goodness has fled.
The land is ruined, though laws are decreed against it,
for destruction is what is done,
and loss is what is found,
and what is done is what is undone:
a man's belongings have been taken from him, and given
        to someone who was an outsider.
I shall show you the lord in sorrow,
and the outsider at peace,
the man who did nothing, helping himself,
and the man who did something, in want.
With hatred, they will give something
only to silence a mouth that speaks,
and answer a phrase with an arm thrusting a stick,
and speak back by killing.

To the heart, spoken words seem like fire;[21]   11 (P 49)
what comes from the mouth cannot be endured.
Shrunk is the land—many its controllers.
It is bare—its taxes are great.

Little is the grain—large is the measure,
and it is poured out in rising amounts.
The Sungod separates Himself from mankind.[22]
He will rise when it is time,
but no one knows when midday occurs, no one can
     distinguish His shadow.
No one's face is bright when He is glimpsed;
no one's eyes are moist with water.
He is in the sky, but like the moon.
His times of nightfall will not stray,
but His rays on the face
are now a thing of the past.

12 (P 54)   I shall show you the land in calamity,[23]
the weak man as the lord of force,
and he who did the greeting greeted.
I shall show you the lowermost uppermost,
the man who followed after, now the man leading a
     generation.
They will live in the necropolis.
The wretched will make riches;
the great will [beg] to exist.
Only the poor will eat bread,
while forced labourers are exultant.
The land will have no Heliopolitan nome,
the birthplace of every God.

13 (P 57)   In fact, a king from the south will come,[24]
called Ameny.
He is the son of a woman of Bowland;
he is a child of Southern Egypt.
He will take the White Crown; he will uplift the Red
     Crown.[25]
He will unite the Two Powers; he will appease the Two
     Lords with what they wish,
with the Field-encircler grasped,
and the Oar in motion.

14 (P 61)   The people of his time will be joyful,[26]
and the gentleman will make his name,
for eternity and all time!

Those who fall into evil and those who plot rebellion
have felled their own speech for fear of him.
Asiatics will fall to his slaughtering,
and Libyans will fall to his flame.
Rebels belong to his rage,
and malcontents to his awesomeness.
The uraeus which is on his forehead
now quietens the malcontents for him.

And The Walls of the Ruler will be built.[27]   15 (P 66)
There will be no letting Asiatics come down to Egypt,
so they will ask for water as suppliants do, to let their
     flocks drink.
Truth will return to its proper place,[28]
with Chaos driven outside.
He who will witness, and who will follow the king, will be
     joyful![29]
The sage will pour an offering of water for me,
when he sees that what I have said has come about.'

So it ends, from start to finish,
as found in writing.

Notes

1. The poem opens as a simple tale. *Sneferu* was the first king of the Fourth Dynasty
   (c.2575–2551 BC). He also features in *The Tale of King Cheops' Court* (q.v., n. 14)
   as a jolly monarch.
2. This morning levée was an occasion for the Vizier to report to the king about the
   state of the kingdom. The *functionary* (literally 'sealer') is an attendant to do with
   palace business, in waiting on the king.
3. The king has already broken the stately pattern of daily custom, by recalling the
   council (anticipating the more drastic changes to come), and he now goes fur-
   ther in adopting a lively tone in describing his whim (*Lads*). There is a sharp con-
   trast between this and the formality of the court which demands that all *prostrate*
   themselves before him. His speech, nevertheless, retains a certain grandeur in its
   threefold pattern, and in its references to high ethical qualities: *clever, perfect,* and
   choice wisdom.
4. *Bastet* is the feline goddess of Bubastis, a city of the eastern Delta. She is a pro-
   tectress of Egypt's borders (a feature relevant to what follows). For the role of the
   lector priest, see *The Tale of King Cheops' Court*, n. 1. *Neferti* is a fictional charac-
   ter, whose name is carefully chosen: *nefer* means 'perfect' and is an element com-
   mon to the names *Neferti* and *Sneferu*, as well as the phrase 'perfect speech';
   Sneferu is literally 'He who makes perfect' the 'perfect' words of the 'perfect' sage
   (which will describe the loss and regaining of perfection (7c)). King, sage, and
   poetry are well matched.

5. The courtiers reply to the king's threefold request with a threefold description. Like many literary protagonists Neferti is a free *commoner*, and his wealth is a tangible result of his wisdom. *With clever fingers* is a standard epithet for scribes (see *The Tale of the Shipwrecked Sailor*, n. 31).

6. Although the king's address to his obedient subject is still strikingly chatty, it is a little less informal than his address to the courtiers (1j and n. 3), as is appropriate. The commoner answers back with a question.

7. As Egyptian texts generally pay respect to yesterday, the king's remark is slightly flippant, although it has a charming irony, given that Sneferu's past fame is being recounted to the audience. His *writing-down* of Neferti's speech is startlingly informal and a great favour (in funerary texts the king aspires to be the scribe of the gods); this shows his joviality, as well as the respect that is due to the poem: a famous king guarantees its textual transmission, and this stresses the truth and importance of what Neferti says. The scene acts out the wordplay on *nefer* (see n. 4).

8. No title introduces the following discourse, but a prelude describes what is to ensue. The description of the sage is once again threefold (see n. 5), and emphasizes that Neferti comes from the *East* (already implied in 2b, see n. 4). The province of *Heliopolis*, the city of the Sungod, was at the eastern apex of the Delta (see also n. 23).

9. After the threefold description of the sage (see n. 8), the description of his thoughts goes beyond this numerical pattern with a sequence of five verses, in which his speech is characterized as a reflective lament. The *East* was vulnerable to invasion from the *Asiatics*, who represent the chaos that always threatened the state.

10. The sage addresses his heart, not the king. Past, present, and future are combined as he speaks in a visionary present tense about the future of the land in which he *began*: his meditation is of timeless veracity. He urges his heart to react, since *silence* in the face of evil is reprehensible—a common theme in Egyptian laments; there is a play between the water of weeping and the *overwhelming* flood of evil. The final couplet provides a précis of the following prophecy, in which order is reversed and authority is destroyed. The prime importance of authority is a constant theme, and the consequences of its absence are developed in the next stanza.

11. The prophecy proper opens with another injunction to his heart to respond. 'Tiredness of heart' is a euphemism for the despair of death. The sage describes the future as an immediate visionary present (cf. 5f). The chaotic state of the *land*—an often repeated word in the poem—is expressed in antithetical statements, which show the breadth of Neferti's concern, ranging from the *Sun* to a *fingernail*. The following stanzas present a vision that covers the social (*officials*), environmental (*the land*), and cosmic (*Sungod*) disruption mentioned here. There is an implied rebuke to the creator-god: his creation is so flawed that he should *recreate* it. This wish will be answered in the final stanzas (13a–15g, esp. 15e).

12. *Destroyed* is a word that acts as a sort of refrain, as does the phrase 'I shall show you': like the various thematic motifs, these elements counterpoint the stanza divisions, and so create complex, superficially chaotic patterns. One sign of the world's ruin is the lack of any response to, or *care* about, evil, such as is expressed by Neferti. The world is indescribable, and left darkling by the *sun's* invisibility. The stanza ends with an assurance that his description of this inexpressible horror is true.

13. After the absence of light, this stanza describes the absence of other basic necessities for life: *water* and (calm) air. In the first half of the stanza, drought leads to an almost apocalyptic description of terrestrial mutability, reversing the basic

elements of the Egyptian landscape, land and river. Here there is a *flood*, although the river was *dry* earlier (6a)—chaos is formulated in increasingly antithetical and contradictory expressions.

14. In the second half of the stanza, the confusion of *winds* allows the invasion of *alien birds*, a metaphor for the foreigners mentioned earlier (3c). This image introduces the motif of 'invasion', which is central to the Egyptian concept of chaos, and brings out the foreigners' symbolic aspect as wild and bestial representatives of chaos. The *people* are Egyptians, who are forced to beg from this cuckoo race.

15. This stanza develops the animal motif and the marsh setting of the previous stanza, but provides a more vivid description of the invasion, contrasting past pleasures with present dangers. *Fishing* and *fowling* are not just recreational activities or means of hunting food, but are symbolic of the destruction of chaos; past feeding is contrasted with present predators. The numerically central couplet of the stanza (7c) curtly summarizes the problem of invasion: the *enemies* from the *East*.

16. In the second half of the stanza, invasion is expressed in vivid detail as a surreptitious military attack on an insecure *stronghold*. All is phrased in passive terms, with sinister effect, and the description is ominously left hanging, as the half-awake guards are brutally woken. (The passage implies the guards are negligent).

17. Invasion is now represented with desert animals which are symbols of chaos, like fowl (see n. 14). Literally they are the flocks of the invaders driven to the Nile by drought, but metaphorically they are the invaders themselves (as opposed to the Egyptians, who are often described as 'the flock of God' (cf. *The Teaching for King Merikare*, 46a and n. 50)). This description contradicts what was said earlier about the *river of Egypt* (cf. 6a and n. 13), and the following triplet describes the confusion of this self-contradictory world. All authority is reversed; the stanza moves from geophysical change to governmental anarchy (*hearer* can mean 'judge').

18. The refrain *I shall show you* begins a series of verses about internal troubles without any reference to the invaders; social responsibility disintegrates into conflict. The verses are full of strong reversals and antitheses.

19. In this stanza the prophecy of uproar is exemplified with specific human examples (as in 7f-i and n. 16). The *copper* was presumably meant for other peaceable purposes. These conflicts lead into descriptions of how funeral rites are disregarded; this is a sign not only of personal selfishness, but also of impiety, and a break with the past. The stanza moves from war to death and murder (which is greeted with gestures of respect), and climaxes in a savage reversal of how familial funerary rites should be. This is the ultimate expression of society's disintegration.

20. This stanza begins and ends with selfishness as expressed in speech and hostile reactions to it. *Ruin* is described in personal terms, with abstract generalizing descriptions and with specific examples—a full range of descriptive possibilities. Antithetical expressions predominate, and there are echoes of earlier passages (the second verse echoes 7c exactly—'goodness' and 'happiness' are homonymous—and *what is done* . . . echoes 4c). In the final four verses communication breaks down in the chaos, and wisdom is rejected. Like the previous stanza, this one ends with a death (cf. 9f), as communication is replaced by violence.

21. The loss of communication continues from the previous stanza. This stanza moves from a personal sense of loss, through social collapse (excessive *taxes* and loss of *grain*, the basic foodstuff), to a cosmic level.

22. Wordplay with *rising* links these verses to the preceding one (11c). The lack of

the sun (cf. 5c) is now not simply on a physical level. This verse alludes to the belief that, after the creation, mankind became so rebellious that the creator-god withdrew from the world. The imperfection of the sundered cosmos is re-enacted by the sun's virtual eclipse, which may presage the end of the cosmos. Time (*midday*) and space (*shadow*) dissolve. The lack of tears (*moisture*) is because there is no dazzling sun, and echoes the earlier lack of pious weeping (9b). The cosmic lack of the sun, and the chaotic fact that it looks like the *moon*, are presented as individual experiences—all is bound together in chaos. Neferti returns to the loss of yesterday's happiness (as in 7a–b).

23. The refrain *I shall show you* now introduces a concluding description of the reversals in society, in which authority is supplanted by anarchy and the wealthy by the poor. This death-in-life is epitomized by having to live in the cemeteries. *Heliopolis* is relevant as being part of the invaded east (Neferti's home (2r–s and n. 8)) and the city sacred to the Sungod, who has abandoned the world; this last couplet is a grand climax, as the environmental catastrophe renders Egypt a godless and unprotected land.

24. *In fact* announces a new sudden turn of events. *Ameny* is an abbreviation of the royal name Amenemhat; it also means 'He who is hidden'. The king is thus also the 'hidden' god who withdrew from mankind (see n. 22) now made manifest. The contrast between the chaos and the redeemer is pointed by the geographical contrast between the northern Heliopolis of the preceding stanza (12g) and the *southern* king, and between the child of the north-east, Neferti (2r–s), and this royal child of the south. The origin of the king is developed in the following verses: *Bowland* is the name of the southernmost nome of Egypt, and can also be a name for the whole far south of Upper Egypt; *Southern Egypt* refers to the seven southern nomes (it is literally the 'Interior of Hieraconpolis', the capital of the 3rd Upper Egyptian nome and a city associated with kingship from the earliest periods). In Egyptian orientation, the south took precedence over the north. The reference to the king's southern mother also develops the motif of the divine as something distant with an allusion to the myth (the 'Distant Goddess') in which the creator's daughter withdrew from Egypt into the far south and had to be lured back for order to be restored.

25. The second half of the stanza describes the redeemer's triumphant assumption of the kingship. The *White* and *Red crowns* are the crowns of Upper and Lower Egypt respectively. The pair, fused as the double crown, are known as the *Two Powers* and are associated with the *Two Lords*, the antithetical gods Horus and Seth, who share Egypt between them. The union of these represents the order of the whole land, and the reconciliation of discordant elements. The accession to the throne seems to have included a ritual run (the *motion*) by which the king symbolically encircled his domain. During this he carried two ritual objects, an *Oar* (symbol of government) and another piece of nautical steering equipment, here apparently called, from this ritual, the *Field-encircler*. The stanza describes the political unity of the whole land in an ancient and stately ritual, with the blessing and presence of the gods.

26. After the king's assumption of the throne, this stanza reaffirms the social status quo in perpetuity, in general (*people*) and individual terms (*gentleman*). A couplet then dismisses the internal evil of *rebellion*, and the distortion of communication (rebellious *speech*). Before the king, evil is no longer dominant but self-defeating. Another couplet turns to the enemies of the east (*Asiatics*) and west (*Libyans*). His *flame* comes from the fiery *uraeus*, which is part of the royal and divine diadem (mentioned in 13c–d). The concluding quatrain dispatches both internal and external disruption. This re-enacts on a terrestrial level the Sungod's destruction of rebellious mankind as he withdrew from the world (see n. 22).

27. The final stanza presents the negation of chaos both in specific and in universal terms. *The Walls of the Ruler* was a fortress on the eastern border, near the present Suez canal, built by Amenemhat I (see *The Tale of Sinuhe*, B 17 and n. 11). All Egypt is now a secure walled enclosure, in contrast to the earlier lack of a secure stronghold (7f–i). This leads to a final reprise of the motif of invasion by *Asiatics* and foreign animals.

28. A central couplet presents the restoration in abstract terms. The phrase is typical of royal eulogies, like much of the final three stanzas.

29. This verse echoes 14a. The restoration is a personal and social triumph for those who witness it, and Neferti concludes by describing his own standing with distant posterity, at the hands of those who will witness his prophecy. The *water offerings* are libations poured by the poem's audience, who are made *sage* by hearing it, in memory of the author; unlike the foreigners (15b–d) Neferti will have no need to beg for water. The poem's prophecy of its reception by its audience provides a conclusion to the framing narrative about how the poem was commissioned; no epilogue is needed to the poet's meditation.

6

The Words of Khakheperreseneb

Introduction

The Words of Khakheperreseneb is a reflective monologue spoken by a priest to his own unresponsive heart. The sage expresses his personal despair at the world's suffering. He begins by lamenting his inability to express the catastrophe, in a rhetorically self-referential introduction about the problems of speech. The failure of communication runs through other literary laments as well as this one, and here the sage stresses the need to find fresh expressions to surpass the language of his predecessors, which was not designed to confront the unsurpassed chaos of his present time. He expresses a desire for literary invention, not innovation, and shows no signs of dissatisfaction with the established literary style, to which the poem conforms. He is a self-tortured writer, troubled by poetry's difficulties in expressing the otherwise inexpressible.

The Words is similar to Neferti's colloquy about the state of the land, but is concerned with Khakheperreseneb's personal experience of present reality, and with the alienation of a wise man in a collapsing world. The self-referential prologue introduces stanzas describing the lamentable state of the land; these are phrased in general universal terms, without particular social examples. The inability of past speech to express the sage's present agony takes on a new dimension, as he laments that evil is so pervasive that the past is no longer a model that can be imitated. The verses give an impression of introverted longing and desperation, as the sage struggles to comprehend the daily misery of life; the tortuous wordplay with 'speak' enacts the difficulties of speech. The style is dense, interwoven, and allusive.

Khakheperreseneb's inner suffering surpasses the suffering of the external world, and, as in The Tale of the Eloquent Peasant, it remains ambiguous whether the cause of his agony is external and objectively observed or is internal and subjective. The name of the sage (see n. 1) may indicate that the words were imagined as being spoken in the settled era of the Twelfth Dynasty, when there would be little specific external cause for his despair, and his complaint is made not to an external figure of authority who could be accused of being responsible, but to his own heart. The sage moves from the difficulties of speaking to the problems of his speech's being received by his heart. He keeps returning to his heart, suggesting increasingly that it is the failure in communication between him and his innermost being that is the source of his distress. His inability to control his own emotions (his heart) is an analogue of man's inability to understand the general imperfection of the world. He laments that people cannot accept the truth, and implies that if he could communicate with his heart, despair would vanish, and it would then be possible for him to come to terms with his misery. Various Middle Kingdom texts present the heart as the source of a persons's suffering, and in a broader context mankind's hearts were the source of conflict in the world.

The sage's aim in speaking is to formulate his agony so that it will gain his heart's sympathy: poetry is a means of reconciling oneself with incomprehensible suffering and with the uncertainty of life. The principal manuscript has no trace of any response by the heart, but the man's final words seem to imply a more hopeful situation, in which the heart will sustain the sage.

The sage's name shows that the composition cannot predate Senwosret II (c.1844–1837 BC); a date has been suggested in the late Twelfth or early Thirteenth Dynasty.

The composition is principally known from a writing board from c.1500 BC (British Museum, EA 5645), which may not be a complete copy, although the extant text seems to form a coherent progression. The front of the board is a writing exercise made up of sections of four to five lines, which may represent stanzas of a complete text or excerpts from a longer one, and the back contains a single slightly longer passage. Part of the poem is also known from an ostracon. Numbers give line numbers of the recto and verso (rt. and vs.) of the writing board.

The Words of Khakheperreseneb

rt. 1   The collection of words, the gathering of verses,[1]
the seeking of utterances with heart-searching,
made by the priest of Heliopolis,
Seni's son Khakheperreseneb,
called Ankhu.
He says, 'If only I had unknown utterances[2]
and extraordinary verses,
in a new language that does not pass away,
free from repetition,
without a verse of worn-out speech
spoken by the ancestors!
I shall wring my body for what is in it,
—a release of all my speech.
For what is already said can only be repeated;
what is said once has been said;
this is no vain boast of the ancients' speech
that those who are later should find it good.

rt. 5   No speaker has spoken yet—may one who will speak
                now speak[3]
and another find what he will speak good!
No one has spoken yet for a matter spoken afterwards,
as they have done long before.
Here is no speaking what is only planned to be said:
this is searching after ruin, this is falsehood—
there is none who will remember his name to others!
I have said these things as I have seen them;[4]
from the first generation until those who come after,
they are now like what has passed away.
If only I knew what was unknown to others,
what is still unrepeated![5]
I would speak this and then my heart would answer me;
and I would enlighten it about my anguish.
I would unload onto it the weight which is on my back,
the utterances that make me helpless.
I would announce to it the anguish I feel because of it.
I would say "Ah!" on account of my relief.

I am meditating on what has happened,[6]
the state of things that have happened throughout the land;
changes are happening—it is not like last year.
Each year is more burdensome than its fellow.
The land is in uproar, has become what destroys me,
has been made into what rests in peace.
Truth is put outside,[7]
Chaos within the council.
The counsels of the Gods are thrown into tumult,
and Their directives are neglected.
The land is ⟨in⟩ calamity,
mourning in every place,
towns and districts in woe,
and everyone alike is wronged.
The back is turned on reverence;
the Lords of Silence are violated;
morning still happens every day,
but the face shrinks from what happens.
I shall give voice to these things, for my limbs are weighed
        down.[8]
I am in distress because of my heart.
It is a cause of suffering, yet I keep quiet about it!
Another heart would show respect.
A brave heart amid pain
is a companion for its lord.
If only I had a heart which knew suffering!
Then I should alight on it,
load it with words of misery,
and drive away my anguish onto it.'

He says to his heart:
'O come, my heart, that I may speak to you,[9]
and you shall answer me my verses,
explain to me what is throughout the land,
how the once bright ones are cast down!
I am meditating on what has happened:[10]
misery has appeared today—
a morning when strangers have not passed away;
everyone is silent about it;
the whole land is in an extreme state.

There is no person free from wrong,
and everyone alike is doing it;
breasts are saddened;
he who commands is as he who is commanded,
and yet the hearts of both of them are calm.
Each day one must wake to it.
Hearts cannot put it aside;
yesterday's share of it is like today's,
because the many imitate it, because of harshness.
There is no one clever enough to understand;[11]
there is no one angry enough to give voice.
Every day one wakes to suffering.
Long and heavy is my anguish.
The pauper has no strength
to ⟨save himself⟩ from the more powerful man.
Silence against what is heard is a disease,

vs. 5   but to answer the ignorant is sorrow,
to oppose an utterance now creates enmity.
The heart cannot accept Truth.
They have had no patience with the reply to a speech;
all a man loves is his own phrase;
everyone is based on crookedness,
and honest speech is abandoned.
I speak to you, my heart, so that you shall answer me.[12]
A heart which is touched cannot be silent.
Look, the servant's lot is like the lord's,
and many things are burdensome for you.'

Notes

1. The title introduces a text which concerns the search for speech; the reference to
   heart-searching is paradoxical, as the sage is seeking how to address his heart. He
   is associated with various positive allusions: his name includes a reference to King
   Khakheperre Senwosret II (it means 'Khakheperre is healthy'); *Heliopolis* is the
   city of the creator Sungod, near modern Cairo. *Ankhu* is the priest's common
   name; it means 'Living one', and make him an 'everyman' figure.
2. In a rhetorical introduction the sage laments the inability of poetry to express his
   woe adequately; he needs a fresh and esoteric style. His approach contrasts with
   many other attitudes to past wisdom, but this aim of surpassing the *ancestors* is
   not unique in Egyptian texts. Renown is the usual aim of speech, which it is
   hoped will not *pass away* so that the future will *find it good*; his aim is no empty
   boasting such as is found in *ancient* inscriptions that cannot now be trusted.
3. The opening of this stanza echoes the end of the preceding one (rt. 4). The sage

now announces his intention to begin speaking, with virtuosic wordplay on *speak*. He will neither speak of what has already been spoken, or of what might be spoken of in the future, but will produce actual vivid speech. The description of intended speech ironically echoes the title (*searching*: rt. 1).

4. In a triplet, he states that he will speak with direct experience, whereas all other speakers are concerned with things that *pass away*; his aim is to emulate what endures. The last verse is ambiguous: the generations both are *like* (i.e. resemble), but also emulate (in speech) transient things.

5. In the rest of the stanza, he reveals the motives for his search: he is seeking to express his despair effectively, so that his heart will respond. The heart's lack of understanding is the source of his agony, and new effective expression will bring relief. This stanza about the difficulties of speaking ends, appropriately, with an inarticulate cry of relief.

6. After the introduction, the sage now denounces the present evil state of affairs in antithetical statements characteristic of the subject (the first verse recurs later like a refrain, in vs. 1). The wordplay is no longer about speaking but about the subject he is articulating, the *happenings* (the word *changes* is a form of the verb *happen*). The need for a new speech is ironically caused by people's neglect of the past (*last year*), which is a common theme of literary laments.

7. This abstract description recalls those of chaotic interregnums in royal commemorative inscriptions. The cosmic aspect is taken up in the *Gods* of the next line; their *counsels* are Truth. These verses are flanked by more concrete descriptions of the *land*. The *Lords of Silence* are the blessed dead, representatives of past order and the virtue of quietness; they are desecrated, literally as well as metaphorically, but humanity goes on regardless. Men shun past values and, unlike the sage, cannot face the reality of what is happening.

8. In the next part of this stanza, the sage returns to his speech and places the responsibility for his suffering on his heart more directly than hitherto. In an earlier stanza he lacked a speech to reach his heart (rt. 7–8), but now the problem is expressed from the other side: if his heart were obedient (and *showed respect*), his suffering would end. He lacks a responsive and sympathetic heart (that *knew suffering*) which could save him.

9. The verso contains a single excerpt, at the start of which the sage addresses his heart directly. This section unites the two themes of the preceding stanzas: the problem of speaking to the heart, and the lament at what has happened. Both result from the human heart. An injunction to *come* often marks the start of a prayer to a god: here he prays to his heart in a prelude to explain things to him. The *bright ones* represent the past authority that is now overturned; the image is from the radiance of the white linen worn by the élite.

10. The sage again laments the invasion of *strangers*, and the omnipresence of wrong which is as inevitable as *morning*. Another theme is everyone's refusal to accept what is happening (and what the sage is saying): people's roles in society are reversed, but this is accepted without complaint. The sage describes the relentless daily drudgery of suffering: evil is so ingrained that the past (*yesterday*) is no longer a model of virtue, and people imitate only past evil.

11. No one (except the sage) speaks out against the happenings. This lack of any communication among people parallels the same lack within the sage: his problems in expressing himself are symptomatic of all humanity's difficulties. He hopes to break the pattern of destructive interaction and lack of attention.

12. The final quatrain returns to the sage's heart. He urges that both the heart and its *lord* (himself) are together in suffering, then presses the claim further, saying that the heart is responsible for much of their suffering. These verses are not necessarily the end of the original text, although here the sage seems more

optimistic that the heart will have been *touched* by his speech; the second verse recalls the title: there the heart was searched for (rt. 1), but now it is *touched*. The phrase *the servant's lot* . . . recalls the end of rt. 13, where a 'brave heart' was 'a companion to its lord', and suggests the interdependence of the sage and his heart.

7

The Dialogue of a Man and his Soul

Introduction

This lyrical composition is an internal dialogue between a living man and his own soul. 'Soul' is a free translation of the Egyptian *ba*, which is one aspect of the personality, and the manifestation of a person after death.

The Dialogue is inspired by a wise man's alienation from the world around him, a theme paralleled in other Discourses. Here, the source of his sorrow is his uncertainty about how to view death, his existential anxiety. Death was respected by the Egyptians, but also feared, and harpist's songs preserved on later tomb walls juxtapose different responses to death and seek to reconcile the audience to both its horror and its blessing, and to the uncertainty about what comes after death. The Dialogue may well draw on this type of song, as well as on pessimistic literary laments and on funerary compositions known as 'Transfigurations'.

The poem is a poetic dialogue on a general theme, and is not a logical analytic argument about a specific aspect of belief, such as the value of funeral rites or the status of a man's soul. Its questioning approach to its subject has a theodic aspect, since the existence of death implicitly calls the justice of the creator-god into question. The Dialogue takes its theme and moves forward through transformations of literary form, imagery, and tone to reconcile its protagonist and its audience with the prospect of death in all its aspects.

In the Dialogue the anonymous speaker and his soul hold opposing views about death. The man is eager to enter the otherworld that is represented by the funeral ceremonies; this was the generally propounded view of death, familiar from funerary inscriptions and other official writings. In one funerary text,[1] the creator-god justifies the existence of mortality as an inspiration to piety:

[1] Coffin Text spell 1130; text: A. de Buck, *The Ancient Egyptian Coffin Texts*, vii (Chicago, 1961), 461–71; recent translation: R. B. Parkinson, *Voices from Ancient Egypt* (London, 1991), 32–4.

I made that their (mankind's) hearts should refrain from ignoring the West, in order that offerings should be made to the Gods of the districts.

The man's soul, however, disagrees and opposes him with the view that death is a painful experience, and that nothing can mitigate its agony. Strikingly, it is the soul that praises this life, while the living man extols life after death. The soul presents a less orthodox view, and is less formal in speech, but its arguments would have seemed pragmatic, valid, and vivid to the original audience.

The start of the poem is lost, but may have included a title such as 'The Dispute of a Man with his Soul'. The man may then have described how he and his soul had a discussion as if in a court of law: grammatical details suggest that the dialogue takes place before an audience, possibly of the gods, even though the man is still alive. In the first surviving verses, his soul is speaking; it warns of the dangers of entering the otherworld, and threatens to desert the man if he persists in his attitude. This would result in the man's utter destruction, the second and final death known from other Egyptian texts.

The man urges his soul to stand by him—a wish found in contemporaneous funerary texts—and he longs to reach the beatified 'West'; the man uses this term for the otherworld, while his soul prefers the more blunt and final word, 'death'. His soul rejects any preparations for death, and thus would consign the man to destruction in the otherworld; it instead pursues the hedonistic 'happy day', as opposed to the 'day of burial'. Their speeches also show two opposing views of the gods who judge the dead: the soul warns of their intransigence, while the man prays to them to justify him.

As the man utters his prayer, his soul interrupts with a sarcastic comment, urging him to value life instead. In an equally biting response, the man warns of the consequences of the soul's attitude. Here the language is particularly rapid and the syntax elliptical, suggestive of an intimate discussion. The man then resumes his topic and eulogizes the West in more stately language, promising his soul that it will benefit by standing by him. The speech ends with a description of funerary rites as an ultimate homecoming.

His soul, however, takes up this description of burial and echoes it point for point. The dialogue proceeds, not with logical argument, but by rhetorical means and through imagery, as the two disputants answer image with image. There are also changes in literary hierarchy, as the soul now lowers the tone to articulate the wretchedness of death. It does this by telling two parables of lowly men in wretched situations, developing the imagery that it used earlier to combat the man's vision of death. For the man, a harbour was an appropriate metaphor for death, but for his soul death is a shipwreck. The generally sordid nature of the parables undercuts the man's claims that death is a noble state, and the events related in them show the vanity of care and of impatience. Both parables are targeted at the man's urgent desire for death.

The man's response retains some of the tone of his soul's speeches, but, instead of a parable, he speaks a lyrical poem which is highly patterned with refrains lamenting his wretchedness. It presents a repetition of extravagant images, which makes it stylistically and formally different from his soul's comparatively simple narratives. Its measured cadences rise above the language of all the previous speeches, but the subject matter remains lowly. The imagery is dominated by stench, crocodiles, fishing, shores, and low life—images taken from his soul's speeches, but which now articulate not the man's folly in longing for death, but his weariness of life. There follows a second poem, which retains a personal concern, but also laments the state of all society. This is the longest and the most forceful of the poems, echoing earlier statements while also echoing itself: this degree of repetition articulates the pervasiveness of evil, and the reflexiveness may also mark a turning-point in the man's interior dialogue. The bleakness of his soul's images and parables now becomes a justification of death, since life is not worth living. The despairing refrain 'Who can I talk to today?' is also a direct rebuttal of his soul's conversation—there is no one for the man to talk to.

A third poem returns to the subject of death, as the man sees it; this is an answer to his soul's injunction to 'call burial to mind', but there is a dramatic change of tone. This intense lyric takes the preceding strands of imagery and transforms them: true life is only to be found in eternity. Immediate, vivid, and fresh imagery gives a sense of release, and a paradoxical feeling that existence can be worthwhile. A fourth lyric concludes the sequence with a description of the blessed Beyond, which moves from the egocentric 'here' and 'now' to a 'future' state 'There'. It is dense in its allusions, and forms a further resonant transformation of the preceding imagery.

Its succinctness contrasts sharply with the seemingly endless laments.

The man's reply, with its four lyrics, kidnaps his soul's images and reformulates them to present his own vision, transforming the conflict between their views into an interplay of opposites. His lyrics overcome his soul's speech both by outnumbering the parables and also by their being a more elevated genre. They transfigure the imagery from a lament into a celebration of the perfection of existence 'There'.

The poem ends with a final speech, in which his soul acquiesces and the two reach an agreement. This speech is not an antagonistic 'answer' like the other speeches, nor is it merely a capitulation or a final attempt to persuade the man. Instead, the imagery in each verse is once again drawn from earlier speeches, and the soul now advocates a balance between the two attitudes towards death. The conflict here reaches a suspension, and the dialogue ends with the two speakers facing death together, with a final allusion to the imagery of voyaging. As the text stands, it is the first time the speakers refer to themselves as 'we'.

Neither vision of death triumphs in isolation: the two sides of death are metaphorically interwoven, as inextricable as death and life are. The consistency of the imagery through the dispute provides a dramatic fusion of opposing views. The problem of death's existence is justified by the perfection of the Beyond, and by the imperfection of this life, which, it is implied, humanity brings upon itself. But this justification is not made in a simple manner (as in the funerary text quoted above); the horror of death is not mitigated, and both aspects of death are found acceptable in a literary resolution.

The Dialogue, with its psychological debate, lyrical style, and elegy-like subject matter, has proved appealing to modern audiences, although its interpretation has been much debated. A late Twelfth Dynasty manuscript (P. Berlin 3024) is the only known copy; it was found together with three rolls containing the Tales of *Sinuhe* and the *Eloquent Peasant*. The start is lost, but the end is preserved. To judge by the language, the Dialogue was probably composed only a few decades before the manuscript was copied. Numbers give line numbers of the manuscript.

The Dialogue of a Man and his Soul

. . . .]'[1]
[My soul opened his mouth to me, to answer what I said,]
'[. . . . .]
[unknown number of verses lost]
[. . . . .]
you will [. . .] to say [. . . . .]   1
[. . . . .] Their [tongues] will not be partial[2]—
that would be cr[ooked] retribution—Their tongues will not
    be partial!'

I opened my mouth to my soul, to answer what he said,[3]
'This is all too much for me today! My soul has disagreed
    with me!
Now this is beyond all exaggeration; this is like leaving me
    alone!
My soul should not depart! He should stand up for me about
    this!
[. . . . . .]! He should [. . .] without fault!
He [may be far] from my body,[4]
from the net of ropes,
but it shall not come about that he manages
to escape on the Day of [Pain].   10
Look, my soul is misleading me—though I do not listen to
    him,[5]
is dragging me to death—though ⟨I⟩ have not yet come to it,
is throwing ⟨me⟩ on the fire to burn me up!
What is he like, [. . .]ing [. . .],
with his back to his [. . .]?
He should stay close to me on the Day of Pain![6]
He should stand on that side, like a praise-singer does
(this is the way to set off so as to return safely)!
O my soul, foolish to belittle the sorrow which is due to life,[7]
you who constrain me towards death, when I have not yet
    come to it—
make the West pleasant for me! Is this pain?   20
Life is a transitory time:
the trees fall.
Trample on evil, put my misery aside!

May Thoth, who appeases the gods, judge me!
May Khonsu, who writes very Truth, defend me![8]
May the Sungod, who controls the bark, listen to my speech!
May Isdes in the Sacred Chamber defend me!
For my need is pressing, a [weight] he has placed on me.
30 It would be a sweet relief, if the gods drove off the heaviness
    of my body!'[9]

What my soul said to me: 'Aren't you a man?[10]
—so you're alive, but to what good?
You should ponder life, like a lord of riches!'

I said, 'So I haven't passed away yet,[11]
but that's not the point!
Indeed, *you* are leaping away—and you'll be uncared for,
with every desperado saying, "I will seize you!"
Now, when you are dead, but with your name still living,[12]
that place is an alighting place,
attractive to the heart.
The West, an [inescapable] voyage,[13]
is a harbour.
If my soul listens to me, without wrongdoing,[14]
40 with his heart in accord with mine, he will prosper.
I shall make him reach the West, like someone in a pyramid
at whose burial a survivor has waited.
I will make a cool shelter for your corpse,[15]
so that you will make another soul in oblivion envious!
I will make a cool shelter, so that you will not be too cold,
and will make another soul who is scorched envious!
I shall drink at the river lip; I shall raise a shady spot,
so that you will make another soul who is hungry envious.
50 But if you constrain me towards death in *this* manner,[16]
you will find nowhere to alight in the West!
Be patient, my soul, my brother,[17]
until an heir exists who will make offerings of food,
and will wait at the grave on the day of burial,
and make ready a bed of the necropolis!'

My soul opened his mouth to me, to answer what I said,
'If you call burial to mind, it is heartbreak;[18]
it is bringing the gift of tears, causing a man misery;

it is taking a man away from his house,
and throwing him on the high ground.
You will not come up again to see the sunlight!
They who built in granite,[19]   60
who constructed pavilions in fair pyramids, as fair works,
so that the builders should become Gods—
their altar stones have vanished, like the oblivious ones'
who have died on the shore for lack of a survivor,
when the flood has taken its toll,
and the sunlight likewise,
to whom only the fish of the water's edge speak.
Listen to me! Look, it is good to listen to men![20]
Follow the happy day! Forget care!

A commoner ploughs his plot;[21]
he loads his harvest into a boat
and tows it along, for his feast day is approaching,   70
and he has seen the darkness of a north wind arise.
He watches in the boat
as the sun goes down,
and gets out with his wife and children,
and they perish by a pool,
infested by night with a swarm of crocodiles.
And at last he sits down, and argues,[22]
saying, "I am not weeping for that mother,
although she has no way out of the West
to be on earth another time;
but I shall ponder on her children,
crushed in the egg,
who saw the face of Khenty before they had lived."

A commoner asks for dinner.[23]   80
His wife says to him, "It's for supper-time."
He goes outside
to relieve himself for a moment.
He is like another man as he turns back to his house,
and though his wife pleads with him,
he does not hear her, after he has relieved himself,
and the household is distraught.'

I opened my mouth to my soul, to answer what he said to
     me,[24]

'Look my name reeks,
    look, more than the smell of bird-droppings
    on summer days when the sky is hot.
Look my name reeks,
    look, more ⟨than the smell⟩ of a haul of spiny fish
90   on a day of catching when the sky is hot.
Look my name reeks,
    look, more than the smell of birds, ·
    more than a clump of reeds full of waterfowl.
Look my name reeks,[25]
    look, more than the smell of fishermen,
    than the creeks of the pools they have fished.
Look my name reeks,
    look, more than the smell of crocodiles,
    more than sitting under the river edges with a swarm of
        crocodiles.
Look my name reeks,[26]
    look, more than a woman
    about whom lies are told to her man.
100 Look my name reeks,
    look, more than a healthy child
    about whom they say, "He belongs to someone who hates
        him."
Look my name reeks,[27]
    look, more than a port of the sovereign
    that utters treason behind his back.

Who can I talk to today?[28]
    For brothers are bad,
    the friends of today do not love.
Who can I talk to today?
    For hearts are selfish,
    and every man is stealing his fellow's belongings.
⟨Who can I talk to today?⟩[29]
    Mercy has perished,
    and the fierce man has descended on everyone.
Who can I talk to today?
    For they are contented with bad,
    and goodness is thrown down everywhere.
Who can I talk to today?

He who should enrage a man with his bad deed   110
   makes everyone laugh ⟨with⟩ his evil crime.
Who can I talk to today?
   They plunder,
   and every man is taking his fellow.
Who can I talk to today?
   For the wrongdoer is an intimate friend,
   and the brother with whom one dealt has become an enemy.
Who can I talk to today?[30]
   The past is not remembered,
   and no one helps him who gave help then.
Who can I talk to today?
   For brothers are bad,
   and one turns to strangers for honesty.
Who can I talk to today?
   People are expressionless,
   and every man's face is downturned against his brothers.
Who can I talk to today?   120
   For hearts are selfish,
   and no man's heart is reliable.
Who can I talk to today?
   There are no just men,
   and the land is left over to the doers of injustice.
Who can I talk to today?
   An intimate friend is lacking,
   and one turns to an unknown man to protest.
Who can I talk to today?
   There is no one who is content,
   and him with whom one walked is no more.
Who can I talk to today?
   I am weighed down
   with misery for want of an intimate friend.
Who can I talk to today?[31]
   For wrong roams the earth;
   there is no end to it.

Death is to me today[32]   130
   ⟨like⟩ a sick man's recovery,
   like going out after confinement.
Death is to me today[33]

like the smell of myrrh,
like sitting under a sail on a windy day.
Death is to me today[34]
like the smell of flowers,
like sitting on the shore of Drunkenness.
Death is to me today[35]
like a well-trodden path,
like a man's coming home from an expedition.
Death is to me today[36]
like the sky's clearing,
like a man grasping what he did not know before.
140 Death is to me today[37]
like a man's longing to see home,
having spent many years in captivity.

But There a man is a living god,[38]
punishing the wrongdoer's action.
But There a man stands in the barque,[39]
distributing choice offerings from it to the temples.
But There a man is a sage[40]
who cannot, when he speaks, be stopped
from appealing to the Sungod.'

What my soul said to me:[41]
'Throw complaint over the fence,
O my partner, my brother!
May you make offering upon the brazier,[42]
150 and cling to life by the means you describe!
Yet love me here, having put aside the West,
and also still desire to reach the West, your body making
landfall!
I shall alight when you are weary;[43]
so shall we make harbour together!'

So it ends, from start to finish,
as found in writing.

Notes

1. One and a half sheets are probably missing from the start of the manuscript—
about forty verses. These would perhaps have included a brief introduction set-
ting the scene, an opening speech by the man in praise of death, and then the
soul's disagreement.

2. The *tongues* belong to the judges of the dead in the otherworld, whose impartiality threatens any hope of a painless death. The soul seems to use this to justify his disagreement with the man. *You* (plural) are the audience hearing their dispute (see introduction, p. 152).

3. The man's speech is rapid, with varied constructions, giving a sense of swiftly changing ideas in debate. He begins by describing the soul's reaction in the third person (this speech may be addressed in part to the audience (see n. 2)). Despite the lacunae, it is clear that by disagreeing with the man about his attitude to death, the soul is—in the man's eyes—trying to mislead him, and if they continue to disagree will in effect abandon him. *Stand* is a keyword (16, 144), later used of a survivor standing at the funeral of a dead man (cf. 42–3, 52–4).

4. The *Day of Pain* is a euphemism for the day of death and judgement, which the soul cannot avoid even though he shuns the man's *body*, and the perils of the otherworld such as the *net of ropes*, which was used by demons to trap men.

5. The man implies that the soul, by urging him to shun the cares of burial (presumably in its lost first speech), is actually leading him to ultimate destruction (*death*), as if the man's corpse was burned rather than being preserved; the enemies of the gods suffered destruction by *fire* in the otherworld, and it was also a means of capital punishment in this life. *Death* is here not just the end of a man's life, but the second, final, death that was inflicted on the dead who were condemned by the gods.

6. The man urges his soul to agree with him and be on his *side* at the judgement of the dead (already alluded to (1–3)). In this court the soul should *praise* the man out of self-preservation, like a traveller who makes provisions for *returning safely*; the image of travel as a metaphor for life runs throughout the Dialogue.

7. In the second half of his speech, the man now addresses his soul directly, and accuses it of underestimating life's suffering and the joy of eternity. He implicitly extols the unchangeable *West*, the land of the dead, in contrast with both the impermanence of earthly life, and ultimate destruction (*death* (see n. 5)).

8. The man invokes various gods to ensure his safety in the otherworld: *Thoth* is the scribe and arbitrator of the gods, who is involved in judging the dead; *Khonsu* is, like Thoth, a lunar god of reckoning; the Sungod is the creator, and the ultimate judge, of the universe, whose *bark* carries the sun across the sky ensuring cosmic stability; *Isdes* is, like Thoth, a funerary god of judgement, and the *Sacred Chamber* is where the deceased are judged. These prayers respond to the soul's warning about the impartiality of the otherworldly judges. They are calmer and more stately than the earlier parts of the speech.

9. His speech ends by begging the gods to free him from the troubles his soul has imposed on him by its dissent.

10. The soul now butts in with a sarcastic question, and tells him to appreciate *life*, rather than wasting it in longing for death; the word 'riches' is homonymous with 'lifetime'.

11. The man replies in the same rather sharp tone, to assert that, even though he is still alive, the final destination—the West—is still the most important concern. Although the soul accuses him of abandoning life, it is the soul who is abandoning his fellow, and as a result it will be defenceless.

12. The man now offers the soul an alternative: death with a funerary cult which will keep a person's reputation *living*, and bestow eternal life. Then the Beyond (*that place*) will be a permanent home to it; *alighting* alludes to the bird-like manifestation assumed by souls.

13. The image of the *West* as a *harbour* is a common expression of eternity's role as man's home and an end to life's voyage. The restoration is uncertain.

14. The man describes, in measured verses, how agreement with him will ensure

the soul's security after death. The soul will be like one of the wealthy and blessed dead (echoing the soul's earlier reference to a 'lord of wealth' (33)), whose immortality is ensured by *survivors* who provide a funerary cult around their *pyramid*.

15. The man also promises to provide for his soul after death and make him enviable (the soul having a *corpse* is poetic licence). *Oblivion* is a term associated with the unresurrected dead who are unprovided for. The first two couplets concern only the soul's felicity, but the third couplet includes both the man and the soul; the *shady spot* is an arbour, such as were used for feasting (and thus will inspire envious *hunger*).

16. The man now threatens the soul with the consequences of condemning him to destruction (*death*). His arguments rely on the paradox that the soul's love of life will lead to death, whereas love of the West, which he advocates (cf. n. 5), would lead to eternal life. For *alight*, see n. 12.

17. He ends his speech by appealing to the soul as a relation, to stay with him until he has prepared for his longed-for death; he offers an attractive—almost homely—description of the *day of burial*; this term is used here rather than the more threatening 'Day of Pain' evoked earlier (10, 15).

18. The soul reasserts the contrasting view of death as painful, and matches the man's description of a funeral point for point. *Burial* is not a homely thing, but an expulsion. This speech reverses the common idea that 'calling the West to mind' inspires piety (see Introduction, pp. 150–1).

19. According to the soul, the horror of death is apparent in the impermanence of funeral buildings, which were designed to immortalize those buried in them. This impermanence means that even the wealthy owners of these monuments are no better off than the poor whose bodies are abandoned beside the river: death spares no one. In a single sentence the soul drags the man from monumental grandeur to corpses. The extended syntax, with its expansive treatment of suffering, contrasts with the repetitive formulations of the man's praise of death; the syntax evolves with the imagery, which echoes earlier passages (e.g. the *oblivious* ones (45 and n. 15)). For the soul, the water and the sun are hostile forces, whereas the man invoked the Sungod (25–6) and spoke of cool drinking water in the Beyond (47–8); a corpse has no survivor to *speak* the funeral rites for it (cf. 41–2), only *fish* ('fish', 'mankind', and 'tears' are all homophones).

20. The soul reminds the man that he, unlike the oblivious ones, has an interlocutor, and it now answers the man's commands to heed him with ones of its own to enjoy life. The terse imperatives contrast forcefully with the convoluted clauses of the preceding sentence. The advocacy of *listening* is characteristic of wisdom literature, and the soul does not advise mindless hedonism: the *happy day* can mean a religious festival as well as more frivolous enjoyment.

21. The soul now tells a parable about the vanity of excessive care, to point out the man's fault in caring too much for the West. The style is looser, simpler, and more rapid. The tale concerns a lowly man, retaining the same social setting as was alluded to in the preceding verses; he is careful not to sail in dangerous weather, and at sunset cautiously disembarks for further safety. His journey is a pious and dutiful one: his *feast day* is a religious feast in which he is to take part (and contribute offerings). The unexpected end to his journey suggests the agony of death, which is not a 'harbour' as the man claimed (38). The climax of this disaster echoes the soul's earlier image of death as corpses on a riverbank (63–4).

22. After the swift series of events, the narrative about the commoner halts with this lament. His debate with himself offers a parallel to the man's debate with

his soul. Contrary to the man's view, the commoner, like the soul, sees the *West* as a country of no return, and for him life is so precious that its loss when mature is no grief compared to loosing it early (*in the egg* is an idiom for extreme youth). Death is here a ferocious predator: *Khenty* is a crocodile-god, a demon of death. The word *ponder* points the moral aim of the parable, by recalling 32-3, where the soul urged the man to *ponder* life in a positive fashion (n. 10).

23. The soul immediately tells another similar parable, which increases the slightly sordid atmosphere. Another lowly man wants his food (*dinner*) before the right time (*supper-time*), just as the man is being over-eager for the West. Such impatience leads to distress and alienation: the lowly man's impatience makes him senseless and unrecognizable with rage. Urinating (the translation is uncertain) can be an image in literary texts for complaining.

24. The man replies in a contrastingly formal tone: he utters lofty lyrics with refrains. He takes images from the soul—the lowly setting (68-70), the river-bank (64-7), crocodiles (74-5), and the smell of excrement (82-4)—to present life as a dreadful swamp. This image shocks because this landscape was often portrayed as a setting for a dead man's rebirth through rituals of fishing and fowling and was given a general positive pastoral value. The *reek* of his name in life contrasts with his earlier hope that the souls's 'name' would 'live' in the West (36-7). His horror of life is implicitly due in part to the soul's disagreement with him.

25. The mention of human workers prepares for the change from vegetable and animal desolation to the human wretchedness which dominates the rest of the lyric.

26. This image recalls the second parable about family dissent. In the following couplet there is another image of family collapse and alienation: although a child is *healthy*, he is disowned (perhaps due to illegitimacy, given the preceding couplet).

27. This lyric ends not on a personal level, but with a description of dissent in the state; this wider horizon is developed in the following lyric. The motif of crocodiles continues indirectly through puns: *sovereign* is normally written with two crocodile hieroglyphs and the verb to *utter treason* is homonymous with to 'be infested with crocodiles' (74).

28. In a second lyric, the man says he can find no one to speak to—he is alone and abandoned, even by his soul. The lack of *friends*, *brothers*, and *intimate friends* embodies the man's lack of an agreeable soul but also extends it further into society as a whole. The refrain occurs elsewhere as the lament of a wise man in adversity: 'And the sage now grasps like an ignorant man . . . the wise man is saying, "Who can I talk to?" ' (the Maxims of P. Ramesseum II, verso ii.4). The man's agony induced by his alienation is no longer personal, but universal, and the Dialogue is concerned, for the first time, with all humanity; the man uses the language of pessimistic discourses such as *The Words of Neferti* (q.v.). This lyric is the longest and most monothematic section of the whole Dialogue. It echoes both earlier statements and itself, and this degree of repetition articulates the pervasiveness of horror. The dreadfulness of *today* rebuts the soul's urgings to 'follow the happy day' (68), and the bleakness of the soul's images and narratives becomes in the man's mouth an implicit justification of death, since life is not worth living.

29. The scribe left a blank here, having mistakenly started to write out the refrain of the third lyric.

30. The *past* is a golden age of values, such as reciprocity and righteousness, that have been abandoned *today*.

31. The lyric ends by proclaiming that *wrong* is endless: the lament could continue for ever.

32. In a third lyric, the man moves to *death today*, rather than today's agonizing life, and he extols *death*. The lyric directly answers the soul's challenge to 'call burial to mind' (56 and n. 18), and is made with a dramatic change of tone. Immediate, vivid, and fresh imagery gives a sense of release after the preceding descriptions of suffering. It is not only an exact reversal of the imagery of the soul's tirades against death, but also the converse of what the man previously used himself.

33. The *smells* and weather are now fair, not foul as in the first lyric (86–103). The image is of a pleasurable sailing trip (unlike the voyage of the soul's first parable (70–5)), but also alludes to the funeral journey to the west bank of the Nile for burial.

34. There is now festivity on the shore, echoing the soul's 'happy day' (68 and n. 20), and reversing its speeches' image of suffering 'on the shore' (64, 75). Smelling *flowers* (lotuses) is an activity characteristic of banqueting scenes. This feast also alludes to the funerary feast celebrated by mourners. *Drunkenness* is imagined as a land, but the image can be paraphrased as 'on the verge of drunkenness'.

35. *Death* is now not just a release, but a homecoming; this contrasts with the disastrous journey of the soul's first parable (70–5 and n. 21) or the 'roaming' in the preceding lyric (129 and n. 31). The images of the second half of the lyric concerns someone (a *man*) whose experiences are what the man aspires to.

36. Death is now a cosmic revelation, in contrast to earlier descriptions of life where all was alien and ignorance (e.g. 124–5).

37. The lyric concludes with an image of death as humanity's *home*, but also on a negative note: mankind is full of *longing*, and life is *captivity*.

38. The man now extols the blessed state of the dead man in the otherworld (*There*) in a final lyric of transcendence. Only there is a man truly alive, and divine. The man's lyrics in praise of death grow increasingly succinct, unlike those lamenting life, which grew more diffuse. This lyric has the whole weight of the Dialogue behind it: in death the man can enact the ideal of Truth in social terms, in cultic terms, and in spoken terms. In the first couplet the wrongdoings that were mentioned before are avenged by the gods.

39. The distribution of offerings is an image of the piety, plenty, and social order that have been lacking hitherto. The image expresses the unity of men and the gods, past and present. (Such piety implicitly includes funerary cults.) The dead man's journeying in the *barque* of the Sungod recalls earlier, less happy, voyages.

40. The dead man's enlightened state is an image of the fulfilment that has been lacking hitherto, and is another guarantee of justice, appropriate for the context of a dispute between the two speakers. The man no longer lacks an interlocutor, but when dead will be able to speak to the Sungod, who now is not a hostile force (as in 65–6); this is the language of funerary texts.

41. The soul answers immediately, and the Dialogue ends in its final, dense speech of conciliation. By adopting the man's imagery, it makes it clear that it has been in part won over by his metaphoric argument. It is now the very *partner* and *brother* that was lacking in the man's second lyric (103–30).

42. The *brazier* alludes to funerary rituals, the image reformulating the earlier reference to the agony of death by fire (12–13), being hot after death (46–7), and scorching weather (65–6, 88, 90). The soul now advocates a balance between the two attitudes towards death: one should love the otherworld, but also love life. The soul expresses this balance with vocabulary that the man has used (the *West* (cf. n. 5)).

43. *Being weary* is an idiom for dying, associated especially with Osiris, the god of resurrection. For the soul, death is now, as it was earlier for the man, a place

of *alighting* (37, 50–1 and n. 12) and of homecoming into *harbour* (38 and n. 13). For the first time the word *we* is used, and the Dialogue ends with the two facing death together, with a final harmonious allusion to the imagery of the riverbank and voyaging.

8

The Dialogue of Ipuur and the Lord of All

Introduction

The Dialogue of Ipuur and the Lord of All is dominated by descriptions of social woe, but the poem is not historical and its laments are—so far as they are preserved—addressed not to a particular king, but to a generalized representative of authority. It is a reflective Dialogue in which the difficulties of existence in the mutable world are debated. Its composition has been dated to the late Middle Kingdom on the basis of various internal features and allusions.

At least one page (about 40–50 verses) is lost from the start of the single surviving manuscript, and many other sections are damaged. The poem probably began with some introduction, perhaps a brief prologue or a title, before a sage named Ipuur started speaking. Details of his speeches show that he is speaking to a king in the presence of the royal court. He addresses the king in his most divine aspect, as the deputy and representative of the creator-god, with the title 'Lord of All', which was variously applied to both the king and the creator-god as lord of the universe. Ipuur himself has no title in what survives, but he features as an 'Overseer of Singers' in a later list of kings and famous ancestors from Memphis. It seems likely that he was introduced as a court poet or orator, who challenges his king with a lament, which he speaks on behalf of all humanity.

Ipuur's first surviving speech opens with a description of social chaos, and comprises a series of short stanzas describing the 'destruction of the land'. These are marked by refrains and are full of savage indignation. The speech is long, virtuosic, and baroque, a highly evolved example of its genre. The sage desires a return to the traditional status quo and, in a denunciation of social anarchy, laments the rise of the poor and the overthrow of the rich. It is a purely descriptive speech and of a single tone; it is also repetitive and very formally consistent, and the subject matter is restricted to social disruption. The long sequence of concise vignettes of specific disasters (interspersed a few times with slightly longer stanzas) gives a sense of the proliferation of evil, and, although occasionally self-contradictory, it is not rambling: some verses repeat individual words from the preceding stanza or are linked by association of ideas to produce a magnificently strong impression of the world spiralling out of control. The formal regularity of the poetry contains and encompasses a vision of chaos.

Immediately after this oration there follows a second lament, which describes the 'changes of mankind' and is essentially in the same compact style as the first. It increases the impact of the first, although it is a little shorter and has a different, slightly blunter, refrain. These two laments occupy most of the surviving poem. They are both patterned by strong antithesis between 'then' and 'now', between the ideal and the actual, between what should be and what is, as manifested in social change. This lyrical form is derived from laments for the dead, such as one preserved in a later tomb:

> You who had many people—you are now in the land that
>   loves loneliness!
> You who had much fine linen, who loved clothing
> now sleep in yesterday's rags![1]

The effect is of a forceful elegy for the life-in-death that humanity is forced to lead. Although the poem laments the woes of the privileged élite, there is a strong element of sympathy for the lower levels of society. As the audience were members of the élite group, the reversals in men's social standing will have been a warning against trusting in the security of their position, and the sage at one point wishes that the Lord would experience this misery himself (see n. 105). These descriptions of reversals were, in part, a rhetorical way of exposing the privileged audience to feel what wretches feel.

After these two major sections, the sage turns from describing the state of the land to urging action, and calls for the destruction of the enemies of the Royal House. Once again he speaks in short stanzas with refrains. A second injunction in similar style follows, in which he turns to positive motifs, urging the Lord to 'remember' the good times of the past. This provides a welcome moment of calm after the unremitting wasteland of what has gone before. The regretful contrast between present woes and past happiness precipitates the next section.

---

[1] Tomb of Neferhotep, late Eighteenth Dynasty; text: E. Lüddeckens, *Mitteilungen des Deutschen Instituts für Ägyptische Altertumskunde in Kairo*, 11 (1943), 111-14.

The injunctions lead into more discursive verses that articulate a complaint to the Lord of All as the representative of divine authority. These passages do not have refrains and develop arguments to present a more direct denunciation of the Lord. The sage directly questions the justice of god, who has allowed imperfection to predominate in creation, and asks why he created humanity. This central complaint grows out of the past speeches: it opens like a stanza from one of the preceding laments, and a note that was sounded earlier—the inefficacy of offerings to the gods—is here brought to the fore. The universal questioning and complaint are interwoven with specific instances drawn from the preceding laments (especially the depleted numbers of mankind), which become justifications of this speech. The use of questions and opposing statements creates a sense of desperately searching for and despairingly destroying ways of justifying the state of things. The sage moves on to accuse the Lord of direct responsibility for society's suffering, and to wish that he would feel some of the suffering himself so that he would act responsibly and restore order on the world.

A series of short stanzas then presents a description of a perfect society, which contrasts sharply with the earlier view of the world. This section is placed in structural symmetry with the earlier section urging the 'remembrance' of good things, which it echoes; this concentric symmetry is unlike the additive patterning of the laments. The problem of lacunae is extreme from this point on, and it is uncertain whether these verses are the sage reminding the Lord of how things should be, or the Lord answering the sage's second injunction and presenting an alternative, positive, view of the world. Up to now the Lord has made no reply.

This section is followed by a discursive reflection, which is certainly spoken by the Lord. He seems to argue that the conflict in the land is the fault not of external enemies, such as the sage earlier urged him to destroy, but of the populace itself; he implies that the Egyptians are their own enemies, and that any blame does not belong to society's leader or creator. In a theodic statement included in contemporaneous funerary texts, the creator-god himself declares:

> I made every man like his fellow;
> I did not ordain them to do evil, but their own hèarts destroyed
>   my pronouncement.[2]

---

[2] Coffin Text spell 1130; see p. 151 n. 1.

This refers to the myth that the world was created perfect but humanity rebelled, forcing the gods to withdraw, leaving an imperfect, sundered world, full of conflict (see n. 95). The creator-god's royal representative seems to advance a similar argument here. The poem, however, does not assert the ways of god to men as absolutely as the funerary text, but uses oblique and allusive arguments.

In his reply to this, Ipuur seems to reject the Lord's speech disclaiming responsibility. He recounts a parable, which apparently tells how mankind can suffer even when it is blameless. He turns from grandiose elegies to a simple tale of a child, which provides the most detailed example of innocent suffering, the implications of which are inescapable.

The extant text breaks off as the Lord replies in a similar vein to his preceding speech. His speeches, which are much shorter than the sage's, seem increasingly pessimistic in their subject matter, and increasingly denunciatory. The end of the manuscript is lost, but there is space for some forty verses after the start of this speech (see n. 122); this may not, however, have been the original end of the poem. The Dialogue is unlikely to have concluded with a narrative section, or to have been resolved with a sudden action. It is probable that the two disputants will have reached a reconciliation, formulated in a short final speech by one of them (as in *The Dialogue of a Man and his Soul*), and that the Lord's reply will have won the sage over to a stoic acceptance of the imperfection of the world.

The Dialogue is preserved on the recto of a single fragmentary papyrus of the Ramesside Period (P. Leiden I.344), of which parts of seventeen pages survive; the start and the very end are lost, and the fragmentary state makes the interpretation of much of the poem uncertain. On the other side are (unrelated) New Kingdom hymns to the god Amun. Numbers give page and line numbers of the manuscript.

The Dialogue of Ipuur and the Lord of All

'................................]
1.1   [................................]¹
       [................................];
       the door-[keeper]s are saying, "Let's go and plunder!";
       the sweet-makers [.............];
       [.............] the [...]er;
       the washerman has no [intent]ion of carrying his load;²
       the rope-[maker ....];
       [................................];
       the bird-[catchers] have raised [their] troops;
       [................................];
       [................................];
       the marsh-[dweller] is carrying a shield;
1.5   the brewers are [..........];
       [................................];
       [.............. is] sad,
       and a man sees his son as his enemy;
       the [.........] is in chaos;
       [................................];
       [................................];
       [one man ...]s himself against someone else,
       "Come with strength!"—
       a message [..................];
       [................................];
       [...........] these things which were ordained for you,³
       in the Time of Horus, in the era [of the Company of Gods];
       [................................].
       The man of character goes in mourning,
       because of what has happened in the land.⁴
       The [man of bad character] goes [carefree];
       [................................]
       everywhere the foreigners have become people.

                              *

1.10   O, but the face is pale [...........];⁵
       [........................].

[O, but] they [. . . .] what the ancestors foretold,
which has reached [fruition; . . . .].

[O, but . . . .]
[. . . . .]

[O], but there is [no] one who can leave [. . .];
[. . . . .].

[O, but . . . .];
[. . . . .].

[O, but . . . .];
[. . . . .].

[O, but . . . .];
[. . . . .].

[O, but . . . must bow down to] the earth, because of gangs;   2.1
a man goes to plough with his shield.

O, but the merciful say, "[My heart] shall suffer [. . .]!";
the [fierce]-faced man is now a well-born man.

O, but [faces] are pale, the archer is settled,[6]
and the wrongdoer is everywhere;
there is no man of yesterday.

O, but the plunderer [rob]s everywhere;
the servant is taking as he finds.

O, but the Nileflood is rising and they have not prepared for it;[7]
every man is saying, "We do not know what has happened
     throughout the land."

O, but women are barren, and no one can become pregnant.[8]
Khnum cannot shape because of the state of the land.

O, but beggars have become lords of wealth;[9]
someone who could not earn sandals for himself is a lord of
     riches.   2.5

O, but their servants' hearts are aggrieved;
the officials cannot fraternize with their people, who shout for
     joy.

O, but the [heart] is savage, plague throughout the land,
blood everywhere.

There is no lack of death;
the shroud is calling out before they approach it.

O, but many dead are buried in the river;[10]
the flood is a grave,
for the embalming-place has become the flood.

O, but the wealthy are in woe;
the poor are in joy;
every town is saying, "Let us drive away the strong from
    amongst us!"

O, but the people are like black ibises,[11]
and filth is throughout the land.
At this time, no one at all is clothed in white.

O, but the land is spinning as does a potter's wheel;[12]
the robber is a lord of riches;
the ⟨lord of riches⟩ has [become] someone who is plundered.

O, but trusted people are like a[ttackers who drive cattle
    away],
and the commoner [says], "How terrible! What shall I do?"

2.10 O, but the river is blood, and they still drink from it;
they push people aside, and still thirst for water.

O, but portals, pillars,[13]
and walls are burning;
the chamber of the Royal House (l.p.h.!)
is enduring and firm.

O, but the ship of the [South] is in chaos, towns are
    ravaged;[14]
Upper Egypt has become empty [sandbanks].

O, but crocodiles are [glutted] with the fish they have taken,[15]
and men go to them willingly.
This is the destruction of the land!
They say, "Don't step there!
Look, it's a net!"
Look, men tread the [ground] like fish;
the fearful man cannot tell what is ground because of his
    heart's terror.

O, but people are few;[16]
the man who inters his brother is everywhere;
the wise man speaks, and then fl[ee]s, without delay.

O, but the [known] gentleman lacks recognition,
while his lady's child becomes the son of his maidservant.[17]

O, but the desert is throughout the land; the nomes are
    ravaged;[18]   3.1
the barbarians of outside have come into Egypt.

O, but they reach [. . . . . . .];
there are no people at all in any place.[19]

O, but gold and lapis lazuli,[20]
silver and turquoise,
carnelian and amethyst,
diorite and ⌊all⌋ our ⌊jewels⌋
[are] strung on the necks of serving-girls;
wealth is throughout the land,
but well-married women are saying,
"If only we had something to eat!"

O, but [liv]ing is a horror for wealthy ladies' [hearts];
their limbs are saddened by their rags;
their hearts sink because [people] greet [them].

O, but ebony chests are shattered,[21]   3.5
the precious tamarisk wood of bedsteads is smashed;
[. . . . . .] the man who [. . .] their [. . .].

O, but the builders [of pyramids have] become field-
    workers;[22]
those who were in the divine barque are at the yoke.
No one at all sails north to Byblos today;
what shall we do
for cedar-wood for our mummies,
with whose products priests are buried,
with whose oil [official]s are embalmed?
From as far as Crete, they do not come!
Destroyed is the gold, and there is an end to storing the
    materials for every work.
Uncovered is the ⟨. . .⟩ of the Royal House (l.p.h.!).

How great a thing it is now when oasis-dwellers come,
bearing their festival offerings:
mats, [animal] skins with fresh palm fronds,
3.10 and [fat] of birds,
for the sake of providing plenty!

O, but Elephantine and Thinis, the [districts] of Upper
        Egypt,[23]
they produce no taxes [because of stri]fe.
Destroyed is grain, kohl, and *irti*-fruit,
maa-sticks, *nut*-sticks,
shrub-wood, and the work of the craftsmen,
colocynth, fenugreek, and the profits of the palace.
What is a treasury for, without its taxes?[24]
For the heart of a king is happy
only when true tribute comes to him,
and then every foreign country would [say], "He is our
        water! He is our prosperity!"
What can we do about this,
when it all has fallen into ruin?

O, but laughter is ruined,[25] and [no longer] sounds.
There is only groaning throughout the land,
mixed with laments.

O, but every nobody is a well-born man,[26]
4.1 those who were people are now aliens,
so that they are packed off.

O, but everyone's hair has [fallen] out,[27]
a gentleman cannot be told apart from a have-not.

O, but [they are deaf] because of noise;[28]
no voice has been righteous in the years of noise;
there is no end [to] noise.

O, but great and small ⟨are saying⟩, "I want to die!";[29]
little children are saying, "He shouldn't have made me live!"

O, but the officials' children are beaten against walls;
babes in arms are exposed on the rocky ground.

O, but those who were in the embalming-place[30]
are [expos]ed on the [rocky] ground:

this is how the embalmers' secrets are overthrown there.

O, but those things that yesterday saw are ruined;[31]   4.5
the land is left to its weakness, like flax being pulled up.

O, but the entire Marshland will not be safely concealed;[32]
the Delta puts its trusts in roads that are now well trodden;
What will anyone do?
"No [escape] exists in any place", is said;
they say, "Down with the Place of Secrets!"
Look, it belongs to those who do not know it, as if they knew it;
foreigners are [skilled] in the works of the Marshland.

O, but families are put to the millstones;[33]
those dressed in fine linen are [wrongly] beaten;
those who never saw the daylight go outside without restraint;
those who used to be in their husbands' beds—   4.10
"Let them sleep on the rafts [bearing] the dead!"
They who said, "It is too heavy for me" about boards
     carrying myrrh—[34]
they are loaded with vessels filled with [water];
the palanquin [no longer] knows them.
Now the cupbearer, he is destroyed.
There are no remedies for this.
Wealthy ladies pity themselves like serving-girls;
musicians are at the looms within the weaving-rooms,[35]
and what they sing to Meret are dirges;
the [story]-tellers are at the millstones.

O, but all the maidservants are full of their own words;[36]
it is burdensome to the servants, when their mistresses speak.

O, but trees are felled, branches stripped.[37]
A ⟨man⟩ has had to abandon the servants of his household.   5.1
People will say when they hear of this,
"Destroyed are the abundant gifts for the children."
There are no unripe or ripe sy[comore figs, or varied fruits].
Today, what is the taste of these like now?

O, but the officials are hungry, because of affliction;
their attendants are attended; [. . . .] are [strong] because of
     woe.

O, but the hot-tempered man is speaking,[38]
"If I [could tell] and know where God was, then I would
     serve Him!"

O, but [Truth] is throughout the land in its very name;
but what they do based on it is Falsehood.

O, but runners are fighting over a [man's] belongings;[39]
5.5   the robber has all his belongings taken.

O, but every flock, their hearts weep;[40]
the cattle are groaning at the state of the land.

O, but the officials' children are beaten against walls;[41]
babes in arms are exposed on the rocky ground.
Khnum is groaning because he is weary.

O, but terror kills;[42]
the frightened man stops anyone acting against your
     enemies.
Of little use, now, are the images and amulets on the small
     man.
Is it giving to Khenty and to the man he has dismembered?
Is it slaughtering for the Lion,
roasting on the fire?
Is it libations for Ptah, taking [materials]?
Why do you give to Him? It does not reach Him;
and your giving to Him is misery!

5.10 O, but servants [rule . . .] throughout the land;[43]
a fierce man has descended on everyone;
a man strikes his close brother.
What can be done?
—I speak of a man already perished.

O, but the ways are [guarded], the paths watched;[44]
they sit in bushes until a night-traveller comes
to seize his load, and what he carried is taken;
he is treated to blows of a stick,
and is falsely slain.

O, but those things that yesterday saw are ruined;[45]
the land is left to its weakness, like flax being pulled up;
commoners wander about because of affliction;

goldsmiths [on commissions are worn out].
If only this were the end of mankind,
with no more conception, no more birth,   6.1
so that the land would be quiet from noise, with no tumult!

O, but ⟨men eat⟩ only plants,[46]
and wash them down with water:
now they cannot find seeds, plants, or birds,
and [fodder] is taken from the pig's mouth.
No one can be benevolent, when they are bent double with
     hunger.

O, but the grain is ruined on every side;[47]
they are stripped of clothes,
unanointed with oil;
everyone is saying, "There's nothing!"
The storehouse is bare,
its keeper stretched out on the ground.
This is such a happy help for my heart! I am completely
     finished!   6.5
If only I had raised my voice in that moment,
it could have saved me from the suffering that happened then!

O, but the Sacred Stronghold, its writings are taken away;[48]
the Place of Secrets which existed ⟨there⟩ is stripped bare.

O, but magical spells are stripped bare,[49]
omens and divination spells are dangerous
because they are recalled by people.

O, but the offices are opened and their lists are taken away;
people who were serfs have become lords of [serf]s.

O, but [the scribes] are killed and their writings taken away;
how bad it is for me, because of the misery of their time!

O, but the scribes of the land register, their writings are got rid of;
the foodstuff of Egypt is a free-for-all.

O, but the laws of the Stronghold[50]   6.10
are thrown outside;
but they walk on them in the public places;
wretches are breaking them up in the streets.

O, but the wretch has reached the rank of the Company of the
    Gods;[51]
those rules of the House of Thirty are stripped bare.

O, but the Great Stronghold staggers to and fro;[52]
wretches come and go in the Great Mansions.

O, but the officials' children are thrown into the street;[53]
the wise man is saying "It is so!",
the fool saying "It is not!"
and the fact that he knows nothing seems fair to him.

*

7.1 And look, the fire has begun to rise—[54]
its flame should break out against the enemies of the land!

And look, things are done that have never happened before,[55]
and the king begins to be removed by wretches.

⟨And⟩ look, he who was buried as a Falcon is out on a bier.[56]
What the pyramid hid will be emptied.

And look, the land has begun to be despoiled of kingship,
by a few people who know no counsels.

And look, they have fallen to rebellion[57]
against the [mighty] uraeus of the Sungod, the Pacifier of the
    Two Lands.

Look, the secret of the land,[58]
of unknowable limits, is stripped bare;
the Residence has collapsed in a single moment.

7.5 Look, Egypt has begun to pour water;[59]
he who should water the earth
has carried the man of mighty arms off into poverty.

Look, the ancestral serpent is taken from its cavern;[60]
the secrets of the Dual Kings have been stripped bare.

Look, the Residence is afraid because of want,
and my Lord will send forth strife, with no opposition![61]

Look, the land is knotted in gangs;
the strong man—the vile man is taking his property.

Look, the ancestral serpent is in the [water like] the oblivious
ones;[62]
he who could not make himself a sarcophagus is a lord of a
tomb.

Look, the lords of the embalming-place are driven away onto
the rocky ground;[63]
someone who could not make himself a coffin is a ⟨lord⟩ of a
treasury.

And look at these changes of mankind!
He who could not build himself a room is a lord of walls.

Look, the councillors of the land are driven away through
the land;
he who was driven away is now in the Royal Quarter.   7.10

Look, wealthy ladies are on boards;[64]
officials are in the Workhouse;
he who did not even sleep on a wall is a lord of a bed.

Look, a lord of property goes to sleep thirsty;
he who begged dregs for himself is a lord of strong beer.

Look, the lords of robes are in rags;
he who could not weave for himself is a lord of fine linen.

Look, he who could not construct himself a cargo boat is a
lord of a fleet;
their lord now looks at them and they are not his.

Look, someone without shade is a lord of shade;
the lords of shade are in the blast of the gale.

Look, someone who knew not the arched harp is a lord of a
harp;[65]
he who could not sing for himself is hymning Meret.

Look, the lords of bronze offering vessels,
no jar is garlanded for a single one of them.

Look, he who slept a widower because of want, he f[inds]
wealth;[66]   8.1
he who was not seen stands making himself important.

Look, a man without property is a lord of riches;
the official now favours him.

Look, the beggars of the land have become the rich;
the ⟨lord⟩ of property is a have-not.

Look, the ⟨butl⟩ers have become lords of cupbearers;
he who was a messenger is sending someone else.

Look, he who was loafless is a lord of a storeroom;
his storehouse is furnished with the property of someone else.

Look, he whose hair had fallen out, a man without oil,[67]
has become a lord of jars of sweet myrrh.

8.5   Look, she who had no box is the owner of a trunk;
she who looked at her face in the water is the owner of a
          mirror.

Look, a man is happy when he is eating his food;[68]
consume your belongings in joy,
having no hindrance!
It is a good thing for a man to eat his food,
and God commands it to someone he favours.

⟨And look, someone ignorant⟩[69] of his God is now offering[70]
with someone else's incense, without his knowing.

Look, wealthy ladies and great ladies,[71]
the possessors of wealth, are exchanging their children for
          bed-linen.

And look, a [fine] man [who was given] a wealthy lady as
          wife,
and was protected by her father,
now a nobody is killing him.

Look, the children of the councillors are in [rags];
8.10   the [calves] of their cows [are given] to the plunderers.

Look, the colonial tenants are butchering cattle;[72]
the pau[pers have become the plu]nderers.

Look, he who did not slaughter for himself is slaughtering
          horned bulls;
he who knew no carving is seeing all [kinds of choice meat].

Look, the colonial tenants are butchering greylag-geese;[73]
they are given ⟨to⟩ the Gods instead of oxen.

Look, maidservants [. . . .] are offering swine;[74]
their wealthy ladies ⟨. . . . .⟩.

Look, wealthy ladies are running away in a single [flight];
their [hearts] are laid low by the fear of death.

⟨Look,⟩ the chiefs of the land are running away;
they have no function because a patron is lacking.

[Look], the lords of bedlinen are on the ground;   9.1
someone who slept squalid smooths a leather cushion for
      himself.

Look, wealthy ladies have fallen into hunger;
the colonial tenants are sated with what is prepared for them.

Look, all the professions—they are not in their proper places,[75]
like a herd straying without its shepherd.

Look, cattle are wandering with no one to look after them;
every man is carrying off for himself
the one now branded with his name.

Look, a man is killed beside his brother
who abandons him to protect himself.

Look, he who had no yoke of oxen is a lord of a herd;
he who could not find himself a ploughing team is a lord of
      cattle.

Look, he who had no seed is a lord of a granary;
he who took out loans of grain for himself is someone who
      lends it out.   9.5

Look, he who had no dependent neighbours is a lord of serfs;
he who was once a ⟨commissioner⟩
does his commissions himself.

Look, the mighty ones of the land,
the state of the folk is not report[ed to them],
and they have fallen into ruin.

Look, all the craftsmen no longer work,
while the enemies of the land have depleted its craft.

[Look, he who recorded] the harvest now knows nothing of it;[76]
he who could not [plough for himself is a lord of fields];

the [harvesting] is happening, but cannot be reported;
the scribe—his arms are [idle] in his house.

*

Destroy the [. . . . .][77]
[. . .] his [. . .] in its time!
A man sees [his brother as] his opponent;
only the enfeebled man now brings cool[ness upon the heat]
[. . . . .]
the [. . .] of the [off]ice is fearful.

9.10 Not [. . . . .]
[. . . . .]
The wretches are [. . . . .]
[. . . . . .] and no day dawns because of it.

Destroy the [. . . . . . who takes] their food from them![78]
[. . . . . .] fear of his terribleness;
the commoner begs [. . . . .]
[. . . .] messenger, but not [. . . in this] time;
he is seized, laden with his belongings,
[and what he has on him] is taken.
The [. . .]—people pass by his door;[79]
[. . . . . . .] outside the walls, in the offices,
and the rooms containing Falcons and Rams;
[. . . . . until] dawn.
Even the commoner will have to watch out,
10.1 with the day dawning for him unready.
They run away headlong;[80]
they who strained through finely woven cloth inside a
        house,
now what they make is tents, like foreigners.

Destroyed are the actions for which followers were sent[81]
on commissions for their lords, and they have no readiness.
Look, they are five men, but they say,
"You go off on a road you know—we have already arrived!"

The Delta should weep, for the Workhouse of the King is[82]
the free-for-all of everyone!
All the Royal House (l.p.h.!) is without its dues.
To it belong grain and barley,

fowl and fish;
to it belong white linen and fine linen,
bronze and oil;   10.5
to it belong reed-carpet and mat,
[water-lily] buds and wheat sheaf—
every good revenue that should arrive in full.
If complaint about these lingers in the Royal House (l.p.h.!),
no one can be free from [the loss] of these things!

Destroy the enemies of ⟨that⟩ fine Residence with splendid
    councillors,[83]
with [. . .] in it like [. . . . .]!
But the Overseer of the City walks, and has no escort.

Des[troy the enemies of that fine Residence] with splen-
    [did . . . .]
[. . . . .]!

[Destroy the enemies of] that fine Residence with many
    laws;
[. . . . .]!
[. . . . .] who [. . . . .]

[Destroy the enemies of] that fine [Residence . . . .]   10.10
[. . . . .] its [. . . . .]!

Destroy the enemies of that [fine] Residence [. . . . . . .]!
None can attend [on it, ...]
[Destroy the enemies of th]at fine [Residence] with many
    offices!
O, but [. . . . .]

*

Remember the washing in [. . . . .],[84]
the [. . . . . .] someone who suffers for the pain of his limbs,
the respect of [a dutiful man, who gives thank]s for his God,
as he guards [his] mouth [. . . . .],
whose upright children range far!

Remember the [build]ing of the shrine, the censing with
    incense,   11.1
the presenting water from the libation vessel in the morning!

Remember the fattened greylag-geese, the white-fronted and
the pintail-geese,[85]
the donating of divine offerings to the Gods!

Remember the chewing of natron, the preparing of white
bread[86]
by a man on the day of anointing the head!

Remember the setting-up of flagstaffs, the carving of
altars,[87]
while the priest is purifying the sanctuaries
and the temple is plastered white as milk,
the perfuming of the Horizon, the endowment of offering
loaves!

Remember the upholding of regulations, the correct
ordering of dates,[88]

11.5   the removing of someone who enters the priestly service
with impure body:
this is doing it wrongly,
this is afflicting the heart [of someone who does it]!

[Remember] the day at the head of eternity,[89]
the months that are cou[nted], and the years that are
known!

Remember the slaughtering of oxen, the [. . .],
and the [. . .] of your very best!

Remember the coming forth clean[sed to a man] who has
called upon you,[90]
the placing of a greylag-goose on the fire, and a [. . .]!

[Remember the . . . . .], the opening of the beer-jar,[91]
the mak[ing of offerings on] the shore of the flood.

[Remember the . . . .],
the [. . .] of the c[ows],
[. . . . .]
[. . . . .]
[. . . . .] garments;
11.10   [. . . . .] giving praise,
[. . . . .]
[. . . . .] to content you!

*

[. . . . .]92
[. . . . . for] the lack of mankind,
because of [. . . . .]
[. . . . .] the [. . .] of the Sungod, so that a command
       may be given.
[. . . . .] respecting Him, the [. . .] of the West
to make little the [. . . . . .], those who are [. . .]ed by the
       [Gods].

Look, why did He seek to shape ⟨mankind⟩,93
when the meek are not set apart from the savage
so that He might have brought coolness upon the heat?
They say, "He is the shepherd of all;94   12.1
there is no evil in his heart,"
yet although He has made the day to care for them, His herd
       is small,
and fire is in their hearts!
If only He had realized their character in the first generation!95
Then He would have struck down opposition, and stretched
       out His arm against them,
and destroyed the flock of them and their heirs.
Birth is desirable for them, but heartbreak comes into being,
and want is on every road.
These things are so, and have not ceased,
although these Gods are in the midst of all this.
From mortal women seed comes forth.
No good can be found on the road—only conflict has come
       forth,
and the driver-off of wrong is now its creator.   12.5
There is no Pilot in their hour of duty—96
where is He today?
So can He be sleeping? Look, no sign of His power can be
       seen.
If we have been saddened, should I be unable to meet you,97
or they unable to call upon you as someone who was free
       from aggression against them? And the heart is in fact
       afflicted!
For the desti[tute] stand over everyone's speech,98
and today fear of them

is more than that of millions of mankind.

No [protectors] from enemies can be seen;

the [temple enclosure has been destroyed, and desecrated] in
  its outer hall,

entered up to the temple, [with evil deeds]

for which the Gods weep [. . . . . . .].

That [. . . . . . .] who makes chaos—

his words [fill everyone's mouths, and good is ignored].

12.10 The land has fallen [into tumult, on its face];

the images have been burnt, their chambers are ravaged.

He who tends his [herd]—he sees the day, and [his he]rd is
  [small].[99]

The Universal Lord has made the sky separate from the
  earth,

and fear is in every face when He comes—

but if He does all this as our attacker,

who will [protest] against this, if you refuse to?

Surely, Utterance, Perception, and Truth are with you—[100]

but it is chaos that you have put throughout the land,

and the noise of tumult.

Look, one man is striking out at another;[101]

they transgress what you have commanded.

If three men go out on a road,

only two men can be found:

the many kill the few.

Should a shepherd really love death?[102]

If so, then you should command that assent be given to
  this!

13.1 Is not the individual who hates another now a loved
  favourite?

The fact is that their forms are few on every road,[103]

and the fact is that your action has created all this—you
  have spoken Falsehood!

And the land is brushwood, and mankind is destroyed—[104]

this cannot be considered living!

All of these years are strife:

a man is slain on his rooftop.

He is watching from his house by the boundary.

Is he strong? Only then can he save himself—such is his
  life!

They set an ambush even against a commoner;
he only goes on the path when he can watch the distance
—they ensnare the road, and he stands still, distressed,   13.5
and what he had on him is robbed, he is treated to blows of
    a stick,
and is falsely slain.
If only you would taste a little of the misery of all this![105]
Then you would say "Patience [. . . . .]
[. . . . .]
[. . . . .] for him, as protector of the walls,
in addition to [. . . . .]
[. . . . .]
[. . . . .] more heated than a generation of
    years,
when a speech is made [as . . . .]."
[. . . . .]
[. . . . .]

*

[It is so] good, when boats sail south [. . . . . . .],[106]
[. . . . .],
[without any thieves] robbing them.   13.10

It is so good when [. . . . .],
[. . . . .].

It is so good, when the net is drawn in,[107]
and birds are trussed, [in the] even[ing].

It is so good, when [. . . . . . .] honours for them,[108]
and the roads are passable.

It is so good, when people's hands build pyramids,[109]
when pools are dug and plantations are made
with trees for the Gods.

It is so good, when people are drunk,[110]
when they drink strong drink and their hearts are happy.

It is so good, when jubilation is in mouths,[111]
and the estates' notables stand
watching the jubilation from their houses,   14.1

clad in linen cloaks,
pre-eminently purified, well provided amidst them.

It is so good, when beds are smoothed,[112]
and the pillows well laid out for the officials;
when the need of every man is filled
with a sheet in the shade,
and a securely closed door for someone who slept in a bush.

It is so good, when fine linen is spread out on New Year's
        Day,[113]
and [. . . .] is on the bank;
fine linen is spread out,
and linen cloaks are on the ground;
the overseer of cl[oaks . . . .]-men,
        [. . . . .]
14.5   [. . . . .] trees,
and the commoners are [sitt]ing [in their shades].
        [. . . . .]
        [*total of 4 verses lost*]
        [. . . . .]

                                    *

        [. . . . .][114]
        [*total of 8 verses lost*]
        [. . . . .]
14.10   [. . . .] they [. . .] a deed of plunder
        [. . . . .] southwards.
The [Delta] is tied up [. . . . .]
[in] the midst of them, like Syrians;
        [. . . . .] to him.
They say that their plans accomplish themselves.
No one can be found who will stand up for their protection,
from [. . .], and the men who [. . .];
every man is wary of his sister, to protect himself.
Is it Nubians? Then we should make our protection,
and make the fighters numerous to beat back the
        barbarians!
Are they Libyans? Then we should have a confrontation,
for the Medjai are as pleased as Egypt is!

But how?—when every man is killing his brother,[115]
and the Youth we raised for ourselves have become
    barbarians,   15.1
fallen to ravaging!
What is now happening to the land is letting the Syrians
    know how to govern it![116]
Now, all the foreigners are still in fear of it,
and the experience of the folk
is that "Egypt cannot be given ⟨to⟩ the sand—
it is strong because of [its] walls!"
[But they will] say of you people after years,
"[A generation of . . .], who ravaged themselves".
Only something that survives [can make] their [houses live];[117]
[. . . . .] the man who is There will make his
    children live.
There is [. . . . .].
What you have made happen is [. . . . .]
[. . . . .] has said.
It is the Youth who [. . . . .]   15.5
[. . . . .]
[. . . . .] for misery.
[. . . . .]
[*total of 13 verses lost*]
[. . . . .]
[. . . . .] fish, [. . . . .]   15.10
[. . . . .]
[. . . . .] you have made contracts [. . . . . . .]
[. . . . .]
bindings [. . . . .] gum resin,
lotus leaves, lotus stems, [. . .],
[. . . . .]
in excess of [all] the provisions [of the land].'

*

What Ipuur said, when he answered[118]
the Majesty of the Lord of All:
'[You are so careful not to speak Truth to] all the flock!
In fact, ignoring this seems pleasant to the heart!
So you have done what seems perfect to their hearts, and
    made people live by this?

16.1 But they still cover their faces for fear of the next morning!
     There was once a man who was old, just before his death.[119]
     His son was a child, still without understanding;
     he had begun to be weaned off the food offered by the
              nurse,
     and he still could not open his mouth to call out to you;
     you carried him off at the death of the deceased.
     He weeps for his father.
     His water reaches the interior of [the Underworld].[120]
     [. . .] the departure of the man [. . .]
     [. . . . .]
     he offers the foreleg of a bull
     [. . . . .]
16.5 [*total of 18 verses lost*]
     [. . . . .]

                              *

16.10 [What the Majesty of] the Lord of All [said][121]
      when [he] answered [Ipuur]:
        '[. . . . .]
        [. . . . .]
        [someone who makes] you people retreat, and the land exist
              [in fear];
        [. . . . .]
        [. . . . .]
        [everyone] is [. . .] on every road;
        if they are called upon, [they do not hear].
        [. . . . . those] enemies—
        weep O Gods!
        Their followers have entered into the funerary mansions,
        and the images have been burnt; [their tomb-chambers are
              ravaged],
        and the bodies of the mummies.
17.1 How evil is the beginning ⟨of rebellion⟩[122]
        [. . . . .]
        [. . . . .]
        [. . . . .] for a Controller of Works;
        [. ,

Notes

1. For the amount missing at the start of the poem, see Introduction, p 166. The surviving text opens with a lament about the various professions, describing how all society is in uproar. The *doorkeepers* should act as guards, not plunderers.

2. This verse may imply that the *washerman* is now carrying something more war-like, or simply that even the most lowly are rebelling against their work. In the following verses workers take up arms, and become leaders.

3. *You* (plural) are the Lord and his entourage (see Introduction). The *Time of Horus* is the primeval past, when the *Company of Gods* ruled the earth and established the laws that the king should maintain. Presumably the *things* belong to tradi-tions that have been overturned by the social chaos.

4. These *happenings* are described in the following lament, for which these verses act as an introduction. By the *man of character* the sage may allude to himself. Egypt is completely overthrown so that *foreigners* become its *people* (the normal word for Egyptians). Social disorder and the threats to property described earlier are signs of this chaos.

5. The sage now begins a long series of short stanzas, marked by the refrain 'O, but'. This is the first of his laments, and is structured with antithetical contrasts and reversals between what was once—the ideal—and what is now—the actual. Aggression, foreigners, and the lowly usurp control of the land.

6. The past (*yesterday*) is an idealized age, in contrast to the present state of the land: the *man of yesterday* is a representative of that ideal, in contrast to the aggressive *wrongdoer* and *archer*.

7. The *Nileflood*, on which agriculture depended, had to be carefully *prepared for*; otherwise disaster followed.

8. The people as well as the land are becoming infertile. *Khnum* is the creator-god who forms children in the womb; the verse implies that the god is rendered help-less by mankind, rather than vice versa.

9. The sage laments the reversal of men's fortunes: the motif of the last becoming the first is an assertion of social chaos, not a cause of rejoicing; the ascent of the poor would have been at the original audience's expense.

10. Throwing bodies into the river instead of burying them both pollutes the river and represents the abandonment of all that funerary preparations stood for in Egypt. Thus the theme of death continues from the preceding stanza: the Nileflood should be a source of life and not a place of death.

11. *White* linen is a common image of Egyptian well-being (cf. 4.8–9 and n. 33), and is a marker of rank. The people are no longer clad in clean linen, but are like *black ibises* grubbing in the earth.

12. This is a demeaning image, derived from a lowly profession; also an ironic reference to Khnum (see 2.4 and n. 8), who should fashion mankind on his potter's wheel.

13. A stanza about prestigious state buildings. The safety of the palace implies a rebuke that the king has isolated himself from the general chaos, which the sage will later make directly.

14. The *ship* is a metaphor for the state, as well as being a literal reference to the loss of riverine communications. The *South* is Upper Egypt.

15. Although *crocodiles* have enough food, men are suicidal and seek them out (*fish* and *men* are homophonous). Land and water are alike dangerous: everywhere seems full of snares (*nets*). The imagery continues to the end of the stanza, where men are as helpless and trembling as fish out of water.

16. Death among coevals is now common, and the verse may even hint at fratricide. The *wise man* has to flee because his advice against chaos provokes hostility.

17. His son and heir—a major concern of Egyptian society—is reduced to the status of his servants, and rendered illegitimate.

18. The *desert* invades the once fertile *land* of Egypt.

19. The *people* are true Egyptians, as opposed to invading barbarians.

20. These materials were used in the jewellery of the élite, who are now deprived even of food, and in the next stanza are ashamed to be recognized.

21. This stanza continues the domestic subject matter of the preceding two stanzas, by describing the destruction of sumptuous furniture.

22. This is the first of two longer stanzas that concern the fall of the élite (including *priests*) and their material achievements (including burials), developing the references to furniture in the preceding stanza. The *divine barque* was the temple boat in which gods travelled in processions; men hoped to travel in its celestial counterpart when dead. The sailing motif continues with the isolation of *Byblos*, an Egyptian trading partner on the Phoenician coast that supplied the *cedar-wood* used in burials in pyramids. There was also trade with the Minoan culture of *Crete*. These stanzas lament the lack of imports and tribute, a sign of Egypt's fall from its accustomed central position in the world. Material culture has disintegrated; the only homage that is now brought is modest, and from the poor oases of the Western Desert.

23. The sage turns from the north to the south: *Elephantine* is at the southern border, and *Thinis* is a sacred town in Middle Egypt. Egypt itself is disintegrating, as well as its 'vassal' states; this is exemplified by the failure to collect the provinces' taxes of goods. The lost revenue includes *kohl* (eye paint), and various unidentified vegetable substances: *irti* is a plant colouring (*Isatis tinctoria?*); the others are types of wood.

24. The despairing sage asks how the state can survive without its revenues. The words *tribute* and 'Truth' are homonymous, and tribute is a sign of true social order. The sage states that the *foreign countries* should bring tribute and acclaim the king as their source of life; the mention of *water* alludes to the idiom 'to be on the water' of a king, meaning to be loyal to him.

25. Here, as elsewhere, the repetition of a word binds two disparate, and often contradictory, stanzas together. The lack of *laughter* recalls the king's lack of happiness in the preceding stanza (3.12).

26. For *people*, see n. 19.

27. In official art commoners are often shown as balding, and elaborate wigs are a sign of status.

28. Quietness is an ethical quality, here engulfed by *noise* (*noise* and *voice* are homonyms, enacting the disappearance of a righteous voice amid the noise). This brouhaha is exemplified in the speeches of the following stanza.

29. The mixture of strong antitheses—*great* and *small*, *die* and *live*—expresses the despair and chaos of life. The following stanzas develop the fate of the children.

30. This stanza moves from the deaths of the newborn to the fate of the dead in general; the repetition of a phrase links it with the preceding stanza (4.3–4). *Embalming* was a privilege of the wealthy.

31. For *yesterday*, see 2.2 and n. 6.

32. The image of flax is continued with a reference to the rich agricultural area of the country, the *Marshland* of the Delta. The access to the Delta is exposed to nomadic foreigners, who now turn to agriculture and pastoral pursuits (the *works of the Marshland*). Restricted access, once maintained by society, is abandoned, first to geographical areas, then to state institutions, and finally to specialized skills and knowledge. The *Place of Secrets* is the private areas of the palace and/or temple.

33. A stanza about social upheaval between the élite and their servants. *Fine linen*

was a prerogative of the wealthy. Those without *daylight* are servants confined in their workplaces. Once-wealthy wives are dismissed with an order to make them sleep on biers.

34. Noblewomen who felt too refined to carry heaps of perfume (*myrrh*) for themselves, and who were carried in *palanquins*, now have to carry large quantities of water as servants.

35. Court singers and other performance artists are lost in the fall of the élite, just as the *cupbearer* is. *Meret* is the goddess of ritual music and harmony. The stanza begins and ends with a reference to *millstones*.

36. In contrast to the high-up servants, the lowly *maidservants* are rebelling.

37. The *trees* implicitly include those from noblemen's plantations; destroying trees is an ultimate symbol of devastation. The next verses are obscure and require emendation; the sense seems to be that a man has to pare his house down, with the result that his children will have no profitable inheritance. No one can remember what food tastes like; hunger is described further in the next stanza.

38. This man's speech is hypocritical, using the lack of god as an excuse for heated action. The next stanza describes the hypocrisy of the entire land, where there is only apparent *Truth*.

39. The *runners* are the wealthy man's messengers. Even the *robber* is robbed: no property is safe.

40. *Flock* is often a metaphor for humanity, the 'flock of God' (see n. 94).

41. The first couplet repeats an earlier stanza (4.3–4). For *Khnum*, see 2.4 and n. 8; here, however, the lament is the reverse of the one there: the god is exhausted at having to fashion enough children to replace those who were slaughtered.

42. Everyone is too frightened for any defensive action which would help the royal audience (*your* is plural). The following verses apparently describe the uselessness of a little man's religious practices (including sacrificing animals, votive *images*, and *amulets*) to ward off terrifying situations. *Khenty* is a crocodile-god and a demon of death; the *man he has dismembered* is his victim, who once dead would also be the object of cult and intercession. The *Lion* is the lion-goddess Sekhmet, another merciless deity; *Ptah*, the creator-god of Memphis, is the consort of Sekhmet. The sage laments that offerings cost mankind dear and do not *reach* the gods effectively; a rebuke to the gods and to their intermediary, the king, is implied.

43. The sage laments man's hostility against man, and that all protest is useless, as society has already *perished*.

44. The attack of the preceding stanza is developed with an ambush.

45. This couplet is repeated from 4.4–5 (see n. 31). Here it is developed as the sage despairs at the created world (echoing the suicidal despair of children and the 'noise' of 4.1–3 (see nn. 28–9)): the way is prepared for his later denunciation of the creator.

46. The scribe left a blank space here, presumably because he could not read the manuscript he was copying. Men who should eat bread and beer, flesh and fowl, are reduced to an animal's diet of *plants* and *water*. No one can be generous when thus deprived.

47. The sage continues to lament the lack of proper food and rebukes himself for not having spoken out sooner.

48. The sage moves from food supplies to other aspects of the administration. This begins a series of more concise stanzas on the destruction of the state's archives of administrative, legal, and religious texts: the lost culture embraces a wide range. The *Sacred Stronghold* is some sort of temple enclosure; the *Place of Secrets* is an area of restricted access.

49. Magic was an integral part of state religion. *Spells* are now remembered and used by common people and are thus made dangerous.

50. The *Stronghold* is an institution that enforced labour duty. The next verses have a double meaning: people trample the *laws* underfoot, and walk freely when they should be detained by these laws.

51. All social order is overthrown, on a cosmic scale. The *House of Thirty* is a law court.

52. The *Great Stronghold* is the central office in charge of labour duty which now is on the point of collapse; the *Great Mansions* are the central law courts, which should be of restricted access.

53. These verses are a formula expressing how social order is overthrown and how the *wise* are contradicted by the rabble (cf. *The Teaching of King Amenemhat*, 14a–b and n. 20). After this stanza the scribe mistakenly copied an earlier stanza (4.4): 'O, but those who were in the embalming-place | are exposed on the rocky ground: | this is how the embalmers' secrets are overthrown there'. This insertion was later marked in the margin as an error.

54. Here the sage starts a second lament, also structured by refrains and short anti-thetical stanzas (the refrain—*Look*—is, if anything, slightly more blunt than that of the preceding lament). *Fire* is elsewhere an image of mankind's destruc-tive tendencies, and the sage wishes that such destruction were reserved for *enemies*. This start to the lament gives a sense of chaos reaching an apocalyptic level, as royalty itself, the centre of Egyptian society, begins to be attacked.

55. The phrase *things are done* can also mean 'goods are acquired', or 'rituals are done': a wide range of possible misdeeds. The *happenings* in the land, the sub-ject matter of the preceding lament, are here surpassed. The royal mummy (the *king*) is *removed* from its pyramid; this climactic wrong is introduced in general terms and developed more explicitly through the following stanzas.

56. The *Falcon* is the king in his full divinity; his regal buried state is contrasted with being carried out on a simple *bier*. The stripping of the *pyramid* forms a climax to the motif of stripping places of state administration in the preceding lament; the sage moves towards a description of how the kingship is being undermined.

57. The *uraeus* is the royal serpent-diadem, a symbol of a deity worn on the fore-head of the king, and is a great protective force. The land rises in anarchy; the stanza alludes to the myth of mankind's rebellion against the creator Sungod, which resulted in the fallen world (see n. 95). The god's epithet presents him as the imposer of order on society.

58. The *secret* is the mystery of kingship.

59. The *water* is funerary libations, but here it is not a sign of piety, only of Egypt's death-like state and neglect of life. The man *who should water the earth* is a farm labourer.

60. The *serpent* is the ancestral spirit of former kings; its *cavern* alludes indirectly to the royal burial places.

61. The sage's *Lord* is the Lord of All, who creates strife without anyone opposing him, although the king's duty is to *oppose strife and not create it*.

62. The royal serpent-spirit is now cast away; the *oblivious ones* are the dead who are left unburied and thrown into the river. The people who should be treated thus are properly buried.

63. The stanzas now move from the subject of burial to the (related) subject of wealth; the élite who once could afford to be *embalmed* are expelled onto the desert when dead (cf. 4.4). Despair is expressed in 'then-now' formulations with direct antitheses. The descriptions are striking and simple, making this lament more forceful than the preceding one, and it moves to wider matters: the way in which the social status quo has been reversed.

64. The ladies now have *boards* instead of beds. The *Workhouse* was an office of forced labour.
65. The people who could not afford the means or time to make music now have them. For *Meret*, see n. 35.
66. *Wealth* was needed to acquire a second wife.
67. For the social significnce of *hair*, see n. 27.
68. This stanza, which interrupts the sequence of antithetical laments, seems to be a sarcastic comment aimed at the Lord, who remains unaffected by the people's suffering.
69. The scribe left a blank space here (cf. n. 46); there may be a full verse missing.
70. The sage moves ironically from describing divine favours to human piety, which is now being usurped by the impious who do *not know* God.
71. Poverty is such that it makes mothers unnatural.
72. The sage moves from *cattle* as property to cattle as food. The subject continues in the following stanzas.
73. The gods are now given only *geese* instead of more prestigious *oxen*, and by *colonial tenants* not priests.
74. *Swine* are inappropriate offerings to the gods; taboos are ignored. In the second verse, the scribe left a blank (cf. n. 46); perhaps restore ('lack anything to offer').
75. The simile of a *herd* is drawn from the earlier descriptions of wrongs involving cattle. The image of the *shepherd* will become still more resonant later (see n. 94). In the next stanza cattle are victims of human greed, suggesting that men's folly is self-destructive.
76. The final stanza of the lament is longer than most and concludes it with a description of the loss of the basic food stuff. The work of the *scribe* is vital to the gathering, *reporting*, and distribution of the harvest.
77. The sage now turns from describing the state of the land to urging the Lord to take action to *destroy* the enemies; the same wish was made at the start of the preceding lament (7.1 and n. 54). A more varied section follows, with stanzas of less regular form. The injunctions are followed by descriptions that justify the need for such action: society is predatory and men only exhaust themselves by trying to bring calm (*coolness*).
78. A stanza about how men are despoiled and degraded; it is more expansive than previous descriptions of this subject, but remains obscure because of lacunae.
79. Perhaps restore 'the [official]', who is ignored. The following fragmentary verses seem to tell how vigilance is needed to protect temple buildings and even a commoner's property. The *Falcons* are sacred images of the king or gods; *Rams* are sacred animals or images.
80. These verses are obscure. The manufacturers of perfume (by *straining*) now use the straining-cloth to make primitive shelters (*tents*); Egyptians are reduced to living like nomadic *foreigners*.
81. The sage moves from longed-for destruction to what has been *destroyed*: he interweaves descriptions of present circumstances and desired reactions. The status of the lords of society is disrupted: even when there are *five* messengers, they refuse to go, and tell their master to go himself.
82. The refrain 'Destroy' is avoided, as the sage instead invokes sorrow at the destruction. His description of the loss of basic life-stuffs summarizes earlier descriptions of the state's impoverishment. The plundering of the *Royal House* does not result in greater wealth for the people: the final couplet implies that if even the palace suffers from lack, all the country suffers the same.
83. The stanzas become more regular as they urge that the *enemies* of the splendid capital be *destroyed*. Retributive action is offered as an answer to the chaos: the second verse in each stanza probably described a sign of chaos to justify the

injunction to *destroy*. The *Overseer of the City* is the Vizier, who should travel in a palanquin with attendants.

84. The sage stops urging action, and instead urges the Lord to *remember* the good things of life, which are based on piety and service. The form of the stanzas is the same as that of the preceding injunctions, highlighting the contrast between the past and the present. These verses are a moment of relief (a similar moment occurs later (13.9 ff. and n. 106)), recalling when god was in his temple and all was well with the world; temple ritual was vital to maintain the order of the cosmos. The first stanza is obscure, but may describe how a pious man is cured (*wash in* is a phrase attested in medical texts) and prospers.

85. These birds were traditionally offered to the gods. The stanza contrasts with the earlier lament about offerings (8.12 and n. 73).

86. The *chewing* is part of the purification required for priestly service: the *bread* is for offerings; the head is *anointed* with perfume for cultic celebrations.

87. Rows of *flagstaffs* flanked the entrances of temples. Temple walls were white-washed as a ground for ritual scenes and texts. The *Horizon* is the temple—the god's dwelling place from which he appears; the idiom adds a cosmic dimension to the general well-being.

88. Members of the élite served periods of time (*months*) as priest, for which purification was important. The mention of ritual impurity is the only negative element in these stanzas, and it is presented as self-destructive.

89. These *days* and *months* are the dates for rituals; these are the most important days of all *eternity*.

90. The ritually *pure* priest is *called upon* to be an intermediary between the people and the gods, an indication of social and cosmic unity. The *fire* recalls the earlier passages where fire was invoked against the enemies of the state: burnt sacrifices of fowl were symbolic of the destruction of chaos.

91. This stanza refers to offerings made at the start of the Nile inundation.

92. This fragmentary passage may have formed a transition from the preceding lyrical section to the following discursive passage, moving from the description of past rituals to a wish for a response from the gods. The *lack of mankind* is a theme taken up in the following section. The *West*, the place of death, was generally considered to be an inspiration to piety, and may have been intended as such here.

93. Another blank (cf. n. 46), but the restoration is fairly certain. The sage now starts a broad discursive argument. The following stanza is different in tone from the preceding ones, although *Look* recalls the refrain of the second lament (7.1–9.8). The sage pursues rapid arguments in complex sequences of clauses, and, instead of addressing the lord's court (you plural), he turns to the Lord himself (you singular). Accusations and questions alternate with descriptions of the land's woes. The sage is inspired by the world's evil and the absence of any divine intervention, and begins to call the justice of both king and god into question; *He* is the creator of the cosmos, the Sungod (already mentioned in 11.11). The lack of any differentiation between the virtuous and the aggressive makes him question the worth of creation; *coolness* is a positive and orderly emotional quality, while heat is choleric and chaotic.

94. What *they say* is a possible answer to the sage's questioning complaint, which he immediately dismisses. The *shepherd* is a metaphor for the creator-god (and king) as the people's protector. The imagery also relates to the earlier description of professions gone wrong (see nn. 75, 99). The *small* size of the shepherd's *herd* (mankind), and its divisive nature, are signs of his inadequacy. The sage notes the dichotomy between the all-powerful creator and his small creatures, and between his supposedly virtuous heart and their aggressive ones.

95. The sage wishes that mankind had been destroyed before it had caused such distress (echoing the wishes expressed through the previous laments). He alludes to the myth of mankind's rebellion, when the creator withdrew from the earth, killing the rebels; part of mankind, however, was saved, which the sage now regrets. It is ironic that the caring shepherd is urged to destroy the *flock*—an irony that is continued in antithetical and paradoxical descriptions of the resultant woe in birth and generation. The phrase *on the road* acts as a sort of refrain for the predominance of evil, while the verse about *seed* is a daringly contradictory evocation of the chaos of birth. The evil state of the land is unchanging; changes were earlier lamented, but now the sage laments that there is no change for the better. All this is despite the presence of the *Gods* in the temples: the divine world does not intervene to save mankind.

96. The *Pilot* who safeguards the ship of state (cf. n. 14) is an allusive metaphor for the creator who guides the cosmos, whose *power* is lacking. A rhetorical question implies that god must be *sleeping*, so inactive is he. The tone of this passage is combative and challenging. *Look* echoes the earlier lament (7.1–9.8) and the start of this section (11.12).

97. A difficult couplet: the rhetorical questions ask whether men should be unable to appeal to the Lord in distress. They imply that mortals only appeal to the Lord for sympathy of necessity when they are *saddened*, and now they suffer much more than sadness—*affliction*. (There is wordplay with the homonyms *call upon* and 'Pilot', 12.5.)

98. The sage continues to lament people's inability to protest freely. The *destitute* who cause this have usurped the king's power, which is often described in official texts as being worthier than *millions of mankind*. The sage then laments the destruction of the sanctuaries of temples, as an indication of the godless state of the world.

99. The shepherd whose flock has been lessened during the night is both an example of the state of the land and a metaphor for the neglectful great shepherd. The sage reverts to denouncing the creator, the *Universal Lord*; this verse repeats the opening of this section almost exactly (12.1). The description of the Universal Lord alludes to the myth of mankind's rebellion which resulted in the withdrawal of the gods and the cosmos being sundered (see n. 95). Rhetorical questions express Ipuur's desperate appeal to his Lord: if the creator seems hostile, who but the king can protest on mankind's behalf? The Lord's abuse of his ability is contrasted with the awesome power of the creator, on a cosmic scale: god has withdrawn from the world in disgust, leaving the Lord as his deputy.

100. The sage now directly accuses the Lord of responsibility for the present catastrophe. *Utterance* and *Perception* are the two great divine forces of the creator, and they and the sum of their creation—*Truth*—are entrusted by god to the Lord, but he fosters their opposite, garbled tumult.

101. Lament-like vignettes exemplify the chaos with specific instances. Mankind's *transgression* of the orders handed down by the Lord recalls a contemporary theodicy (see Introduction, pp. 168–9).

102. A difficult passage (one could also render 'Should the loving shepherd be dead?'). A *shepherd* (a metaphor for the god and the king as the people's protector (see nn. 94, 99)) should protect the *few* of the preceding verse. The sarcastic question implies that, if a shepherd should love death—an obvious absurdity—only then should the Lord promote death. In the next verse, the sage ironically points out that selfish aggressors are now favoured by the court, and society is based on *hate*, not love.

103. *The fact is* . . . strengthens the affirmations that answer the preceding

rhetorical questions and denounces the Lord directly. Mankind is now depleted to a *few* creatures: the king, in contemporary eulogies, is meant to 'increase those born with him'. The homonyms *forms* and *created* tie the verses together, and present the Lord's responsibility forcefully. *Speaking Falsehood* is the opposite of the creative wisdom the Lord should have (cf. n. 100).

104. After these accusations, the sage returns again to laments, describing the results of the Lord's actions for the *land*. This couplet alludes ironically to the idiom for the earth, 'the land of the living': life is meaningless now. All of created time (*years*) has become conflict (unlike earlier (11.5–6 and n. 89)): vignettes follow of danger and destruction, describing the loss of home and property by both rich and poor. There is no refuge except in brute strength.

105. He begs the Lord to stop being aloof from mankind's woe: direct experience would move him to pity and make him intervene. The sage imagines a speech from the Lord, which would (presumably) offer some promise of consolation.

106. The following stanzas present a contrasting view of a harmonious society. The refrain here is expressive of order, rather than the inescapability of woe, and these stanzas provide a vision of the world alternative to that of the preceding laments. They reverse the earlier descriptions both of woe and the *good* things that have been lost, answering and echoing the laments; they recall the earlier injunctions to 'remember' the happy past (10.12 ff. and n. 84). This ideal is probably voiced by the sage (although the lacuna is just sufficient to restore a change in speaker, making the Lord speak these stanzas). The first stanza recalls the earlier descriptions of boats disintegrating (see n. 14), and imports failing (see n. 22), and the numerous references to robbery (see n. 104).

107. This stanza evokes idyllic country life, and recalls the earlier references to lack of food and misappropriated offerings (e.g. n. 73).

108. This stanza recalls the descriptions of wayfarers being robbed (13.4–5 and n. 104).

109. This stanza echoes both the earlier laments about the desecration of the royal burials (7.2), and the injunction to 'remember' the temple cult (11.1 ff.). The *pyramids* are the central monuments of the state, the burial places of the kings and members of the court; the *Gods* include the royal deified dead. These stanzas offer a vision of the whole of society ordered and united.

110. Drunkenness had a positive value, and accompanied many religious celebrations.

111. The acclamation of the clean and well-fed rich by the rest of society is a sign of social stability; this contrasts with the earlier accusations that society is in disorder. *Linen* recurs throughout these stanzas as an ideal of Egyptian life (cf. n. 33).

112. This stanza is intimately domestic; the final verse reverses the 'then–now' formulations of the laments in both form and content (cf. 7.10). *Pillow* is literally 'headrest'.

113. *Linen* (see n. 33) is spread out to bleach it; this may also be part of the celebrations for the New Year. The *New Year* is, according to mythology, a dangerous time, an allusion that broadens the image to a cosmic dimension, without losing specific application. The New Year contrasts with the earlier mentions of 'years of strife' (13.2–3 and n. 104).

114. After the lacuna, there comes a more discursive section, spoken by the Lord; in the lacuna one should probably restore '[What the Lord of All said, | when he answered Ipuur:]'. Although this section describes social chaos in similar terms to the preceding laments, there is emphasis on the self-destructive nature of the chaos. The Lord argues that, although people claim to be acting effectively, this is not so: men are too selfish to protect the country, and suspect

even their *sisters*. The Lord evokes a full range of enemies: first come the *Syrians* who are Egypt's inveterate enemies to the north-east, and then the *Nubians* to the south, the *Libyans* to the west, and the *Medjai*, who are nomads of the eastern deserts of Nubia, and warlike enemies. The Lord argues that it would be possible for Egypt to maintain itself in order, if only humanity did not turn against itself. The people are responsible for the social chaos, not their rulers.

115. The aggression witnessed in families is now worse than that in earlier verses: the sage cited family murders as evidence of general disorder (9.3), but here the Lord cites them to show how men bring chaos on themselves. The men raised as paramilitary troops (the *Youth*) to oppose the foreigners of the preceding verses are now *barbarians* themselves.

116. The Lord announces that the foreigners (*Syrians*) are becoming aware of Egypt's troubles. While there may still be complacent confidence in Egypt's security abroad and at home (the desert *sand* is the contrary of Egypt), he prophesies that posterity will realize that the people wrought their own ruin (*ravage* echoes 15.1). He implies that present events, provoked by mankind, will destroy any security.

117. The Lord seems to argue that men should not just lament the present, but should act to ensure the safety of the future. In a generalizing couplet he affirms continuity through death, evoking endurance as opposed to 'ravaging'. The *man who is There* is one of the dead, who could intervene in human affairs to help their relatives (letters to the dead show that appeals were made to them). The passage probably went on to blame mankind for what has happened, but is very fragmentary. His speech seems to end with a list of good things, including tribute. The *contracts* are evocative of law and order.

118. For the title *Lord of All* see Introduction, p. 166. The sage now makes a short but violently sarcastic reply, reverting to the imagery of men as a *flock*. He dismisses the Lord's arguments, and accuses him of pretending to act for the people's good, while spreading falsehood and terror.

119. The sage now resorts to a parable to make his point about the fearful state of mankind. The parable concerns an innocent *child*, who is left helpless by his aged father's death and who is seized by the state before he is old enough to protest at being made into a servant or some similar fate. The sage implies that such a child at least cannot be blamed by the Lord for destroying himself.

120. The *water* is both the son's tears and a libation poured to the dead. The parable seems to imply that, even if the son cannot appeal to authority, the dead will hear (the mention of the dead takes up that made by the Lord in 15.3–4 (see n. 117)); the sage warns that the dead, if not the living, can take vengeance on the Lord's folly. The *foreleg* is a funerary offering.

121. The Lord's reply seems to allude to mankind's negligence in making any response to calls for help; the phrase *call upon* echoes earlier passages where superiors were invoked (11.7, 12.5 and nn. 90, 97). The gods and the dead are weeping at mankind's folly (as opposed to the sage's parable where a victim of injustice wept for them to hear (16.2–3 and n. 120)). The Lord's lament concerns the same woes that the sage lamented earlier, but he implies that the gods are blameless for mankind's woe and cannot help, as they themselves are attacked by men (the passage echoes 12.10).

122. The scribe left a blank space here, presumably unable to read what he was copying, as in several other passages (cf. n. 46). The omission is restored tentatively from a parallel phrase in *The Teaching for King Merikare*, 1f. Only the top right-hand corner of page 17 is preserved. There is space for ten more manuscript lines, as there are traces of a different hand by 17.13, i.e. for *c*.25 verses. It is uncertain how much of the original composition is lost.

TEACHINGS

9

The Teaching of King Amenemhat

Introduction

Teachings are one of the most important genres of Egyptian litera-
ture. They are instructions in wisdom addressed by an elderly father
to his eldest son and other children, who are about to succeed him;
these testaments of a lifetime's experience give advice on the means
of success in public life, and articulate the continuity of ethical and
social values. They are, however, fictional, and do not give practi-
cal injunctions for real life, although the teacher is often a histori-
cal figure of rank, and, in the case of the present teaching, a king.
In royal teachings, narrative and reflection have a larger role than
in the Teachings of non-royal officials, relating as they do to the spe-
cific events of individual reigns and to the central role of kingship
in articulating Egyptian culture. Their commands, therefore, have
less immediate relevance to the lives of the audience.

The Teaching of King Amenemhat is spoken by the founder of the
Twelfth Dynasty for his son and successor, Senwosret I; in The
Words of Neferti Amenemhat I was acclaimed as an idealized
restorer of order, but this poem gives a more intimate, and strik-
ingly dark, portrait. The king is speaking to his heir from the grave:
father and son are separated by death. Amenemhat was clearly not
the actual author of the poem, which may have been 'ghost-
written' some time after his death. Some 700 years later, New
Kingdom scribes attributed it to a master scribe called Khety.[1]

The historical Amenemhat I died after a thirty-year reign
(c.1938–1908 BC), a death which is described as unexpected in The
Tale of Sinuhe (q.v.). In his Teaching he appears to his son in a dream
and tells him of an attempted assassination, which the poem implies
caused his death. The conspiracy seems to have originated in the
royal harem; the family of the Vizier Intefiqer, who subsequently fell

[1] P. Chester Beatty IV 6.11–7.2. Text: A. H. Gardiner, *Hieratic Papyri in the British
Museum*, 3rd ser., *Chester Beatty Gift*, ii, pp. 20–1.

from favour, may have been implicated. From historical evidence, it seems that there was a ten-year co-regency between the king and his son, but the poem represents things otherwise and emphasizes the perils of sudden succession. At the start of the Twelfth Dynasty, co-regency was a new institution which, although it had obvious practical advantages, was difficult to reconcile with belief in a single king who was both unique and divine; the poem rewrites political history in order darkly to affirm the royal succession in a manner uncompromised by the awkward reality of the co-regency.[2]

The Teaching's stated aim of instructing the prince in how to rule is disingenuous, for much of it is reflective rather than didactic in tone, and addresses an audience of all mankind. The poem has clear political overtones, and it can be read as a veiled justification of co-regency or of reprisals following the old king's death. However, it primarily explores the wider issues of the humanity and divinity of the king, and of the duties of rulers. The theme of the interregnum between two rules embodies broad Egyptian concerns about the instability of order and the threat of chaos, ones not restricted by the policies or intrigues of the Twelfth Dynasty. Manuscripts of the poem show that it was still being read in the fourth century BC.

The title states that the late king appears to his son as the latter is about to ascend the throne, and tells him of the duties and responsibility of kingship. In the first five stanzas he warns against trusting anyone, and alludes to his own fatal experience of humanity's treachery. This pessimistic attitude is not just determined by the specific and dramatic situation, but is part of the generally negative Egyptian concept of human nature, in which society was viewed as tending to the wild, and man as needing to have order imposed on him from above. It was a royal duty to re-enact the creator's imposition of order on the cosmos at creation. Many of the stanzas are dominated by repetitive syntax, giving an air of imposed force and monumentality, while antithetical statements express the sudden eruption of disorder, and many verses have a prominent caesura. The first thematic section ends with impassioned pleas to mankind to benefit from the king's bitter experience.

In a central section Amenemhat describes his assassination in intimate and human detail: even within the circle of the court this

---

[2] There is also no mention of any political difficulties Amenemhat may have encountered in originally seizing the throne; opponents of the new dynasty could have interpreted the assassination as retribution on the new king.

would have been a deeply shocking passage for the original audience—the sordid death of someone whose role was that of a god. The narrative account explains the reason for the king's cynicism, but also provides a justification for his fallibility in allowing himself to be surprised by his enemies. In his defence he cites the unexpected nature of the attack, while the detail that he was overcome at night-fall adds a cosmic dimension to the disaster: sunset was a time of universal danger. The traumatic death of the old king and the accession of the new is presented as part of a cosmic struggle against chaos, and an instance of the pattern of death and rebirth, sunset and sunrise: Amenemhat's day is done.

In a third section, the king moves to his positive achievements. It was, paradoxically, his invincible achievement that made the attack unexpected, and this legitimizes his apparent fault of lack of foresight. His success as the defender and sustainer of the country makes him an epitome of Egyptian kingship. This self-presentation recalls the language of monumental commemorative inscriptions and non-royal autobiographies, and culminates in a description of his memorial, a magnificent funerary temple. This image of stability is, however, undercut by a vision of disorder in the streets, which is part of the unrest of the interregnum. In a dramatic manner the king departs from his son with a final address, half-despairing, half-triumphant, in which the new king is assured of his right to office, and of his father's intention to have him rule. The true culmination of Amenemhat's reign is this succession rather than his assassination.

The Teaching begins and ends with the theme of the king rising to divinity, and includes both his divinity and his humanity. To the ancient audience it would have provided a discussion of the nature of kingship, the centre of Egyptian culture; to a modern audience, it offers a rare and dramatic insight into the uneasiness of ancient kings.

There are many New Kingdom copies of the work, but the most complete manuscripts are the New Kingdom P. Millingen (now lost) and P. Sallier II (P. British Museum EA 10182). Numbers give the stanzas of Wolfgang Helck's edition (letters indicate the lines of these sections), with the page and line numbers of P. Millingen in parentheses.

The Teaching of King Amenemhat

1 (M 1.1) Beginning of the Teaching[1]
made by the Majesty of the Dual King, Sehotepibre,
the Son of Re, Amenemhat, the justified,
when he spoke in a revelation
to his son, the Lord of All.
He said, 'Rise as a god![2]
Listen to what I tell you,
that you may be king of the land, and rule the Banks,
increasing the good.

2 (M 1.3) Concentrate against subjects who prove non-existent,[3]
in whose respect no faith can be placed!
Do not approach them when you are alone!
Trust no brother! Know no friend!
Make for yourself no intimates—this is of no avail!

3 (M 1.5) You should sleep with your own heart watching over
you,[4]
for a man will have no supporters
on the Day of Pain.
I gave to the beggar, I raised the orphan,[5]
and I made the man who had not end up like someone
who had.

4 (M 1.7) It was someone who ate my food who caused trouble;[6]
someone to whom I had given my help was raising plots
with it;
someone clad in my fine linen was looking at me as if
needy;
someone anointed with my myrrh was pouring water in
return.

5 (M 1.9) O my living images, my partners among men,[7]
make for me mourning, such as was never heard before!—
the greatest fighting, such as was never seen before!
When one fights in the arena, forgetful of the past,
the goodness of someone who ignores what should be
known is of no avail.

It was after supper, when darkness had fallen,[8]   6 (M 1.11)
and I had spent a happy time.
I was lying on my bed, since I was tired,
and my heart had begun to follow sleep.
When the weapons at my disposal were wielded,
I had become like a worm of the necropolis.[9]

As I came to, I woke to fighting,[10]   7 (M 2.2)
and I found it was an attack of the bodyguard.
If I had quickly taken weapons in my hand,
I would have made the back-turners retreat with a charge.
But no one is strong in the night; no one can fight alone;[11]
no success will come without help.

Look, my passing happened when I was without you,[12]   8 (M 2.5)
when the entourage had not yet heard that I would hand
      over to you,
when I had not yet sat with you, that I might make plans
      for you;
for I was not prepared for it, I did not foresee it,[13]
and my heart had not thought of servants' negligence.

Had women ever before commanded troops?[14]   9 (M 2.7)
Are people of tumult ever brought up in the Residence?
Is water that destroys the fields ever let forth?
Do commoners ever bring folly on themselves by their
      actions?
Since my birth, evil had not come near me;[15]
my deeds as a strong hero were inimitable.

I strode to Elephantine,[16]   10 (M 2.10)
and I travelled to the Marshes;
I stood firm on the limits of the land, having seen its
      midst.
I attained the limits of strength
with my strong arm, and my manifestations.

I was a maker of grain, beloved of Nepri.[17]   11 (M 2.11)
The Nileflood honoured me on every plain.
No one hungered in my years; no one thirsted then.
Men could relax through what I had done, and told of me.
All that I decreed was as it should be.

12 (M 3.1) I tamed lions, and I captured crocodiles.[18]
I subjugated Nubians, and I captured Medjai;
I made Syrians do the dog-walk.

13 (M 3.3) I made myself a mansion adorned with gold;[19]
its portals were of lapis lazuli,
with walls of silver,
a floor of sycomore,
doors of copper,
bolts of bronze,
made for all time,
prepared for eternity.
I know, for I was the lord of it, of all!

14 (M 3.6) But now the children of the masses are in the street,[20]
the wise saying "It is so!"
the fool saying "It is not!"
for he cannot know anything, lacking regard for you.
O Senwosret, my son![21]
My feet are departing, but my very heart draws near,
and my eyes are looking for you,
to whom the children of a happy time,
beside the sunfolk, offer praises!

15 (M 3.9) Look, I made a beginning, so that I might secure the
              end for you.[22]
I alone have brought to harbour my heart's desire for
              you:
you wearing the White crown, divine progeny!
This is as it should be, as I began it for you.
I have descended into the barque of the Sungod.[23]
Ascend to the kingship created aforetime,
for it is what I achieved, in the midst of all this!
Raise your monuments, endow your tomb shaft!
May you fight for the wisdom of the wise-hearted,[24]
for you loved him beside your Majesty (l.p.h.!)!'

So it ends, from start to finish,
as found in writing.

Notes

1. Amenemhat I, Sehotepibre, was the founder of the Twelfth Dynasty, who died *c.*1908 BC. He speaks his Teaching not on the point of death (the usual setting) but after it, in a dream to his heir. His son, Senwosret I, is not named, but is addressed with the title *Lord of All*, which presents him as the king in his most divine aspect.

2. The command to *rise* has overtones of appearing both as the newly crowned king and as the Sungod. The poem concerns the manifestation of the potential of kingship and divinity, and the duties of the king.

3. The duties of kingship are presented in strongly pessimistic terms, as combating humanity's fallibility. In contrast to the divinity and ideals of the last stanza, humanity is presented in negative terms, as faithless and unreliable, as if they were a chaotic force (*non-existent*). A forceful series of injunctions, all of them involving negative phrases, stresses the lonely and dangerous role of a king.

4. In this stanza, the king changes briefly to positive injunctions, advocating self-reliance. One would expect vigilance to be urged, rather than *sleep*: this advice prefigures the disaster that the king is about to relate, and the need for sleep hints at the king's mortality. The *Day of Pain* is the day of death.

5. The king expounds his virtuous acts, using formulae from commemorative funerary Autobiographies. The *beggar* and the *orphan* are alienated individuals, continuing the negative characterization of humanity. The antitheses of these lines are reversed in the following stanza (4a–d), where the good he does turns sour.

6. This stanza continues with antithetical statements, describing directly the undeservedness of the evil which struck the king. The people rewarded with *linen* and *myrrh* look at the king with envy, as if *needy*. The idiom *pouring water* seems to mean 'pouring funeral libations' for him (i.e. preparing for his death), but it can also mean figuratively 'passing complaints' like urine; the verse gains in piquancy from the contrast between *myrrh* and *water*, and is very resonant: it also suggests that people were literally 'pissing on', or spitting at, the king. *Myrrh* and *linen* are signs of privileged living, but can also have funerary overtones, relevant to the king's death.

7. The king now addresses a wider humanity than his son: the invocation to mankind reflects both the king's divinity and his humanity—men are both the *images* of the creator-god and thus of the king's divinity, but *partners* of the king's humanity. The relationship between the two poles of divinity and humanity reflects human responsibility to uphold order. This involves making *mourning* for the king and avenging him. The more varied sentence structures in this stanza combine injunctions and generalizing reflections and prepare for the change to narrative in the next stanza. The *fighting* to avenge the king becomes an image of combat which expresses the necessity of learning from past experience and harkening to what the king is revealing, without which all virtue is in vain.

8. In a movement to personal narration the king now relates what he has only alluded to before. The mention of *after supper* shifts from a public and abstract sphere to a more intimate level; it is also significant as a time when cosmic order is at its weakest. *Tired* is a word often used of the languor of the dead. The king's *sleep* recalls his earlier warning and injunction (3a). The *happy time* may have involved sexual pleasure.

9. The *worm* is an image of sluggishness: in later funerary spells it 'sleeps and is reborn daily' (*Book of the Dead*, spell 87), an allusion to the cosmic cycle of death and rebirth that is also evoked to by the mention of the *necropolis*.

10. The references to fighting and arms reach their climax in this stanza describing the attack. *Back-turners* is a term of abuse for enemies of the state, with a sexual edge—they are effeminates.

11. The king moves to generalizing negative statements, arguing that his weakness was not a personal fault, but partook of human vulnerability. The verses ironically reflect the earlier injunction to remain solitary (2c–e), which is both a strength and a weakness. The duties of kingship make a king vulnerable whatever he does.

12. *Passing* is the most direct reference to the king's death (the Egyptian word can mean an 'injury', but also the 'withdrawal' of the mummy into its tomb). Even here, however, he narrates his assassination allusively: it is an almost unspeakable event. In this, the central stanza of the poem, he continues to justify himself with a more specific threefold description of his solitary state. The only one whose help he could have trusted was his son, who was away (as also mentioned in *The Tale of Sinuhe*, R 11–13). These verses stress the uncertainty of the transfer of royal power (see Introduction, pp. 203–4). Negative forms predominate.

13. The king admits his lack of the foresight that should be a royal duty; he relates it, however, to the failings of his servants, as if justifying his fallibility by theirs. The next stanza offers further justification for his lack of readiness (9a–f).

14. This stanza returns to a repetitive style, with a series of rhetorical questions. The questions imply that the attack could not have been foreseen, even by the king. The *troops* are the treacherous bodyguard; the mention of *women* suggests that the conspiracy originated in the royal harem. The second question asks who would expect revolt to originate in the centre of government, and the third presents the problem in cosmic terms: *water* is associated with the forces of chaos. The fourth question asks who could expect that the people would self-destructively destroy their own protector.

15. The questions are followed by a descriptive couplet that points their rhetorical nature. The king's mistaken confidence is justified by descriptions of his absolute power, as he begins to give an account of his reign in positive terms.

16. The king describes his achievements as reaching first geographical *limits*, then abstract ones. *Elephantine* is the southernmost town of Egypt, and the *Marshes* are the northern Delta: he dominates the land to its edges.

17. His achievements guaranteed the well-being of Egypt; the stanza alludes ironically to the fact that people who thus benefited attacked him (see 4a). *Nepri* is the god of grain; the god of the *Nileflood* is the provider of growth and of water (echoing the image of 9c): these allude grandly to the necessities of existence, bread and water.

18. A relentlessly repetitive stanza on the king's protection of Egypt from enemies. The two animals are representatives of the chaotic forces of the desert and of the flood, and are juxtaposed with two hostile peoples, the *Nubians* of the south, and the *Medjai* of the south-east. Animals and enemies are fused in the final verse, with the description of the north-eastern *Syrians* crawling submissively like *dogs*.

19. An extremely simple and stately stanza now describes the temple dedicated to his funerary cult—an eternal mansion that represents the permanence of his achievement and his universal authority. It is described as being made of precious things: usually doors had architectural elements of blue glazed composition, not *lapis lazuli*, and walls were white with plaster, not *silver*. The *all* of the final verse alludes to the royal title 'Lord of All' (1c; see n. 1).

20. A new stanza marks a sudden contrast—from the mansion to the common *street*, and from the god-king to the confused *masses* of humanity. The street is

full of quarrels and unrest (see *The Dialogue of Ipuur and the Lord of All*, 6.12–14). These are the chaotic forces which undermined Amenemhat and which threaten to predominate in the interregnum. Only the presence of the new king can set them right.

21. Amenemhat's son is named for the first time in the poem (this cry is at the numerical centre of the stanza). The deceased king reluctantly leaves him for the otherworld, separated from him as he was when attacked. The stanza ends, however, on a positive note, describing the son as the restorer of all that has been wrong: the people of his reign will no longer be the unsettled children of the start of the stanza (14a), but *children of a happy time* (this regains the happy time lost in the assassination (6b)). They are joined by all mankind who live under the sun (the *sunfolk*).

22. A stately stanza follows with a final summary of the son's role as successor. To *bring to harbour* is also a metaphor for death, as well as one for a succesful completion. This stanza implies that the disaster of the king's death is finally acceptable, since it resulted in his son's accession, which is his crowning achievement and intention, and compensates for his assassination in his son's absence. The *White crown* is the crown of Upper Egypt, and the principal single crown of the Egyptian king.

23. He has *descended* into the otherworld in the barque in which the Sungod travels through the night. His descent is paradoxically the ascension of the new king (1d; see n. 2); both attain a sun-like godhead. This accession is the true achievement of the king in the midst of all *this* misfortune, and is associated with the orderly, golden past (*aforetime*). He urges his son to continue to create enduring monuments like his own (13a–d); such works are a sign of piety.

24. This *fighting* echoes the assassination and the revenge for it, and the earlier image of combat (5c–d): all previous struggles are subsumed in the new king's struggle to uphold wisdom. The *wise-hearted* person is the dead king, whose dearly bought *wisdom* is the centre of the Teaching; the poem ends with a personal appeal to his son's *love*. Appropriately the final word is the *Majesty* of the new king.

10

The Teaching for King Merikare

Introduction

This Teaching is spoken by a King Khety to his son and designated successor Merikare; it is imagined as part of a continuous tradition of wisdom passed down through the royal line. The Teaching is set in the turbulent Heracleopolitan Period, c.2081–1987 BC, when the country was divided between rulers in the north and south, before the Middle Kingdom was established. The teacher may possibly be the same king as Nebkaure Khety, in whose reign *The Tale of the Eloquent Peasant* is set. The position of him and his son, the future King Merikare Khety, in the dynasty is unsure. The date of the poem's composition is also uncertain, although it is not contemporaneous with the Heracleopolitan Dynasty. From its length and style it can perhaps be dated to late in the Middle Kingdom, considerably later than the more concise *Teaching of King Amenemhat*.

In contrast to royal inscriptions, the Teaching portrays a king as a troubled shepherd struggling to uphold order, and it seems that King Khety is speaking at the end of his life (see n. 56), reflecting on the causes of his downfall. This rather pessimistic presentation could be interpreted as a means of legitimizing the absolute rule of the Twelfth Dynasty. Chaotic circumstances justify harsh actions by the élite and the state, and it is likely that the Heracleopolitan Period was regarded by the Middle Kingdom audience as a sort of troubled interregnum writ large across history. The poem, however, is not limited to specific programmatic concerns; it is in part a study of statesmanship comparable to Machiavelli's *The Prince*, but it rises to yet more universal themes. The difficulties facing kingship were integral to the Egyptian world-view, of a universe threatened with chaos.

The Teaching opens with advice to the king's heir on how to restrain potential rebellion, a theme that suits its setting in a period of internal war. The king takes a negative attitude to the populace, and portrays them as a rabble tending towards evil. Words are as important as actions, and are extolled as embodiments of true wisdom. The rather cynical policies advocated are justified in terms of absolute Truth, and are then presented with more positive instances; although the advice is often brutal, the king also urges restraint in vengeance. Dealing with practical issues is entwined with concern to act by the laws of eternity, which will be manifested in a man's reputation with posterity, and in his judgement by the gods after death.

The opening seven stanzas concern specific instances of rebellion, but the poem then considers broader issues in more generalizing and reflective stanzas both about the role of wisdom and about actions related to social and eternal justice. The interweaving of injunctions and reflections, as well as the development of various lines of argument with the repetition of certain themes, parallels the concerns of the subject matter: the king's actions do not exist in isolation, but take place within a cosmic setting which ranges from the divine to the lowly, the ideal to the actual. The king himself embodies these concerns as the intermediary between the gods and mankind. The motif of wisdom, which occurs throughout the Teaching, articulates the dichotomy between the all-knowing wisdom of god and the more partial, fallible nature of the king and the folly of humanity. Despite these broad aspects, the teacher rarely steps outside the dramatic context of addressing his heir. His Teaching is very specific in the historical detail it uses—though there is no means of knowing how historically accurate it is—to present the human and individual side of the divine king.

The poem advocates 'doing Truth' as a means of ensuring endurance on earth. This theme is developed in a central series of stanzas dealing with the king's historical deeds and achievements that reflect his attempts to create an enduring legacy. Prominent among these, however, is a fault on the part of the king. The details of this event were presumably familiar to the audience, and at first it is alluded to only in general terms, as an example of why one must act with a view to the future. The event is mentioned several times with increasing directness, and it gradually becomes clear that it was the destruction of hallowed tombs in the necropolis of Thinis by the king's troops during the war with the rival Theban dynasty to the south. The king, however, presents the need for such

conflict in terms of the 'enemy', who is associated with areas out-
side Egypt, and is thus allied with the forces of chaos that continu-
ally face the cosmos from outside. Despite this universalizing
justification for his actions, the sacrilegious event reveals the king's
fallibility and the limits to his knowledge. His responsibility for this
deed seems to be viewed as having caused the end of his reign.

The references to this misdeed are nevertheless interwoven with
descriptions of the king's positive achievements, by which he guar-
anteed the safety of the kingdom for his heir. None the less, the
poem does not provide any simple positive summary of the king's
reign. The description of the land's prosperity continually alludes to
the dangers of royal responsibility, although less pessimistically
than these threats are formulated in *The Teaching of King
Amenemhat*. The king's failure at Thinis does not undermine his
achievement as a whole, but remains an untoward event, both in
that it involved royal fallibility and in that it meant that, as the
upholder of justice, he suffered for his misdeed. The qualification of
human fallibility, which lessens the king's responsibility for the sac-
rilege, paradoxically puts in general terms one conclusion that is
drawn from the episode: that the world is imperfect. This untoward
event in effect questions the benevolence of the gods, since they
allowed this injustice to occur unwittingly and still punished the
king for it; at first sight, this is grounds for pessimism. The king,
however, takes his own misfortune as an indication not only that
faults are inevitable and are punished, but also that the gods are
watching over everything, and are not hostile to mankind. The uni-
verse is, despite appearances, 'bound together' through laws of eter-
nal justice.

It is characteristic of the poem that the king's oversight is
described most explicitly as part of a eulogy of the 'perfect office' of
kingship and the wisdom of kingship. The stanzas move with a con-
tinual ebb and flow between the ideal and the actual that underlies
the structure of the whole, and is made explicit in the final stanzas.
In these the poem moves through a description of the invincible
might of god against sinners towards what is arguably the climax
of the poem, a eulogy of creation. The cosmos was created to care
for mankind, and it is centred around men's hearts; this alludes to
the belief that provided an answer to the questions of suffering and
of the apparent injustice of the gods: that men's hearts were the
source of evil, and that they brought suffering upon themselves

despite the gods' benevolence (see pp. 168–9). Creation is a struggle against primeval chaos, and mankind is inherently tending to wild, and by nature tearful. Thus, restraint is necessary on a cosmic scale, even including the punishment and slaughter of men by the gods. Suffering, paradoxically, can be the consequence of the creator's benignity, as in the mythical past when he destroyed most of mankind in order to restrain their rebellion (see n. 46). This formulation validates both the need for kingship and the untoward events caused by King Khety's failings and his consequent downfall.

The problem of divine justice is presented in terms of a royal individual's experience but is validated in terms of all mankind's. The poem moves from the sacrilege done in the name of the king to an epiphany of the creator-god whose care is made manifest through the retribution for the royal misdeed. At the centre of the Teaching, however, remain the ambiguous troubled heart of man and the fallibility of the all-too-human king. The whole poem extols the responsibility of rulers to impose order on a complex and chaos-ridden world. Although the responsibilities necessitate harsh actions, the king's awareness of the difference between the ideal and the actual also gives his teaching an air of humility. In a final stanza Khety returns to the theme of teaching his heir, and urges restraint once again: total power is God's alone, and, while the king must emulate him, he must not overstep his limited ability.

The most complete surviving manuscript (P. St-Petersburg 1116A) was copied *c.*1400 BC in Memphis by 'the scribe Khaemwaset for himself, the truly quiet, good of character, patient, loved by people . . . for his dear brother whom he loves . . . the scribe Mahu'; the manuscript is rather corrupt, but other more fragmentary copies supplement it. Numbers give the sections of Wolfgang Helck's edition (letters indicate the lines of these sections), with the line numbers of P. St-Petersburg in parentheses.

The Teaching for King Merikare

1 (P 1)   [The beginning of the Teaching[1]
          made by the Dual King, . . . Khet]y,
          for his son Merikare.
          [He says, '. . . . .][2]
          [. . . . .]
          Do not be lenient about a misdeed which you have
                caught!
          You should punish [. . . . .]
          [. . . . .] their [. . .] in every respect:
          this is the beginning of [rebellion]
          [. . . . .].

2 (P 4)   [. . . . .] created,[3]
          when the malcontents are made many, [. . . . .]
          [. . . . .]
          [. . . . . .rebel]s with their plans against you.
          [. . . . .]
          [. . . . .]
          Someone who speaks a repor[t . . . .]
          [. . . . .]
          After your words exist against e[vil. . . . . . .]
          [. . . . .]
          [. . . . . that is brought] low is partial.
          [. . . . .]
          [. . . . .]
          He makes half of it as a heap.
          Then [one shall . . . . a lord];
          he [. . . . .] division [with] my supporters.
          The Y[outh. . . . . say the like],
          [. . . . . .] seem many to you.
          You should ⟨not⟩ stray from the path of [. . . . . .]!
          [. . . . .]
          [Do not be lenient] to him! You should kill those who
          [owe] him [allegiance] for this,
          for you know his supporters, who love him!

3 (P 13) If you encounter a [mighty man who] is the [master] of a
                town,[4]

and is the lord of a clan,
care for him, and then [he] will not [. . . . . . .] your many
    100,000s!
Do not destroy a man for the sake of principle, not [. . . .]
[. . . . .]
[He is in charge of the] Great Mansions,
and [. . . .] bread [. . . . .]
he [. . . . .]; he [care]s for the clan.
Take care not to [. . . . .]

[. . .] the men who guard for us the living![5]   4 (P 18)
A month has passed and [. . . . .]
[. . . . .] he [. . .]s himself.
He speaks, takes concern, remembers—
O a man on earth who is mighty
in every limb of his body!
[Punish] the people who are con[spiring]!
But be kind to him, when your heart is satisfied;
then everyone says, "This is his rebirth!"
and they [become] contented.

If you encounter someone who was once without [many]
    neighbours,[6]   5 (P 21)
whom the townspeople did [not] know,
but whose supporters now amount to many
and [love] him [for] his goods, and also for his knowledge,
who has entered into hearts,
and who makes himself seem fair to his servants,
yet who continues to be an agitator and a talker—drive
    him away!
Kill his children! Erase his name!
[Destroy] his neighbours! Drive away memory of him,
and of the supporters who love him!

The tumultuous man is a disturber of the townspeople.[7]
He raises up two parties among the Youth.
Now, if you find that he belongs to the townspeople,   6 (P 26)
a hasty-[mouthed man] whose actions ignore you,
accuse him in front of the entourage!
Drive [him] away! He is a rebel also.
The talker is an agitator of the town.

Curb the masses! Drive away the heat from them!
He who drives the rebel away should not blame the
      poor man whose father made him rebel.

7 (P 28)   A dependant can put the army that [follows] you in
              chaos.[8]
           His end will be made in the confusion which he began;
           the masses rage, and they will be put in the Workhouse.
           But be lenient [to . . . . . .] when you punish!
           You thus change [the citizen]s into rejoicing.

8 (P 30)   You should be righteous beside God,
           so that men will speak [according to] your thoughts!
           You should punish in accordance with the off[ence]!
           Good nature is a man's heaven.
           The angry-hearted's cursing is his pain.

9 (P 32)   Be skilful with words, and you will be victorious.[9]
           The strong arm of the king is his tongue.
           Words are stronger than any weapon.
           No one can get round someone who has a skilful heart.
           [He acquires effectiveness] effortlessly.
           A man of understanding is a [shelter] against even
              officials.
           They who know that he knows cannot attack him.
           [Misfortune] cannot exist near him.
           Truth comes to him distilled,
           like the counsels of ancestral speech.

10 (P 35) Emulate your forefathers, your ancestors,[10]
           and work will be done [successfully] with [their]
              wisdom!
           Look, their words endure in writings.
           Open, and read,
           and emulate the wise!
           A skilled man becomes an educated man.

11 (P 36) Be not evil! Patience is good.[11]
           Make your monuments last through love of you!
           Make the cor[vée-workers] whom the city has gathered
              have plenty.
           They will thank God for this bounty—
           watch over your [repute],

give praises for your goodness,
and pray to [the Gods] for your health.

Respect the officials! Make your people well![12]   12 (P 38)
Strengthen your borders and your patrols!
It is good to act for the future.
The life of the clear-sighted man will be respected;
he who trusts will suffer.
Make people watch over [you], through your good
    nature!
Vile is he who binds the land to himself, [to make it his].   13 (P 40)
The man who is rapacious when something belongs to
    someone else is a fool,
for [life] upon earth passes—it is not long.
Being remembered because of it is success.
Even a million men cannot benefit the Lord of the Two
    Lands.
It is for eternity that a [man] will be alive;
the departure of him who issued from the Creator will be
    like the release a favoured man.

Make your great ones great, so that they will enact your
    laws![13]   14 (P 42)
Someone wealthy of house cannot be partial.
Someone who does not suffer want is a lord of goods.
A poor man cannot speak truthfully.
He who says "If only I had!" cannot be righteous,
but is partial to a man who endears himself,
and inclines to a lord who pays him.
Great is the great one whose great ones are great.[14]   15 (P 44)
The king who is the lord of an entourage is strong.
Someone wealthy in officials is a rich man.
You should speak Truth in your house,[15]
so that the officials who are in the land will fear you!
Righteousness is proper for a lord.
It is the public rooms which give out fear of the private
    rooms.

Do Truth so that you may endure upon earth![16]   16 (P 46)
Quieten the weeper! Do not oppress the widow!
Do not expel a man from his father's property!

Do not destroy the officials in their seats of office!
Beware of punishing wrongly!
Do not smite! It is not good for you!

17 (P 48) You should punish with beaters and with guards![17]
This land will be founded through this—
except for the rebel who is devising plans.
God knows the malcontent.
God will impose his doom with blood.
Only the lenient man [will increase] his lifetime.

18 (P 50) Do not kill a man whose excellence you know,[18]
with whom you used to chant the writings,
who was brought up to be someone recognized [as . . .
      be]fore God,
with free-striding feet in the Place of Secrets!
The soul will come back to the place it knows,
and it cannot stray from its ways of yesterday.
No kind of magic can beat it back.
It will reach those who offer it water.

19 (P 53) The court that judges the man who is wanting—[19]
you know that They are not lenient
on that day of judging the wretched,
that hour of doing Their office.
It is painful when the accuser is someone wise.
Trust not in length of years,
for They see a lifetime as an hour!

20 (P 55) After death a man remains,
and his deeds are placed beside him in a heap.
Now, being There is eternity:
the man who does what angers Them is a fool;
the man who reaches Them without doing wrong,
he is There like a God,
free-striding like the Lords of Eternity.

21 (P 57) Raise your Youth, so that the Residence will love you![20]
Make your supporters plentiful among the veterans!
Look, your town is full of new growth.
These twenty years, the Youth has been happy, following
      its heart;
and the veterans are now going forth once again;
the recruits are recruited into it

as children [raised up for service].
It is the ancient past that fights for us;[21]
on my accession I raised up troops from them.
So make your great ones great! Advance your [fight]ers!   22 (P 60)
Increase the Youth of your following,
equipped with amounts,
established with fields,
and endowed with cattle!

Do not treat a gentleman differently from a commoner![22]
Take a man to yourself for his actions,
so that every work of craft will be done!
The [territory] of the lord of strength will [prosper].
Protect your border! Marshall your fortresses!   23 (P 62)
Troops are good for their lord.
Make [many] monuments for God;
this makes the name of him who does it live.
A man should do what is good for his soul:[23]
performing the monthly service, putting on white sandals,
joining the temple estate, keeping confidential the
      mysteries,
entering into the sanctuary,
eating bread from the temple!

Make the offering tables flourish, make the provisions
      great,[24]   24 (P 65)
increase the daily offerings!
It is a good thing for him who does it.
Strengthen your monuments according to your power!
A single day gives to eternity,
an hour benefits the future.
God knows the man who acts for Him;
your images, of which they can make no compilation,
will spread to a far foreign country.
He who is unconcerned about the enemies' affairs suffers.
      The enemy cannot be calm within Egypt.   25 (P 68)

The Youth will attack the Youth,[25]
just as the ancestors foretold it.
Egypt will fight in the necropolis,
destroying tomb-chambers in a destruction of deeds.

26 (P 70) I did the like, and the like happened,
           as is done to someone who goes against God in this way.
           Do not deal badly with the southern region![26]
           You know what the Residence foretold about it.
           As such things happen, these happened.
           Those things could not go otherwise, even as they said it.
           I got to Thinis, opposite its southern border at Tawet.[27]
           Like a cloudburst I seized it;
           King Meri[ib]re, the justified, had not done this.

27 (P 74) Be lenient about this to the governed![28]
           Make them content with this! Renew the treaties!
           No pure water lets itself be concealed.
           It is good to act for the future.

28 (P 75) All is now well for you with the Southern Region,[29]
           which comes to you bearing produce, bearing tribute.
           I did the like for the ancestors.
           Someone had no grain, and I gave it to him.
           Be kind to those who yield to you,
           so that they are satisfied with your bread and your beer!

29 (P 77) To you comes granite unhindered.
           Destroy not the monuments of another;
           you should hew stone in Tura!
           Build not your tomb-chamber from ruins,
           for what is done will be what will be done!

30 (P 79) Look, the king ⟨is⟩ the lord of joy.[30]
           You should be lenient, and then you can sleep secure in
               your strength!
           Follow your heart, for this is what I have done:
           there is now no enemy in the midst of your borders.

31 (P 81) Then I arose, a lord of the city,[31]
           whose heart grieved because of the Delta,
           Hutshenu to Sembaq,
           with its southern border at Two-Fish Canal.
           I appeased the entire West—
           as far as the sand dunes of the Lake.
           It labours of itself and it produces cypress;[32]
           whatever juniper can be seen, it produces for us.
           And the East is rich with the barbarians,
           and their labour-dues are [arriv]ing;

the Middle Islands have turned back respectfully, and
    every man from amongst them;
the temple estates are saying to me, "You are so great!"

Look, the [land] which they had destroyed is made into
    nomes;[33]   32 (P 85)
every great town [is refounded];
what one man ruled now belongs to ten;
officials are appointed, and granted labour-dues,
with knowledge of every duty.
There are freemen granted a plot,
and they work for you like a single team.
This means that there will be no malcontent among them.

The Nileflood will not be sick for you, and fail to come;[34] 33 (P 87)
the labour-dues of the Delta belong to you.
Look, the post which I have made in the East is driven in,
from Hebenu to The Ways of Horus,
founded with townspeople,
full of people,
of the choicest of the whole land, to beat back attacks on
    them.
O to see a man strong enough to equal this,[35]
and increase what I have done!
Down with a vile heir!

But now, these things are said about the barbarian:[36]   34 (P 91)
the vile Asiatic is the pain of the place where he is—
lacking in water,
difficult with many trees,
whose roads are painful because of the mountains.
He has never settled in any one place,
lack of food making him wander away on foot!
He has been fighting since the Time of Horus.
He cannot prevail; he cannot be prevailed over.
He does not announce the day of battle,
like a thief whom a gang has rejected.

But as I shall live, and shall be what I am,[37]   35 (P 94)
these barbarians were a walled fortress,
whose fortifications were open, and which I had isolated!
I have made the Delta strike them,

have plundered their underlings, and taken away their
    cattle,
to horrify the Asiatics who are against Egypt.
Do not worry about him!
The Asiatic is a crocodile on its riverbank
that snatches from a lonely road
but cannot take from the quay of a populous town.

36 (P 98)   Secure Mednit to its di[strict]![38]
Flood its side to Kemui!
Look, it is the lifeline against the foreigners—
its walls and fighters are many;
the supporters in it know how to take up clubs,
as well as the freemen within.
The region of Djedsut totals ten thousand men,[39]
commoners and freemen who are without labour duty.
Officials have been in it since the Time of the Residence;
the borders are fixed, its strongholds are mighty;
many northerners irrigate it as far as the Delta,
taxed in grain in the manner of freemen.

37 (P 103)   For those who do this, this is the way to surpass me.
Look, it is the door to the Delta—
it has acted as a dyke for Heracleopolis.

Plentiful towns mean integrity.[40]
Beware of being surrounded by supporters of the enemy!
Wariness renews the years.

38 (P 106)   Arm your border against the South—
they are barbarians who take up the war belt!
Build mansions in the Delta!
A man's name will not be little, being what he has
    done.
A well-founded town cannot be destroyed.
Build a mansion for your image!
The enemy loves grieving the heart, and vile deeds.

39 (P 109)   King Khety, the justified, decreed as a teacher,
"Someone silent against the savage is someone who
    destroys the offering tables.
God will attack someone who rebels against the
    temples."

It will come upon him, even as he does it.[41]
He will be sated with what he ordains to be snatched for
    himself;
but no one loyal to him will be found,
on that day of arrival.
Enrich the offering tables! Respect God![42]
Do not say, "The heart's too vile", and do not slacken
    your actions!   40 (P 112)
Now, to make revolt against you is to destroy heaven.
Security is a monument for a hundred years.
If the enemy were wise, he would not destroy this;
but no one is free from enemies.
The ⟨Lord⟩ of the Two Banks is a sage;[43]   41 (P 115)
the King, the lord of courtiers, cannot be foolish.
When he came out of the womb he had understanding,
and God has set him apart before a million other men.

Kingship is a perfect office;[44]
it has no son, it has no brother, who can make its
    monuments endure:
it is one individual who restores another's.
A man should act for his predecessor
for love of his achievements' being restored by another
    succeeding him.
Look, a vile deed happened in my time:[45]   42 (P 119)
the nome of Thinis was destroyed.
It happened, but not as my action,
and I knew of it only after it was done.
See my shortcoming, which is pre-eminent in what I did.
Now, destruction is vile.
It is no good for a man to refurbish what he has
    wrecked,
to restore what he has defaced—beware of it!
With its like is a blow repaid:
all that is done is bound together.

Generation passes generation of mankind,[46]   43 (P 123)
while God, who knows their character, has hidden
    Himself.
Yet there can be no resisting the Lord of the Hand:
He can attack whatever eyes can see.

Respect should be shown to God on His path,[47]
made of jewels, fashioned from copper,
like a flood repaid with a flood:
no river lets itself be concealed,
but it opens the dyke in which it hid.

44 (P 127) The soul also goes back to the place it knows;[48]
it cannot stray from its ways of yesterday.
Make good your place of the West,
furnish your mansion of the necropolis,
with rightness, with doing Truth—this is what Their
     hearts rely upon!
The character of the righteous-hearted is more accept-
     able
than the ox of the evil-doer.

45 (P 129) Act for God, and He will do the like for you,
—with great offerings for a flourishing altar, with
     inscriptions!
This is a guidance for your renown:
God is aware of the man who acts for Him.[49]

46 (P 130) Mankind is cared for—the flock of God.[50]
For their sakes He made heaven and earth,
and drove away the rapacity of the waters.
So that their nostrils should live He made the winds.
They are images of Him, come forth from His flesh.[51]
For their sakes He rises in heaven.
For them He made plants and flocks,
fowl and fish to feed them.
He has killed His enemies and He has destroyed His
     children[52]
for thinking to make rebellion.

47 (P 132) For their sake He shines.[53]
To see them He sails.
He has raised for Himself a shrine around them.
They weep and He is listening.
He has made for them rulers from birth,[54]
commanders to sustain
the back of the weak.
He has made for them magic, as a weapon
to resist the events that happen,

watching over them, both night and day.
He has killed the malcontents amongst them,[55]
like a man striking his son for the sake of his brother.
God knows every name.

May you do no ill ⟨against⟩ my pronouncement,[56]   48 (P 138)
which gives all the laws about the kingship,
which instructs you how to sustain men!
So may you reach me, without anyone accusing you.
Do not kill a single man who is close to you,[57]   49 (P 139)
for you have favoured him, and God knows him!
He is one of those who should flourish upon earth.
The followers of the king are Gods.
Place love of you in the whole land.
A good character is memory, when the years have
    passed.
You are to be called the Destroyer of the Time of Ill[58]
by those who are posterity in the House of Khety,
with the prayer "May he come again today!"
Look, I have told you the virtue of my generation.   50 (P 143)
May you act by what is set down for you!'

So it ends, from start to finish,
as found in writing.

Notes

1. The opening is very fragmentary. The name of the teacher is uncertain. *Khety* is the dynastic name of the Heracleopolitan kings, but it is uncertain which one is meant here (see Introduction, p. 212); the lacuna may have included the teacher's throne name.
2. The first stanza concerns the restraint of *rebellion*, a theme that is developed in the following six stanzas describing the proper responses to various types of citizen. This topic is almost entirely absent from official inscriptions.
3. The second stanza advocates the power of the spoken word in responding to opposition. The opening verse can perhaps be restored '[If you encounter a city whose . . . are]'. For the *Youth*, see n. 7. The final verses concern reprisals against a particular type of rebel described by the stanza; the future king is urged to kill both the leader and his allies.
4. The king now urges caution in punishing a powerful man; the whole Teaching has a strong pragmatic streak, and he advises that different circumstances demand different responses. The *100,000s* are numerous underlings; the *Great Mansions* are the central law courts.
5. This stanza turns to a commendable type of subordinate (wordplay links this stanza with the last: *take care* and *guard* are homonyms). The final verses affirm

that if such a mighty man is in charge of people who conspire, a king should not punish him as part of his reprisals; then everyone will acclaim the royal benevolence.

6. The king next urges merciless punishment for a man who has acquired influence and *goods* only in order to stir up dissent. A forceful series of commands embraces his present power, his heritage, his future repute (*name*), and his survival in the next life (*memory*). The practice of *damnatio memoriae* is widely visible on monuments. One manuscript inserts a verse at the start of this stanza: 'May you [punish an agitator] like God'.

7. The king turns to a more lowly townsman, who *ignores* royal authority and is a rabble-rouser. The echoes of the vocabulary of the preceding stanza suggest his similarity to the other rebel, despite the difference in their status. The *Youth* is paramilitary companies. The concluding verse advises a king to punish the rebel but not his dependants, who were forced to follow him by their poverty (inherited from their *father*).

8. This stanza is more reflective and concerns a yet more lowly man, who nevertheless can make trouble for an entire *army*. Disturbance among the poor leads to their being sent to the *Workhouse*, the office of forced labour. The king warns against being harsh towards the lowly, and urges that one should punish only in proportion to the provocation. Such justice is *good nature* and brings bliss and security (*heaven*); to do otherwise causes the punisher to suffer.

9. The king moves from specific opponents to more general injunctions about wisdom. Wise speech is a way of avoiding rebellion, rather than punishing after the event; describing speech as strength brings out the contrast with the acts of strength described previously. As the king turns to positive commands, more metaphorical and less aggressive images follow. *Words* are also the means of acquiring virtue, and are the only refuge in a tumultuous society. After listing various types of rebel, the Teaching now describes the single value of *Truth*.

10. This stanza develops the previous one's preoccupation with wisdom as the ideal of the ancestral past; wisdom endures in *writings*, and the stanza considers how royal virtue and achievements can be made to endure through wisdom and patience (a central social virtue). The verse about an *educated* man implies that one has to be *skilled* to benefit from teaching.

11. After a central verse urging *patience*, the second half of the stanza advises a king to plan enduring defensive action. The king's forces should be well rewarded, so that they will be grateful. After a passage on emulating established virtue, the future is cited as a reason for virtue. This stanza moves from the present act of reading *writings*, through the enduring *monuments* of the reign, to a king's future reputation. The next stanza continues this movement into eternity, and describes how enduring renown is gained by ensuring that social prosperity is continued.

12. The king now warns against blindly trusting in the terrestrial future and ignoring the responsibilities of authority. This stanza develops the contrast between *good nature* and the selfish use of power, which is *vile* (a keyword) and will bring no renown. Virtue is the only stability—acquiring property (even as much as the whole *land*) is useless. Without wisdom, human plenitude (a *million men*) is of no use to a king (the *Lord of the Two Lands*); this verse ironically evokes official statements that the king is worth more than a million men (cf. n. 43). Virtue and renown are presented *sub specie aeternitatis*, and in the light of the otherworldly judgement of God. The stanza progresses from concern with the *future* and life *upon earth* to all *eternity*, which is the lifetime of the virtuous man; for him, death (*departure*) is a painless transition to a more perfect state. (The *Creator* is literally 'He who created Her', i.e. Truth').

13. Another stanza on officials, which returns—like the start of the preceding one—to specific and practical considerations in enacting eternal principles. The following verses, however, imply that the pragmatism of this advice is not materialistic: to be *wealthy* enough to be impartial does not require great wealth, only no *want*.

14. The second half of the stanza develops the argument of the first, as the king affirms the unity of the élite with wordplay on *great*. This is then explicated: the king's security depends not on acquiring personal wealth, but on the well-being of his *entourage*—if members of it are great, he will be truly great. Thus generosity is true *wealth*. His greatness is his ability and responsibility to articulate and enact Truth, as the poor cannot.

15. A concluding quatrain develops the idea of the king's spreading *Truth*, as a means of power. Public behaviour will earn respect for an individual.

16. The king now moves gradually from these reflections on wealth to consider the virtue of consideration for society's oppressed. This is integral to order and *Truth*; the reflections on the *widow* echo claims to virtue in funerary inscriptions. This stanza moves from the specific and this-worldly to the otherworldly and absolute, returning to the theme of endurance (from 13c–h).

17. After warnings against harsh measures, the king now advises how to protect the land with limited reprisals—with imprisonment rather than with execution (*smiting*). Almost in an aside, the theme of rebellion reappears, but here *God* is the absolute avenger of any wrong; thus the king (his deputy) should be lenient. Caution and mercy are urged, as part of a general movement towards admitting royal fallibility.

18. The king warns against action towards an acquaintance who was educated with the royal children (an actual practice with the children of the provincial élite). The *Place of Secrets* is an area of restricted access, the private apartments of the palace; it can also refer to a temple, moving the subject into the next world, as in the following verses. (*Free-striding* is also used later of the blessed dead (20g)). The *soul* represents the dead, who can avenge themselves on the living, as agents of retribution, and who can overpower any *magic* used by the living to defend themselves. *Water* was offered to the dead, by a living intercessor claiming justice. Reciprocity and retribution continue beyond the grave.

19. This *court* no longer consists of earthly 'officials' (as in 14a–g), but of otherworldly judges who are absolutely impartial; eternal judgement is infallible, unlike royal vengeance, and being *someone* absolutely *wise* is an attribute of God (as in the preceding stanza). *They* are the accusing Gods who judge the *heap* of a man's riches and achievements (*heap* is homonymous with *lifetime*, as are *deeds* and *remain*). *There* is the otherworld, where the virtuous are rewarded, in contrast to this world, which is a mere *hour*. The concluding verses contrast the fates of the unvirtuous and virtuous man (the epithet *free-striding* echoes 18d). Although the description of judgement is couched in generalized terms, the context makes it clear that the king himself will also be judged by absolute standards.

20. This stanza returns to the here and now and the effects of the last *twenty years* rather than future eternity. The king urges care for the human resources that can defend the realm; he has ensured that the *Youth* (see n. 7) is happy to perform its military service; the phrase *following the heart* can imply an ethical following of one's conscience as well as enjoyment.

21. In the second half of the stanza the king affirms that royal success depends on previous achievements, and on the earlier generation of *veterans* (the *them* of the verse after the cue). These stanzas interweave futurity, the present, and the antique past into one continuum, to emphasize the responsibility of the new king, which is expressed in paramilitary terms.

22. The king develops further the theme of human resources, and of cultivating allies regardless of their social status. There is a progression from the specific to the universal, moving from the treatment of subjects, through military protection, to an injunction about piety and temple procedure. Temple ritual was also a protective measure, since it enacted and maintained the stability of the cosmos. The unity of these actions, all of which will ensure security, is reinforced by the homophony of the words *fortresses* and *monuments*. The king should deal well both with his servants and with his divine superiors.

23. The king was the universal protagonist of the temple cult. These verses refer to the practice whereby members of the élite served as temple priests in *monthly* shifts. *Bread* that was offered to the gods was afterwards distributed for the priests to *eat*.

24. This stanza continues the theme of cultic piety: earlier God was said to know the malcontent (17d), but here he acknowledges the virtuous. This affirmation of reciprocity in the seventh verse echoes the start of the preceding stanza (22f), where the king was urged to reward a man for his 'actions'. Here the benefits of virtue extend geographically as well as through time by spreading royal *power* abroad (represented by numberless images of the king). This provides a transition to the following contrasting themes of barbarism, chaos, and conflict: the stanza ends with a description of the contrary of a vigilant and virtuous ruler. *Enemies* require continuous warding off, and are an eternal threat to *Egypt*.

25. The opening verse develops the preceding affirmation that the threat of disorder is always present and that neglect of this brings conflict between troops in Egypt (echoing 5l). The king cites the authority of *ancestors* for this; although a specific prophecy or teaching may be alluded to, he probably refers to general knowledge that conflict is unavoidable. He now describes a historical event, a fault of his own—the references to himself increase in this passage—that is a specific instance of the laws of retribution and the need to act virtuously. A hallowed cemetery was destroyed during the conflict of his accession, and this misdeed was punished with divine retribution (answering *the like* with like). A mixture of future, present, and past tenses suggests the eternal relevance of the event.

26. An injunction to deal well with the south (the scene of his misdeed) leads to a description of past historical events. An ancestral prophecy is ominously alluded to once again to show the inevitability of the workings of retribution (*happen* and *go* echo the preceding verses 26a–b). *They* who *said it* are the royal ancestors of the *Residence*.

27. The town of *Thinis* is the capital of the 8th Upper Egyptian nome, near modern el-Girga, over 300 km south of Heracleopolis; nearby was the site of the most famous necropolis in Egypt (modern Abydos). *Tawet* (reading uncertain) is apparently a place south of Thinis, perhaps near modern Nag al-Tud. King *Meribre* was a predecessor of the teacher, whom he surpassed by gaining territory from the rival kingdom to the south. The taking of Thinis is recounted initially as if a positive achievement, as in a commemorative inscription, but the context is ominous.

28. The king again urges leniency towards those who were overthrown in the southern kingdom (in contrast to the destruction done in his reign). The proverbial-sounding image of *pure water*, suggesting that responsibilities must be acknowledged, contrasts ominously with that of the violent 'cloudburst' of 26h (and is later developed as an expression of irresistible divine power (43g–i)). The stanza ends with a verse (repeated from 12c) on the *future* benefits of virtue.

29. The king now describes the stability he has achieved and his virtuous generosity to his ancestors and dependants; it is part of his addressee's duty to

maintain this status quo and build on his experience. This stanza continues the
concern with the *South*, but in an unqualified, positive vein; the contrast
between the positive reciprocity here and the retribution of the preceding stanza
is pointed by the repetition of *I did the like* (from 26a). *Granite* was a product
characteristic of the far south; this sign of prosperity inspires general reflections
on building and relationships. He urges the new king to build fresh monuments
rather than usurping or reusing material from his ancestors' (this recalls the
activities in the necropolis of 25e–f). This was a common practice, and graphi-
cally relevant to the themes of retribution and reciprocity: those who usurp
monuments will have theirs usurped; the repetition of *what is done* expresses the
acting out of retribution. *Tura* is a renowned limestone quarry on the east bank
of the Nile, 12 km south of modern Cairo.

30. In a concluding quatrain, the king assures his heir of his security (*joy* is
homonymous with 'largess', and the epithet *lord of joy* is a standard royal one).
Sleeping securely and *following* pleasures (cf. n. 20) are signs of well-being. The
final verse, proclaiming the lack of any enemies (recalling 25b), assures the heir
that the king has repressed disorder, both by his kindness and by his active poli-
cies.

31. This stanza continues to recount the king's achievements after his capture of
Thinis, but turns from the south to the north and north-west. The extent of his
rule increases through the stanza, from his city to a much larger harmonious
region. Middle Kingdom hymns acclaim the king as 'lord of his city'—as per-
sonal local rulers. The idiom *heart grieved* contrasts with the 'following your
heart' that the king's efforts have guaranteed for his son (30c and n. 30).
Hutshenu and *Sembaq* are unknown locations, probably delimiting the Delta or
its western edge. *Two-Fish Canal* is in the Delta, west of Heliopolis, near modern
Zat al-Kom. The *sand dunes* are perhaps the ridges around the *Lake* of the
Fayyum, i.e. at the southern end of the western boundary.

32. In the second half of the stanza the king describes how he has ensured that these
areas freely pay taxes, of whatever is *seen*; such tribute is a sign of the order
that covers the north, west, and east. The *Middle Islands* are the islands or
watery regions of the north, in the Delta or Mediterranean. The king now
receives the acclamation of the provincial *estates*; this affirmation of centralized
authority leads into the next stanza.

33. The king presents his rule in the usual ideological terms, as a recovery from a
chaotic interregnum, a refounding of what had been *destroyed*; local tyrants
have now had their monopolies divided between a proper number (*ten*) of local
governors. Such harmonious prosperity prevents *malcontent* (a keyword).

34. The king moves to the north-east and concentrates on the efforts needed to
secure prosperity, described in the broad geographical terms of the *Nileflood* (for
whose success the king is ideologically responsible). The *post* is literally a border
marker, but also a metaphorical 'mooring post' by which the ship of state is
securely landed; this image also has a funerary sense of securing an eternal
landfall. *Hebenu* was the capital of the 16th Upper Egyptian nome (near modern
Kom el-Ahmar); *The Ways of Horus* refers to the royal road leading eastward
from Sile (modern Tell Abu Sefa) towards Palestine. The king claims to have
defended the eastern border from the northern edge of Middle Egypt to the Delta.

35. The account of the teacher's reign ends in a directly expressed wish—such as
occurs in royal inscriptions—for an heir to equal him (that is, Merikare). The
vile heir in the concluding curse leads into the next stanza, where the apogee of
vileness is revealed as the ever-chaotic barbarian, the contrary of royal virtue.

36. The description of the *Asiatic* continues the theme of the east. He is a *vile* enemy
in a vile land, and is the worst of its many hostile features. The *Time of Horus*

(the royal god) was the period of primordial harmony when the gods ruled Egypt, a contrast with the Asiatics' chaos. The king warns that the enemy is always present, and attacks unexpectedly, though he is ultimately disorderly and ineffectual.

37. An oath opens a second stanza about barbarians, which provides a résumé of the king's struggle against enemies; this passage is similar to those found in commemorative inscriptions where the king recounts his victories, swearing that they are true. The king has made the *Delta* a force against the Easterners; their helplessness is described with the metaphor of a siege. The next metaphor reduces the Asiatic to a wild predatory non-human being. The *town* contrasts with the earlier image of an open—that is, ineffective—fortification, and represents organized society as proof against such chaotic forces.

38. This stanza returns to a didactic tone, and urges the new king to maintain and extend the eastern defences around *Mednit*, the 22nd Upper Egyptian nome, *c.*30 km north of Heracleopolis. *Kemui* (modern Tell Atrib) is the capital of the 10th Lower Egyptian nome, near the apex of the Delta, *c.*160 km north of Heracleopolis. To *flood* is a metaphor for possessing, as well as irrigating.

39. The protection of the kingdom's northern border results from maintaining the prosperity of the ancient city of *Djedsut*, which protects Heracleopolis (like a *dyke*) and secures access to the Delta (like a *door*). *Djedsut* is a name for Memphis, derived from the name of an Old Kingdom pyramid at nearby Saqqara. The *Time of the Residence* is the Old Kingdom, when Memphis was the royal Residence.

40. The king warns of the necessity of vigilance: the state's security is ensured by caution and virtue, and by towns that have been made prosperous. He then summarizes the injunctions about the north and the south, reflecting on the totality of his achievements, which is exemplified by the founding of settlements and shrines, including those dedicated to statues of the king (*your image*). He draws an abstract moral, and moves towards universal truths, citing ancestral authority: *Khety* is one of the earlier kings of the dynasty, perhaps its founder. His maxim asserts that there will be divine retribution against the enemy of piety: inaction is as bad as active sacrilege.

41. Retribution emerges as the dominant theme as the king moves towards discussing his own fault in generalizing terms. Retribution will *come upon* man on *that day* when death arrives for him. *Sated* may be meant ironically, to suggest bad deeds rebounding on their doer.

42. The king urges virtue and persistence in virtue: the *heart* is here the conscience and will, the sense of the quoted speech being 'I can't be bothered'. The speech echoes the earlier description of the enemy (38g), which is resumed in the next figurative couplet. The sense seems to be that rebellion is like trying to wreck *heaven* itself (which was earlier said to be a man's good nature (8d)), but *security* (to be obtained by repressing rebellion) is like a lasting monument. A *hundred years* is the ideal lifetime as an adult, although the sage earlier advised against 'trusting in length of years' (19f). The following couplet warns of the inevitability of folly and enmity. (After this line all manuscripts have the verse 'for love of his achievements' being restored by another succeeding him', an erroneous insertion from 41i).

43. The king should be the opposite of such folly and enmity. Wisdom gives security, and the king must be wise to protect the *Two Banks* (Egypt); this quatrain allies him with god, who is alone all wise. The comparison with a *million men* is the language of royal eulogy, expressing the king's superhuman duty (earlier such men could not avail the king (13e)).

44. The king now pronounces a generalizing eulogy of kingship. The unique perfection of kingship, however, makes it vulnerable: the lack of a *son* is striking in

the context of the Teaching, in which the king is addressing his son. The endurance of kingship implicitly involves respect for individual solidarity (as witnessed in the maintenance of monuments (cf. n. 29)). This is the other side of the retribution that was described earlier. From the mention of this reciprocity, the king moves to evoke in the rest of the stanza the misdeed that brought retribution on him.

45. The area of Abydos in *the nome of Thinis* was particularly sacred, and the king's misdeed was to desecrate others' monuments (see n. 27). His *vile deed* is described explicitly here for the first time; the word *vile* associates it with the preceding descriptions of barbarism. The stanza moves from the perfection of kingship to the fact that this individual king was fallible. The king accepts his responsibility, even though he was unaware of the sacrilege: he should, however, have been a sage (41a-b and n. 43), not unaware of what was being done. The couplet on the vanity of repenting and of trying to restore a misdeed echoes the earlier imagery of unavoidable reciprocity (29a-e). The final verses assert reciprocity in broad abstract terms.

46. This stanza has a wide chronological sweep, encompassing all *generations* of mortal men; this develops the specific historical events of the preceding stanza into more generalizing pronouncements. Men are transient and fallible, whereas god is absolute in his knowledge of men. His *hidden* quality alludes to the myth of the 'sundered world', according to which the creator-god, angered at mankind's rebellion against him, slaughtered them and then withdrew from earth and from mankind, separating heaven and earth. The *Lord of the Hand* is the creator-god: the epithet alludes to his creation of the cosmos by masturbating—a relevant epithet in that the creator was unique and alone, like the king; it also refers to his active force in general.

47. Despite the sundered world, divine power is still manifest on earth in temple images. The injunction refers to the processions of god's image (*on His path*; this is also an allusion to the path of wisdom, 'the way of God'). Divine power is as irrepressible as a flood: like water it is *concealed* but has power to burst forth. *Flood repaid with a flood is* an expression for the swiftness of flowing water, but it also alludes to reciprocity and repaying like with like.

48. Reciprocity is as unalterable as the nature of god, and is exemplified, as earlier (18e-g), by the case of the *souls* of the dead who are bound by it, and who enact retribution. The theme of the dead continues an injunction to funerary piety in preparation for eternal judgement. *Make good your place* (i.e. tomb) is a phrase from *The Teaching of Hordedef* (see p. 292). The king stresses that true monuments are achieved by virtue and not by material wealth; the piety of the poor is expressed with wordplay: *the character* of the virtuous is homophonous with 'the loaf'—a humble offering in contrast to an *ox*.

49. This stanza about reciprocity concludes with an affirmation of god's wisdom. Earlier god was said to know the malcontent (17d), the virtuous (24g), and humanity (43b); here his power is articulated positively, and the next stanza hymns His benevolence to the world.

50. A calm stanza now describes god as the shepherd of mankind, the ideal that the king must imitate. Humanity is at the centre of the created cosmos (*for their sakes* is literally 'for their hearts'). The passage recalls a Twelfth Dynasty funerary text, in which the creator describes his creation as comprising 'four good deeds', and in which the ways of god are justified (see pp. 150-1). Divine creation is presented as a process of restraint, just as a king's harsh rule must be. The creation of *heaven and earth* alludes to the 'sundered world' (see n. 46). The *rapacity of the waters* may be a monstrous personification of the chaotic nature of the primeval waters from which creation arose.

51. In a funerary text (see n. 50) humanity is said to have come forth from the creator's 'tears'; 'mankind' and 'tears' are homophones, and the wordplay articulates the imperfection and sorrowful nature of man, which is alluded to in the next stanza (47d).

52. The concluding couplets allude to the mythical rebellion of mankind (see n. 46). God's slaughter of the rebels is a precedent both for the action of the king against his subjects and for the action of god against the king. The retribution that befell the king is now a sign of god's care for his *children*, not of his anger.

53. This stanza continues the eulogy of the creator, concentrating on the maintenance of the cosmos, rather than its establishment. The Sungod *sails* across heaven in the sunbarque as part of the daily renewal of cosmic order. Egyptian *shrines* were figurative recreations of the cosmos: the whole created world is a dwelling place for the numinous, in which mankind can appeal to god. For mankind's *weeping*, see n. 51.

54. Rulership is an institution of the creator to maintain his order; this justifies the actions of the king to suppress dissent, despite his fallibility. *Magic* is another gift from god: it is a positive religious force, used by the state, and one originally used by god in creation. With magic and kingship the creator provides for mankind's adversity.

55. Both of the eulogistic stanzas end with a reference to mankind's rebellion (see n. 52). His *killing* of rebellious mankind is presented as a paradoxically caring action, to protect the loyal members of the family of mankind; violence and strife—a recurrent theme—are here evidence of god's absolute knowledge—another recurrent theme—and of his care and control of every individual. The final verse provides a climax to the description of god's intimate care.

56. The final stanza provides a coda to the whole poem and returns to the specific setting of teacher and pupil. It is linked to the preceding eulogy by a mention of *kingship* (and by an echo of 47f: *sustain*). The phrase *may you reach me* implies that the old king has reached the goal which the new king should aspire to—i.e. he is either deceased (as in *The Teaching of Amenemhat*) or at the end of his life; he urges his son to end his life without any reproaches.

57. The injunctions to avoid reproaches are further developed, providing a summary of the motifs of restraining slaughter and of wisdom. Human fallibility both makes the exercise of power necessary and makes discretion and caution essential in exercising it. The king turns to positive topics, however, as the warning against executing courtiers is transformed into a statement about their future felicity as *Gods* (i.e. the blessed dead): loyal mankind is here well tended by the king, and the *whole land* is united in love of him.

58. The teacher assures the new king of the benefits that his wisdom will bring. The *House of Khety* is the Heracleopolitan Dynasty, and the *Time* is the preceding troubled period, including the old king's reign. At the end of the poem the king and his heir are placed in their specific historical context, viewed and judged from the future. A final injunction to benefit from experience concludes the work; the text and the country are both *set down*, or established, for the new king.

[11]

The 'Loyalist' Teaching

Introduction

The name of the teacher to whom this poem was ascribed is not preserved in any of the surviving copies, but he is certainly a man of high rank from the royal court. He tells his children of the 'way of living truly' in society and presents a vision of social solidarity in the Two Lands of Egypt, and of the responsibilities of enacting the ideals of Truth and order.

The Teaching falls into two halves. The first half opens with commands for the audience to respect their ruler. Teachings are often concerned with resolving tensions between the audience's concerns and experiences and the public ideals of society. This one presents these tensions in specifically political terms, embodied in the relationship between the audience and the centralized state. When dealing with this theme, Egyptian poetry is at its closest to official discourse. Loyalistic writings were common in Egypt, and articulated the absolute control of the king over society, but made little mention of any events or features of society that did not conform to traditional ideology. The king was regarded as a god and his power united individual bodies into a single prosperous society. Many of this Teaching's stanzas resemble a praise song to the king, such as were performed at court, although in the Teaching the royal power is extolled in strongly personal and intimate terms. The style is appropriately formal, and the verses are patterned in an even sequence of epigrammatic couplets, with many statements describing the king. He is presented as an ideal, generalized figure, the absolute embodiment of divine perfection, to which the audience is urged to enact its allegiance. The opening stanzas are monolithic and generally positive in tone; they are highly metaphorical—a feature that is developed in a different way in the second half of the poem.

The stanzas of the first half largely comprise generalizing

statements, and are not overtly very didactic: all injunctions are dis-
tilled into the single implicit command to choose between loyalty
and rebellion. The contrast between order and chaos, which domi-
nates literary Discourses, is here formulated as one between the
loyal man and the rebel, and both virtue and order are defined
exclusively in terms of the king. His power has a correspondingly
dual aspect, as he is assimilated with both protective and destruc-
tive cosmic agencies.

The second half of the Teaching turns to 'another matter', the
treatment of one's social inferiors. While the first half concerns the
relationship of the audience to the king, the second deals with
the audience's responsibility to the rest of society. The two halves
are marked as distinct with introductory formulae, but they also
form a unified whole, linked by the repetition of various phrases and
images. This integration is very appropriate, as a central subject is
social solidarity. The poem acknowledges that the state is dependent
on the labouring classes, and, although loyalism and an official's
duties to his subordinates are common themes of many texts, this
acknowledgement is unparalleled in official discourse of the Middle
Kingdom.

Just as the first half admitted the possibility of rebellion against
the king, in the second another danger is presented—that labour-
ers may prove fugitive, and rebel against their immediate masters.
The style matches the change in subject matter: it is more diverse
than that of the first half, as it is concerned with the populace,
rather than the unique king, and with a wider range of experience,
including a more forceful and detailed presentation of the dangers
of life.

The theme of an integrated world is embodied in imagery of cat-
tle and herdsmen. Literally, this extols the value of peasant shep-
herds, but metaphorically it extols the value of the 'shepherd' of
society, who is in the first instance the official who is being
addressed, and ultimately the king, who is in turn the representa-
tive of the divine shepherd whose flock is mankind. The interde-
pendence of society was an important aspect of the idea of Truth
and order, and of the principles of retribution and reciprocity by
which that ideal was enacted in the world. This solidarity existed
not only throughout society, but also across time and through suc-
ceeding generations, and the Teaching describes at the end of both
halves how the reader's sons will ensure the continuity of wisdom

and social values. The final stanza concludes with a man's burial. At the end of the first half this was presented as a royal reward for loyalism, but here it also depends on a man's virtue being remembered by his underlings. Social integrity continues after death and spans the whole course of civilization, uniting the world with eternity in an affirmation of ultimate togetherness. The king is the representative of this unity, but the nexus through which it is achieved is the ethical choice of the audience.

The text was first discovered in a version inscribed on a cenotaph stela (Cairo CG 20538) erected at Abydos by the Treasury official Sehotepibre in the reign of Amenemhat III (c.1790 BC); he appropriated the authorship and addressed the royal eulogy specifically to his patron. This ancient edited version consisted largely of the first half, the loyalistic topic of which provided the Teaching with its modern title. The poem may originally have been composed early in the Twelfth Dynasty. The text is complete thanks to the scholarship of Georges Posener, who pieced together numerous partial New Kingdom copies. Numbers give the sections of Posener's edition (and the individual lines of these sections).

The 'Loyalist' Teaching

1 Beginning of the Teaching[1]
  made by the Patrician and Count,
  the God's Father, whom the God loves,
  the Privy Counsellor of the Palace (l.p.h.!),
  the Head of the Entire Land,
  Sem-priest and Controller of Every Kilt,
  [. . . . .].
  He speaks a Teaching before his children,
  'I shall speak a great matter, and shall cause you to hear,[2]
  cause you to know the counsels of eternity,
  the way of living truly,
  the passing into blessedness.

2 Praise the king within your bodies![3]
  Be close to his Majesty in your hearts!
  Put terror of him throughout the day!
  Create acclamation for him at every season!
  He is the Perception which is in breasts:[4]
  his eyes probe every body.
  He is the Sungod under whose governance one lives:
  the man under his shade will have great possessions.
  He is the Sungod by whose rays one sees:[5]
  he illumines the Two Lands more than the sun.

3 His heat burns more than a tongue of flame.[6]
  He consumes ⟨in⟩ his moment more than fire.
  He makes thrive more than the great Nileflood:[7]
  he has filled the Two Lands with the strength of life.
  Noses are blocked when he falls into storm.
  He is calm, and then the air is breathed.
  To those in his following he gives sustenance;[8]
  he feeds the man who keeps to his way.
  The man he favours will be a lord of provisions;
  his adversary will be a nobody.
  The king's supporter will be someone blessed.
  [He secures] the Two Lands, and he casts his opponents away.

4 It is his power that fights for him.[9]
  His ferocity emits dread of him.

The man who looks upon [him will be . . . .].
Our [well-being] is based on praising his beauty.
He will reveal [his] appearance [to . . . . .].
[. . . . . .] love [. . . . .] his heart.
He is life to the man who gives praise to him.
His opponents will sink [into distress].
[Their] corpses [are to be thrown into the water].

The king is Sustenance; his speech is Plenty.[10]   5
The man he makes is someone who will always exist.
He is the heir of every god,
the protector of his creators.
They strike his opponents for him.
Now, his Majesty is in his palace (l.p.h.!)[11]—
he is an Atum of joining necks:
his protective might is behind the man who promotes his
          power.
He is a Khnum of every limb,
the begetter and creator of the folk.
He is a Bastet who protects the Two Lands:
the man who praises him will be sheltered by his arm.
He is a Sekhmet against the man who transgresses his command:
the man he disfavours will sink to distress.

Fight for his name! Respect his oath![12]   6
Make no opposition against a reward of his giving.
Acclaim the Red-king! Worship the White Crown!
Pay homage to the uplifter of the Double Crown!
You should do these things, so that your limbs may prosper![13]
You will find this good for all time—
being on earth, without sorrow,
passing lifetime in peace!

Enter into the earth which the king gives![14]   7
Rest in the place of all time!
Join with the eternal cavern!—
with your children's homes full of love for you,
your heirs remaining in your positions.
Conform ⟨to⟩ my example! Do not neglect my words!
Make good the rule of my making!

8   May you speak to your children![15]
    Speech has taught, since the time of the God.
    I am a noble to be listened to,
    whose understanding is recognized by his lord.
    Do not overstep my example! Do not be indifferent to my
            pattern!
    You should be free from disloyal action!
    The son who hears will be a faultless man.
    Can any plan of his not succeed?

                                    *

9   You will praise these things after years,[16]
    for their soundness gives landfall.
    Another method for developing your hearts,
    —which is even better—concerning your servants:
    care for men, organize people,
    that you may secure servants who are active!
    It is mankind who create all that exists;[17]
    one lives on what comes from their hands.
    They are lacking, and then poverty prevails.

10 The professions are what provide provisions.[18]
    A house is empty, with its foundations uprooted,
    and the very sound of them re-establishes its walls!
    The man who sleeps until dawn is a lord of many;[19]
    there will be no sleep for the solitary man.
    No one sends a lion on a mission.
    No herd can isolate itself from the walled enclosure;[20]
    its voice is like the thirsty creature's outside the well,
    with [decay] around it, and the wailing of birds.

11 One must long for the Nileflood, then one profits by it;[21]
    no ploughed field exists of itself.
    The cattle who belong to a cowherd are great:
    it is the cattleherd who can drive the wild bull.
    it is [the herdsman] who brings [the animals] across to land.
    [The shepherded] will be a plentiful flock, without number!
    To God, [these are] excellent professions.[22]
    Someone who is capable in them is a clever man.
    Do not make a field-worker wretched with taxes—

let him be well off, and he will still be there for you the next
    year.
If he lives, you have his hands;
you ruin him, and then he plans to turn vagabond.

The man who fixes the taxes in proportion to the barley[23]   12
is [a just] man in God's eyes.
The riches of the unjust man cannot stay;
his children cannot benefit from any remainder of his.
The man who afflicts is making the end of his own life:
there are no children of his close to him.
Serfs belong to the man who passes over himself:[24]
there are no heirs for the man with a restless heart.
Great is the reverence paid to the master of his temperament;
the vociferous man is unjust in all eyes.

It is the evil man who destroys his own mound;[25]   13
a town is founded for the man who is loved.
Patience is a man's monument.
Quietness is excellent, [calmness] is good.
The man who foresees what will come [has never been
    thwarted];
the man with powerful authority prevails.
The merciful—the cow bears for him;
the bad herdsman—his herd is small.

Fight for men in every respect![26]   14
They are a flock, good for their lord.
Evidently by them alone one lives;[27]
they are good also when joining the earth.
You should look to [your . . . who . . .]!
You should watch over your funerary priests:
the son is disloyal, but the priest remains!
It is a kind man who is named "heir".
Lay the noble dead to rest; make invocations in their name;[28]
[honour] the blessed dead; bring food-offer[ings]!
[This is better for] the doer than for the man for whom it is
    done—
the beneficiary protects the man who is still on earth.'

So it ends, from start to finish,
as found in writing.

Notes

1. The teacher is introduced by a series of high-ranking titles (see *The Tale of Sinuhe*, n. 1). *God's Father, whom the God loves* is a priestly title. The next two epithets with were often applied to viziers. The *Sem-priest* acted in rituals as the son of the god; he was associated with the rites of clothing the god and the king, hence the title referring to the ritual *Kilt*. The titles suggest that the teacher was a vizier, holder of the highest office in society after the king. His name, however, is lost. One possible, if unlikely, candidate is the historical vizier of Senwosret I, Montuhotep.

2. A rhetorical introduction proclaims the Teaching's importance and its eternal concerns. The verses envisage an easy progression from speech to obedience, and hence to a wisdom through which eternal principles are embodied in daily life, enabling the pupil to enter *blessedness* as one of the dead.

3. The first stanza of the Teaching proper opens with injunctions to *praise the king*. The first half of the Teaching advocates loyalty to the king, since this will guarantee success and ensure that virtue is rewarded. The loyal relationship ranges from the very intimate and personal to the cosmic.

4. Having urged homage, the stanza continues to eulogize the king as a personal force, who is all-knowing, and whose *Perception* penetrates every heart. *Perception* is a divine power used in creation by the *Sungod*: this divine aspect is developed in the following verses. The assimilation with the Sungod takes up the earlier allusion to *day* (2.3); the complementary evocation of *shade* is an image of royal protection, the reward for virtue. The sequence of sentences beginning 'He is . . .' is characteristic of eulogies; the identifications with gods express the various aspects of the king's power; although the king was in many senses divine, they are metaphorical.

5. From describing the king's power as a personal force, the stanza progresses to images of his power as universal and cosmic, embracing the whole of Egypt (the *Two Lands*).

6. This stanza continues the imagery of the fiery sun, and develops the theme of royal fearsomeness. The two sides of kingship—love and ferocity—are juxtaposed throughout the subsequent stanzas.

7. The *Nileflood* and the Sungod are often associated as the two forces controlling life (the association is expressed by repetition of *Two Lands* from 2.10). Both are potentially dangerous forces, but here the sage gives assurance of their revitalizing force. *Noses are blocked* in the dusty dry season when the Nileflood was absent (according to a contemporaneous hymn to the Nile). The imagery presents a sequence of light, water, and air, basic life forces which the king can give and withhold.

8. The assimilation to the Nile colours the rest of the stanza, which describes the king, like the Nileflood, as supplying provisions. The stanza moves from principles of royal power to its realization in deeds, described in antithetical verses. The final couplet provides a summary.

9. This poorly preserved stanza continues the balanced descriptions of the king's life-or-death *power* over his subjects, expressing this as physical might. At the end of the stanza his power is broadened to include the otherworld: his *enemies* are not only slaughtered, but are deprived of a burial on land that would ensure otherworldly survival; this resumes the imagery of water (3.3–4), which can give life or death.

10. A final stanza of royal eulogy extols the king as the quasi-divine benefactor of mankind. The opening verse takes the motif of provisions (3.7–9) onto a more elevated level, that of creation: *Sustenance* has a spiritual edge, and *Plenty* is

homonymous with 'Utterance'—one of the powers of creation. These powers recall the earlier mention of another, less material, creative power, Perception (2.5 and n. 4). The teacher now turns to the king's relationship with his divine superiors, as opposed to his mortal inferiors. He is the linchpin of society, conceived in the grandest terms, both temporal and hierarchical. The gods legitimize his actions against his enemies.

11. The king at his most divine (in the *palace*) is again assimilated with the gods; as the heir of the ancient gods he is the present people's god. *Atum* is the All-lord creator, who created people's bodies (*joining necks*). Each divine assimilation is followed by a verse on the results for humanity. *Khnum* is another fashioner of men's bodies: the king creates individuals, and is literally the father of his country. *Bastet* and *Sekhmet* are complementary feline goddesses, cat and lion, who can be aspects of the same deity: one is protective, the other aggressive and destructive. The two aspects of the king are manifest in his treatment of the two types of underling, loyal and disloyal.

12. After the implicit advice in the preceding three stanzas, this stanza returns to explicitly didactic verses, and prescribes appropriate behaviour towards the king. The first half urges loyalism (*fight* echoes 4.1): *oaths* were taken on the king's *name*. The second verse implies that the king is inclined to generosity, and is frustrated only by mankind's rebelliousness. Dual expressions suggest the totality of royal power: the *Red-king* is the king who wears the Red Crown of Lower Egypt, while the *White Crown* represents Upper Egypt. The *Double Crown* symbolizes the unity of the state under single rule: the king is presented in his essential regalia.

13. The second half of the stanza describes the enduring personal rewards of virtue in two couplets.

14. In this stanza, the sage moves to discuss prosperity in the future life, which is also dependent on the king: a full state burial was literally in his giving. A triplet on funerary preparations employs phrases from mortuary inscriptions referring to the tomb (*earth, place, cavern*). A formulaic wish follows for social continuity in offices held in the family, and a final couplet implies that such success will result from obeying the Teaching. The Teaching is itself a means of social continuity—a theme developed in the next stanza.

15. The advice to *speak to your children* recalls the context of the Teaching. The injunction at the end of the previous stanza (7.7) is developed: obedience involves passing the Teaching (the *speech*) on to the next generation. Wisdom ensures and comprises social continuity, from the primeval rule of the gods to mankind's descendants. The following verses give three reasons for obeying the teacher's advice: its antiquity, the personal authority of the teacher, and the resulting success. The stanza ends with a rhetorical question, that is answered in the second half of the Teaching.

16. This injunction sounds like the conclusion of the Teaching, with its reference to *landfall*, which is both success in this life and burial. The teacher, however, now turns to people who are socially inferior, rather than superior, to his audience, and the pronoun referring to the audience is now singular (an individual official in charge of his *servants*) rather than plural (a group of officials collectively exhorted to loyalism). *Another method* is a phrase found in medical texts: wisdom is the remedy for society's ills. This subtitle introduces the second half.

17. A grandiloquent verse states that the created world owes its existence to workers. The following verse explains this statement, and a third summarizes the élite's dependence on workers in pragmatic terms.

18. A more elaborate stanza develops the notion of society's dependence on lowly *professions* with an increased use of metaphor. In the first triplet, the way in

which they sustain a household is considered. The *sound* of them represents their presence, and the image gives their support a miraculous aspect—their voices are enough to restore and revive a ruined house.

19. Being able to *sleep* is a sign of security and prosperity: the antithesis of a man with many servants is the *solitary man* who isolates himself from society. He is antisocial like the *lion* (a solitary and proverbially unsleeping animal), and will not thrive on social tasks, or reap their rewards.

20. From the animal imagery of the preceding verse, another triplet develops the image of mankind as a *herd* that needs a shepherd (i.e. a leader, king, or god): the herd outside its shelter is prey to animals such as the lion. In the description of a doomed animal, society is presented as a man-made shelter (*walled enclosure* and *well*). The stanza ends on a starkly negative note.

21. This stanza describes a man's need for peasants to tend his land, but it also affirms metaphorically that care is needed for society to flourish, just as one must prepare for the annual *Nileflood* and plough fields to gain from the harvest. The opening mention of the Nile continues the imagery previously used to extol the king (3.3–4 and n. 7). The imagery of cattle presents the need for order to be imposed from above on creatures (including mankind). Read literally, the verses deal with the officials' need of peasant shepherds to tend their cattle, while metaphorically they allude to mankind's need for a ruler; this double reference expresses the inseparable nature of all living beings. The happy *flock* is in sharp contrast with the situation portrayed at the end of the preceding stanza (10.7–9).

22. The second half of the stanza demonstrates the practical value of social solidarity in the worth of labourers. The *professions* are literally the peasant shepherds, who are servants to be valued, but metaphorically they are the official and his king who control society. Care for society and the principle of reciprocity are expounded in pragmatic terms; the problem of people becoming *vagabonds* in order to flee labour duty is well attested in contemporaneous documents.

23. This stanza describes the results of being just or unjust to one's inferiors. The first couplet evokes a wide range of reference from *taxes* to God. In a following quatrain on the consequences of injustice, the imagery alludes to the idea that Justice and Truth are the only true means of life; all other wealth is transient, and time brings retribution on the unjust.

24. A second quatrain, structured antithetically, demonstrates the various qualities that the official must possess and shun. Selflessness and justice towards servants are associated with success for one's *heirs*. The final verse reformulates the second verse of the stanza (12.2) in negative terms: the opinion of society is in perfect accord with that of god. The stanza starts at an abstract level in *God's eyes*, moves though future survival (*children* and *heirs*), and ends with the general attitude of society (*in all eyes*).

25. This symmetrically structured stanza, which begins and ends on evil, continues to develop the subject of the preceding one on a wider social scale, to affirm that evil is self-destructive. The *mound* is a settlement (towns were built on mounds to avoid the flood waters of the Nile). The stanza centres around a quatrain on the enduring value of virtue and ends with a couplet that returns to antithetical structure and the metaphor of cattle.

26. The opening of the stanza echoes 6.1, where the audience was urged to fight for the king: the official has responsibilities to society both above and below him. This injunction is justified by the next verse, in which men are *good*, just as the shepherd seems excellent and is beneficial to god; the metaphorical aspect of the cattle motif (11.3–6 and nn. 21, 22) is made explicit here. Men are a benefit in both life and death, present and future. This final stanza moves into the next

world, with reference to society, just as the final stanza of the first half did, with reference to the king (7.1–5).

27. The teacher now turns to another group of underlings—funerary servants. The survival of a man after burial depends on the maintenance of his funerary cult, which requires the continuing goodwill or obedience of his *priests* and his children. The teacher affirms that virtue transcends family bonds, a sentiment which suits the wide perspective of the teaching, but which is striking in a teaching addressed to children. The *heir*—a representative of social continuity—was ideally the son, but here he is instead a loyal servant.

28. Reciprocity functions not just within society, but through time—from generation to generation, as well as between the worlds of the living and the dead. The *beneficiary* is a dead man for whom a funerary cult is performed. A final quatrain begins with injunctions and ends with generalizing statements on the mutual benefits of virtue and reciprocity. The style matches the content, since these phrases are also found in tomb inscriptions.

12

The Teaching of the Vizier Ptahhotep

Introduction

The Teaching of the Vizier Ptahhotep is spoken by the vizier of the Fifth Dynasty King Isesi (*c.*2388–2356 BC). Although the Vizier Ptahhotep was a historical figure, the earliest manuscripts date from the middle of the Twelfth Dynasty. It seems that the Teaching was composed in the first reigns of that dynasty, and was merely set some four centuries earlier in the Old Kingdom, a golden age in the eyes of the Middle Kingdom.

After the title, a short prologue locates the sage in the grand court. It opens with his address to the godlike king, which paints a dark picture of the vizier's condition, in contrast with the usual ideal of a good old age expressed in official inscriptions. He is almost on the point of death, and he proposes to teach his son, so as to enable him to support his aged father. The poem itself becomes a restorative against the onslaught of time, and a process of renewal is enacted by the pronouncing of the Teaching: in the final stanzas, the vizier describes not his decrepitude, but a vision of how wisdom ensures the health of a wise man. Between these two descriptions of age comes the main substance of the Teaching: a series of maxims, which are introduced by a second title describing their aim of teaching men to be wise. Although the prologue states that the Teaching is addressed specifically to Ptahhotep's son, this title proclaims that it has wide concerns.

In the chosen setting of a perfect Old Kingdom, world virtue should be automatically rewarded, by society with wealth, and by the gods with a healthy old age. The sage can thus advocate an apparently pragmatic and self-interested approach to virtue: do good and you will be rewarded. Each of the thirty-seven maxims deals with a social situation that can exemplify wisdom. Many of these situations are presented in a diagnostic fashion, in the manner of a medical text: if such and such is the case, then this is the appropriate response. A common pattern for a maxim is an introduction giving a particular context, a personal injunction, and a concluding summary in reflective generalizing terms. Wisdom is a restorative for the ills of humanity. The style is consistently epigrammatic, spare, and dense, with verses patterned in couplets.

The sage's morality is social rather than purely personal: the central maxim (298–315) is about greed and selfishness, which is an official, social, and family fault as well as a personal one. The wider aspects of ethical issues are not presented with metaphors, as in *The Tale of the Eloquent Peasant*, but are embodied in the specific situations. This formulation can make the Teaching seem opportunistic and materialistic, but the interweaving of situations with accounts of broad ethical principles presents an image of social behaviour in which every detail is informed by eternal Truth. This technique of expansion from the particular to the general allows consideration to be given to the interplay between ethical ideals and the practicalities of actual life. Much of the maxims' import is conveyed by wordplay, drawing parallels between associated ideas, and occasional use of double meanings.

The Teaching places value on social advancement and respect for social rank, which presumably reflect the original audience's dependence on their social superiors and patrons. Despite this, the sage's attitude is far from complacent: he emphasizes the responsibility of rank towards those lower in society, as well as warning against ambition. His moderate and humane wisdom is, in this respect, immediately appealing for a modern audience. He advocates not merely conformity but also a stoic quietist acceptance of 'what happens' and of one's social role, as well as self-improvement in terms of wisdom and patience.

Each maxim is self-contained, but they are linked into short series by subject matter and language; this is particularly evident in the opening sequence. However, there is no rigid overall progression in the sequence of maxims, and the unity of the whole should be assessed in the context of the Egyptian tradition of wisdom texts as collections of wise sayings. Two versions of the Teaching are known from Middle Kingdom manuscripts, and this variation may relate in part to the choice of a loose structure for the Teaching. While the diverse situations express a basic unity of ethical attitude, the artful disorder of the sequence of maxims builds up into a more complex whole. Within the distant and idealized setting, the sage affirms that virtue will be rewarded, but the maxims also mobilize the audience's actual experience that this is not always so. Although virtue should ensure success in life, and although society and the divine order of things run in parallel, the variety of the maxims presents a variety of possibilities: success might be virtue rewarded or might be the result of crime; the virtuous might be rewarded, but are not necessarily, and might remain poor. The sage's son would be expected to succeed to the vizierate, but the Teaching covers a wide range of possible careers for him. Some maxims envisage him as subordinate to great officials, or even wretched. The sage is thus advising not merely social conformity or opportunism, but a trust in virtue for its own sake. Despite the Teaching's positive affirmations, and despite the setting in the Old Kingdom, there is an undercurrent of assertions that the world is uncertain, and full of social mobility, social competition, instability, and complexity. It is impossible to know what will happen; the role of chance in life is acknowledged, alongside that of the divinely sanctioned law of reciprocity. The series of maxims begins and ends with instances of unexpected virtue: the first maxim acclaims the 'perfect speech' of maidservants, whose talk is treated with disdain in other texts, and the last asserts the worth of an unconventional woman as wife. The world of the Teaching is unexpectedly varied.

Although the Teaching lacks the problematic setting of the literary discourses, it nevertheless articulates a complex sensibility, very different from the more straightforward presentation of similar ethical matters in funerary official Autobiographies. The choice between good and evil that has already been made there is here still to be made, and is a perilous one. The first maxim makes this complexity immediately apparent, warning of the folly of having pride in the very quality that it teaches—wisdom—and praising lowly maidservants, whose virtue has brought them no social rewards. The sage's realization that absolute wisdom and virtue are unattainable runs through the Teaching, and his often pragmatic attitude springs from the fact that a little good is sometimes all that is possible in an imperfect world.

The unity of the maxims is affirmed and developed in an epilogue, in which the general principles are expounded around the idea of hearing—that is listening, understanding, and obeying. Repeated wordplay on 'hear' enacts the unity of these principles in a dense and dramatic manner. As the train of thought becomes both more unified and more interwoven, the style becomes correspondingly more elaborate. The rewards of transcendent virtue and wisdom are presented unambiguously, but are counterbalanced by descriptions of the fate of the 'fool'. The ethical choice between good and evil, obedience to the gods and disobedience, is determined by a person's own heart. The variety of such choices previously presented becomes here a central choice between good and evil, hinging on the dual nature of the human heart, a theme that is expounded more darkly in the Discourses.

The epilogue moves away from particular situations in a dizzying spiral from past to future wisdom, presenting the latter in broad terms in which the act of teaching a son embodies the cultural continuity of society as well as the individual's survival in eternity. This emphasis on obedience returns the audience to the dramatic setting, and the teaching concludes with the sage describing himself in old age, no longer suffering but on the point of becoming one of the blessed dead. In this resolution there is no uncertainty. His achievements in the court of his king validate his authority and the wisdom he has expounded.

Two Middle Kingdom manuscripts provide two slightly different versions of the Teaching, only one of which is attested in later New Kingdom copies. Here the other, from Papyrus Prisse (Bibliothèque Nationale, Paris) is followed, as it alone is completely preserved. Numbers give the lines of Eugène Dévaud's synoptic edition (which numbers all phrases from variant versions), with the page and line numbers of P. Prisse in parentheses. The notes give the modern maxim numbers, which are sometimes used to refer to individual sections of P. Prisse.

The Teaching of the Vizier Ptahhotep

1 (P 4.1)   The Teaching of the Lord Vizier Ptahhotep,[1]
            under the Majesty of the Dual King Isesi,
            may he live for all time and eternity!
            The Lord Vizier Ptahhotep
            said, 'Sovereign, my lord![2]
            Elderiness has occurred, old age descended;
            woe is come and weakness is renewing itself;

10 (P 4.3) the heart passes the night in pain, every day;
            the eyes are shrunk, the ears made deaf;
            strength now perishes because of the heart's weariness;
            the mouth is silent and cannot speak;
            the heart has stopped and cannot recall yesterday;
            the bones hurt because of their length;
            good has become evil;
            all taste is gone.

20 (P 5.2) What age does to people
            is evil in every aspect;
            the nose is blocked and cannot breathe,
            because of the difficulty of standing and sitting.
            May One decree for this humble servant that a Staff of
                Old Age be appointed,[3]

30 (P 5.3) so that I may tell him the words of the hearers, the
                counsels of the ancestors
            who once listened to the Gods.
            So may the like be done for you:
            may sorrows be driven off from the folk,
            may the Two Banks serve you!'
            And the Majesty of this God said,[4]
            'Teach him according to the speech of the past,
            so that he will be a model for the officials' offspring!

40 (P 5.5) May hearing enter him, and all honesty. Speak to him!
            No one is born already knowledgeable!'

                              *

            Beginning of the verses of perfect speech[5]
            spoken by the Patrician and Count,
            the God's father, whom the God loves,

the eldest King's Own Son,
the Lord Vizier Ptahhotep,
in teaching the ignorant to be wise,
and to be the standard of perfect speech,
good for him who will hear,
woeful for him who will transgress it.   50 (P 5.8)
And he spoke before his son,

'Do not be proud because you are wise!⁶
Consult with the ignorant as with the wise!
The limits of art are unattainable;
no artist is fully equipped with his mastery.
Perfect speech is more hidden than malachite,
yet it is found with the maidservants at the millstones.

If you encounter a disputant in his moment,⁷   60 (P 5.10)
an authoritative man, who is better off than you,
bend your arms, bow your back!
When your heart defies him, he will not support you.
You will make little of such a one who speaks evil,
by not opposing him in his moment.
He will be summoned as "this ignoramus",
your self-restraint having matched his riches.

If you encounter a disputant in his moment,⁸
a man like you, who is a match for you,
you should better him by silence,
while he is speaking evil.   70 (P 5.13)
Great will be the acclamation by the judges,
and your name will be good in the officials' assessment.

If you encounter a disputant in his moment,⁹
who is poor, not a man like you,
do not be aggressive to him because he is vilely poor!
Ignore him, and he will oppose himself.
Do not address him to lighten your heart!
Do not vent your feelings on the man facing you!
The man who destroys the poor-hearted gets pain,   81 (P 6.2)
but what is in your heart will be done:
you will beat him through the officials' punishment.

If you are a leader,¹⁰
ordaining the disposition of the masses,

seek out for yourself every worthy deed,
so that your disposition will be faultless!
Great is Truth, enduring in potency;
it is undisturbed since the time of Osiris.

90 (P 6.5) The man who transgresses the laws is punished—
it is a transgression even in the eyes of the selfish.
Baseness can carry off riches,[11]
but wrong has never yet brought its deed to land.
A man says, "I will snare for myself",
but he cannot say, "I will snare because of my
    occupation".
When the end comes, Truth endures;
a man will then say, "It is my paternal heritage".

You should not make schemes about people;[12]
100 (P 6.8) God will punish with the like.
A man says, "I shall live by these"—
he lacks bread for his mouth.
A man says, "I shall be powerful by these",
and says, "I shall snare for myself whatever I notice!".

111 (P 6.9) A man thinks to rob another—
he ends by being given to a stranger.
The schemes of men have never yet come about.
Only what God ordains comes about.
Plan to live in deep calmness;
what They give will come by itself.

If you are a man among those who sit[13]
120 (P 6.11) at a place on your superior's table,
take what he gives, when it is placed under your
    nose.
You should look at what is in front of you—
do not pierce him with many looks!
Imposing on him is a horror to the spirit.
Do not speak to him until he calls!
One cannot know what seems evil to the heart.
You should speak only when he addresses you.
130 (P 7.1) Then what you say will seem perfect to the heart.
A great man, when he is at food,
behaves as his spirit commands.
He will give to the man he favours.

This is how night-time behaviour happens:
it is the spirit which extends his hands.
A great man gives, when a man does not exert pressure. 140 (P 7.2)
Eating bread is according to the counsel of God.[14]
Only the fool will moan about this.

If you are a man of close trust,[15]
whom one great man sends to another great man,
be entirely exact when he sends you!
Do the commission for him as he says!
Beware of making evil with a speech
which embroils one great man with another great man! 150 (P 7.4)
Hold fast to Truth! Do not exceed it!
An outburst is not to be repeated;
do not speak out against anyone!
Great or small, it is a horror to the spirit.   160 (P 7.4)

If you plough and there is growth in the countryside,[16]
and God causes it to be great with you,
do not satisfy your mouth right beside your neighbours!
Great is the respect paid to the quiet man.
The lord of character who is a lord of property
seizes in the court like a crocodile.
Do not make a claim against someone without
     children!
Do not degrade anyone, do not boast about it!   170 (P 7.6)
There is many a father who suffers,
and for many a mother who has given birth there is
     someone happier.
It is the solitary whom God brings up;
a lord who is prayed for by his kin comes second.

If you are vilely poor, follow an excellent man![17]
Then all of your condition is good before God.
Do not acknowledge to yourself that he was little before.
You should not be proud against him
because you knew about him before.
Respect him because of what has happened to him,   180 (P 7.8)
for no property comes by itself:
it is Their law for those They love.
His plenty, he gathered it himself.

It is God who made him excellent,
and He protects him while he sleeps.

Follow your heart as long as you live![18]
Do no more than you are told!
Do not shorten the time of following the heart:
to destroy such a moment is a horror to the spirit!

190 (P 7.9)   Turn away no chance in the course of a day,
beyond the needs of establishing your household!
Property will exist regardless, so follow the heart!
Property is of no avail, when the heart is disregarded.

If you are a man of excellence,[19]
you should beget a son to please God.
If he is upright, takes after your character,

202 (P 7.11)   and cares for your property in the proper way,
do all that is good for him:
he is your son; he is of your spirit's seed!
You should not withdraw your heart from him!
Progeny can cause quarrels.

210 (P 7.12)   If he goes astray and transgresses your counsels,
having defied all that was said,
his speech coming out with vile words,
you should belabour him for his speech as is fitting.
Strike out at someone whom They detest—
he is someone on whom doom was imposed in the
            womb!
The one whom They guide cannot go astray, the one
            whom They leave boat-less cannot find a crossing.

220 (P 8.2)   If you are a member of the law courts,[20]
stand and sit according to your duties,
which were ordained for you on the First Day.
Do not overstep, or you will come to be opposed!
Intelligent is the man who enters when announced,
and wide is the access for the man who has been
            summoned.
The law court is according to the standard;
all behaviour is by measure.
It is God who advances position;

231 (P 8.5)   the jostler is not appointed.

If you are with people,[21]
make supporters for yourself by being trustworthy!
The trustworthy man, who is not led by his temper's
    urgings,
becomes his own commander,
and a lord of property because of how his behaviour is.
And so your name is good, and no one speaks out
    against you;   240 (P 8.8)
your limbs sleek, you are held in regard by your
    neighbours,
and boasted of without your knowing.
The heart of someone who listens to his temper is such
that it replaces love of him with disdain;
his heart becomes worn away, and his limbs parched.
The heart of God-given people is great;
the man who listens to his temper belongs to the enemy.

Report your conduct without dissimulating,[22]
when your counsel is given in the council of your
    lord!   250 (P 8.11)
As for gushing when speaking,
there is no pain for the messenger of a report.
Nor can a great man reply "So who does know it?"
when the messenger's knowledge fails.
If the great man plans to punish him for this,
he should be quiet, saying, "I have spoken."

If you are a leader,[23]
and wide-ranging the affairs at your command,
you should do distinguished things.
Remember the days that come after!   260 (P 9.1)
No matter comes awry in the midst of favours—
but the lurking crocodile emerges, and resentment exists.

If you are a leader,[24]
be calm while you hear a petitioner's speech!
Do not prevent him from purging his body
of what he planned to tell you!
A wronged man loves to pour his heart out
more than achieving what he came for.
About someone who prevents petitions, they say,   273 (P 9.5)

"So why does he thwart it?"
Everything for which a man petitioned may not come
           about,
but a good hearing is what soothes the heart.

If you want to make friendship last[25]
inside a house you enter—
whether as lord, or brother, or friend,
280 (P 9.9)   wherever you enter—
beware of approaching the women!
There is nothing good about the place where this is
           done;
there is nothing intelligent about the man who
           uncovers them.
A thousand men are turned away from their good—
a little moment, the likeness of a dream,
and death is reached by knowing them!
292 (P 9.12)   It is a vile matter, conceived by an enemy;
one emerges from doing it
with a heart already rejecting it.
Someone who fails through lusting after them,
no plan by him can ever succeed.

If you wish your condition to be good,[26]
save yourself from every evil!
300 (P 10.1)   Beware of the selfish man's deed!
It is a painful disease of an incurable.
The man who catches it cannot survive:
it alienates fathers and mothers,
and even the closest brothers;
it drives apart husband and wife.
It is a compound of all evil;
310 (P 10.4)   it is a sum of all that is detested.
A man will last when he uses Truth aright.[27]
The man who goes according to his duties makes a
           legacy by this:
there is no tomb-chamber for the selfish.

Do not be selfish in the division![28]
Do not be greedy, not even for your portion!

Do not be selfish against your neighbours!
The claim of the mild-mannered is greater than the
    mighty's.
The man who shuns his neighbours is diminished,   320 (P 10.7)
deprived of the gift of speech.
A little of what is craved
is enough to make the quarrelsome man cool-tempered.

If you are excellently well off, you should establish your
    household,[29]
and love your wife with proper ardour:
fill her belly, clothe her back!
Perfume is a restorative for her limbs.
Make her joyful as long as you live!
She is a field, good for her lord.   330 (P 10.10)
You should not have her judged.
Remove her from power, suppress her!
When she sees anything her eye is a storm-wind to her.
Restraining her is how to make her remain in your
    house;
a female who is under her own control
is rainwater:
when one enquires after her, she has flown away.

Gratify your close friends with what comes to you,[30]
which has come to someone favoured by God.   340 (P 11.1)
Of the man who fails to gratify his close friends,
they say, "Isn't he a lovely spirit?"
What will happen cannot be known, when thinking of
    tomorrow.
The upright spirit to whom people are grateful is truly
    a spirit.
If occasions of favour come,
it is close friends who say, "Welcome!"
If there are no means of contentment brought into
    harbour,
then there are still close friends, even though there is
    ruin.

You should not repeat gossip about something you did
    not hear direct![31]   350 (P 11.5)
It is the outpouring of the hot-tempered

to repeat a matter that is only seen from a distance
    and not heard direct—
ignore that, do not tell it at all!
Look at the man before you, by whom excellence is
    known!
When theft is ordered, that act is made into some-
    thing hateful
against the taker, according to the law.

360 (P 11.8)   Look, gossip is a self-destructive dream, at which one
    covers the face.

If you are an excellent man,[32]
who sits in the council of his lord,
concentrate on excellence!
You should be quiet! This is better than a potent
    herb.
You should speak when you know that you under-
    stand:
only the skilled artist speaks in the council.
Speaking is harder than any craft:
only the man who understands it puts it to work for
    him.

370 (P 11.12) If you are powerful, promote respect for yourself,[33]
by wisdom, by calmness of speech!
Give no instructions except according to
    circumstances!
The provoker always begins to go wrong.
Do not be haughty, lest your heart be humiliated!
Do not be silent—but beware lest you offend
when you answer a speech with ardour!
Turn away your face! Govern yourself!
The flame of the hot-hearted disperses.
Even the pleasant man, when he offends, has his
    way blocked.

380 (P 12.4)   The man who is sullen all day long[34]
cannot spend one happy moment.
The man who is light-hearted all day long,
he cannot found a house; while the man who aims
    at completion
is like someone who steers a deed to land,

and another deed is secured.
The man who listens to his heart will feel "If only!"

Do not let yourself oppose a great man in his moment.[35]
Do not be wrathful-hearted to him when he is burdened;
his ill-will will be against someone who quarrels with
     him.   391 (P 12.7)
The spirit will be free with someone who loves him.
He is a giver of sustenance, together with God.
What he loves is what should be done for him.
Compose your face after tumult!
Peace is with his spirit,
ill-will with the enemy.
Cultivating love is sustenance.

Teach the great man about what is good for him![36]
Create support for him among the people!   400 (P 12.10)
You should cause his knowledge to strike his lord.
Food for you comes from his spirit.
The favourite's body will feel content.
Your back will be clothed with this.
Your support of him will be the life of your house
through your noble, whom you love.
He lives through this, and he will be a great help for
     you also.   410 (P 12.12)
Now, this is how your love will last in everybody that
     loves you.
Look, the man a hearer loves is a spirit.

If you have the rank of a gentleman who belongs to
     the council,[37]
someone commissioned with appeasing the masses,
shun negligence in judgement!
You should speak, but do not distort!
Beware lest someone tells his thoughts—"Officials,   420 (P 13.2)
he has distorted the matter!"—
and your action is prevented from reaching judgement!

If you are merciful about a misdeed that has
     happened,[38]
and incline towards a man on account of his usual
     righteousness,

pass over this! Do not remember this,
since he was quiet to you on the First Day!

If you are great after being little,[39]
and you acquire property after former want,

431 (P 13.7)   in a town you know, which is aware of what
                    happened to you previously,
do not trust in your riches,
which came to you as a gift of God!
Then you will not lag behind another man like you,
to whom something similar has happened.

441 (P 13.9)   Bow your back to your superiors,[40]
and your overseer from the palace!
Then your household will endure in its property,
with your rewards where they should be.
The man who opposes a superior will feel pain.
One lives for as long as he is merciful.
The arm is not sprained by baring it.

450 (P 13.12)   Do not rob a neighbour's house!
Do not take the property of someone close to you!
Let him have no cause to denounce you, before you
                    hear it!
The man who is stubborn has a defective heart.
A heart that is experienced in this will create
                    quarrels.
An opposer in the neighbourhood suffers pain.

You should not have sex with a woman-boy, for you
                    know that what is condemned[41]
will be water on his breast.
There is no relief for what is in his belly.

460 (P 14.5)   Let him not spend the night doing what is
                    condemned;
he will find relief only when he has abandoned his
                    desire.

If you investigate the character of a friend,[42]
do not question someone who is close to him,
but deal with him alone,
until you are no longer pained by his manner!
Dispute with him after a while!

Broach his heart in conversation! 470 (P 14.8)
If he lets slip something he has seen,
and does a deed at which you are angry,
be friendly with him still! Do not remove your regard!
Be composed! Do not reveal the matter to him!
Do not respond with uproar!
Do not turn away from him! Do not trample on him!
His time has never yet failed to come.
No one can escape his destiny. 480 (P 14.12)

Be benevolent as long as you live![43]
What has come out of the storeroom cannot return.
It is bread for sharing that can inspire greed:
the man with an empty belly is an accuser.
An opponent becomes someone who inflicts suffering—
do not appoint him as someone close to you!
Kindness is the memorial of a man,
in the years that come after the staff of office.

Acknowledge your former associates, and your
    property will exist![44]
Do not be vile-natured to your friends: 490 (P 15.3)
they are a riverbank which is fertile,
are greater than its riches!
The property of one man can belong to another;
a gentleman's qualities are excellent for him alone.
Good character will be a memorial.

Punish promptly![45]
Instruct absolutely!
The restraint of wrongdoing will establish a good example.
An act not in response to evil
is what makes grumbling become opposition.

If you take to wife a plump woman,[46] 500 (P 15.6)
someone light-hearted, well known to her town,
who is volatile, to whom the moment is fair,
do not reject her! Let her eat!
The light-hearted woman provides fresh water.

*

If you listen to these things I have told you,[47]
all your affairs will advance.
Their Truthfulness is their value.

510 (P 15.9) Memory of them will not depart from the mouths of
                   men,
              because of the perfection of their verses. Every word
                   will be attained;
              none can perish in this land for all time.
              When well uttered, it should be enacted, so that the
                   officials will speak of it.
              This is teaching a man to speak to the future.[48]
              If he listens, he will become an artist of hearing.
              It is good to speak to the future; it will listen.

520 (P 15.11) If a good deed happens because of someone who is a
                   chief,
              he will be excellent for eternity.
              All his knowledge is for all time.
              Only a wise man sustains his soul with what ensures
                   permanence,[49]
              so that his soul is happy with him on earth.
              The wise man will be satisfied through his wisdom.
              Only the official who is about his good deed
              twines together his heart and his tongue;
              his lips are righteous while he is speaking,

530 (P 16.1) his eyes see,
              and his two ears hear what is excellent for his son—
              a doer of Truth, free from Falsehood!

              Hearing is excellent for a son who hears.[50]
              Hearing enters the hearer,
              so that the hearer becomes someone who is heard.
              Good is hearing; good then is speaking;
              the hearer is a lord of excellence.

540 (P 16.4) Hearing is excellent for the hearer.
              Hearing is better than anything, so that perfect love
                   comes into being.
              How good for a son to receive his father's speech!
              He will have an old age through it.
              Someone who hears is loved by God. Someone hated
                   by God does not hear.

It is the heart which makes its lord[51]   550 (P 16.7)
a hearer or a non-hearer—
a man's heart is his life, prosperity, and health!
It is a hearer who hears speech.[52]
The man who does what is said is someone who loves
    hearing.
How good for a son to listen to his father!
How joyful is someone of whom this is said,
"This son is a fine lord of hearing."
The hearer of whom this is said   560 (P 16.11)
has a splendid person,
and is blessed before his father.
He is remembered in the mouths of the living,
those on earth and those who will be.

If a gentleman's son receives his father's speech,[53]
no plan of his can miscarry.
You should teach a hearer in your son,
someone who will seem excellent to the official's
    hearts,
guiding his mouth by what is said to him,
and regarded as a hearer.
Such a son is excellent, his actions distinguished,   570 (P 17.2)
while the installation into office of a non-hearer will
    miscarry.
The wise man will rise early to establish himself;
the fool is hard-pressed.

As for the fool who does not hear, he can do nothing.[54]
He will see wisdom as ignorance,
excellence as harm.
He does everything detestable, so that he is complained
    about every day.   580 (P 17.6)
He lives on that by which one dies.
Distorted speech is his sustenance;
and this character of his is known to the officials,
who say "Every day, a living death!"
His deeds are passed over,
because of the many evils due to him every day.

And a son who hears is a Follower of Horus.[55]
It is good for him when he hears.

590 (P 17.10) He will attain old age; he will reach blessedness.
He will tell the like to his children, renewing what
    his father taught,
every man being taught as he was.
He will tell it before his offspring,
so that they will speak to their children.
Set a good example! Give no offence!
Make Truth strong, and your offspring will live!
The first of them who will be involved with injustice,

600 (P 18.3) people who see will still say, "They are exactly like
    him",
and they who hear this will have said, "They are
    exactly like him" too.
Everybody looks to them, and the masses are pacified.
Without them, riches are of no avail.
Do not chop, do not change a word![56]
Do not put one in the place of another!

611 (P 18.8) Beware! Do not let loose the restraints in you!
Watch out lest a sage tells you to listen,
when you wish to establish yourself in the mouths of
    the hearers!
You should speak when you have entered into the art,
and you will speak to good effect;
then all of your affairs will be as they should be!

Suppress your heart, control your mouth,[57]
so that your affairs will be amongst the officials'!

620 (P 18.13) Be entirely upright before your lord;
act so that they say to him, "He is the son of that
    one,"
and say to those who will listen, "Now, favoured is
    the man to whom he was born!"
Be patient as long as you speak!
You should say distinguished things, so that the
    officials who hear will say,
"How good is what comes out of his mouth!"

Act thus, until your lord says about you,[58]
"How good is his father's teaching,

with which he came out of his flesh, 630 (P 19.4)
which he told to him even when he was in the womb!
What he has done is greater than what he was told."
Look, a good son is a gift of God—
one who increases what he was told before his lord!
He will do Truth, his heart having acted according to
his duties;
even thus you will reach me, with your limbs healthy,
the king content with all that has happened.
You will achieve years of life!
What I have done upon earth will be no small thing.[59] 640 (P 19.7)
I have achieved a hundred and ten years of life,
as a gift to mé from the king,
with favours beyond the ancestors',
by doing Truth for the king, until the state of
blessedness.'

So it ends, from start to finish,
as found in writing.

Notes

1. The initial title sets the scene that is developed in the prologue. *Lord Vizier* is literally 'The Overseer of the (capital) city, and Vizier'. *Isesi* was the penultimate king of the Fifth Dynasty (c.2388–2356 BC). Two viziers Ptahhotep are known from this period; the first (Ptahhotep I) is probably the historical basis for the character here. Both of their tombs may show signs of later reverence, suggesting that they were regarded as culture heroes by the start of the Middle Kingdom.
2. The prologue opens with a comprehensive description of old age and its evils; this contrasts with what the audience might expect—a description of a happy old age as a reward for virtue. The failure of the sage's *heart*—the organ of wisdom—is striking; its inability to remember the past (*yesterday*) is a bitter irony, since the past is when wisdom originated (cf. 31–2) and for the original audience it is the time to which Ptahhotep belongs. The passage ends with the absence of the most basic necessity of life, breath, which was often referred to as being in the king's giving; this allusion to the sage's death-in-life prepares for the subsequent request to the king (28–32).
3. The *Staff of Old Age* is an office held by the son as his father's helper, agent, and named successor, who will support Ptahhotep in his infirmity; the role of the sage's speech in training his son is underlined by wordplay: *Staff* and *words* are homophonous. *This humble servant* is the vizier himself (see *The Tale of Sinuhe*, B 175 and n. 44). The continuity between the primordial past of the *Gods* and his heir offers a chance of immutability, and affirms the value of ancient things in contrast with the decline of *old age*. The sage then turns to the future with a reciprocal wish for the king. The *Two Banks* are the totality of Egypt.
4. The king is divine like the gods, who are the origin of wisdom; later in the Teaching 'God' refers to the undifferentiated divine, rather than a specific god or

the king, and is often resumed with 'They'. The king's speech affirms that teaching is needed to supplement the imperfection of mankind.

5. A full title now introduces the Teaching proper; for the sage's titles, see *The 'Loyalist' Teaching*, n. 1). *Perfect speech* refers to ethical as well as rhetorical perfection: it is the spoken embodiment of the ideal of wisdom. The title establishes the ostensibly pragmatic tone of the subsequent maxims, in which the effects of virtue are manifest in material prosperity and success, and raises the question of ethical choice and obedience.

6. In the first maxim the limitations of wisdom are stated: absolute wisdom and virtue are impossible *unattainable* ideals. Wisdom and wise *perfect speech* are likened to *art*; this (like *mastery*) is a term also applied to the efficacy of magic. *Malachite* (literally 'greenstone') is a semi-precious mineral. Complementary to this is the idea that social success and wisdom are not necessarily correlated: wisdom can belong to lowly *maidservants*, who cannot hope to benefit from their virtue, unlike the privileged audience of the Teaching.

7. The second maxim begins a sequence of three on how to deal with disputants in a law court. These return to the specifically official setting after the general opening maxim, but reveal the Teaching's concern with all levels of society: they are ordered hierarchically from social superior to inferior. *In his moment* refers to the moment of confrontation, the climax of a person's case. The sage advocates deference to a social superior. Wordplay with *riches* (homonymous with 'lifetime') gives the maxim a wider perspective, but also helps establish a tension between the material status quo and ethical qualities (such as *self-restraint*), although the sage relies on society's judgement.

8. The third maxim concerns an equal in a court case, who is to be silently opposed. The sage again trusts in the state's official judgement of the case to uphold virtue, and advocates passive inaction. (*Judges* and *officials* are synonymous here.)

9. The fourth maxim advises that one should not take action against social inferiors who are in the wrong: they will defeat themselves in the eyes of society if one is patient.

10. The fifth maxim asserts the absolute and eternal value of *Truth*, in contrast with the relative values advocated in the second and third maxims; it moves from social concerns to eternal and abstract ones. *Truth* is order—both social and ethical—and right, on which the world, the state, and its *laws* are based. Enacting Truth with *worthy deeds* is the responsibility of any official. *Osiris* is a god who ruled the earth in primeval times, whose death and resurrection are archetypes for the vindication of Truth (there is also wordplay between his name and the homophonous divine epithet 'He who created it (Truth)'). He is the judge of the dead, and the theme of otherwordly judgement is taken up in the following verses.

11. The sage now uses allegorical personifications to affirm the impermanence of ill-gotten *riches* (homonymous with 'lifetime'); to *bring to land* is both to reach a successful conclusion and to reach eternity after the voyage of life. The following speeches affirm that no man can prey on others while justifying himself by his official position, and that *Truth* belongs to a virtuous man like an inherited estate.

12. The sixth maxim warns against predatory scheming. As in the stylistically similar preceding maxim, ignoble actions have their consequences, as is shown by a series of hapless schemers. The antithetical statements give a sense of human futility, which must be *calmly* borne, in the face of the gods' laws of reciprocity which alone can avail. Prosperity comes of itself as the reward to virtue from the gods (*They*), and cannot be forced by man. Human life is governed by absolute forces.

13. The seventh maxim urges patient respect towards one's social superiors as well as towards the gods; both will *give* to the virtuous man. *Those who sit* are privileged people of high rank. The principles of the preceding maxim are presented in the more pragmatic terms of human society. (A person's *spirit* and *food* are homonyms).

14. The concluding couplet affirms the relationship between social order and abstract ideals. Etiquette and *night-time behaviour* embody eternal principles of reciprocity—the *counsel of God*: if you behave properly, then you will be rewarded (*behaviour* and *counsel* are the same Egyptian word). These principles are inevitable, and protest is useless.

15. The eighth maxim is about discretion when acting for a superior. The mention of a *great man* and the *horror to the spirit* recall the preceding maxim (120, 125). *Truth* as an abstract principle involves moderation, and excess is alien to it; the sage advises against repeating truth indiscreetly and maliciously.

16. The ninth maxim is also about temperance, but in a context of power rather than subservience. The *ploughing* of the first verse is metaphorical for the growth of an official's prosperity and progeny. The *crocodile* is a positive image of ferocious capacity and retribution, but its darker undertones are developed in the warnings against preying on the lonely in the second half of the maxim. A man *without children* was considered socially unfortunate, as he lacked an heir to ensure his continuity in this world and the next, but he is not to be despised for that reason, as god may still make him more fortunate than a man with a family and vindicate him. The final verse means that the man who has a faithful family can, despite this, come second to the virtuous *solitary* man.

17. The tenth maxim concerns attitudes towards power in others. The sage warns that the parvenu and those who have risen by merit should not be despised, as their success is a reward that has been earned. The sage implies that social position may not be stable and that wealth may prove transitory—which is taken up later in the thirtieth maxim (428–40). *They* are the gods, who here give prosperity, as well as caring for the socially alienated (as in 173). This and the preceding maxim are linked by *follow* (174), and by the general reference to vileness: these maxims also imply that the dispossessed may be more excellent than the wealthy.

18. In the eleventh maxim, the pupil is urged to *follow* not his superior, but his own *heart*, or desire. This is an injunction to hedonism, but as the heart is a moral force and the seat of wisdom—the conscience—free-thinking and self-reliant morality is also encouraged. After two maxims on the value of material goods, this maxim puts the question of wealth into a broader perspective; all three, however, advocate a lack of immoderate concern for property and wealth.

19. The twelfth maxim deals with how to react to a good son—who is not to be spurned—and a bad son—who is to be cast off. The structurally central verse warns that a son (like *property*) can cause trouble (*progeny*—literally 'seed'—wordplays with the homonym 'poison'). Once again, ethical qualities are here more important than social links: *excellence* is taken up from the last maxim but one (175, 184), and is a concern parallel to 'following the heart' in the preceding maxim (186, 188). Virtue is foreordained, and the maxim, like others, ends by affirming man's dependence on the gods (*Them*).

20. The thirteenth maxim asserts the value of the social status quo. *Stand and sit* is an expression for 'behave'. Social order is presented as part of divinely ordained creation (for the *First Day* as the moment of creation, see 425 and n. 38), and the maxim warns against social ambition, as this disrupts the justice established in society. Once again, the maxim concludes with a reference to the divine, and to man's helplessness.

21. The fourteenth maxim concerns social responsibility; it describes the effects both of trust and of self-willed indiscretion (the latter description echoes that of old age in the prologue (8–27 and n. 2)). At the centre is a description of the rewards of discretion and of society's recognition of unassuming virtue. The maxim concludes with a couplet summarizing the contrast between the selfless and the selfish with reference to the divine. To *belong to the enemy* means 'to fall prey to' as well as 'to be one of'.

22. The fifteenth maxim advocates honesty. In the first part, the sage affirms that no harm will come to a messenger who repeats all his report, and in the second, that no punishment will befall a messenger who repeats all he can, even when his knowledge is incomplete. *Quietness* is a positive ethical quality in other contexts.

23. The sixteenth maxim describes the leader's position (cf. the fifth maxim (84–98)) and the effect of his actions on his fate. It warns against complacency: a leader should act virtuously even when he has no apparent need to. The final verse asserts that everything can go sour for a man when adversity suddenly strikes; the *crocodile* is often an agent of retribution (cf. n. 16). Implicit in this is the belief that a man's *distinguished things* will be remembered by society and will ensure goodwill towards him even in adversity.

24. The seventeenth maxim presents virtuous leadership more specifically and very pragmatically, in terms of an official's responsibility for the happiness of those who petition him.

25. The eighteenth maxim is a warning against interfering with another man's women. In Egyptian literature, sexual desire can be irregular and undermine the social structure, of which the possession of women, as wives or as servant girls, is an integral part. Two triplets state the fatal consequences of sexual pleasure in broad terms (as affecting a *thousand men*) and describe the transience of the pleasure itself (as opposed to the lasting harm it can cause). *Knowing* and *conceive* can have a sexual meaning.

26. The nineteenth maxim is numerically the central maxim, and concerns the sin of selfishness (literally 'graspingness of heart'). Like the preceding maxim, it concerns social ties (the phrasing reinforces this: 298 echoes 277), but with an even wider perspective and with as absolute a condemnation. The sin is presented as a fatal disease; *compound* and *sum* are medical terms, but continue the metaphor ironically, since they are terms for remedies. The imagery of wisdom as health runs throughout the Teaching.

27. Truth and unselfishness, by contrast, bring eternal well-being, both in this life—with the continuity of property (*legacy*)—and in the next (the *tomb-chamber*, which is a desirable possession). The disease of the selfish reaches its fatal conclusion here.

28. The twentieth maxim continues the subject of *selfishness* with the specific example of distributing provisions; this was a duty of administrative officials and landowners. After three warnings, a triplet affirms that a *claim* by a good-natured official will be heard, and that ignoring the needs of others can lessen a man's well-being; he is deprived of the benefits of communication (*speech*). The final couplet offers the pragmatic advice that a *little* generosity will calm opposition.

29. The twenty-first maxim continues the sequence of domestic references, contrasting in subject matter with the eighteenth (277–97; cf. also the twelfth and twenty-fourth maxims (197–219, 362–9)). The restricted role of women in Egyptian society is reflected here. The first half of the maxim asserts the benefits of a wife to her husband, while the second asserts the need to keep a woman under control. Being *judged* alludes to divorce proceedings. Both halves of the

maxim mobilize agricultural imagery, but the prosperity of a well-irrigated *field* (an image with sexual overtones) becomes *storm-wind* and inadequate *rainwater*, which damage crops.

30. The twenty-second maxim about generosity reformulates the twentieth maxim (316–24) in positive terms. It draws a contrast between the gains of temporary wealth (mocked by ironic comment) and *contentment*, and the more enduring benefits of *friends*. The equivalence of generosity and virtue is expressed with wordplay: *spirit* is homonymous with 'sustenance'.

31. The twenty-third maxim warns against gossip and slander (cf. the eighth maxim (145–60)). The sage's advice to repeat only what one has experienced directly leads to a reference to his own acknowledged wisdom (the *man before you*). The final verses present two analogies for the effects of gossip—an act of plunder that rebounds on the plunderer, and a terrifying nightmare (this latter recalls the dangerous dream of 287).

32. The twenty-fourth maxim develops the preceding maxim's reference to the sage's excellence (355). Wisdom and intellectual *excellence* requires skill and humility before it can be put into effective speech by a man advising his superior in his *council*. The *potent herb* is the unidentified *teftef*-plant, which may have had medicinal properties.

33. The twenty-fifth maxim urges modesty and restraint in the mighty. The sage warns against passionate behaviour and speech; passion is, like a *flame*, short-lived and ineffective, and it can create opposition against even a *pleasant man*.

34. The sage now affirms that either of two extremes of character (*sullenness* and *light-heartedness*) cannot bring success; the success of the moderate man is expressed with the metaphor of voyaging: he lands achievement after achievement. *Steering* is often a metaphor for social responsibility. The *heart* and its passions are here a source of evil, and of regret.

35. The twenty-sixth maxim urges respect towards one's superiors, and warns against reacting intemperately to a superior's troubled behaviour. It is linked to the preceding maxim by mentions of opposition and wrath, and is similar in sentiment to other maxims that concern *great* men's favour and support (e.g. the seventh (119–44)). The central couplet affirms that social and divine order are complementary. For the *enemy*, see 248 and n. 21; *sustenance* and *spirit* are homonyms, expressing the dependence of favours on goodwill.

36. The twenty-seventh maxim is also about relations with one's superiors, but is more positive than the twenty-sixth (388–98; the mention of *love* and *spirit* echoes 397–8). It advises helping and supporting a superior, since this will lead him to reciprocate. *Teaching* is appropriate for the didactic context of the poem. The *love* that this fosters spans society from the superior's master, through the superior, the audience, to the audience's household, and is reciprocal. The concluding verse means that the man who follows this advice will be provisioned and blessed by his superior (*hearer*, i.e. judge).

37. Two maxims, the twenty-eighth and twenty-ninth, concerning judgement and behaviour in court cases and disputes follow. In the twenty-eighth the sage advises that *negligence* or *distortion* will rebound on the unjust and discredit them.

38. The twenty-ninth maxim admits that one case where partiality is acceptable is when showing leniency to a fundamentally *righteous* man, but it urges that leniency should not be granted only in order to exert pressure later. The *First Day* is an allusion to the moment of creation (cf. 222): unconditional leniency without recriminations can provide a return to primordial calm.

39. The thirtieth maxim begins a sequence of maxims dealing with social relations with various types of people that continues until the last maxim; it recalls the

tenth maxim about how to treat a superior with a lowly past (175–85), and the
twentieth maxim (316–24). It warns against trusting in good fortune and
asserts that a prudent attitude towards gain will ensure respect from society.

40. The thirty-first maxim once again urges respect towards social *superiors* (cf. the
seventh maxim (119–44), and the twenty-sixth (388–98)), which will ensure
their reciprocal support for the pupil and his property. *Baring the arm* is a ges-
ture of reverence that costs nothing. The second half of the maxim urges respect
towards the property of others, in similar terms. *Stubborn* disrespect for others
will create a hostile environment.

41. The thirty-second maxim warns against venting sexual desire on a *woman-boy*—
apparently a boy prostitute who takes the female role in sexual intercourse. The
act does not reflect on the character of the active partner, and has no social con-
sequences for him (unlike the socially unacceptable sexual intercourse with
women in the eighteenth maxim (277–97)). The boy's desire is perverse, and
socially unacceptable, and must not be encouraged. His physical desire (*what is
in his belly*) cannot find relief except by being renounced (the image of sexual
gratification as being sprinkled with cool *water* wordplays with 'semen').

42. The thirty-third maxim is the first of three on social relationships with depend-
ents and associates, that are concerned with increasingly wider social spheres.
This maxim, which is dominated by imperatives, recommends trust when deal-
ing with a *friend*. In the second half, the sage advocates a restrained response to
a friend who has been indiscreet or infuriating. A generalizing couplet concludes
the maxim, asserting that a friend who does wrong will be found out eventu-
ally; the phrasing suggests that this might take place only after death and not
in this life.

43. The thirty-fourth maxim urges generosity. The sage advises that, once goods are
issued from the *storeroom*, they may as well be distributed freely, as they can-
not return. Memory of a man's generosity will sustain him in old age and in
death, after leaving his *office*. As the maxims reach their conclusion, there are
several references to future memory. Lack of generous treatment will stir up
social unrest and create enemies.

44. The thirty-fifth maxim affirms, like the preceding one, that generosity brings its
rewards. A distinction is drawn between material goods and the true prosperity
of *friends* and virtue; success is not defined in simple terms of *property* or the like.
The paradox of the first verse—that generosity to one's *former associates* will
bring wealth—is explicated with imagery that recalls that of the twenty-first
maxim (330). The sentiment is similar to that of the twenty-second maxim
(339–49), and the final verse recalls the preceding maxim (487–8).

45. The thirty-sixth maxim advises immediate punishment to correct faults, but it
is also a final warning about unwarranted correction. The sage asserts that
undeserved punishment will make a minor fault into a major one, and cause
social unrest (*opposition*).

46. The thirty-seventh maxim returns to the subject of marriage. The series of max-
ims ends with an affirmation of the importance of *light-heartedness*, which was
earlier condemned (in the twenty-fifth maxim (382)). *Plumpness* in women was
not usually considered admirable. *Fresh water* is an image of prosperity (well-
watered ground and drinking water), and pleasure (the relief of cool water).

47. An epilogue of more reflective stanzas follows, in which the specific wisdom of
the Teaching is presented in more generalized terms, and its eternal values are
articulated more explicitly. The epilogue begins with a conditional clause, like
many of the maxims, and the opening verses proclaim the effective virtue of the
maxims: they affirm Truth and their wisdom is true. The *perfection of the verses*,
both rhetorical and ethical, results in their transmission, which is a transmis-

sion of cultural values—which will be acknowledged by society—through suc-
ceeding generations of sons to the future and to eternity.

48. A triplet affirms that *hearing* the Teaching induces a man to speak it again to
future generations. *Hearing* is a sign of understanding, obedience, and wisdom,
and *hearers* is a term for the officials' role in society as judges. These verses
develop the opening statements of the epilogue; a second triplet then affirms the
eternal value of the wise *deeds* which result from this listening.

49. The sage states that wisdom is the only means of enduring, and is its own
reward. First a triplet describes the *wise man*. Then the *official* who enacts Truth
is presented in an image of physical well-being. Virtue's reward is not presented
merely as material advancement, but as something inherent—personal fulfil-
ment (to *satisfy* is homophonous with 'to be knowledgeable'). The old age suf-
fered by the sage in the prologue (8–27 and n. 2) is here regenerated by the
speaking of wisdom; the description ends with a reference to hearing as ensur-
ing continuity through the hearer's *son*. The epithets in the final verse resemble
those found in praise songs and funerary inscriptions, and describe the wise man
in broad abstract terms.

50. The second stanza of the epilogue describes the benefits of *hearing* a father's
wisdom, developing the theme of the preceding stanza (507–33). A virtuosic
and repetitive passage plays on the word *hear* (and on how hearing enables
speech and creates love), in the manner of a toccata, teasing out the possi-
bilities of the thematic material. The passage returns to the specific context
of the Teaching—a father speaking to his son (1–41)—and extols hearing for
how it provides a good old age and favour from *God*, such as the sage has
gained.

51. After a verse suggesting that a man's ability to *hear* is predetermined by god,
comes a triplet which forms the centre of the stanza. This triplet states that an
individual is himself responsible for whether he is virtuous or not: the human
heart has potential for good and evil. *Life, prosperity, and health* (i.e. well-being)
is a grand phrase, originally used as a wish for the well-being of royalty: the
heart can elevate a man. The two contrasting views of responsibility for ethical
choice—predetermined by the gods or taken by man—are juxtaposed to suggest
the uncertainty of how a man's nature is determined.

52. In the rest of the stanza, the sage returns to the motif of the son, symmetrically
echoing the first section. *Hearing* and *speaking* are increasingly interwoven in the
epilogue, as the sage extols the consequences of wisdom; hearing is not just a
passive virtue. A concluding couplet extols how a virtuous man will be *remem-
bered*; in this the sage uses a phrase that was earlier used of the Teaching itself
(510 and n. 47), to imply that the pupil's reputation is, in a sense, the essence
of the Teaching.

53. The third stanza explicates the preceding stanza's affirmations, presenting those
claims in a more practical, worldly manner. A conditional clause, reminiscent
of the start of many of the preceding maxims, marks a return to specific
instances. The sage again addresses the pupil directly, and extends the Teaching
into the next-but-one generation. The stanza ends with a generalizing verse on
the benefits of seeking after excellence, and thus avoiding the hardships of the
fool (*fool* is homophonous with 'night', pointing the contrast with the *wise man*
who *rises early* at dawn).

54. A fourth stanza has the *fool* as subject; the description balances the preceding
stanza's presentation of the virtuous man (564–74), and develops the antithesis
of that stanza's final verse (573–4). The sage now warns against folly rather
than affirming the benefits of virtue. He ironically echoes the title of the
Teaching (47–50): while the sage teaches how to live truly, the fool makes life

like *death*. He is transient, a parody of the true way of life, and as such is despised, with his *deeds* being ignored by the officials.

55. The fifth stanza resumes the description of the son's increasing wisdom, and elevates him to a courtly and almost semi-divine level: the *Followers of Horus* are both the king's courtiers (*Horus* is the kingly god), and the semi-divine associates of the god himself. This stanza places wisdom more explicitly than before in a grand chronological frame, moving from the teacher—who will achieve *blessedness* in death—to his descendants in a spiral of regeneration and continuity. Society will recognize this continuity, and people who witness how a wise man's children behave will favour them for being like him, even in misfortune (*involved with injustice*). Obedient children are the essence of success through the generations.

56. The second section of the stanza turns from the value of children to the value of carefully transmitting the wisdom enshrined in the Teaching. The continuity of textual transmission complements the continuity of children, and is merged with *speaking* the wisdom with *art*. *Speaking* Truth is the archetypal active virtue, the enactment of the passive virtue of listening to wisdom.

57. The sixth stanza continues the movement from hearing to speaking. Advice to be restrained in speech is interwoven with the motif of wisdom passing from father to son to their mutual renown. The son is urged to behave in a manner worthy of his father. This stanza returns to a more consistently didactic mode, and turns from considering the pupil's children to the pupil's role as the teacher's child, citing speeches by officials who witness his deeds of wisdom (as in the preceding stanza (600–3)).

58. The final stanza takes up the didactic themes and interweaves generalizing descriptions and injunctions in a final rhetorical flourish about hearing and wisdom. There are reprises of motifs such as speaking before one's *lord*, the complementarity of *Truth* and social position, and well-being as a result of virtue. These are described with reference to an ideal *son* who will surpass his ancestors and develop and increase the sage's wisdom and teaching. The sage then returns to the actual setting, referring to his own good fortune in making the Teaching before the *king*. The prominence of the king in the final verses of the epilogue returns the audience to the courtly setting (1–41). At the start of the poem the king stated that 'no one is born already knowledgeable' (41), but here the son is born with wisdom derived from his father.

59. The sage's own reputation will endure as proof of his personal virtue and wisdom. Wisdom is presented as ultimately guaranteeing happiness, without any qualification. *A hundred and ten* was the ideal age to reach; it is a gift from the gods and the king in return for virtue. *Blessedness* is the state of the deceased élite, whose burials were in the gift of the king; it is a resonant term in wisdom literature and funerary inscriptions.

13

The Teaching of Khety

Introduction

Over 250 New Kingdom manuscripts survive of parts of *The Teaching of Khety*, since the Teaching's subject made it a quintessentially suitable exercise for apprentice scribes. The text, however, is corrupt, and at least one important manuscript is still unpublished. For these reasons only a very tentative translation is given here.

The teacher is a man named Khety, who has no prestigious title; in a later literary text a sage named Khety is praised for having written *The Teaching of King Amenemhat*, when the king 'was at rest and united with the sky'.[1] Khety may thus be a historical figure from the early Twelfth Dynasty, but this is very uncertain.

The Teaching has a specific setting, since it is spoken to justify Khety's taking his son to be trained as a scribe. It does not extol generalized virtue or wisdom, but the value of the scribal profession, which is illustrated with a series of scornful vignettes of other lowly professions and occupations; these have led modern scholars to call it the 'Satire on Trades'. Although the Teaching shows concern for general human activities, like other Teachings, its selection of occupations is very specific and partial. The selection and presentation of the trades may derive in part from a 'folk' tradition. The vignettes are linked together by recurring elements, such as the workers' common exhaustion, and their lack of proper clothes. The different types of labour are supremely wretched in various ways, and the phrases 'more than . . .' and 'more so than any other profession' occur several times. This bureaucrat's view of the lower orders is very different from the idealized representations of obedient and efficient workers on tomb walls, and contrasts sharply with the benevolent attitude towards society offered by élite poems such as *The 'Loyalist' Teaching*. It develops, instead, the pessimistic descriptions

[1] P. Chester Beatty IV, 6.11–7.2; see p. 203 n. 1.

of society that are found in the Discourses, as well as the bleak view of mankind as tending towards rebellion that is found in *The Teaching for King Merikare*, into a grim satire.

Although the poem is more episodic in structure, and more lowly in content and in its implied audience of apprentice scribes, than the other Teachings, it is part of the same literary tradition as these more elevated works: the Ramesside writers seem to have considered both it and *The Teaching of King Amenemhat* to be by the same author. The formal structure of introduction, specific vignettes/maxims, and a more generalizing series of stanzas, forming a sort of epilogue, recalls that of *The Teaching of the Vizier Ptahhotep*, and there are also strong similarities with *The 'Loyalist' Teaching* and *The Teaching of a Man for his Son* (pp. 292–3). Nevertheless it is hard to escape the impression that this is a more culturally peripheral work.

The date of composition is uncertain, and cannot be easily determined by linguistic criteria, since the text is corrupt; the lack of any reliable manuscript may be a result of its peripheral status in the Middle Kingdom. The distinctive 'lowly' tone and subject matter also make a comparison with other texts problematic. Although the work is usually assigned to the beginning of the Twelfth Dynasty, on the basis of its supposed author, it may be later. It seems to have been influential in the New Kingdom and to have acted as a model for the Miscellany texts extolling the scribe's profession that are one of the major genres of Late Egyptian literature.

The vivid vignettes of the Teaching need little elucidation, and only limited comment is provided here. The translation draws on the readings of Wolfgang Helck, Günter Burkard, and Alessandro Roccati (see Select Bibliography). Numbers give the sections of Helck's edition (letters indicate the lines of these sections).

The Teaching of Khety

Beginning of the Teaching[1]   1
made by the man of Sile
called Duaf's son Khety
for his son called Pepy,
while journeying south to the Residence
to place him in the scribal school,
in the midst of the children of the officials
and as the foremost of the Residence.

Then he said to him, 'I have seen beatings!   2
Set your heart to writings!
Observe how it rescues from labour!
Look, there is no excelling writings—
they are a watertight boat![2]
Read at the end of the *Compendium*,
and you will find these verses there, saying,
"A scribe in any position in the Residence—
because of it, he will never be wretched".

He fills another's want[3]   3
even before that person can leave the court content.
I can see no other profession like it,
one about which those verses could be said.
I shall make you love writing more than your mother;
I shall make its beauties be shown to you.
Now, it is greater than any other profession.
There is not its like in the land.
The scribe begins to flourish when he is a child;
he will be greeted, and will be sent to do missions,
before he has arrived at the age to wear a kilt.

I can see no sculptor on a commission,[4]   4
no goldsmith being sent.
But I have seen the metalworker at his labour
at the mouth of his furnace,
with his fingers like a crocodile's,
and stinking more than fish roe.

Any craftsman who grasps an adze[5]   5
is more wearied than a corvéed land-worker;

his fields are the wood,
his hoe is the bronze tool.
At night, he is still occupied,
although he has already done more than his arms can do.
At night, he kindles light.

6   And the jewel-worker is boring with his chisel[6]
in all kinds of hard jewels.
He has finished inlaying things,
and his arms are perished, and he is weary.
He sits down to his daily food
with his knees and back still bent.

7   And the barber is still shaving at evening's end.
He takes his bag, takes it onto his shoulder,
and takes himself from street to street
in search of people to shave.
He must exercise his arms to fill his belly,[7]
like the bee which can eat only as much as it has worked.

8   The reed-cutter goes north to the Delta,[8]
to carry off arrows for himself;
he has done more than his arms can do,
the mosquitoes have killed him,
and the sandflies have butchered him,
so that he is cut to pieces.

9   And the maker of pots is under earth,[9]
though standing up with the living.
He grubs in the meadows more than pigs do,
to fire his pottery,
and his clothes are stiff with mud,
and his loincloth in rags;
the air enters his nose,
after coming straight out of the burning kiln.
He is pounding with his feet,
and is crushed up by himself—
grubbing the yard of every house,
treading public places!

10   I shall tell you about the wall-builder:
his sides hurt,

for he must be outside in the howling wind,
building without a kilt—
his loincloth is a cord of the weaving shop,
a string for his backside;
his arms are covered with earth,
and mixed with all kinds of shit.
Though he eats bread with his fingers,
he can wash himself only once a day.

Vile is the carpenter, working at a ceiling;[10]   11
it is the roof of a chamber,
a chamber of ten by six cubits.
A month passes after the beams are laid,
and the matting is spread out, and all the work on it is done.
The provisions which are then given for his household—
they cannot be handed out to his children.

And the gardener is bringing a yoke,[11]   12
with each of his shoulders bearing old age,
with a great swelling on his neck,
which is festering;
he passes the morning watering the vegetables,
and his supper-time by the coriander,
having spent the midday in the orchard.
Because of this, it happens that he only rests when dying,
more so than with any other profession.

And the field-worker laments more than the guinea fowl,[12]   13
his voice louder than the ravens',
with his fingers swollen
and with all sorts of excessive stinks.
He is weary, having been assigned to the Delta;
and so he is always in rags.
He's well—well among lions!
The hippopotami are painful for him;
his forced labour is trebled by them.
He goes out,
and only arrives back at his house in the evening,
shattered by the walking.

The mat-maker within the weaving shop[13]   14
is worse off than a woman,

with his knees against his stomach,
and unable to breathe air.
If he wastes a day without weaving,
he is beaten with fifty whips.
He has to give provisions to the door-keeper
to let him look on the daylight.

15   The arrow-maker is made very feeble[14]
by going out to the foreign land.
He has to give his donkey more
than its resulting labour's worth.
He has to give more to the rustics
who put him on the road.
He arrives at his house in the evening,
shattered by the walking.

16   And the courier goes to the foreign country,[15]
having handed over his property to his children,
in fear of lions, and Asiatics.
He knows himself only when he is in Egypt.
He arrives at his house miserable,
shattered by the walking.
Whether his house is of cloth or of brick,
he will not come home happy.

17   The stoker—his fingers are putrid,[16]
smelling of corpses,
his eyes scorched by the smoke;
he cannot get rid of his dirt,
spending the day in cutting reeds.
His clothes are his horror.

18   The sandal-maker is very badly off,[17]
under his vats for eternity.
He's well—as well as a corpse,
chewing on hides!

19   And the washerman washes on the riverbank,[18]
and he is near to the crocodile.
"Father, come out of the flowing water!"
say his son and daughter.
This is no profession that anyone can be content in,

more so than any other profession;
his food is mixed with shit,
and no part of him is clean.
He puts himself to the underskirts of a woman
who is in her period;
he weeps, spending the day at the washing board.
The washing stone is by him;
he is told, "Here's dirty clothes! Get over here!"
and the edge sinks under their weight.

The fowl-catcher is made very feeble,[19]   20
by watching the flying birds.
If a flock of waterbirds passes over him,
he says "If only I had a net!"
God does not let this happen to him,
so that he is made feeble by his own plans.

I will tell you about the fisherman.[20]   21
He is made feebler than any other profession—
whose labour is in the river,
who consorts with crocodiles.
Even if the total of his reckoned catch comes to him,
he is still lamenting;
he cannot even realize that the crocodile's waiting,
being blinded by fear.
Even if he comes out of the flowing water,
he's as if smitten by God's anger.
Look, no profession is free from a director,[21]
except the scribe's—the director is he himself.

But if you know writings, all will be well for you,[22]   22
more so than with these professions I have shown you.
Look at them, at their wretchedness!
one can not call a field-worker a man: beware of this!
Look, what I have done in coming south to the Residence—
look, I have done for your sake.
A day in school is good for you—
it is for eternity, its works are mountains.
The enforced workers I have told you of hurry by,
risen early and resisting.

*

23 I shall also tell you other things,²³
    to teach you wisdom.
    Such as: If you attend a place of conflict,
    do not approach those who are quarrelling!
    If a brick is seized by the hasty-hearted
    and it is not known how to lower the temperature,
    with witnesses before the judges,
    make answer to him with due hesitation!

24 If you walk in attendance on great ones,²⁴
    approach from afar, behind the end rank!
    If you go in to the lord of the house in his house,
    and his hands are to someone else before you,
    you should sit with your hand to your mouth!
    Do not demand anything when you are beside him,
    but behave to him as he says!
    Beware of going up to the table!

25 Be weighty in yourself, and great of respect!
    Speak no secret matters!
    The discreet man makes himself a shield.
    Speak no reckless matters;
    you should be relaxed with someone who is defiant!

26 If you leave the school,²⁵
    after you are told it is midday,
    going and coming in the public places,
    negotiate the result of what is yours!

27 If a great one sends you on a mission,²⁶
    speak as he spoke!
    Do not delete or alter anything concerning this!
    The hasty-hearted man produces oblivion;
    he has no enduring name.
    He who is intelligent in all his character
    has nothing hidden from him;
    there is no dismissing him from any position of his.

28 Speak no falsehood with your mouth, it is the horror of the
      officials.²⁷
    Now after a meal is prepared,
    both your hands should be placed at your nose.

Do not take enjoyment with the troublesome:
the man whose appetite is listened to is vile.
If you are fed with three loaves
and two jars of beer have been drunk
without ending appetite—resist it!
If another is being fed, do not wait around;
beware of going up to the table!

Look, you will send multitudes, and hear the discourse of the
    great ones;[28]   29
so that you will acquire the nature of the well-born,
following in their steps.
A scribe is regarded on account of hearing;
hearing will create a champion.
You should resist a word of "Welcome!":
do not hasten your limbs as you go; do not be overtrusting!
Associate with someone who is more distinguished than you!
Be friendly with a man of your Youth!

Look, I have placed you on the path of God,[29]   30
for the Fortune of a scribe is on his shoulder,
on the day of his birth.
He will achieve office,
the council of the Residence.
Look, no scribe lacks food,
or property from the palace (l.p.h.!).
Destiny is ordained to a scribe—
She who advances him before the council.
Thank God for your father and your mother
who put you on the path of life!
Look at these maxims that I have put before you,
and before the children of your children!'

So it ends, from start to finish,
as found in writing.

Notes

1. The name of the author is not certain. The lowly title describes him as a com-
   moner from *Sile*, a frontier town on the north-eastern edge of Egypt, near mod-
   ern Tell Abu Sefa (the reading is, however, uncertain; 'cabin' has also been
   suggested instead of *Sile*). See p. 203 n. 1.

2. This image of easy travelling—a common metaphor for success in life—is dramatically appropriate, as they would travel to the Residence by water. The *Compendium* was a didactic text used in scribal training; see p. 293.

3. Khety now describes the benefit of the scribe's skill, beginning with the scribe's ability to satisfy his clients before their legal case is completed. The reference to the pupil's *mother* is echoed in the final stanza (30f). The present stanza ends by stating that the office is so great that a scribe will prosper even as a *child*—evoking eulogies of the king as someone who conquers 'in the egg' (e.g. *The Tale of Sinuhe*, B 69 and n. 22)—and will have authority before reaching adolescence, when he would start to wear a *kilt*.

4. Khety begins by mentioning three craftsmen who work with valuable materials, whose labour is nevertheless no better than that of field-labourers. *Commissions* were jobs for literate men, and involved deputized power. The *metalworker* is scorned because of his smell.

5. This and the following vignettes stress the exhaustion of workers, which, it is implied, the scribe does not suffer. The carpenter hacking wood is compared to a farmer hacking the earth—an even lowlier and more strenuous trade (cf. the farmer of 13a–f). He has to *kindle light* to continue work after sunset. He and the next three workers all labour with metal tools (adze, chisel, razor, and reed-knife).

6. The *jewel-worker's* exhaustion is made worse by the fact that he cannot move from his working posture by evening, due to cramp.

7. The simile likens the flapping arms of the *barber* to a *bee's* wings.

8. The *reed-cutter* cuts reeds for *arrows*, and is attacked by insects as if by arrows; the insects recalls the bee of the previous stanza (7e).

9. This and the next stanza concern people who work with earth. The *maker of pots* carries earth for clay, making him *under earth* as if dead, and gathers clay like a *pig* grubbing (*meadow* and *pig* are homophonous). He kneads clay with his feet, which batters him as well as the clay. Such labour is self-destructive.

10. Khety moves to a second type of builder. The first verse is very corrupt, and some critics have suggested that the following lines continue the description of the builder. The chamber measures 5×3 m. The end of the stanza states the craftsman is paid only after the job is finished, and then his earnings are so meagre that his children get no provisions.

11. Two vignettes about people who work the land follow. The *gardener* has to carry heavy water pots to irrigate the plot, an endless task.

12. The *field-worker* has a long journey to reach the land which he has been assigned to cultivate. The stanza is full of raucous and dangerous animals. *Hippopotami* were a threat to crops.

13. The *mat-maker* suffers from the opposite of the travelling field-worker: his work confines him in a single room. He is *worse off than a woman* because of his posture which resembles a woman in labour.

14. The woe characteristic of the *arrow-maker*, who has to go out into the desert to gather flints for arrow-heads, is that his travelling expenses exceed his income. His lack of profit recalls the carpenter's (11e), and his travelling the field-worker's (13f). This and the following vignette concern workers abroad.

15. This second travelling worker has to go into dangerous areas, and so makes a will each time he leaves home. He is unhappy whether he is abroad in a *cloth* tent or in Egypt in a proper *brick* house. The *lions* echo 13d; his *shattered* state echoes 13f and 15e.

16. The *stoker* smells repulsive, since most of his fuel is dung. This and the following stanza are linked by the stink of *corpses*; the motif of smell echoes 4c and 13b, and continues into the following stanza (19).

17. The *sandal-maker* is involved with stinking vats for tanning leather (suggesting the process of embalming a *corpse*), and uses his teeth in working the leather.

18. The *washerman's* is another profession dominated by human filth. This and the following two vignettes are linked together by the mentions of water animals (*crocodiles* and fowl), and the riverine workplace.

19. The *fowl-catcher's* birds recall the images of the field-worker's distress (13a). His profession is god-forsaken, and self-destructive, since his own *plans* are what afflict him. As the series of vignettes nears its end, there are several references to *God* (see n. 29).

20. The *fisherman*, like the washerman (19a–h), works in a dangerous environment, and like the fowler is not helped by god (20c), even if he is lucky to survive his work in the water. Towards the end of the series there are several references to the premature deaths caused by the occupations.

21. The stanza and the series of vignettes end as Khety moves to consider the autonomy and prosperity of the *scribe*, who is not forced to labour so excessively, and whose work is self-controlled rather than self-destructive.

22. Khety ironically echoes the claims that the professions are superlatively bad by extolling the scribe's superlative qualities (cf. 12e, 19d, 21b); this resumes the earlier assertion that scribedom is greater than any other trade (3d). He returns to the setting of the Teaching, the journey to the *school*. The image of *mountains* expresses the rock-like stability of writings, as opposed to the transient lowly professions.

23. General advice on ethical behaviour follows in a concluding section. These pieces of wisdom are similar to those of the other Teachings in form and content. Here Khety advises restraint in dealing with legal and/or administrative disputes, including heated arguments when a *brick* is taken to throw at an opponent. Such restraint is an appropriate virtue for clerical staff.

24. A stanza enjoining respect for one's superiors; the scribe associates with elevated circles, unlike the earlier labourers (only the élite would have eaten at *tables*). *Sitting hand to mouth* is to sit quietly and respectfully, with due deference while one's *lord* is attending to *someone else*. The same qualities are advised in the following stanza.

25. An obscure stanza, but one relevant to the setting of the Teaching. It either means that time spent in *school* will give benefits in other *public places*, or possibly warns that anyone who leaves school early will have to negotiate against opposition.

26. Another stanza extolling careful speech, recalling the last but one stanza (25a–c).

27. A stanza advising respect for one's elders and betters, particularly while at table (developing the advice of 25a–c). To have one's *hands at the nose* is apparently a gesture of self-restraint and respect; it also contrasts with the strenuous activities of the labourers' arms (5c, 6b, 7d, 8b, 10d).

28. The first half of the stanza describes the benefits of the scribe's position, and his ability to rise in society. The second half warns against becoming too proud and trying to be greeted (*Welcome*) as a prominent person. Being in a position to *hear* is the virtue of the scribe's role. The scribe should associate with people both higher and lower than himself: the *Youth* are paramilitary bands.

29. A final stanza proclaims the benefits the pupil will gain from being placed in school: literacy is acclaimed in generalized terms as a great and holy virtue— the *path of God* and of *life*. *Fortune* and *Destiny* (Meskhenet) are goddesses of birth and good fortune, who attend on the scribe; the *shoulder* is where the scribe slung his equipment to carry it. The stanza is full of references to the divine, unlike the preceding stanzas that depicted godless or god-afflicted work (20c, 21g). The advice looks to perpetuity in two ways: Khety's son will have progeny, and the Teaching will last down the generations.

PHRASES AND FRAGMENTS

[14]

Phrases and Fragments

The preceding poems are the best preserved from the Middle Kingdom. Many more survive only as odd fragments, and a selection of these is translated here.

Tales

The most tantalizing of these fragments are perhaps the Tales, especially *The Tale of the Herdsman*. Twenty-five lines of this were accidentally preserved by the scribe who wrote the only extant copy of *The Dialogue of a Man and his Soul*. To strengthen the end of the roll he cut a section from a manuscript of the *Herdsman*, partially cleaned both edges of it and joined it to the end of the *Dialogue*. A short episode in the middle of the section was not erased; a herdsman is telling his colleagues how a terrifying goddess approached him from a pool. He proposes that they should escape across the river to another pasture, invoking a spell to ensure a safe crossing. However, as they prepare to leave, he returns to the pool and the goddess surprises him with her erotic overtures. The whole episode is as follows:

> [. . . . .],[1]
> ['Look, I . . . .]
> [. . . . . . long . . . .]
> [. . . when I come . . . .]
> Look, I went down ⟨to⟩ the pool,   I
> which is close by this low-lying pasture,
> and I saw a woman in it: she was not of human form.
> My hair stood on end when I saw her tresses,[2]
> and the smoothness of her skin.
> I'll never do what she said, and dread of her still runs through
>   my limbs!
> I say to you: So bulls, let's return!
> So let the calves cross over and the herd spend the night

         on the edge of the grazing land,
10   with the herders looking after them!
         Our skiff for the return!
         With the bulls and cows behind it,
         and the herders' sages reciting a water-spell.[3]

         Speaking thus, "My spirits rejoice,
         O herders! O men!
         I will not be driven from the water-meadow,
         even in a year of a great Nileflood who issues the order to the
             earth's surface,[4]
         when the pool cannot be told from the river!
         Be well within Your house![5]
         The cattle stay in their proper place.
         Come! Fear of You has perished,
20   dread of You is driven away,
         even until the storminess of the Mighty Goddess,
         and the fearsomeness of the Lady of the Two Lands will perish!" '

         When it was dawn, very early,
         they did as he said.
         This goddess approached him[6]
         when he appeared before the pool.
         She came stripped naked of her clothes,
25   with her hair let loose. [. . . . .][7]
         [. . . . .]

She advances alluringly, but nothing further is legible. Seduction by
a spirit is suggestive of a folk tale, but the water-spell is also found in
a late Eleventh Dynasty funerary text, and this suggests that the Tale
belongs, like *The Tale of the Shipwrecked Sailor*, to the élite sphere.

Other Tales survive in even smaller fragments, mostly single scraps.
Many of these are reminiscent of *The Tale of King Cheops' Court*, with
its lighter tone. There is, for example, an apparently humorous *Tale
of Horus and Seth* found at the town of el-Lahun, in which Seth, the
god of chaos, tries to seduce his rival Horus with the words 'How
lovely is your backside!' Of another Tale from el-Lahun, *The Tale of
Hay*, only the ending survives; in this a man called Hay is buried,
and a feud is ended. In *The Tale of King Neferkare and Sasenet*, known
from several fragmentary copies, a king is having an amorous li-
aison with a general, and a 'pleader of Memphis' tries to denounce
him before the court, but the king's musicians drown out his

speeches. Later the king is noticed by a courtier called Tjeti as he

> goes out at night,
> all alone, having nobody with him

to visit the general secretly for four hours of pleasure:

> Hent's son Tjeti waited,
> thinking, 'So this is it!
> What they said is true—
> he does go out at night.'
> Hent's son Tjeti then went
> behind this god—
> without letting his heart have misgivings—to see all that he did.
> He then arrived
> at the house of General Sasenet.
> Then he threw a brick, and stamped his foot,
> so that a [ladder] was let down for him.
> He then ascended,
> while Hent's son Tjeti
> waited until his Majesty should proceed.
> Now after his Majesty had done what he desired with him,
> he proceeded to his palace, and Tjeti went after him.

The conclusion of the intrigue is lost.

A Tale on Papyrus Lythgoe from el-Lisht involves a Vizier who goes

> to the field of the Vizier Weḥau,
> which was on the east of the Residence,
> and he loaded a sea-going boat of the palace (l.p.h.!)
> [with] every good thing.

There is also a *Tale of the King and the Ghost*, the most coherent fragment of which is almost as tantalizing as that of *The Tale of the Herdsman*:

> He (the ghost) was not in the sky,
> He was not in the earth;
> his feet were far from the ground
> [. . . . .]
> [. . . . .]
> [. . . . . . the Fair of] Face![8]
> Never will you weep [. . . . .]
> [Let] him [speak] to me!'
> And this ghost said, 'I am Khentyka's son Snefer,
> sovereign, my lord!'

Discourses

Partially preserved reflective wisdom poems include the magnificent but tattered *Discourse of the Scribe Sasobek*. A narrative prologue describes how a scribe was imprisoned wrongfully, and then released without full restitution, to his grief. His lament is introduced with the title:

> Discourse spoken by the scribe
> Hotephathor's son Sasobek,
> his mouth moving according to what had happened,
> and what was presented to mankind:[9]
> 'This life of a span—what happens in it is unknowable;
> [its beginning] happens suddenly;
> its end is destruction.'

Only short sections can be read, but the sage's speeches seem to have been similar to those of *The Tale of the Eloquent Peasant*, and full of reflections on the uncertainty of life:

> 'Behold! it cannot happen—yet it happens!
> Hidden are the counsels of God.'

The same style occurs in *The Discourse of the Fowler*. In this a countryman is left helpless as his countryside is destroyed, and he petitions a superior to restore him to his former state:

> 'May you renew action, according to your knowledge!
> Look, our condition is before you—
> the water-meadow has flowed away into the land, but there is no
>   leaving it.
> Its margins and districts are now under the herdsmen of the foreign
>   countries,[10]
> the stillness now under cattle byres,
> the huts for hiding now under town-dwellers' grain.'

Some forty verses of this are preserved, very faintly, on the back of a manuscript of *The Tale of the Eloquent Peasant*. Of another reflective work, *The Discourse of the Priest Renseneb*, only the opening title remains.

Teachings

The Teachings are perhaps the best preserved genre, thanks largely to the numerous copies made by New Kingdom apprentice scribes (see p. 4). Nevertheless, many are incomplete, including *The Teaching for Kagemni*, which is known from a single copy at the start of the principal manuscript of *The Teaching of the Vizier Ptahhotep*. *Kagemni* is also set in the Old Kingdom and is addressed to a famous historical vizier of the Sixth Dynasty (although the Teaching ascribes him to the Fourth Dynasty). It reveals the same concerns with etiquette and eternal principles as *Ptahhotep*:

1.1 'The meek man prospers, and the honest man is favoured;[11]
the tent is open for the quiet man,
and wide is the access for the calm man.
Do not talk! Knives are sharp for someone who errs from the path.
There is no hastening except at its due time.

If you sit with many people, scorn the bread you love![12]
Restraining the heart is a little moment.
1.5 Gluttony is wrongdoing. It is pointed at.
A cup of water quenches thirst.[13]
A mouthful of herbs makes the heart firm.
One good thing serves for goodness.
A few little things serve for greatness.
Vile is the man who has a greedy appetite when the fit time is past,
and who has forgotten that the appetite has free range only at home.
If you sit with a glutton,
you should eat when his fever has passed.
If you drink with a drunkard,
you should take when his heart is contented.
Do not attack meat beside a voracious man;
1.10 take only what he gives you, do not reject it! That is the way to soothe.
A man who is free from reproach about food—
no words can prevail against him.
He who is mild-mannered to the point of being indulgent—
the harsh are kinder to him than his mother is.
Everybody is his supporter. Cause your renown to spread thus:
2.1 you are quiet with your mouth even when you are summoned.

Do not be proud because there is strength among your Youth![14]
Beware lest you are opposed! What will happen,
what God does when He punishes, is unknowable!'

*

And the Vizier had his children summoned,
after he had understood the nature of mankind,

and its character had come upon him.
And at last he said to them,

2.5   'All that is written down on this roll—
listen to it as I have said it!
Do not go beyond what is ordained!'
And now they prostrated themselves.
And now they read it out exactly as it was written down.
And it seemed more perfect to their hearts
than anything in this entire land.
And they behaved accordingly.[15]
Then the Majesty of the Dual King Huni passed away.[16]
Then the Majesty of the Dual King Sneferu ascended
as the worthy king in this entire land.
Then Kagemni was appointed as Lord Vizier.
So it ends.[17]

Partial copies are also extant of *The Teaching of Prince Hordedef*, a prince who features in *The Tale of King Cheops' Court*. In the second stanza, the prince urges his audience to prepare themselves for death, and tells how death and life are inseparable:

'You should build your house for your son;
then you will have made a place in which you will always exist.
Make worthy your house of the necropolis![18]
Make excellent your place of the West!
Accept a humiliation for us—death!
Accept an exaltation for us—life!
The house of death belongs to life!'

Another fragmentary teaching is *The Teaching of a Man for his Son*, which is very similar to *The 'Loyalist' Teaching*.[19] The Teaching begins as follows:

Beginning of the Teaching[20]
made by a man for his son.
He says, 'Hear my voice! Do not pass over my speech!
Do not neglect what I tell you!
Enact good character, with no transgression!
A man of understanding cannot be negligent.
Be exact, silent, and respectful!
Be excellent of heart! Do what is said!

Deploy words before strength! . . .'

The first half is loyalistic, praising the king, and urging the son to 'Turn not your heart from god! | Praise the king!' The final stanzas are more concerned with speech in a social context. The end extols calmness:

> 'He who is unresponsive and does not quarrel is relaxed.
> A man himself can cause his enemies to succeed;
> but he who masters his mouth succeeds.
> Accusations are words to provoke fighting.'

A literary letter called the *Compendium* (*Kemit*) is quoted in *The Teaching of Khety* (2d–e, p. 275). The *Compendium* was used in scribal training later in the New Kingdom and possibly also in the Middle Kingdom. It is highly formulaic, and reads like a model letter. It tells a tale of an errant and amorous son, and the letter-writer draws a didactic moral. It was perhaps a paradigm for learning both literacy and literature.[21]

Other Compositions

Among what survives, there are a few indications of a wider set of genres than those of the relatively well-preserved classical canon.

One person's collection of manuscripts (the 'Ramesseum library'), which contained *The Discourse of Sasobek*, *The Tale of Sinuhe*, and *The Tale of the Eloquent Peasant*, also included a papyrus with a random collection of short proverbial maxims, all very generalizing, and most now very cryptic:

> He who fails the drowning man, fails everyone.
>
> He who drives away his protection is protection-less.
>
> A man does what he does, without knowing that someone is
> doing the same against him.

Fragments of two long compositions survive on a group of very broken New Kingdom papyri in Moscow: *The Account of the Sporting King* and *The Account of the Pleasures of Fishing and Fowling*. They seem to belong to a mixed genre. One is a narrative which frames a set of highly metaphorical eulogies, probably similar to actual royal praise songs, acclaiming a sporting king. A sample reads:

> Words [spoken to his Majesty (l.p.h.!)] at the foot of the throne;[22]
> the Treasurer of the Red-king, the Royal Document Scribe of the
> Presence,
> Sehotepibreankh, [said to] his [lord],
> 'Take unto yourself this your red shaft,[23]
> ruddy of colour, the [. . .] of your [Majest]y (l.p.h.!);

> may it extend its protection to you!
> It is like the Red Crown when placed in coronation,
> when the [. . .] has received the Coil which is in Pe,
> and the Coil which is in Dep!
> Like the horns of the staff of the Coptite!
> Like the [. . .] of his breastplate!
> Like the Horizon-dweller when he shows himself at dawn!'

The other poem is narrated by a man speaking to his lord, and
extols pastoral pleasures:

> 'A happy day, as we go down to the water-meadow,[24]
> as we snare bi[rds and catch] many [fish] in Two-Waters,
> and the catcher and harpooner come to us,
> as we draw in the net[s full of] fowl;
> we moor our skiff at a thicket,
> and put offerings on the fire
> for Sobek, Lord of the Lake,
> the [. . . of] the Sovereign (l.⟨p.⟩h.!).
>
> . . . .
>
> My lord! My lord!
> Spend the night in the hide!
> Success will be given to the man who draws the net
> when it is dawn [on the] midmost [isle].
> The Marsh-goddess has been kind to you;
> your fishing rods have been kind to you.
> Every water-meadow is green, and you have fed on the countryside,
>
> . . . .
>
> If only I were in [the country]—
> [I would do] what my heart desires,
> as when the country was my town,
> when the top of the water-meadow was [my dwelling];
> no [one could part me from] the people my heart desires and from
>   my friends;
> I would spend the day in the place of [my] longing,
> [in the . . . and] the papyrus clumps.
> When it was dawn, I would have a snack,
> and be far away, walking in the place of my heart!'

These long episodic pastoral poems probably date from late in the
Middle Kingdom, and in many respects they look forward to the lit-
erature of the New Kingdom.

The oral compositions of the Middle Kingdom, which probably included love-songs, secular harpist's lyrics, and other genres, are lost to us. It is, however, some consolation that the poetry we have is that which the scribes wished us, the future, to read, and is the art that they considered worthy of eternity.

Notes

1. Traces of four erased lines are almost, but not quite, legible. A new stanza seems to start in the first erased line, and then the herdsman speaks.
2. *Tresses* of hair were often objects of erotic interest; from this and from what happens later, the goddess presumably had invited him to sleep with her.
3. The *sages* are rustic wise men and magicians. Their *spell* opens with a pun: *spirits* and 'bulls' are homophonous.
4. During a year when the annual *Nileflood* was high, the meadow would be under water, and the *earth's surface* under the control of the flood.
5. *You* is the Nileflood, whom the sages conjure to stay in its course and not threaten the crossing. They urge the river to be a friendly force, whose fearsomeness will now be as non-existent as the *fearsomeness* of the *Mighty goddess* is imperishable. The *Mighty Goddess* and the *Lady of the Two Lands* are titles of the goddess of the royal uraeus; the mention of a goddess is appropriate, given the reason for the herdsmen's departure.
6. Probably to wash or drink, before setting off.
7. For the erotic implications of *hair*, see n. 2. After the end of l. 25, the text is erased, with traces of four more lines that are illegible apart from one or two signs.
8. An epithet of the king or a god, most commonly Ptah, the creator-god of Memphis. The king is now speaking, and hoping to talk with the ghost.
9. A grandiose way of saying 'according to his experience'.
10. The quiet marsh that was once an idyllic hunting ground is now pasture and agricultural land. The *huts* are the hiding places used in catching fowl.
11. The first surviving stanza urges quietness, moderation, and deliberation.
12. A section on table manners, which expands from these specific examples into reflections on restraint in general.
13. These verses recommend moderation in eating, but also explicitly formulate the theme that virtue in this world is relative; thus to limit evil may be as near as one can get to absolute virtue. The following verses describe the man who ignores restraint, and then acclaim the *quiet* man.
14. The Teaching concludes with a warning against trusting in (paramilitary) might, as the future cannot be known.
15. Literally, 'stood and sat'.
16. *Huni* was the last king of the Third Dynasty (*c.*2599–2575 BC) and predecessor of *Sneferu* (for whom, see *The Words of Neferti* and *The Tale of King Cheops' Court*). *Kagemni* seems to be the old Vizier's son, who now succeeds his retiring father. The name of the teacher is lost, but he may have been one Kaires, who is mentioned as a sage in a later list of ancient writers.
17. A short version of the standard colophon.
18. This building is the tomb, as opposed to the house for one's living descendants. The two spheres of existence—*death* and *life*—are united in the final verse through the tomb which will ensure eternal life.

19. The text is being reconstructed by H.-W. Fischer-Elfert (see Select Bibliography).
20. The title alludes to the phrase 'son of a man', which means a 'gentleman'. This suggests that the teacher is no common man, even though he is a sort of generalized 'everyman'.
21. A recent translation with references to publications is by E. F. Wente, in his *Letters from Ancient Egypt* (Atlanta, Ga.; 1990), 15–16.
22. The name of the speaker, *Sehotepibreankh*, contains the name of Sehotepibre Amenemhat I; the king who is addressed may be Amenemhat II.
23. The *red shaft* is a hunting spear used in sporting rituals; the following verses describe it in elaborate terms. Its colour allies it to the *Red Crown* of Lower Egypt, which has a *Coil* as a distinguishing feature. *Pe* and *Dep* are twin royal cities of Lower Egypt, at modern Tell el-Far'in (classical Buto, in the 6th Lower Egyptian nome). *The Coptite* is the god Min, lord of Coptos and a god of virility, beside whose shrine stood a horned pole emblem. The *Horizon-dweller* is the Sungod, who is red with the *dawn*.
24. *Two-Waters* is a place in the Fayyum, location unknown. The monologue about hunting is set in a pastoral marsh landscape, presided over by the *Marsh-goddess*. *Sobek* is the crocodile-god of the Fayyum (the *Lake*); the burnt *offerings* are thanksgiving for a successful hunt.

GLOSSARY

Autobiography a commemorative tomb inscription, in which the deceased man addresses the passer-by with an idealized description of his virtues, as manifested in his life and career (see p. 21)

cubit a unit of measure, equal to 52.3 cm

Delta the 'Papyrus land' or Lower Egypt, the northern part of Egypt, marshy and fertile

Dual King a title, literally perhaps 'He of the Reed, He of the Bee', which refers to two aspects of the kingship that were paired with Upper and Lower Egypt, so that it is often rendered 'King of Upper and Lower Egypt'. It introduces the royal prenomen (throne name)

electrum a naturally occurring alloy of gold and silver, highly prized

Golden Horus the third element of the royal titulary; it refers to the king as the triumphant god Horus

Horus the first element of the royal titulary, acclaiming the king as the royal god

the justified literally 'true of voice', an epithet referring to judgement after death, thus indicating the person as 'deceased'. Often applied by copyists to names of characters from the past, regardless of whether it would have featured in the original manuscript

(l.p.h.!) an abbreviation for 'May he live, be prosperous, and healthy!'—an invocation of well-being for superiors, especially the king—written after names. It is partly a graphic convention, applied differently by different scribes

Lower Egypt the northern part of Egypt, the Nile Delta

Majesty literally 'Person', a term referring to the physical presence of the king

nomes the administrative districts or provinces of Egypt

ostracon a flake of limestone used as a writing surface

P. Papyrus, followed by a name or museum number

recto the 'front' of a papyrus sheet or roll (and of a writing board)

Red-king the king of Lower Egypt, distinguished by the red crown

Residence the capital or royal residence, which in the Twelfth Dynasty was at Itj-tawi, probably near modern el-Lisht, south of Memphis

Son of Re a title of the king, prefacing the nomen (birth name), and alluding to his divine lineage

Truth a schematic translation of Egyptian *Maat*; its range of meanings includes truth, right, justice, equity, reciprocity, and social and cosmic order (see p. 13)

Two Ladies the patron goddesses of Upper and Lower Egypt, who appear on the royal diadem; a royal title, introducing the second element of the titulary

Two Banks/Lands Egypt: the strips of land on either side of the Nile, the two halves of the country

Upper Egypt the southern part of Egypt, the Nile Valley

uraeus an image of a serpent worn on the royal brow, a protective symbol to strike down the king's enemies

verso the 'back' of a papyrus sheet or roll (and of a writing board)

The Oxford World's Classics Website

www.worldsclassics.co.uk

- Browse the full range of Oxford World's Classics online

- Sign up for our monthly e-alert to receive information on new titles

- Read extracts from the Introductions

- Listen to our editors and translators talk about the world's greatest literature with our Oxford World's Classics audio guides

- Join the conversation, follow us on Twitter at OWC_Oxford

- Teachers and lecturers can order inspection copies quickly and simply via our website

www.worldsclassics.co.uk

American Literature

British and Irish Literature

Children's Literature

Classics and Ancient Literature

Colonial Literature

Eastern Literature

European Literature

Gothic Literature

History

Medieval Literature

Oxford English Drama

Poetry

Philosophy

Politics

Religion

The Oxford Shakespeare

A complete list of Oxford World's Classics, including Authors in Context, Oxford English Drama, and the Oxford Shakespeare, is available in the UK from the Marketing Services Department, Oxford University Press, Great Clarendon Street, Oxford OX2 6DP, or visit the website at www.oup.com/uk/worldsclassics.

In the USA, visit www.oup.com/us/owc for a complete title list.

Oxford World's Classics are available from all good bookshops. In case of difficulty, customers in the UK should contact Oxford University Press Bookshop, 116 High Street, Oxford OX1 4BR.